From The Women's Press Ltd
34 Great Sutton Street, London EC1V 0DX

SUZY McKEE CHARNAS

WALK TO THE END OF THE WORLD
and
MOTHERLINES

The Women's Press
sf

This volume published in Great Britain by
The Women's Press Ltd 1989
A member of the Namara Group
34 Great Sutton Street, London EC1V 0DX

Walk to the End of the World first published in the
USA by Ballantine Books, 1974
First published in Great Britain by Victor Gollancz
Ltd, 1979

Motherlines first published in the USA by Berkley,
1978
First published in Great Britain by Victor Gollancz
Ltd, 1980

British Library Cataloguing in Publication Data
Charnas, Suzy McKee, 1939–
    Walk to the end of the world.
    I. Title
    813'.54 [F]

ISBN 0-7043-4154-9

Typeset by MC Typeset Ltd, Gillingham, Kent
Printed and bound in Great Britain by
BPCC Hazell Books Ltd
Member of BPCC Ltd
Aylesbury, Bucks, England

WALK TO THE END OF THE WORLD

To Stephen

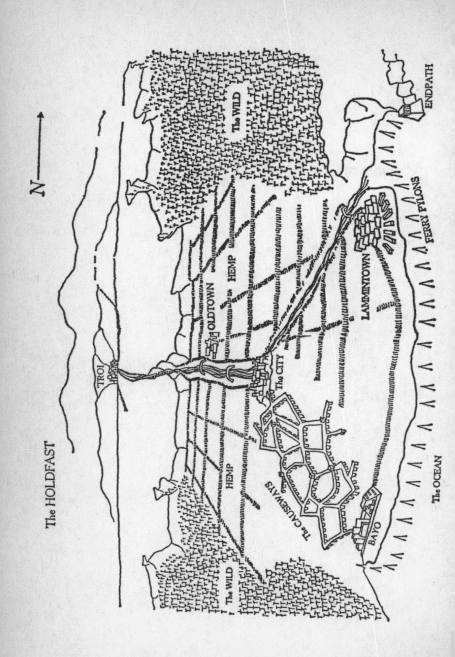

Contents

PROLOGUE

The predicted cataclysm, the Wasting, has come and – it seems – gone: pollution, exhaustion and inevitable wars among swollen, impoverished populations have devastated the world, leaving it to the wild weeds. Who has survived?

A handful of high officials had access to shelters established against enemy attack. Some of them thought to bring women with them. Women had not been part of the desperate government of the times; they had resigned or had been pushed out as idealists or hysterics. As the world outside withered and blackened, the men thought they saw reproach in the whitened faces of the women they had saved and thought they heard accusation in the women's voices. Many of these women had lost children in the holocaust.

The men did not notice their own shocked faces and raw voices. They had acted, they thought, responsibly, rightly – and had lost everything. They did not realize they had lost their sanity, too.

They forbade all women to attend meetings and told them to keep their eyes lowered and their mouths shut and to mind their own business, which was reproduction.

Among themselves, most of the women thought as women were taught to think: it would be proper and a relief to think of nothing but babies any more, and while the men were crazy with grief, guilt and helplessness it was support they needed, not antagonism. These women said to one another, let's do what they say for now.

A few objected, saying, no, these men will enslave us if we let them; no one is left to be their slaves except us! They tried to convince the others.

The men heard, and they rejoiced to find an enemy they could conquer at last. One night, as planned, they pulled all the women from sleep, herded them together, and harangued them, saying, remember that you caused the Wasting. It was a Black female's refusal to sit in the back of the bus that sparked the rebellion of the Blacks; female Gooks fought against our troops in the Eastern Wars; female terrorists made bombs side by side with our own rebel sons, whose mothers had brought them up to be half-men; female vermin of all kinds spewed out millions of young to steal our food-supplies and our living space! Females themselves brought on the Wasting of the world!

And the men, armed with staves and straps, reminded them and saw to it that these things were not forgotten again.

It is their male descendants who emerge from the Refuge to find the world scoured of animal life and beggared of resources. They continue the heroic, pioneering tradition of their kind: they kill the few wretched mutants who have persisted outside and clear the spiky brush from a strip of river-valley and seacoast where they establish a new civilization. They call their land the Holdfast, after the anchoring tendril by which seaweed clings to the rocks against the pull of the current.

Seaweed is an important source of nourishment to these new men; so is the hardy hemp plant, a noxious weed to the Ancients but now a staple crop that furnishes fiber, a vision-giving drug, and, because the new men are of necessity ingenious, food. Bricks are made from earth; machine graveyards are mined for metal; a vein of soft and greasy coal yields fuel; wood is brought from the low and thorny forests of the Wild beyond the Holdfast's borders. Nothing is abundant, but men live. They have not completely forgotten technology or culture, and they adapt what they can.

What else do they remember? They remember the evil races whose red skins, brown skins, yellow skins, black skins, skins all the colors of fresh-turned earth marked them as mere treacherous imita-tions of men, who are white; youths who repudiated their fathers' ways; animals that raided men's crops and waylaid and killed men in the wild places of the world; and most of all the men's own cunning, greedy females. Those were the rebels who caused the downfall of men's righteous rule: men call them 'unmen'. Of all the unmen, only females and their young remain, still the enemies of men.

CAPTAIN KELMZ

1

In an alley of the silent Pennelton compound in Lammintown, a man waited, his hands tucked into his sleeves against the night's chill. He was a Rover Captain in full uniform under his disguise of blanks. He stood alone in the shadow of a doorway.

Most of the lamps fixed to the corners of the buildings had been smashed. By the light of one that still burned he could discern obscene and insulting figures scratched into the granite walls. The Pennelton Company was assigned away south this five-year, and young men of other Lammintown companies had turned the empty compound into a temporary skidro. He had followed a group of wild lads down here, seekers of illicit pleasures.

The one whose services they had hired tonight was the one he was after; d Layo the DarkDreamer, a young man too, but of no company, no order, and no legitimate use to his fellows.

Heavy-muscled, smooth-moving, a tawny-colored night-slinker, a prowling predator with a broad, blunt-nosed face and wide-curling mouth, d Layo padded before his mind's eye. D Layo really did look like that, though it wasn't manly for the captain to think of even such a corrupt man as an actual beast.

The Lammintown trumpets brayed, as they did every quarter-hour. The captain began silently reciting the Chant Protective, to drive away visions. The chant opened with a reckoning of the size and reach of the Holdfast and of all the fellowship of men living in it; not a great or impressive tally, but it served to remind a man of his brothers and of what they expected from him.

The Holdfast was a strip of plain bisected by a river. A good runner could cross the plain north-to-south at its widest point in three days or run the length of the river from the coast to 'Troi in seven. The river descended from 'Troi on the high inland plateau. Further east, the City overlooked the river's fork: the southern branch reached down over the flats to Bayo; the northern branch emptied in Lammintown under the pale cliffs. These were the holdings of men — bastions of order, clear-thinking and will — to which the rest of the world one day would be added again.

But not, the captain thought morosely, if the Reconquest depended on men like himself. He let the chant drop. It wasn't because he stood alone in the dark that he saw beast-ghosts, though darkness encouraged such lapses in the manliest of men. At night the earth could be felt stretching away on all sides, its vast stillness stirred only by the currents of wind and water. The mind, shrinking from such expanses of emptiness, tended to supply populations of spirits.

However, the captain's personal vice was to envision other men — even decent, manly men — in beast shapes. Not many benefits derived from the Wasting that had turned the world into scrub-desert; the extinction of all creatures lower than man was one. To think of the beasts was like willfully calling up the ghosts of dead enemies.

He glanced up at the sky, hoping the DarkDreamer would come out before moonrise. The moon was the ally of brutes like d Layo. The captain, without his usual complement of Rovers, had no allies.

Trumpets blared; a pot shattered somewhere along the stone-paved streets. D Layo emerged from a narrow passage between two buildings. He was alone and seemed to be in a state of mild dreaming-shock, for he veered as he walked and ran one hand along the wall for guidance. Not many DarkDreamers would venture out still dream-dazed; but d Layo was reputed to be a rash young man.

The captain had the urge to clear his throat of the tightness that commonly afflicted him just before a clash. He waited until d Layo had meandered past. Then he sprang at him, clamping a forearm across the DarkDreamer's throat and a leg around his legs to prevent him from kicking, and he threw himself and his captive backward seeking to brace his own shoulders against the wall.

The DarkDreamer plunged like the ocean; he seemed to have no alley so that both their heads smacked against the opposite wall. The captain grunted and tightened his grip. He scrabbled for a foothold on the cobbles and used his weight to hurl the Dark-Dreamer down with force. D Layo's head glanced against stone; he made a muffled sound and went slack.

Kneeling on the DarkDreamer's back, the captain glanced quickly around. There was no one. He thought longingly of the knife sheathed on his thigh. It would be gratifying to carry out his original assignment and simply kill this brute.

Instead, he took hold of d Layo's thick hair and pulled his head up. 'A Senior wants to talk with you,' he said to the blank, handsome face.

D Layo groaned. The groan turned into hiccups. There was the sweet scent of manna, the dreaming-drug, on his breath.

In a harsh whisper, the captain repeated his message. Then he got up and stepped clear. He felt exhausted. This sort of work was better done in the bright, clean light of the sun, and by younger men.

D Layo sat up. He rubbed at his face and held up his hand to see if there was blood. A thick, compartmented bracelet of metal slid down his lifted arm, glinting. He said, unsteadily, 'Are you the cunningcock that's been sniffing after me for the past two months? To give me that message?'

'Until last week, my orders were different,' the captain growled.

'You're Captain Helms, aren't you?'

'Rover Captain Kelmz, of Hemaway Company.'

'Ah.' D Layo got up, making ineffectual brushing-off motions with both hands. There was some blood; in the feeble lamplight, the captain could see the dark line weaving down around the socket of d Layo's eye. 'Tell your Senior to meet me on the beach, in the sheds. Only one is in operation; tell him to follow his nose.'

'No. You're to come with me to meet him.'

'Hell-ums,' d Layo crooned, putting an irritating softness into his speech, 'be rational. You don't need my cooperation to kill me, but you do need it to talk with me. So we'll do this my way – unless you feel like another round?'

The captain did not feel like another round. He felt worn out and heavy in the hands.

'It's a let-down, I know,' the DarkDreamer added, 'after you've tagged along behind me all this time hoping for a taste of my blood.Forget it, Hell-ums. You have managed to cause me a good deal of inconvenience recently; settle for that.' The dreaming-shock was gone now. D Layo's voice was as the captain had first over-heard it months ago: light, lazy, and sweet with malice. 'You may have another chance to kill me sometime, cheer up. By the way, which of my many good friends told you where to find me tonight?'

'Go eat femshit.'

D Layo laughed.

Lammintown was a storm-battered, cold-gnawed place, 'rock on rock' its men said, boasting of their halls made of blocks hewn from the cliffs. They said that Lammintown men carried the Holdfast on their tough shoulders, because no one could survive without the harvests of long kelps, called lammins, from the bay.

There was an edginess in Lammintown these days. For several seasons and more noticeably this past summer the lammin-take had been alarmingly scant. The Lammintown Juniors who had charge of the offshore waters this five-year blamed the moon's influence over the shifting currents of the sea. They claimed that unusually warm water had impeded the maturing of the young kelps. But the Seniors maintained that the young men had mistimed the placing of rocks on the bay floor during the previous autumn, so that the new lammin spores had found no footholds and had died or drifted elsewhere. This crop failure came on top of a long series of econ-omic setbacks in the Holdfast.

Seniors had begun turning up on the work-turfs of the Juniors without warning, hoping to catch them in the act of stealing por-tions of the scarce harvest for themselves. These Seniors came with escorts of Rovers, often dispensing with the formality of bringing officers to command them. Rovers were powerful defenders of the Seniors and their interests, but they were hard to control, and most Seniors were not skilled in handling them personally.

There had been incidents, and rumors.

The young men of 'Ware Company, whose work-turf that five-year was the whole waterfront complex of lammin-works, had grown more and more restive. Between their resentment and the suspicion of the Seniors, a moonlit night was hardly the time for prudent men to venture into the sheds of Lammintown beach.

To keep the heat under the vats high without tending all night the wall-mats of the shed had been rolled down and secured. The waiting men were confined with the bitter stink of boiling lammin and the roaring of the furnaces under the two working vats.

A brace of Rovers, under Kelmz' command, flanked the Senior whom they escorted. They were nervous in this strange atmosphere, but they would answer to Kelmz' voice and hands. The Senior himself looked no different here than he looked when at ease in his home-compound in the City. He stood with his stumpy legs planted apart, his hands folded neatly on his belly. Despite the heat, he hadn't even bothered to draw the starched folds of his mantle down from around his neck and shoulders. His round, balding head was tilted back.

High above them, a network of taut, heavy ropes webbed the mouths of the vats. Two young men ran barefoot over the lines, flickering like visions. Now and then one of them would pause for an instant to cast a wide and measuring glance over the heaving surface of the 'soup' they tended. The metal hooks they carried swung gleaming from each hand. Their skins were sweat-bright and smudged with smoke. They shaved themselves hairless to keep the soup clean, and they wore only shorts. The hooks, part of their balance, hung as naturally from their hands as fingers from the captain's own. 'Lose your footing and lose the soup,' warned the workchants of the sheds.

It was unarguably the dirtiest work men had to do in the Holdfast. Periodically, proposals were made to turn it over to fems instead, but this phase of the processing of a staple of men's diet was considered too important to be entrusted to fems. Besides, attachment to the sheds for a time was a handy punishment for insolent young men. Only one of the pair now running wore the 'Ware Company sign, sewn to the hip of his shorts. The other wore no emblem and was doing time.

Hooks smacked suddenly into the heavily wrapped handle of one of the vat-ladles. The runner's body arced out in a leap from one line to another, by its weight and momentum turning the ladle in the soup. The captain looked hastily away. It made his stomach lurch to see one of those gleaming bodies suspended in the steaming air, like a beast that in Ancient times had leaped in the branches of tall trees . . .

The Rovers stirred uneasily: d Layo had entered the shed. He must have somehow bought himself the freedom of the 'Wares' work-turf, for the runners never even bothered to look down. That was the worst of brutes like d Layo, they corrupted others.

'Servan,' said the Senior, projecting his voice above the roar of the furnaces without actually shouting, 'where can we talk?'

'Right here, Senior,' the DarkDreamer replied. 'It's safe. The patrols keep the beach clear at night now, and the lads up there can't hear us.' He sat down on the lid of a fuel-box and patted the space beside him.

The Hemaway Senior stood where he was and took a deep, deliberate breath.

'Now, Senior — Bajerman, is it?' d Layo said, before his breath could be expelled in speech. 'It's been some time since our last meeting. Oh, please, let's have no apologies over all that, the past is the past. In the interests of brotherly harmony, let's comport ourselves like men newly met. You don't mind the suggestion coming from a younger man, I hope.' He beamed amiably. The Senior ignored his impudence, and d Layo went smoothly on, 'Now, what can this humble young man do for so great a Senior? Nothing too strenuous, I hope? Your messenger found me at an awkward time; I'm all dreamed out for the moment.'

'It's not d Layo the DarkDreamer I've come to see,' the Senior said calmly.

'Servan the outlaw, then?'

The Senior said, 'You romanticize yourself.'

'Which laws do you want broken, Senior?' d Layo smiled. 'It must be very important for you Seniors to give up wanting my blood and start negotiating for my services.'

'Some laws must be bent, so that they may spring back into firmer shape than before.'

'I hope,' d Layo said piously, 'that the years will bring me wisdom as great as your own.'

Knowing things that were not his business had never brought the captain anything but trouble. He withdrew into his own thoughts, yet kept alert. An officer's eyes were trained to be ceaselessly on the move. His success depended on his ability to notice and counteract any inadvertant cues that might set his Rovers off, especially in unfamiliar surroundings.

D Layo and the Senior could arouse the Rovers themselves with harsh tones or sharp gestures; but they weren't arguing. Far from it. The DarkDreamer teased and mocked with both voice and gestures. The Senior sat back stiffly, resisting; again and again he spoke with the insistence of a man trying to restate the serious core of a wandering discussion. Both men knew this game well and played it with pleasure. They ignored even the rumbling of a ladle rolling in its socket overhead, intent as they were on the levels of their game.

The captain's own game began in his head; he saw the Senior as a large, horn-headed beast. The red-and-black mantle became the burnished hide of a thick-shouldered creature, slow but strong, confident and patient, ready to outlast the subtle prowler opposite him, the tawny hunter d Layo. Come to my teeth and my claws, coaxed d Layo; come to my horns and my hooves, lowed the other. They smiled and played their strategies of menace and attraction.

Kelmz shook his head; but he could no more shake free of these visions than he could shake the roar of the fires out of his ears while he stood within reach of their heat. He hugged his ribs with his elbows, blotting the tickling runnels of sweat on his skin. He was bruised from his struggle with the DarkDreamer. Kelmz was too old for such tussles.

It looked as if Senior Bajerman had gotten what he wanted now. He was winding up the conversation, expounding on the need for the raw strength of young men to be curbed by the wisdom of their elders.

'So true,' murmured d Layo. 'You'll permit me to take a mature man with me on this journey so that I can have the benefit of his wisdom? A man with experience running Rovers would be most helpful.' His dark eyes mocked the captain.

'No!' Kelmz blurted, but he had to pause to calm the Rovers, who reacted to his own agitation. This pause gave him time to steady himself as well. He said, 'I mean, Senior, if d Layo means me, I'd rather not.'

'D Layo means you,' the DarkDreamer said. He rose and arched his back, as if bored with a matter already settled.

'Your are commanded, Captain,' the Senior said.

Kelmz bent his head in submission and to hide his angry face. It was clear from the Senior's smug look that he had expected d Layo's request.

The Senior said he would take over direct control of Kelmz' two Rovers for his trip back upriver to the City, adding in a kindly tone, 'It should be welcome to you, Captain, to be relieved of your ordinary responsibilities for a time.'

Saying nothing, the captain unclasped his bracelet of office and surrendered it to the Senior. In its compartments were the carefully measured doses of manna with which an officer bound his Rovers to him. Kelmz looked at the Rovers, the best of the new squad. He didn't think he would command them or their like again. His arm felt as light as if he had given up its bones.

'Hero!' said the Senior to the Rovers. 'I need your escort through danger!'

They stepped forward, speaking passionately and both at once of their prowess as escorts through danger. There was no actual resemblance between them, but the eagerness of their expressions made them look alike. They were very tense; transferring command was always a touchy business. The Senior spoke the traditional calming responses several times; this would serve until he could take time to bind them formally under his control with a manna-dream.

The imagined dangers dream-fixed in the Rovers' minds made them not only alert and fierce, but indiscriminately dangerous unless skillfully handled. Each Rover, in his isolated vision of himself as a hero constantly on guard, imagined all orders to be for his ears alone and himself to be the sole subject of all events. Rover-egotism was considered a sign of healthy, manly individualism and was encouraged, so that getting even two to work efficiently together as a brace was difficult.

Kelmz momentarily wished that the Senior wouldn't be able to hold them; but whatever happened to Senior Bajerman in that case, the Rovers would have to be destroyed as rogues, so it was hardly a thought worthy of an officer.

'Safe journeys,' said the Senior. He drew aside his mantle for a parting salute. The skin of his shoulder was elaborately patterned with the dark dyes of high rank.

Kelmz and the Rovers all touched their own shoulders and bowed. But the DarkDreamer smiled.

'Have you forgotten your salutes?' the Senior said, sharply.

'Have you forgotten that when a man is expelled his shoulder is stripped? He has no salute to give. It's one of the charms of being without standing in the companies.'

'Do this job, and you'll have standing again.'

'Provided the Senior remembers me when the job is finished.'

'I'll remember you,' Senior Bajerman said drily. 'You are a memorable young man.'

He turned and left them, the Rovers pacing alertly at his back.

2

'We'll give him time to get off the beach,' d Layo said. 'We have one stop to make that doesn't concern a person as important as the Senior; and then we're off.' Kelmz remained silent, 'Don't you want to ask me where we're going? I could see you weren't listening to us just now.'

'Nobody was talking to me,' Kelmz said.

'I'm talking to you now.'

Kelmz discovered painfully that though he was older, he lacked the store of haughty tones and cutting phrases used by mature men to keep their juniors in place. None of that had ever been necessary; he had lived with his Rovers, among whom age meant nothing. Now he found himself unarmed against d Layo's mockery and shaken by what the DarkDreamer had to say. Their mission had to do with Endpath.

Apparently a party of pilgrims had returned from there early that same afternoon with the unprecedented news that Endpath was closed. Now it happened sometimes that pilgrims found the Endpath Rovers standing sentry on the roof of the building and a black flag snapping from the mast. That meant that the Endtendant in service had died and would have to be replaced. Alone with four stone-headed Rovers and a stream of death-bound pilgrims, each Endtendant eventually succumbed to the temptation of mixing an extra cup of death-drink for himself. Some young criminal was always speedily appointed to his place. Being chosen for the job was in fact a death sentence, though merciful; the wrongdoer was given time to purge his wicked soul by service until he himself was ready to die like a man.

Never, however, had pilgrims found the flagmast bare, the doors barred and the parapet deserted. It seemed that the present Endtendant had simply withdrawn, locking the pilgrims out.

The purpose of Endpath was to provide Seniors whose souls were ripe for departure with a simple, painless release and remembrance in the Chants Commemorative. To dream into one's death at Endpath was said to assure the life of one's name among younger generations for as long as the sun shone on the manna-bearing hemps that made all dreaming possible. Closing Endpath to death-seekers was an appalling act.

What d Layo had agreed to do for Senior Bajerman was to go to Endpath and dig the Endtendant out of it – no easy feat, since the place was so constructed that one man could hold it against hundreds. Historically, there had been some attacks on Endpath – by Juniors avenging young friends who had gone there prematurely, driven by shame or by the despair of lost loves. Old men, some said, could maneuver young rivals into death on the Rock instead of meeting them fairly in the Streets of Honor, like men.

'Scared?' d Layo inquired.

Of course Kelmz was scared. He had run Rovers too long and survived too many intercompany skirmishes to retain any fascination with death or any illusions about it. In fact, he had been advised more than once by his age-superiors that his own soul was ripe for release at Endpath. But Kelmz had no desire to join his peers – not in wearing the mantle of Seniority, not in walking with stately tread to a dignified death on the Rock. Seniors were not officers; it was, in ordinary times, beneath their dignity to run Rovers. So, as Kelmz had declined to take his mantle on turning thirty years and each year thereafter, he had several times declined the pilgrim robe also. He would not give up running Rovers for the privileges of higher rank or for the dreaming-death. Both meant being cut off from the only company that gave him any pleasure, that of his mad-eyed Rovers.

When d Layo judged it was time they walked out under a lattice from which bunches of cooked lammin were hung to drain – like little gray beasts that had once hung in clusters from the walls of caves, Kelmz thought with a shiver. A melancholy dripping sound surrounded them, and an acrid seastink had soaked permanently into the sand underfoot.

The moon was up, brightening the beach. Rows of small clay lamps dotted the sand. A few were still alight among the crouching forms of fems who were wringing moisture from the lammins with cord-nets. Young men walked in pairs among them, carrying switches with splayed ends. Occasional snapping sounds, followed by yelps, punctuated the plaintive, blurry singing of the fems. The young men wore their hoods up, being nervous about the moon, which was the mistress of all fems and of the evil in them. Older men outgrew such timidity.

These were hags too worn out for other work. Each squatted with her carry-cloth stretched out from her head and over one extended knee, to make shelter from the wind for her hands and for the flickering lamp-flame by which she worked; each fem's fingers shone darkly with the juices of the lammins.

The sky was wide out here. Kelmz preferred to see the night tamed into neat rectangles between compound rooftops. He searched out the four stars that marked the cross-sign and traced it on his own chest. It signified the opposed wills of Father and Son. Though the odd religion was discredited, the sign had survived as a recognition and acceptance of its one great truth.

They walked between rows of extinguished lamps. On the left, the town sloped upward in lamplit tiers. On the right, the black sea shuffled emptily under the stars. Kelmz put up his hood. He was glad that Endpath was beyond sight.

D Layo walked bareheaded, humming to himself. He said, casually, 'Have your Seniors been trying to get rid of you for long? Well, it's obvious that they must want to. A man like you with gray hair and nothing but Junior-stripes on your shoulder must make them nervous, wondering why you persist in standing out of order, so to speak. Maybe they feel insulted that you hang back as if the company of your peers isn't good enough for you.'

'I like my work,' Kelmz said.

'Too much for your own Seniors' taste; though others are more appreciative. Did you know that there are men of the Chester Company here in Lammintown who boast that their second squad of Rovers was trained by Captain Kelmz of the Hemaways? You must have earned your company a fortune in the renting of your services. They show their gratitude very oddly, I'd say.'

Muffled thumping sounds and the drone of fems' voices came faintly from the shredding-shed ahead of them. In the moonlight the shed's walls were nearly black with the stencilled emblems of the companies that had succeeded one another in charge of it, five-year after five-year.

'Does Bajerman want to unload you because he's jealous?' d Layo pursued thoughtfully. 'Does our esteemed Senior have his eye on some young Rover of yours?'

'Rovers make poor lovers.'

'Or have you an admirer outside Rover-ranks whom Bajerman wants for himself?'

'I haven't the looks for it.'

'But the lads love scars,' d Layo began, raising his voice above the growing noise from the shredding-shed. He stopped. Someone was beckoning to them from the open doorway. 'Now what's this? I keep some things of mine in the back here, things we'll need.'

He advanced again, warily. Kelmz walked behind him and to one side; he had no intention of catching anything that was meant for d Layo.

The man at the shed door was one of a pair of young 'Wares in charge of the shredding-gang. He peered out of the yellow light and said irritably to d Layo, 'Somebody's in back waiting for you.'

'What kind of somebody?'

The 'Ware wrinkled his nose. 'One of the pilgrims that got turned back from Endpath today, and by the stink of him they should have let him in. He's been sitting in the storage room all afternoon. I hope he hasn't contaminated the place with some famishing disease. See you get him out by morning, and if any of your stuff's missing, don't blame me; he's the only one been back there.'

D Layo nodded. 'Thanks, Jevv.'

'Thanks yourself,' the 'Ware muttered. He turned and shouted down the length of the shed, 'Pull it in, you bitches! If you make the masters touch you in passing, you'll pay for it!'

He cracked his switch down on the table-end. The fems, working in teams across the narrow surface, pressed their lean bellies against the table's edge. They didn't miss a note of their song. The two-handled shredding-blades jumped without pause between them, chopping and feeding the lammin-fragments steadily back into collecting sacks at the far end.

The storage room smelled strongly of the pickling-tubs along one wall. A pyramid of lammin-packets occupied the center of the floor. Beside the mound a lamp burned, and a man sat straight-backed at the edge of the glow.

'Christ-God-Son!' cursed d Layo. 'Shut the door, those bitches have ears and so do the 'Wares.'

The sounds of the shredding were reduced to a low, vibrant drumming. D Layo bent and lifted the lamp so that its light fell on the stranger in pilgrim gray. The man's hair was black, and his face appeared startlingly pale except for the bruise-blue shadows around his eyes and the dark stubble on his jaw. It was a young face, mid-twenties at most, but it was as hard and cold-looking as a limestone mask.

'How did you know where to find me?' d Layo asked.

'Who is this with you?' The stranger spoke haltingly, as if out of the habit.

'A man of mine,' d Layo said off-handedly, obviously pleased with the idea. 'Captain Kelmz of the Hemaways.'

The stranger's mouth turned down. 'So the Hemaways have mixed into this already.'

'It was Bajerman who came to see me, remember him? He used to teach Deportment when we were in the Boyhouse. Now he claims to speak for the entire Board of Seniors. Thus is virtue rewarded with advancement.'

Kelmz knew, unhappily, who the stranger must be. During the previous five-year the Hemaways had taught at the Boyhouse. They had lost control of two boys to the extent of having had to expel them: one to become Endtendant at Endpath, and the other – d Layo – to his presumed death in the Wild. Kelmz had been training Rovers in Lammintown at the time, but the entire Holdfast had buzzed with the news.

'You've made a deal with Bajerman,' the Endtendant said.

'We dealt together, yes. I'm to get you out of Endpath and deliver you to him in the City, to be handed over to the Board's discipline committee for abandoning your post.' The Endtendant made an abrupt, impatient movement of his head. 'If you have other plans,' d Layo added, 'you'd better tell me.' He settled himself cross-legged on the floor and with an expansive gesture invited Kelmz to sit, too.

These were the kind of smart lads Kelmz had never felt comfortable with. Besides, they had been boys together, which shut Kelmz out. He remained standing.

D Layo shrugged and turned again to the other, studying him critically. 'Jevv was right,' he said, grimacing. 'You do stink. You're not really sick, are you?'

'It's the robe,' the Endtendant replied. 'I took it from one in the last group of pilgrims to be admitted. The smell of illness discourages curiosity.'

'Who knows you're here?'

'No one. A few men know that a pilgrim has been asking for you, that's all. Tell me what the Hemaways have offered for me.'

D Layo grinned. 'They offer Senior status on the Board! How do you like that? Think what I could do, under a Boardman's immunity! They think they could keep me in hand with their plots and alliances, but with a little imagination and nerve there's no limit to what I might do from a position like that!'

'Now tell me how it's all more complicated than I think.'

'Simpler. Mishandling of our cases has cost the Hemaways a great deal in standing. They want us both dead, Servan.'

D Layo glanced up at Kelmz. 'I know they don't like me, but they seem to have found a use for me anyway.'

'Yes, to deliver us both into their hands.'

'Oh, I can get what I want from them and leave them stumbling over their own feet,' d Layo said, carelessly. 'I've made a bargain, Eykar. Can you stop me from going through with it?' He coughed delicately behind his hand. 'We must consider my manly honor, after all.'

The Endtendant gave him a long and chilly stare, and d Layo smirked derisively back at him. Yet some alternative deal hovered in the air between them. They approached that alternative with the easy indirection of men who knew each other well. This was not d Layo baiting Senior Bajerman; these two young men were building on something long established. What they built would have no place in it for Kelmz.

'Come on, Eykar, bribe me,' d Layo said. 'There must be something you can offer that would make it worth my while to hide you from them.'

'I don't want to hide,' the Endtendant said. 'I only want to stay out of their hands long enough to find my father.'

Kelmz looked away uncomfortably. This pale young stranger had been a unique person in the Holdfast long before becoming Endtendant. In a society that took pains to sink the identities of individual fathers and sons into the mass-division of Seniors and Juniors, this man knew his father's name.

In all the Holdfast, no blood-ties were recognized. All men were brothers – that was the Law of Generations – though some were older brothers and some younger. Thus, men avoided the fated enmity of fathers and sons, who once known to each other must cross each other even to the point of mutual destruction. The sons of the Ancients had risen against their fathers and brought down the world; even God's own Son, in the old story, had earned punishment from his Father. Old and young were natural enemies; everyone knew that. To know your father's identity would be to feel, however far off, the chill wind of death.

In a sense, however, the Endtendant was himself the chill wind of death. He did not seem afraid.

D Layo said, 'You got tired of waiting for the old man to come to you at Endpath?'

Rubbing at his forehead as if it ached, the Endtendant answered, 'I caught myself mixing an extra cup, the last time. For myself.' He looked up. 'I can't wait for him to come.'

'I don't understand why he hasn't,' d Layo said. 'Knowing your name and where to find you, why hasn't he had you killed to safeguard his own life?'

'That's what I mean to ask him.'

Incredulously, d Layo said, 'You want to search him out so you can have a polite conversation with him?'

'I'm a man first and his son second,' the Endtendant retorted. 'The proper approach of one rational being to another is through words, not mindless violence.'

'Spare me,' pleaded the DarkDreamer, holding up his hand. 'I should have guessed; finding him is just another test you've decided to set yourself –'

'Alone,' the Endtendant continued, coldly, 'I'll never get to him. I need your help.'

Kelmz felt as if he were dreaming this talk of matters never openly spoken of; but the Endtenant was real. Though young, his face was clearly marked by inward struggle, bleached by the effort of discipline even to the icy irises of the eyes. The pallor of the skin was spectral, set off by the brows and closehugging cap of black hair. Sharp-boned, etched in black and white, it was a fanatic's face, as befitted one bent on smashing the law.

D Layo's voice was tender. 'Suddenly, Eykar, it's you who are the tempter, and I the tempted.' For him, it would be the danger that attracted: the lure of unformed possibilities as opposed to a settled deal with Bajerman. 'To find Raff Maggomas,' he went on, naming the Endtendant's father quite casually, 'we would have to go south to Bayo and try to pick up his trail there. It's been years since he dropped out of sight – as many as our own years out of the Boyhouse. He may go into hiding, if he hasn't already, when he hears that you're on his track. It won't be easy to find him.'

'If that worries you,' the Endtendant said, 'then those years have changed you a great deal more than they've changed me.'

'Eykar,' the DarkDreamer said, 'they haven't changed you at all.' He allowed one beat of silence to mark the existence of agreement between them. Then he pointed at Kelmz with a tilt and thrust of his chin.

'And what about this old Rover-runner here? Now that the plan is changed, it seems to me I owe him for the sleep and the work he's cost me lately, with his cursed snuffling around after me through every dive in town, though I'm sure he's enjoyed himself. Do you have any objection, Eykar, to my settling with him before we start out?'

3

Fickle as a fem, Kelmz thought bitterly, or as devious as one, to plan this all along. Either way, d Layo was wolf enough to take Kelmz on here and now, and never mind official standings or the Streets of Honor.

The Endtendant was looking at Kelmz with a steady, cool regard, though it was to d Layo that he spoke: 'So this is the man who won't take his mantle. Did Bajerman send him with you to get rid of him?'

'That's right,' d Layo said cheerfully, producing a knife from his sleeve; a thin-bladed, well-balanced weapon honed to a bright-edged, satiny finish, Kelmz noted – a professional item. ' "Gray head yields to young blade," as they say.'

'Captain Kelmz,' the Endtendant said, 'if Senior Bajerman were here now, he would insist that you try to enforce the terms of the original bargain. To do that, you must fight Servan here at the outset. In spite of your reputation, I think Servan would kill you. I suggest that you turn your back on those who have turned their backs on you. Come with us. There's no shame in a fighting death, but I would rather have you as an ally than leave you as a corpse on this fem-stinking beach.'

'Eykar, you're being reckless,' d Layo reproved him. 'He'll say yes and turn on us later. Don't you think other men have tried to buy him over from the Hemaways before this? In the end, he'll be loyal to his company, whatever he says now to save his life.'

'Treachery is *your* style,' the Endtendant snapped. 'That's why I need a man like the captain. I'm not such a fool as to travel the Holdfast alone with you, Servan.'

The DarkDreamer put on a hurt expression. 'I try to help, and what do I get in return? Insults!' He grinned at Kelmz. 'Come on, Captain, you can't resist the call of duty: 'Hero, I need your escort through danger!" '

Ignoring him, Kelmz said, 'I have a question.' He cleared his throat. 'What happened to the Endpath Rovers? There have always been four of them, specially trained, with standing orders from the Board to keep the Endtendant safe – inside of Endpath.'

'That's correct.' The Endtendant stood up. He wasn't tall, and his build was light, but well corded with muscle. Kelmz knew the type: frail-looking and nervy, cable-tough under strain. He held his head back so that he seemed to look at Kelmz levelly, eye to eye. 'The Endpath Rovers wouldn't have allowed me to leave, but they were vulnerable. One of their duties was to dispose of the dead. The central chamber at Endpath is a domed circle, where the drink is mixed and dispensed to the pilgrims. Then each man goes apart into an individual cell to dream his death properly, as he would any other dream – in private. My part ends when I've handed the last man his cup and put his name down for inclusion in the Chants Commemorative.

'Later, the Rovers enter and bring the bodies back into the central chamber, where there's a chute leading down to an incinerator under the floor. When the corpses are cleared out, the Rovers leave and seal the chamber behind them, and I open a sluice-gate from outside. The sea floods the chamber and scours it out.

'This last time, I locked the Rovers in while they were still working, and I opened the sluices. They drowned.'

'Did you watch?'

'Yes, from the gallery above.'

Sometimes an officer had to kill his own Rovers if they were maimed or went rogue; Kelmz had accepted that necessity long ago. He felt that any man who would not look at his own lethal handiwork was no man at all.

'Then you traveled down here alone?' he said, frowning. It was reckless for a man to risk his mental balance between the emptyness of sky and land.

'No,' the Endtendant said. 'I waited outside Endpath until the next group of pilgrims came. They began milling around in confusion when they saw that something was wrong on the Rock. I slipped in among them, dressed like this, and came back with them on the ferry.'

He looked at the captain, waiting. His eyes were disquietingly clear and steady; Kelmz could not return their gaze for long. The dull black of the Endtendant's uniform showed at the breast and cuffs of the pilgrim gown.

'Are you satisfied?' the Endtendant demanded.

The captain saw a night-plumed being, nervous and awkward on the ground but in the air a dark and wheeling grace, lacing the wind with harsh cries.

'Oh, Kelmz is satisfied,' d Layo said, sulkily. 'Look at him, he's half in love with you already.' He put away his knife and rose neatly to his feet, yawning. 'I'll get together the things we'll need; you two rest, we don't leave till morning.'

'I've rested enough,' the Endtendant said. 'Captain, will you walk outside with me?'

'Of course he will,' d Layo leered. 'But come back before sunrise; it's better that no one sees either of you.'

The beach was empty; even the shredding-shed was silent now. The Lammintown horns shouted periodically over the hissing of the sea. They walked by the water. The Endtendant held the skirts of the pilgrim robe clear of the wet sand by bunching his fists in the pockets. He looked eastward over the water, as if there were something to see out there.

With the moon up so bright there weren't even any netting-crews out sifting the tides; the plankton that they sought only surfaced on dark nights or if it were roiled up from the bottom by storms. It was too early in the fall for bad weather. Kelmz wondered where he would be when the storms began. He couldn't see his way at all as a companion of these two. He didn't think he would ever be comfortable in the Endtendant's company.

They walked without speaking for some time until, brushing up against the Endtendant's arm by accident, Kelmz felt a tremor in him.

'It's cold,' the captain said. 'Let's turn back.'

'I will; you don't have to.'

Kelmz stopped and looked up at the paling sky. 'I'm committed to come with you. I won't try to turn you over to Bajerman or to the Board, my word on it. I'm a man, not a boy. You can't trust me.'

'What choices do I have?' The Endtendant uttered hard cracks of sound not much like laughter. 'Of course I must trust you, and Servan, and who knows how many other unlikely types before our journey is over. But I can try to minimize my risks. You must be nearly my father's age; whether you wear a mantle or not, Captain, the years make us enemies.'

'The way things stand,' Kelmz observed, 'you don't have anything but enemies. Even your age-peers would sell you to the Board for extra points, anything to enlarge their share of the lammin-harvest, lean as it is. If you think my age makes me a special risk, why didn't you let d Layo cut my throat just now?'

'I don't like Servan's attitude toward killing,' the Endtendant said, drily. 'He's too casual. I can manage alone with him if I must.'

'Look, I have no place else to go but with you.' Kelmz fell abruptly silent, feeling the heat of shame on his cheeks. What a thing to admit to a younger man!

To his relief, the Endtendant merely said, 'All right.'

Only age-peers shook hands. They gave each other a short nod of assent and turned back down the beach. Already a fem-gang could be heard approaching from the town; the low weave of their plaintive voices made a walking rhythm of intersecting tones.

The Endtendant said, 'They shouldn't be allowed to sing. Don't you find their voices disturbing?'

Most men were entirely too preoccupied with the creatures, in Kelmz' opinion. 'No.'

'I do.' The Endtendant put up his hood.

Beyond the silent shredding-shed, the pier reached out over the water. Netters' boats tied to the tall pilings bobbed all along its length. At the far end, where the ferry pylon reared up against the sky, the winch-housing of the coastal ferry was visible. One winch-arm angled darkly up across the dawn.

Some one was standing there, urgently waving: d Layo.

They glanced at each other and stepped up their pace, walking swiftly past the shed. As they cleared it, a man straightened from examining footprints in the sand. He was a highmantled Senior. At his shout, two other men came charging around the side of the shed:

Rovers.

On the run, the captain veered toward the water, shouldering the Endtendant into it. They plunged through the icy tide and clambered into the first of the netting-boats. There was rope coiled in the prow, with a grapnel fixed to one end. Kelmz swung the grapnel and hurled it upward. The cross-arm caught behind the head of a piling above them.

The Endtendant climbed up, the sea-soaked skirts of the robe clinging to his legs. Kelmz followed.

As he had intended, the Rovers had been thrown off by the change of footing. They were pelting around the long way, up the steps into the pier from the landward end. Kelmz held back a pace, racing down the pier, to cover the Endtendant if he had to, for the Rovers were closing hard. A yard ahead of them, Kelmz and the Endtendant dashed across the gangway onto the deck of the ferry. Someone kicked away the gangway, and gouts of cold water shot up over the rail.

The two Rovers stood panting on the pier, eyeing their trapped quarry. Kelmz' Rovers would have jumped the gap and made the enemy secure. It was a sign of the times that these Rovers did not do so, though Kelmz knew them (by their gear, knives sheathed on the left hip for a slicing crossdraw) to be products of a first-class training officer in 'Ware Company. They were slightly unsure of themselves and should have had an officer in charge of them, not the 'Ware Senior who stood far down the pier talking with another man.

D Layo, ignoring the Rovers and their master, presented the newcomers to a ferryman who leaned stolidly on the railing. This man, bulky in salt-stiff clothing, studied them both from his single eye. The other socket was closed by a discolored veil of skin. He was a young man still, but nearing the top of Junior status by the look of him, nudging the crucial age of thirty years. His name was Hak. A salt-eaten Chester symbol was stitched crookedly to his cap.

He stabbed his thumb in the direction of the two 'Wares, who were striding toward the ferry now: 'Friends of yours?'

'Hardly,' said d Layo.

The white-haired Senior came emphatically first, though not in haste. Seniors never hurried.

Hak looked Kelmz up and down. 'What are you, man, under that blank-coat?'

'Hemaway.'

The authoritative voice of the approaching 'Ware Senior rang out: 'You, on the ferry!'

'Not Captain Kelmz?' Hak said, with mild interest.

'Yes,' Kelmz said.

'Right.' The ferryman winked his eye and turned to gaze coolly up at the 'Ware Senior. Apparently what d Layo had said was true: there were Chesters who remembered the work Kelmz had done for them once, to which they owed several recent skirmish-victories against their rival, 'Ware Company. Blandly, Hak said, 'Do something for you, Senior?'

'Give me those three men.'

Hak looked thoughtfully down into the water. 'My gangway got knocked overside, Senior. There it is, floating.'

The Senior did not look down. He wore a beard in the fashion of Lammintown Seniors and had singed his eyebrows to make them grow in thick and spiky. Frowning, he looked impressively fierce. 'This isn't the first time we've had trouble with you Chesters this five-year. Your superiors will not be pleased.'

'Never are,' Hak said, sadly.

There was a short pause. The morning wind plucked at the ferry cable that swooped down from the top of the pylon to the deck wheel. Two ferrymen lounged at the winch, looking bored.

The Senior said menacingly, 'This is no game, Boyo.'

To this insulting term, Hak responded merely by spitting carefully into the water between the ferry and the pier.

The other 'Ware, a Junior, hung unhappily in the background, pretending to be blind and deaf for fear he would have to pay later for having witnessed the scoring-off of the Senior at a Junior's hands. In theory, the Senior should not have entered into any game-point rivalry with the young man, since for anyone over the age of thirty the simple accretion of years measured personal worth on an absolute scale. But informally, fierce competition was the rule among Seniors as well as Juniors, though normally it was confined to verbal games like this one. Older men found in the accumulation of gamepoints (which they affected to despise) a way of unofficially offsetting the implacable order of the age-scale among themselves.

This 'Ware Senior mastered his anger carefully to avoid further losses in his encounter with the Chester ferryman.

'Listen,' he said, 'you'd better understand what you're mixing into. There have been reports of unlawful use of my company's work-turf. These are the offenders. They are two unknowns, probably Skidro drifters going home via Bayo with whatever they've lifted in Lammintown, including some packets of prime lammin that are missing from storage. The third one is the DarkDreamer d Layo, who's long overdue for burning. The price on his head is enough points to buy you free of your duties for a five-year.'

The ferryman took off his grimy cap and scratched his head. He squinted down the coast toward the next pylon, and the ones beyond that; they marched parallel to the beach in single file as far as the eye could see.

'Who says I don't do my job right?' he demanded suddenly. 'What man in the Chesters? Or is it just you 'Wares that say it?'

The Senior's bristling eyebrows rose. 'I didn't criticize the way you do your job —'

'Then what's this talk about getting me off my boat? You trying to score me off, Senior? Taking advantage of a rough working lad that's been at sea too long?'

Turning on his subordinate, the Senior curtly ordered him to get the Rovers out of earshot of the discussion. The older man plainly appreciated the difficulties of his position, and he was giving himself time to think. He could hardly send for a Chester Senior, for he would incur enormous humiliation for himself and his company by appealing for help in dealing with an uppity Junior.

The Senior leaned out over the piling and said balefully, 'A man who helps a thief is worse than a thief, in these lean times. You might remember that you are no Pennelton, to walk off this boat in Bayo and sleep safe for the rest of the five-year with the whole coast between us. You'll be coming back here on your return run, and when you do, I'll have your standing stripped. You're compounding an injury done my company on its own work-turf, and that's injury to all. It will cost the Chesters a lot to make it good. It will certainly cost them you.

'Think about that, Junior, and consider: who should pay the price of theft, you or the thieves?'

'There's a lot of things lying crooked between the 'Wares and the Chesters, Senior. Maybe it's time it all got put straight. Then we'd find out who owed whom.'

Without another word, the Senior turned and stalked off, with his entourage hurrying after him.

'Go stick it up a fem,' Hak muttered. Giving Kelmz a sour grin, he stumped off toward the winch deck, shouting at the men standing there. They leaped up onto the winch housing and laid hold of the handles with their gauntleted hands.

D Layo sighed. 'Well, Captain,' he said, 'I suppose I must grant you some usefulness after all.'

4

No Seniors rode the ferries, except occasionally as passengers. Skilled administrators (some were even literate), they were in charge of record-keeping ashore. Aboard the ferries, the older Juniors were responsible for the crew, passengers and cargo between dockings. One-eyed Hak had been crew chief on the coastal run since the beginning of the five-year.

The ferry itself was a converted river craft which had replaced the legendary ocean-goer lost long ago. The story was that a Senior had insisted on taking Rovers on a sea trip with him and that one of them had gone rogue and cut the cable. The ferry had drifted out onto the empty immensity of water and had never been seen again. The largest of the river craft had been altered to take its place, for by that time the building of ships was an art that had vanished with the trees cleared from the Holdfast.

There were tales, of course, of ships of the Ancients which had been driven by fire and by secret and strange substances that could kill a man on contact. These legends ranked with stories of craft, carrying human cargo, that could hurl themselves through the air for great distances. That had been in the days when the world was so rich in metal that there was plenty for the fashioning of mighty machines.

In the Holdfast, requests for metal went through the company hierarchies to the Board, which might pass them on to the town of 'Troi. Not many orders were filled; the furnaces of 'Troi could only turn out so much metal goods per five-year. Tools, weapons, and replacement parts for the few machines still in use had priority. Extra work-time and material tended to go into luxury items like jewelry, which only Seniors could afford.

The ferries were powered by machines. 'Troi engineers had designed a system of gears by means of which the strength of men on the winch was amplified and transferred to rotary blades at the rear of the craft. Certainty of staying within sight of land was assured by the long cable which fed down from the pylons through a wheel fixed to the midships decking. The whole arrangement was slow and clumsy, but free of the perils of fast-moving, free-ranging boats. The Holdfast could not afford to lose another ferry.

All that remained of shipyard skill was the ability to patch and trim existing vessels with wood won from the Wild. Each bit of the precious material was polished and shaped by the hand of every man in a given crew before being ceremonially installed. The names of the men who dared the empty lands beyond the borders of the Holdfast to obtain wood went into special Chants Celebratory concerning the ferries. Every step of the patching process was, like most of the things the ferrymen did, part of a fabric of custom intended to hold ferrycrews together in manly order, despite their isolation between empty sea and empty sky.

The huge hold of the coastal ferry was lit by hanging lamps and stray sunlight that entered the high-set ports. The air was hot, moist and permanently impregnated with the reek of sweat, lammins and beer. The noise never stopped.

At the center of the hold was the play-pen, a pit of sand that was the scene of the perpetual contests and games with which ferrymen filled their off-deck hours. Something was always going on in the pen and at the tile gameboards that made up the apron around it. Every match drew its mob of shouting spectators.

Forward, the sweating sloppers tended cook-tubs sunk into the tops of great clay fire-boxes in which fires roared day and night. Aft, past the cargo-space and the rows of crewmen's hammocks, someone was always playing the part of story-box to whatever audience he could keep, bellowing out his tale in order to be heard above the general din. The entire ship reverberated ceaselessly to the growling of winch and propeller blades.

The gleaming skins of the ferrymen, who went about in shorts or nothing at all below decks, reminded Kelmz of insect armor. Even the interminable activity and racket struck him as mimicry of the meaningless scurryings of those strange, tiny beasts of the Ancients' times.

He had never travelled by water before, except under awnings on the decks of river barges. His journeys had commonly been overland, with a brace or two of Rovers in his charge. There were no Rovers on the ferry; there was nothing familiar or easy. The heat made him dizzy; the stuffiness choked him; the constant rolling cost him several meals. It was impossible to sleep in all the noise, but he didn't need much sleep, having nothing active to do; and he didn't eat a lot.

The food — never enough of it here any more than elsewhere at Juniors' tables — was invariably blue-stew with dollops of the hemproot starch called taydo in it; thin slices of hempseed bread smeared with plankton jelly; and pale beer to wash it all down. The only relief was the occasional fresh salad made with the lammins that d Layo had turned over to the sloppers on first entering the hold. That gesture had won him friends from the start.

He had built on this beginning by becoming an enthusiastic participant in the games at the play-pen. As a DarkDreamer and an outlaw he lived outside the company system of work- and game-points, so he took his winnings in cash. This should have made trouble for him since Juniors were always short of cash, their only means of buying any sort of luxury beyond the subsistence distributed to them by the companies. Yet without apparent effort, d Layo shortly became so popular with the young Chesters that he influenced their private status structure.

Officially, work-points determined a company's subsistence portion every five-year, and game-points converted into individual shares of spending cash for the Juniors. But among themselves young men vied for standing on the basis of scars. This system had begun as a defiant glorification of the marks of corporal punishment. By the time the Board had substituted more subtle forms of discipline, the Holdfast Juniors had established an underground hierarchy based not only on verbal contests but on scars gotten in fights. It was rare for a young man not to be marked up, even if he had to inflict wounds on himself.

To Kelmz' surprise, the DarkDreamer had very little to show under his shirt other than the pallid discolorations of an acid-bleached rank-tattoo on his shoulder and a few faded wound-weals that he did nothing to enlarge or freshen up. Smooth skin should have worked against d Layo; but something in his manner and his impressive showing in the ferrymen's games converted it into an asset. Within a few days of leaving Lammintown, it became the fashion on the ferry to modestly cover one's scars with a shirt. The theory was that a man who stood ready to prove his courage in action had no need to show off evidence of past bravery.

Similarly, because d Layo wore no jewelry but his manna-bracelet, the younger ferrymen soon put away their own highly prized ceramic earrings, pendants, anklets and studded belts. D Layo mockingly ascribed these changes to Kelmz' influence, not his own.

By professional habit the captain sported no ornaments. He continued to wear his patched and threadbare suit of blanks, saving his uniform. It was not a Rover's way to display his body like a boastful boy. Kelmz was hoping the anonymity of blanks would help him spend the voyage in quiet obscurity.

However, on the first morning out he woke from a fretful doze to find a ribby, freckle-skinned lad, ostentatiously scarred on chest and arms, waiting silently by his hammock. This Junior politely requested that Captain Kelmz come join a group at the story-box. Once Kelmz accepted out of courtesy, he found himself trapped into a pattern that repeated itself daily, to his intense embarrassment.

The young men would begin complimenting him. By reputation, it seemed, Kelmz was strong, skillful, efficient, loyal, brave, honest, and on and on until he couldn't tell whether they were describing some mythical paragon of the manly virtues or trying to make a fool of him. He would sit among them with a flush in his seamed cheeks and his big hands clenched, until he could bear no more of their bright-faced praise. When he finally started to rise and leave them, someone would say, 'Will the Captain tell about the time two Rovers went rogue on him on the river-road near Oldtown?' Or about the skirmish with Birj Company at the City breweries, or a fight in a Lammintown Street of Honor, or even the time he had carried his friend Danzer, fatally injured, five miles on his own back?

These lads knew Kelmz' life better than he did himself, and they pressed him unabashedly about events that he would have preferred to forget. By convention, a man could not refuse to tell a story that he knew or to come back next time and finish one that had been interrupted. Kelmz' stories were always interrupted.

D Layo claimed that some of the regular Chester story-boxers were angry because Kelmz was stealing their audience. Kelmz said he didn't understand how the young men knew so much about him.

The DarkDreamer laughed at that. 'Kelmz, you are an innocent. Haven't you ever looked past your Rover-brutes at anything? Man, you're a walking legend, and for once there are no Seniors around to check the lads' demonstration of their feelings. How would you expect youngsters to regard a famous fighting man who sticks by his Junior status and his dream-doped Rovers in spite of all customs and pressure?'

'They don't know anything about it,' Kelmz muttered and refused to discuss the matter further. He felt as if he had won the young Chesters' respect falsely.

The situation grew serious when the freckled lad turned up one morning with a gold-glazed earring which he pressed on the captain as a gift; then he asked for a story that was part of a courting-series. Kelmz didn't care about the jealousy of the lad's prior friend, an older Junior chiefly noticeable these days for his sullen looks; but he felt he had no right to divert the young Chester from companionship within his own company and age-group. Though Kelmz was not an officially mantled Senior, by any biological reckoning the freckled lad was on the Junior side of the age-line. The appropriate attitude of an older man toward a younger was wary concern, not lust. A man could hardly have a relationship of equals with one less mature than himself. Kelmz had no intention of descending to the vice of boy-stealing. Besides, after the years with Danzer, Kelmz had formed the habit of avoiding close bonds with other men.

He retreated; he went up on deck, where he found the Endtendant standing at the rail.

The Endtendant spent daylight hours alone there, with all that bleak sky overhead and fathoms of water below and nothing but the line of the land, gliding past, to look at. He even kept his back turned to the chanting ferrymen on the winch, as if he actually enjoyed solitude in the open. He was slightly tanned by sun and wind. His eyes were the same pale windows on the chilly place behind the mask.

Kelmz nodded a greeting, which was curtly returned, and leaned on the worn rail a little distance away. He watched the water slide by below. That was a mistake.

The sight of the shifting surface in whose depths nothing lived any more brought horribly to mind all sorts of stories that no decent man should even recall from his Boyhouse lessons, let alone picture in vivid detail: house-sized fish that ate ships, many-legged bladder-beasts skittering along the bottom of the sea to gobble the bodies of drowned men . . . Kelmz closed his eyes and turned his face up to the cleansing light of the sun.

Fortunately, that afternoon they sighted the tall marshgrass that grew between Bayo and the beach. That was also the day that the Endtendant was recognized.

Thanks to ceaseless prodding by the freckled lad's friend, certain Chesters who were contemporaries of d Layo and the Endtendant had worked out who the DarkDreamer's companion must be. When Kelmz and the Endtendant came belowdecks for the evening meal, they found a meeting in progress. Hak was addressing the assembled men with some heat, while those who had precipitated the crisis stood in a group at his right, headed by Sullen-face and the freckled lad.

Hak was saying that he had extended the freedom of the ferry to the strangers on the strength of Kelmz' reputation and because of a natural sympathy for any young men in trouble with Seniors. He had not counted on one of the fugitives turning out to be an outlaw Endtendant.

D Layo got to his feet, brushing sand from his chest and arms. Though his skin was blotched with red marks from a play-pen match, he seemed unruffled and spoke in a tone of light incredulity. 'Leaving aside for the moment the question of identities, is it seriously suggested that these young Chesters refuse to help other young men – or maybe even turn them over to the cloth-cocks for cash?'

The listeners guffawed; young men sometimes called Seniors that, meaning that the only thing an old man could still get up was his mantle.

Sullen-face retorted, 'If there's a reward, why not? It's not every day that men have a chance to do their manly duty and get paid well for it besides.'

At that point someone noticed the two new arrivals, and a cry was raised: 'There's the man!'

Hak called, 'Are you Eykar Bek, Endtendant of Endpath?'

And the Endtendant said, 'Yes.'

'Ah, Christ,' Kelmz said, with deep disgust; to throw away their lives so simply was a crime. He set his hand on the hilt of his knife.

'Then something has to be done,' Hak declared. 'I know who gets blamed by those here when this five-year ends and the work-points and game-points presented by this company are discounted by the Board because we've helped a renegade Endtendant. There won't be plenty to go around to begin with. The Board will be looking for reasons to cut shares where they can.'

There were mutterings at this. The Chesters shot sidelong looks at the outsiders or frowned at the floor and avoided looking at them at all.

D Layo smiled. 'Brothers,' he said, stepping forward with casual grace, 'I have a story to tell.'

5

By these words, he took on the role of story-box, and with it the right to speak.

'When I was some years into my education,' he began, 'a certain boy was put into my class. Everyone talked about him, not because he was smart and was being moved ahead of his age-peers, but because he was special in another way: he knew his father's name, and his father knew his.'

They groaned; he had them. Not one of these young men could fail to recall the fear of his own early years, that somehow his father would identify him and have him destroyed. There were a few well known historical cases of Seniors arranging the deaths of boys whom they suspected to be their own sons. This was the basis of the insecurity that afflicted every boy as soon as he understood the natural enmity between generations. That insecurity was never fully outgrown.

It made sense, after all: sons, fresh from the bellies of fems, were tainted with the destructiveness which characterized their dams. Therefore they were dangerous. It was natural for fathers to protect themselves from their sons' involuntary, irrational aggression by striking first.

On the other hand, the Holdfast needed these sons to live long enough to outgrow the fem-taint and join the world of mature men in their turn. This was the reason for the existence of the Boyhouse and the justification for the strict lives led by its inmates. The rules were harsh, designed not only to wipe out the unmanly streak as soon as possible, but to protect boys from the righteous wrath of their fathers in the meantime.

There had been times when adult men had organized deadly raids on whatever concentrations of boys they could find. This sport had served as a reminder that men would not forget the Freaks, the sons of Ancient men who had turned against their fathers in the Wasting and paid for their treachery with their lives. The raids no longer occurred. The Boyhouse kept the boys, and with them the future, safe; here their souls were beaten into a hardness that would be fitting to the souls of men.

Later, men grew old enough to breed and to search the faces of young boys for likenesses to their own. But no one ever forgot his own time within the Boyhouse walls, hiding in the anonymous mob of his peers.

The young Chesters squirmed in their places, thinking of the boy who had known his father's name and whose father had known his.

'Now, how could this be?' d Layo said. 'It goes against the Law of Generations. This man – the father – who was a Tekkan from Lammintown called Raff Maggomas, took a fem from the Tekkan breeding rooms the first night of her heat and kept her with him in a secret place until she had cooled again. He marked her neck, here at the back just under the hair, with blue rank-dye –' The Chesters buzzed with outrage at this. '– and slipped her back into her place. During the time Maggomas kept her for himself, no one noticed that a cold fem had been substituted for her in the breeding-rooms, one fem being very like another. This man Maggomas had put together enough standing and favors-owed to accomplish the deed.

'Next, he arranged to be in the City when that fem was sent to the Hospital to drop her young. Now, what do you think would have happened if the bitch had dropped a fem-cub?'

Laughter; someone called out, 'He'd have gone home again a lot faster than he'd come!'

'Since you ask me, I'll tell you,' d Layo said. He was good at this, making a play of expression and gesture to wring the full degree of delicious disgust from the unnatural events of which he told. 'Maggomas had a confederate at the Hospital, and that man marked the cub with the same blue mark that was on the neck of the fem that had dropped it. So when Maggomas sneaked into the Boyhouse next day, he found the marked cub and read off the name the

Teachers had inscribed on its boy-tags.

'But having accomplices means sharing secrets, and you all know how the cloth-cocks talk, sitting with their lumpy old feet up to the hearth-fire day and night. Some years later, word got out.

'By that time, nothing could be proven, and there was always the chance that some youngster had started the rumor as a way of getting at Maggomas for a private reason.' Knowing nods from the young Chesters, who were familiar with such private reasons. 'Maggomas himself had nothing to say on the subject, though I doubt he was ever asked point blank. He was a Senior himself, and among themselves they are so standing-proud and courteous that they don't even have words to frame such a question. So the fem was burned on suspicion of having witched a man into breaking the Law of Generations, and the Board left it at that.

'Now, think a bit about the son, Eykar Bek. There he was, knowing that something set him apart from his peers and wondering what it was. When the rumors reached him, he heard the name of his father for the first time. Think about living with that: listening for the footfalls of a murderer at night, studying the faces of the Teachers for one who had been paid to strike for Maggomas . . .

'Well, if such plans were made, they never came to completion. What did happen was that an unfortunate friendship was permitted to develop between Eykar Bek and another boy – a bad boy, a boy of clearly corrupt character, a boy who was in fact destined to become a DarkDreamer.'

D Layo bowed facetiously, and some of the Chesters applauded.

'Now, what do you think came of this attachment? Why, trouble came of it, as any fool could have foreseen. The bad boy's curiosity led him to explore the art of the DarkDream. He involved Eykar Bek in his activities; they were caught; they were punished. One of the boys was dumped into the Wild to die. The other – Raff Maggomas' son, as it happened – was exiled to Endpath to become Endtendant, even though he was not yet invested as a Junior.'

Suddenly d Layo shot out a pointing hand: 'And there he is. While he's here among you, you might ask him why he abandoned his assigned work-turf. Ask him why he turned away a mob of sick-stinking whiteheads (with perhaps a few broken-spirited lads mixed in among them) and left the death-manna for someone else – or no one else – to brew. Ask him where he's going and who he's looking for and what he means to do when he finds him!'

The sullen-faced man gnawed at his thumbnail, saying nothing. No one spoke. They all looked at the Endtendant.

Kelmz heard Bek's voice rattle rustily in his throat a moment, before the words came out: 'I have a question for Raff Maggomas.'

'Only one question?' a Chester shouted. It wasn't a joke; nobody laughed.

Another cried, 'Why hasn't he had you killed?'

'Have you any real, blood brothers that you know of?'

'My question,' the Endtendant said, over their excited murmuring, 'is this: I want to know why I was singled out from among those who otherwise would have been my peers. I want to know the reason for blackening my whole life with the shadow of another man, of another generation.'

A Junior stood up and said, 'I have a question I'd like asked too, as long as you're going to be asking questions. This Maggomas must be an old man now, maybe he'll know the answer. I'd like to know how come Seniors live on limitless credit for doing nothing while working men have to get by on the pitiful rations they give us. That's what I'd like to know.' He sat down again.

Other questions followed. The Chester Juniors asked what they would never have dared to ask any Senior to his face: how was it that the cloth-cocks took the most powerful manna to dream themselves into fitting strength of mind and virtue, but still acted with spite and self-indulgence when awake? How was it that they said one thing and did another, all the time cursing the Juniors for famishing deceitfulness? Enforced the age-line except where it cut them off from the objects of their own lusts? Would hear no petition from younger men unless in the presence of the Boardmen, whose power over young men's lives was utterly intimidating? Ruled that a young man had to carry all his life a name picked from a list drawn out of the Boardmen's dreams, though he might wish to call himself after some friend or hero in respectful memory?

Their voices raw with fury, the Chesters gave the Endtendant no chance to speak. He stood silent, ice-eyed, like a personification of the cold heart of their rage.

When the excitement began to die down, Hak made one last try: 'How do we know that this DarkDreamer has told us the truth?'

'Ask one you trust,' d Layo rejoined. He nodded at Kelmz. 'What does the first fighter in the Holdfast, the man who won't take his mantle, have to say?'

Kelmz cleared his throat and said he thought truth had been spoken.

The Chesters set up a roar and a storm of clapping. Hak bowed to it; he promised on behalf of the whole company to do what was needed to speed the Endtendant on his way. Immediately, d Layo outlined what he wanted.

'When the rumors of his having claimed a son got out, Maggomas left the Tekkans and went off to Bayo, and we haven't heard of him since. We can't go to the Board and ask them where he is, and the men at Bayo are Pennceltons assigned there this five-year, so they won't know anything. Some of the older Bayo fems might remember, though, and anything they know we can get out of them – if we can reach them and deal with them privately. We need you lads to see to it that we won't be disturbed in Bayo.

'Set us down on the coast a little way north, and you go on upriver and dock at Bayo as usual. We'll make our way there through the marshes and try to enter the fems' quarters after dark. All you have to do is to make dinner in Bayo such a drunken, enjoyable affair that no Pennceltons come wandering outside while we're looking for a way into the fems' section.

'After that, we're on our own – but the longer you can keep our visit among you secret, the better for us and for you.'

'Done,' said Hak, promptly, before any more could be asked. 'Done!' shouted the Chester Juniors. Someone added, 'And a Dark-Dream to seal it,' a cry which others took up.

Ferrymen were only permitted to dream between runs, under the auspices of their Seniors. Now they were daring in their excitement. Learning that d Layo had only enough manna to serve a few, they quickly put together a group of eight to represent the complicity of them all in the fugitives' lawlessness. Sullen-face and the freckled lad were both included.

For the others, Hak had kegs of beer broken out to go with the scanty evening meal. Supplies were apt to run short at the end of the coastal run, and the only ferrymen to escape the grip of hunger tonight would be those lucky enough to be caught up in a dream. Some of the more talented chanters performed around the play-pen, improvising lyrics and obscene pantomimes, a welcome distraction to the others.

Hak was a good chief; he knew how to pull his people together. Kelmz was ashamed of d Layo's blatant theatrics, and he hoped that the one-eyed ferryman wouldn't suffer for all this in the end. For a man who bore no responsibility himself, d Layo was adept at maneuvering those who did.

The dreaming-group went back to the story-box area and hung mats from the ceiling for privacy. A ferryman brought a pitcher of beer and some mismatched mugs on a tray; another supplied a mixing-whisk of straws bound with cord. D Layo squatted by a brazier and heated the beer, not bothering with the Chants Preparatory. The others, seated in a circle around him, began to murmur the Chant Thankful, which extolled the virtues of the hemp: it provided fiber to clothe men's bodies, food for their nourishment, and manna for the dreaming of their souls. Sullen-face sweated a lot, and stuttered every time he chanted the refrain.

It was, Kelmz thought, going to be one sorry excuse for any kind of a dreaming.

D Layo used the doubled-over hem of his shirt to pad the hot handle of the pitcher. A sweet scent rose as he shook powder from the compartments in his bracelet into the steaming liquid. He whipped the mixture in the cups before taking the ceremonial first sip from each one.

A man could grow attached to the rituals, especially if (like Kelmz) he was accustomed to being dream-giver to Rovers who were utterly dependent on him in that role. The Chants Commanding, which went with Rover-dreaming, kept running through Kelmz' mind. He glanced at the Endtendant, whose angular face showed nothing at all.

It was absurd to impute nostalgia to him, of course. The dream he had given had always been death. He could hardly have put off his own bracelet of office with any feeling but relief.

D Layo began handing out the cups. Bek refused with a wordless shake of his head, and no one made anything of it; but when Kelmz hesitated, he noticed that several of the ferrymen were watching him anxiously. Perhaps they had never DarkDreamed before. They trusted Kelmz' judgment and were waiting for him to drink.

This wouldn't be the first time Kelmz had DarkDreamed. He had indulged once or twice to no great effect, with fellow officers. That had been before he had started seeing beasts, a thing that had come upon him suddenly soon after Danzer had died with his throat torn out by a rogue Rover. Kelmz had not DarkDreamed since then. His waking visions were DarkDream enough.

Now he looked into the cup, warming his hands on the glazed surface, and thought, why not? He was an outlaw among outlaws, his legitimate life was over. He drank.

The manna-beer tasted gluey; d Layo hadn't taken time to mix it properly, the slovenly brute.

The others drank too. They hunched closer together and listened to d Layo, who had begun a low, singing-chant.

A man was supposed to be an individual. He was supposed to go apart and strengthen his soul with a dream from among those taught in the Boyhouse, which were all on the same heroic themes: dreams of victorious battles against monsters, dreams of power and wealth bent to the good of lesser men, dreams of manly love and lifelong loyalties, dreams of endurance and achievement – an endless selection of patterns keynoted to the manly virtues. In this way the soul could be schooled independently of the drowning flesh. Each man, in command of his own dreaming, chose the proper dream for his own needs and weaknesses.

D Layo told them to forget all that and give him control. He would show them how to free their souls for the delight of knowing what they were, not what they ought to be. It was seditious nonsense that undermined manly self-discipline and integrity, but he made it attractive.

'Let me teach you,' d Layo murmured, 'to relax your mind and soul, to open the dark core of yourself and free what lives there. Every soul is equal before a DarkDreamer, and every soul is unique; what is your soul?'

The insidious lure of DarkDreaming lay partly in this deliberate abolition of hierarchy. D Layo led them into the void of their hidden selves, where any mad chaos was possible. He was skillful, nothing like the fumbling fools Kelmz had encountered before. Gently, the DarkDreamer touched Sullen-face, drawing out the hesitant movements of his limbs and his slowcurling fingers. The man's mouth simpered open, his hands began to stroke downward on his own chest and thighs. He cringed, he melted, he was a fem.

Revolted, Kelmz looked away. For himself, he realized, he had hoped to see beasts – real beasts, hot-hided, pungently scented alien beings – not the pathetic perversions of other men.

Now d Layo was working on Hak. One-eyed Hak, chief of the crew on the coastal run, tumbled over and rolled on the floor, shielding himself from invisible kicks and blows, yammering. The DarkDreamer seemed to dance over and around him, perfecting the ferryman's performance with a touch, a whisper, a tug at the sleeve.

Kelmz began to shake.

He couldn't understand the meaning of the upright-walking being that came toward him, sniffed at him, put its hot, smooth touch on him. Panicky, he reared back to escape, but there were barriers. He struck out. The tall-walker evaded him and withdrew. Alone, penned in, he squeezed his eyes half shut and swung his head away from the bright, flaring heat and burning smell. Deep tremors of fear shuddered through him. He swayed from side to side, nosing the air for a familiar scent. There was none.

A sound found its way out of his throat, a whimper. He rocked his weight from shoulder to shoulder and moaned out his despair and isolation; but there came no answering voice.

It was day. Close by, a man slept all asprawl, snoring. Another had burrowed his way under a pile of woven mats so that only his haunches stuck out, collapsed sideways over his bent legs.

'Stand up, Captain,' the Endtendant commanded.

He was right to give that order, though he was only a Junior. Kelmz stood, blinking.

'Sun's fire!' he croaked; 'I was a beast!'

D Layo was laughing. 'Look at him, he's upset because his secret is out. What a secret! He should know as many men as I do who dream themselves a coat of fur or feathers when they get the chance!'

SERVAN D LAYO

6

Servan was high as a flag. Each go-round with manna was a gamble for him; his tolerance for it was undependable. When it left him exalted he was the victor. He shook the empty bracelet along his arm as he walked. He would have to see about getting hold of some more good stuff, now that he'd used up his supply on that pack of ferry-punks.

The ferrymen had let them off at midday. The three men made their way through the marshes in the still, warm afternoon. The hike gave them time to emerge from the after-effects of the dreaming. Kelmz, in particular, needed that. He was in a black, bewildered mood and walked apart from the others.

As for Servan, he held onto his euphoria; he was practiced in keeping alert enough to function well in spite of his intoxication. That their destination was the fem-center of the entire Holdfast increased his good humor. He had always intended to visit Bayo, in order to fill a gap in his professional background – as he explained several times to his companions, between snatches of song. Inside his head an on-running paean of praise to his own good luck rippled along, woven of scraps of songs he had wrung from various fems who had passed through his hands. Completely unable to produce a true note of his own, he had spent a period of his life pursuing others' music. That craze was over now, but he had learned a lot and still liked to sing, however tonelessly. Besides, one thing he still had a craze for was needling Eykar, and he knew perfectly well that his singing needled Eykar.

There was no one to hear him but themselves. The grass of the marshes was allowed to grow undisturbed to head height, curing in the salty mud. The Bayo fems were sent to harvest it as needed for weaving, and you could always hear them coming a mile off, singing their work-chants. The scattered stands and thickets were deserted now.

The footing was soggy, but Servan liked the hiss and rustle of their passage through the tall, yellow stems. Stripes of gold and shadow glided over their skins and clothing, giving a fantastic, underwater motion effect. The sunlight struck obliquely toward them between the ribbons of grass; they must have been slogging along like this for some time. He'd hardly noticed.

Soon there came the piping of the flutes of Bayo, which were said to skirl as ceaselessly as the horns blew in Lammintown. There was a song that said the flutists' indrawn breath sucked up the spirits of dead fems and that it was these ghost-voices which sang so sadly from the instruments. An interesting conceit. Servan was eager to see fems on what must be considered their homeground.

Bayo had begun as nothing more than a crude outpost of the City, which lay forty miles inland. The flats between the City and the southern mouth of the river were perfectly suited to the growing of lavers. These freshwater weeds, both tasty and nutritious, grew best in nutrient-rich, shallow waters. So the south channel of the river had been dammed into ponds, into which the City's sewage was fed. Then stone causeways had been built bestriding the ponds and linking Bayo with the City. Lastly, the structures of Bayo itself had gone up, to house a permanent fem labor force and whatever company of men was assigned to supervise them.

Surrounded on the seaward side by the golden grass, the thick crescent of Bayo buildings crouched, compact and unadorned, between the southern margins of the ponds and the river's mouth where the ferry docked. Bayo's walls were of mud-brick, fired to withstand the summer rains. All the structures had been erected on a ramp of similar brick that sloped noticeably upward from the dockside warehouses to the farther horn of the crescent, where the pyramidal men's compound reared up overlooking everything. The quarters of the fems comprised the curved centre.

This evening, from the bright-windowed men's compound came cheerful rills of flute notes and a drum beat reinforced by the stamp of dancing feet. The Penneltons' greeting-feast for the ferrymen was in full swing. Hopefully, the Chesters would maintain the secret of their complicity with the fugitives outside for some hours yet.

The three of them squatted in the high grass, weary and coated to the knees in marsh mud. An unpleasant odor hung in the air, penetrating even the dank salt-smell of the marshes. Probably the odor was connected with the cloudy emissions from the chimneys clustered on the rooftops of buildings adjoining the warehouses. Those would be the workrooms, a good place to enter, if they could get past the guards.

Three pairs of Rovers patrolled the lighted gallery which ran along the inside curve of the crescent. Servan considered Rovers to be highly overrated as fighting men. Once you figured out that they worked on the principle of the pre-emptive strike, it was easy to deal with them. Acting out of fear themselves, they interpreted others' fear of them as a presage of aggression and responded by attacking first. Seen in this way, theirs was a reasonable sort of behavior. Servan had a theory that the famous 'mature' composure of Senior men was primarily protective, to prevent the unintended triggering of Rovers against the Seniors themselves. Servan had adopted the show of serenity in his own contact with Rovers quite successfully.

A man like Kelmz, however, was not to be wasted in a situation like this. Servan waited while Kelmz sized up their position independently and came, naturally, to the same conclusion. The captain made a stay-put sign and moved off silently toward the warehouses. For a big man, he could travel very neatly when he chose to.

Servan sat back to wait, turning his mind firmly from considerations of food. They had eaten nothing since morning, and now that the manna-high had worn off, he was hungry. He hummed part of a song concerning 'Rovers, red-handed, mad-eyed warders, dreadful and deadly to fems.'

The two Rovers guarding the workroom and warehouse end of the crescent came swinging down the gallery in step, bald-headed and thick-bodied like two rough clay men made from the same mold. That their features could not be discerned in the shadows of the thatch overhead seemed only fitting; their anonymous madness was their most formidable aspect. Servan knew from experience that they were so nearly soulless, like the mechanical men of Ancient legend, that they were a disappointment to kill unless fully aroused

— something that at present was to be avoided.

He thought he knew what Kelmz had in mind. If successful, it would save Servan trouble. If not, he would do what was called for. He never liked to plan too tightly for the future.

The Rovers wheeled and marched back the way they had come. A shadow rose from the darkness behind them, and Kelmz fell silently into step at their backs. They stiffened visibly, but didn't turn or break stride. Kelmz would be matching their tread so exactly that each of them would hear only his own steps amplified by his companion's in a manner that he had been taught not to fear, so that he could work as a member of a brace or squad.

Servan would have to tell Kelmz later what an artist he was. His praise would certainly irritate the captain — art was a famishing untrustworthy attribute — and at the same time it would have the virtue of being true. Kelmz had an artist's luck, too: the Chesters were doing their part well, for no one stepped outside the men's compound to piss or settle a bet. There was no break in the pounding rhythm of the Penneltons' dancing.

Smoothly, the captain moved up and put his hands on the Rovers' shoulders. He wheeled with them and they came back down the gallery, secured by his authoritative touch. If he had hesitated, they would have turned and cut him down. By the time Servan and Eykar gained the gallery themselves. Kelmz and the Rovers were again at the far end of their patrol, backs turned.

The doors to the work-buildings were not locked, for no fem would try to get past a Rover-watch. The two men simply walked in, entering a huge room full of hot, sour air.

The cement floor was cluttered with machines, bins, tables, and chutes. At the far end, layers of stuffed hempen sacks mounted toward the ceiling, presumably containing some of the finished product. Most of the equipment seemed to be idle. A few fems were present, wearing sweat-rags bound around their heads and stained aprons that reached from armpit to knee. Three of them stood nearby, fixing a piece of wire mesh over the opening of a pipe that stuck out of the wall. The pipe and the trough under it seemed to be the prime source of the pervasive sour stink. From this group and others came the murmur of voices; that was surprising. Though normally fems sang at work, the majority of them were held to be incapable of any but the most limited fem-to-master type of speech.

There were no men about at all. This was the first time Servan had ever seen any number of fems together without at least one pair of Juniors overseeing their activities. It made his hair prickle.

Some signal must have been given; suddenly every fem in the place acquired a slight stoop or cringe. The faces of the nearest ones went slack and foolish before his eyes. Witchery? He almost laughed. He had seen a dormful of boys change in just such a way when a Teacher walked in on them unexpectedly in the Boyhouse.

One of the fems tending to the pipe came toward the intruders, her calloused feet rasping on the concrete floor. She knelt to kiss the ground in front of them. There were scars on her lean back. Nobody bothered about pretty appearances in the workrooms of Bayo, it seemed. She had wide shoulders for a fem and a strong neck, and she was almost the size of a fair-grown boy.

Servan addressed her close-cropped head. 'Where are your masters?'

'This fem feels that they are all in the men's compound, please-you-master,' she whined, slurring her words in the manner of fems. She sat back on her heels, so that now that he had acknowledged her presence, he might see her face if he wished to. 'Is there something this fem might offer these masters?'

A trickle of white fluid ran off the lip of the pipe into the trough, setting off a to-do of shouting and wall-rapping from the fems working with the mesh.

'She can offer her full attention,' Servan snapped to the one before him. She kissed the ground again in apology. 'Is there some fem here who's been in Bayo for the past three five-years?'

'This fem can try to take the masters to one such,' she said, using the proper formula that avoided any suggestion of actual competence on her part. She arose at his gesture to guide them.

Then the outer door opened and Kelmz walked in. The two Rovers strode ahead of him, heads up and nostrils flaring.

Every fem in the room froze.

'Christ,' Servan groaned, 'and his unfortunate father!'

Close up, the Rovers were impressive. Their heavy torsos gleamed, and the short capes they wore strained across their shoulders. They stood with their legs bent in an aggressive crouch. Each Rover had a knife in his right hand, and his defensively gloved left hand tensed before his belly, ready to lash out with a metal-studded blow or to turn the slash of an enemy's weapon.

'Kelmz, you're moon-mad to bring them in here!' Servan said.

'I can hold them,' said the captain.

Eykar said sharply, 'Will they be missed?'

Kelmz shook his head. 'They're fresh, probably just on duty an hour or so. Nobody will check them for a while. I think they're worth the risk to us. You want to keep these bitches shivering when you have to go among them.'

His hands rested lightly on the Rovers' shoulders; he stroked them a little, calming them. But he had an odd, abstracted air, as if he touched them from a great distance.

7

In his time Kelmz had done enough guard duty among workgangs of fems to be unfazed by them now. He attended to the Rovers, who padded warily along rolling their eyes and quivering under their scarred hides. To them, fems were drug-distorted demons.

Servan watched Eykar as they all proceeded through the fems' quarters. Eykar's eyes, that Servan knew to be remarkably keen and untiring, missed nothing; but his face remained austerely uncommunicative. Probably he was holding in his disgust. What he had been taught about fems in the Boyhouse (as Servan knew, having had the same lessons and having had opportunities since to prove them against reality) was not enough and not even particularly accurate. It was one thing to be told that fems were smelly, misshapen and alien-minded. It was another to be surrounded by them.

No fems ever went to Endpath. They had no souls, only inner cores of animating darkness shaped from the void beyond the stars. Their deaths had no significance. Some men believed that the same shadows returned again and again in successive fem-bodies in order to contest for the world with the souls of men, which came from light.

It was hard to connect these crude mud walls and their stunted inhabitants with the great witch-fems who had overthrown the Ancients' mighty civilization. The Chants Historical told the tale: at the peak of their power, the men of Ancient times had been so fascinated with their own technical prowess that they had neglected the supervision of their treacherous fems. Technics had seemed to offer the promise of overcoming the sullen chaos of the void itself by the extension of manly will from the face of the earth out among the stars. The Ancients had concentrated first on attacking the moon, through which the forces of the void were focussed on the world.

The Moonwitch had not been destroyed by the missiles the Ancients had hurled; she had fought back through her minions, the fems. With her magic the fems had inspired the natural inferiors of the Ancients to join in a coalition to overthrow the rule of order and manly reason. There was some question as to the exact apportionment of blame for the rebellion of the Wasting among the various kinds of lesser beings (collectively known as the unmen). Each kind had a proper place, after all, under the authority of men: the beasts of all elements furnished men with raw materials; labor could be forced from the lazy, savage Dirties; even the fems had certain minor skills to offer their masters in addition to giving them sons.

To the logical mind, however, the answer was obvious: there had been beast-fems, and fems among the Dirties, and the sons of men had turned Freak under the tutelage of their dams. The common denominator of corruption and rebellion among all the unmen had been fems.

Even at the time, there had been names for fems indicating some understanding of the danger they represented. One Ancient book used in the Boyhouse mentioned fems as 'bra-burners.' Since 'bra' was a word in an old language meaning 'weapon,' clearly 'bra-burner' meant a fem who stole and destroyed the weapons of her masters.

The weapon of the fems was witchery, and that could only be destroyed by burning the witches themselves. The Ancients had begun by burning other kinds of rebellious unmen, out of a reluctance to recognize the power that the fems had accumulated. By the time the fems' primary responsibility for the wars of the Wasting had been openly acknowledged by the Ancients, the world had already begun to slip from the grasp of men.

Yet it never fell into the hands of their enemies. The fems' witchery was by nature irrational, utilizing epidemics, uprisings of crazed Dirties, destructive storms (to which the Ancients properly gave fem-type names), and poisons released into air, earth and water. These weapons were so virulent and undiscriminating that they also killed the unmen themselves. That anyone survived at all was due to the foresight and tough-mindedness of a handful of ruling men.

Shelters had been prepared earlier against the aggressiveness of the most powerful of the Dirties: Reds and Chings across the ocean and Blacks at home. Seeing at last that the light of manly reason was doomed to be overwhelmed by the forces of chaos, the wisest leaders of men withdrew to these shelters, taking a handful of fems with them for breeding purposes.

Outside of this Refuge, as the area of the shelters was called, men and unmen fell to the plagues and disasters that wasted the world. In helpless horror the men in the Refuge watched (by means of wonderful distance-instruments) the ruin of the civilization they had once commanded but were powerless to save. Some of the refugees went mad, but the strongest among them (many were military men) organized an interim life of discipline and sturdy optimism. They had faith that someday the surface of the earth would be habitable again. Meanwhile, at least the vermin responsible for earth's ruin were dying along with their victims.

The descendants of the refugees (and the properly tamed fems) emerged eventually to reclaim and make usable the territory now known as the Holdfast. It was the first step in the Reconquest of the whole world in the name of light, reason, and order. The descendants of the surviving fems, however, would never again be allowed to become an active danger to the hegemony of their masters. The only type of unmen to have been saved from the Wasting, fems were now closely controlled; modern men were taught never to forget that these beings were by their nature the hereditary and implacable enemies of everything manly, bright and clean.

Servan was disappointed to find no signs of witch-power here in the recesses of Bayo. On occasion he had sensed something secret about certain fems, a holding-back that had challenged him. He had never been able to extract anything from them other than a song or two, and often the fem who sang only half-comprehended the words, which were merely lamentations over hard work and the vagaries of the masters' desires. Though he had considered dosing a fem with manna as an aid to interrogation, when it came down to it he never could bring himself to waste good stuff on them.

In the Holdfast, fems accused of exercising powers inherited from the terrible fems of Ancient times were burned as witches. Here in the dull yellow light of the wall lamps of Bayo, the existence of such powers seemed preposterous. Servan congratulated himself for his own scepticism.

Yet, moving among so many of these bent, dull-eyed figures, he wasn't sorry to have the Rovers along.

Their guide stopped and indicated with a cringing gesture that their goal lay through the doorway to the right. The room beyond was sparsely furnished with clay tables and sitting-blocks. One old fem sat eating curdcake from a chipped bowl. She arose at once and hurried toward them, wiping her mouth and fingers on the hem of her smock so that they wouldn't have to smell fem-food about her. She knelt in front of Servan. So far, all was in order.

'Fossa presents herself, please-you-masters, with important news.'

Servan was no kind of fanatic about fems and their proper place, but by addressing them first this old bitch (who should have known better) had committed a serious breach. Kelmz looked ready to break her skinny neck. It was not out of anger but to maintain propriety that Servan slapped her, hard.

She rocked back from the blow, but went right on with the same astonishing forwardness: 'Word came from Lammintown. The Pennelton masters watch for you masters. They seldom come to these quarters after sunset. Tonight, they have come twice.'

The men looked at each other; Senior Bajerman must have heard about their encounter with the 'Wares and guessed something of their intent and their destination.

Servan said, 'Is there a place where the men never come?'

'There is a place where they have never come before, please-you,' replied the crone. She was even using hard-edged, manly speech, instead of the slurred softspeech of fems, so that there would be no misunderstanding.

'Take us there,' Servan said.

Fossa was leathery from weather and work; teeth were missing from one side of her mouth so that her cheek had sunk in and her jaw was crooked. She scuttled ahead of them, bowed with age and humility. Yet something in the bearing of other fems towards her as they passed seemed to indicate respect. Servan was intrigued.

They entered a series of low-ceilinged, dimly lit dormitories. Fems slept or reclined in slit-eyed torpor in the beds. Some had small, blanketed bundles lying next to them. Servan was reminded of the brief trip that all boys made to the Hospital adjoining the Boyhouse, to be instructed about the grossly swollen fems due to drop cubs. The lights had been brighter in the Hospital, but the somnolent atmosphere had been much the same.

One of the bundles began kicking, and it raised a thin cry. The fem next to it hiked up on her elbow, eyes still shut, and put her hand over the source of the sound. The kicking continued, but the wailing diminished to small grasping sounds that were succeeded by quiet. The fem rolled on her side and went back to sleep.

Fossa gave Servan the cringing, ingratiating smile of a fem imparting information, so that he should be reassured that she claimed no credit for knowing something that he did not. 'We teach fem-cubs to be quiet. It's a good first lesson in obedience.'

A number of fems were without cubs. Servan pointed to one of them and asked why she wasn't back at work, having dropped her young and apparently lost it.

Apologetically, the old fem said, 'There are ways to continue the flow of milk even when there is no suckling cub. If a dam's capacity is high, she stays here in the milkery. Some stay all their lives, for fems have a great need of this milk now, in their well deserved deprivation.' She was referring to the drastic reduction of the sea-weed ration allotted to the fems, which dated back several five-years. At that time, successive failures of the laver harvest had earned a rather freehanded rage from the men, resulting in fewer fems (and the deaths of the witches responsible for the blight, since the crops had stabilized again, though at lower levels). Now the fem population was built back up in number, but their food supply had not been expanded. Apparently they were finding their own sources of sustenance, as Fossa explained.

'The masters entered through the curding room, where the milk from these fems is made into the curdcake which fems eat.'

Kelmz said grimly, 'If I'd known so many of them could talk I'd have been more careful working around them. But this old bitch can't even describe what we saw with our own eyes without lying: that stuff they eat is brown and gelid, not white.'

The old fem responded, after a pause, 'Other things are added, to give fems strength for the tasks set them by the masters.'

An alcove at the far end of the dormitory complex served as an office. Strings of tally-beads hung from pegs in the walls, presumably to keep track of the workings of the milkery. Here they stopped. Servan drew up a worn sitting-block, turning so that he could look back the way they had come. The place fascinated him. It was a DarkDreamer's dream, with its sleep-heavy air, its quiet, the lumpish figures large and small under their coarse, gray covers, the dull light from basket-shaded lamps.

Kelmz used the pause to get better control of the Pennelton Rovers, rubbing them down carefully with his hands as their officer would do, to check for injuries that their inflamed minds would never notice. He kept them facing away from the milkery.

' "The moon's unpredictable daughters",' Servan quoted softly. 'That's from the fems' own songs. And here they are, in full mystery. Eykar, turn your back; you're just a boy where these creatures are concerned; you have no defenses. They might witch you right out of your high purpose.'

Eykar stopped pacing and turned his pale gaze on Servan. 'In pursuit of which, do you think you might bring yourself to find out what we came to find out?'

Doing so turned out to be simple. Servan asked Fossa about Raff Maggomas, and she told them. He had come; he had stayed with the Quarterback Company assigned here at the time (a hard time, marked by laver failures); he had returned to the City with the Quarterbacks when the five-year was over.

Years later, word had gotten about that Maggomas' son was in trouble in the Boyhouse. The son had been sent to become Endtendant, and Maggomas had vanished. At once, a new scandal had broken. Maggomas had apparently had a lover across the age-line, a Junior Quarterback who was moreover much sought after (however covertly) by an Angelist Company Senior superior to Maggomas; a Boardman, some said. The young man, whose name was Karz Kambl, had also disappeared, presumably to join Maggomas in hiding. Enraged by this turn of events, the Board had passed a resolution barring Maggomas from returning to any company of the City in any capacity.

So far as was known, he had never tried to return and had not been seen or heard of since by any reliable witness. And that had been six years ago. The younger man, now a Senior, was said to be living more or less in hiding in the City.

Aside from one or two breaks (profusely apologized for) when Fossa was called to confer with some fem in the dormitory, the report was a model of concise information, clearly delivered. Servan complimented the old fem on the effectiveness of her intelligence network. She was remarkably well informed. These rumors of an affair had never come to Servan's notice, possibly because he was too closely involved through his connection with Eykar.

He was beginning to be amused by this old fem and was not offended when she went on unbidden: 'If the master is pleased with this fem's service, perhaps he will condescend to do a small thing for this fem?'

She didn't say, favor for favor, but she might as well have, the presumptuous hag. Servan burst out into a delighted guffaw. This episode was more entertaining than he could have hoped. He inquired with exaggerated courtesy into the nature of this 'small thing.'

'Will the master accept a fem to travel with him and serve him?' She was making a gift to a master of another fem! It was marvelous.

Eykar snapped, 'Servan, this is too much!'

'It is pretty odd,' Servan admitted, 'but perhaps this bitch has other help to offer than information – if we cooperate. Besides, think, man: cash is only cash, and we may have to spend high in the City to locate this man Kambl. Like them or not, fems are a form of wealth.'

Kelmz objected. 'They're also a form of trouble. She could cost us more than she's worth. Fems are stupid and spiteful; you can never even tell just why it is they've betrayed you to your enemies. I know them well. But I have these Rovers on my hands now, so who's to keep an eye on some fem besides?'

'Servan,' Eykar said, 'since she was offered to him, and if he still thinks it's worth the trouble.' Kelmz shrugged reluctant assent, and Eykar turned sharply on the old fem: 'What extra aid comes with this gift?'

Fossa kissed the ground to him. 'Such poor help as mere fems have to offer,' she fawned. 'Yet the masters may find it useful.'

A bell tinkled somewhere close by. Some of the sleeping fems sat up, reaching for the swaddled cubs beside them or for the clay pitchers kept under their beds. Each of the cubs was put to the breast for a moment only, then handed on to the nearest waking fem who had no cub of her own to start her milk. Some of the fems didn't even open their eyes as they went through the motions of what was obviously a well established routine. The pitchers, now containing fresh milk, were set on the floor to be picked up by fems who pushed carts down the aisles between the beds. Those whose milk-shift had not yet been called slept through it all.

'Let's get on with this,' Eykar said, hoarsely.

'Please-you-masters,' murmured Fossa, 'this fem will go and fetch the one spoken of from another place.'

Servan stood up. 'We'll go with you.' It would hardly be to her advantage to betray them. She would get no reward, for fems were invariably punished for anything found to be out of order. Yet it paid to be wary of their irrationality.

'This fem feels the masters would be happier waiting here,' she said.

He laughed. 'We're tough enough for anything you or your kind can offer, gray bitch. Lead on.'

They crossed a hallway beyond the milkery and stepped between two heavy doors into the embrace of a hot, acrid roil of stench and noise that stopped them in their tracks.

Right at their feet, a hopper was set into the concrete floor. A huge screw-shaft, bedded in a chute, angled up out of it. The screw-thread was gleaming sharp, and wedged into the hollows of its spiral were fragments of flesh, bone and fat. Above the level of the men's heads, a fem stood on a ladder, carefully scraping this detritus into a bucket. The screw-chute led past her to a row of drums mounted on a platform. The drums turned slowly, driven by a crank shaft at which the fems labored with bent, straining backs. Another fem-crew tended the furnaces under the drums, stepping to and fro with scoops of coal over a gutter in the floor. The gutter flowed with a yellow fluid that drained through a pipe from the drums overhead.

Fossa put her head close to Servan's and said at the top of her voice, 'This is the Rendery, please-you-master.'

8

The Rovers began to shiver and snarl; Kelmz turned and thrust them back out into the corridor. Eykar, who never ran away from anything, followed the old fem to the end of the central structure. Not to be outdone, Servan went too, dizzy with the effort to breathe through his skin or his ears, eyes streaming.

The other side of the machinery featured a broad, sloping table onto which the drums could be emptied. From there, the contents were screw-driven again into an enclosed grinding-mill. On the floor under the mill's outlet was a conical heap of dark, damp-looking particles. A large, tight-woven basket on wheels stood nearby, with ceramic scoops hung from pegs fixed along the rim.

Through the half-open lids of the drums, Servan could see fragments dropping from the fixed blades inside back into the churning material below. The end-drum rotated more slowly and loudly than the others. Its lid had been opened completely and fastened back, so that the contents could be drawn out with long-handled hoes. Two fems were working the heavier dregs to the lip of the drum, to be tumbled off onto the steaming hill on the table beneath.

Servan's DarkDream-trained mind made the connection between this noxious operation and what the old fem had said about adding other substances to the milk-food, which obviously wouldn't be plentiful enough to go around unless it were stretched; and what more nutritious additive than the flesh of dead fems and of fem-cubs who did not survive the milkery? What was reputedly poisonous to men, the fems had learned to consume safely, having no other choice but starvation.

Some man must have designed the process; it was too beautiful, too efficient to be a product of the fems' own thinking. The concept of making them literally self-sustaining had a certain gruesome sophistication impossible for fems' thinking. He had to admit, though, that a sort of manly hardness was argued by the ability of fems to accept such an arrangement; unless they were not hardened so much as merely too depraved to be horrified.

Fossa tapped on the lowest of the footplates leading up onto the platform. The fems working up there looked down. She shouted something. The nearer of the two fems went to the edge, handed down her hoe to one of the furnace-feeders below and descended. At the bottom of the steps, she untied a filthy rag from the railing and wiped off the greasy fragments that spattered her skin. Then, stepping carefully over and around the scraps lying on the floor, she came toward the men with downcast eyes.

There was no point in trying to speak in these surroundings. When they emerged into the hallway, Kelmz turned from the Rovers and looked the young fem icily up and down, saying with undisguised revulsion, 'Must we travel attended by a thing that reeks of its own dead?'

The choice of words was unfortunate. Eykar said in a tight, bitter voice, 'You great fool, don't you recognize punishment when you see it?' Imaginative of him, to see a similarity between Endpath and the Rendery.

Still staggered by the impact of the Rendery, the men were moved smoothly through the fems' washroom – it was a relief to scrub off the dank muck of the swamps and the lingering Rendery smell – and out again. They found themselves surrounded by a dozen fems armed with cloth, needles and thread, who cut and stitched, outfitting the men as a party of Hemaways from the City. Using Kelmz' uniform as a basic pattern, they transformed the Pennelton Rovers into Hemaways; Kelmz held the brutes calm in spite of the fems' hands darting about them.

Servan had underestimated the resources at Fossa's command. The men's clothes, from Kelmz' worn blanks to Eykar's uniform, were completely reworked or replaced. The one item that the fems could not supply was a manna-bracelet. Since a Senior in charge of

Rovers would certainly be wearing one, Servan grudgingly lent the captain his own.

The work was done in the kitchen, the only place where the light was good enough and yet not easily noticeable from the men's compound. From some corner a pack basket was produced, and food was brought. While the men ate lightly of leafcurd and beer, fems filled the basket with supplies for the journey: a white crock of curdcake at the bottom for the fem who would go with them, two jugs of beer, a bar of lamminchew, a square of hempseed bread wrapped in a damp cloth for freshness, and even a small box of dry laver-flakes of seasoning – that last a real luxury these days. There wasn't enough to feed the men well for the whole trip, but they were all used to going hungry. What was astonishing was that the fems had access to any amount of men's food at all.

There was also a razor, some earthenware eating gear, a mending kit, firestones and tinder, and a pair of spare sandals that could only be meant – by the size of them – for Kelmz.

Fossa drew a diagram on the floor with soot from the cookstoves. The causeways which linked Bayo and the City were easily navigable in daylight, but at night they formed a baffling maze. She drilled the men, ever so respectfully, until they could have picked their way in their sleep. Then she scuffed out the drawing with her heel.

The other fem, the young one, returned from washing the stink and grease of the Rendery from her skin and hair. She was introduced as Alldera, the old one's hold-mate, which meant that Fossa's master had at some time owned this young fem as well. Whoever he was, he seemed to have interesting requirements in his personal femhold. Both fems could speak; neither was in any way beautiful, and in addition the young one had been schooled as a messenger.

Alldera had one other unusual, visible, attribute: her legs and buttocks were strongly developed (Fossa lifted the young one's smock to point this out). She had been speed-trained, which was illegal and added to her value. Speed-training was confined to men who specialized in racing competitively for their companies. In any case, no fem should be able to outrun Rovers.

Though as a runner she was more fluidly muscled than most labor fems, her looks were not appealing. The wet hair clinging to her head only emphasized the breadth of her jaw and cheekbones.

She had wide-set eyes of an unremarkable pale hazel color, a nose that had been broken and healed flatbridged, and a heavy-lipped mouth with a sullen turn to the corners. The best that could be said of her face was that the skin was of good quality, though verging on a Dirty coppery cast.

Servan would have preferred a prettier fem, but there were few of them to be had in Bayo. Anyway, as she was she would lend an added touch of authenticity to their group disguise. A fem of no great beauty but specially skilled was just the sort of property that a man like Kelmz might be expected to acquire, once he took his mantle and with it the right to own fems personally.

The four of them were to be Senior-Kelmz-and-party come on one of the unannounced spot-checks of work-turf so common lately in the Holdfast. Kelmz would play himself, promoted. Any Penneltons they might encounter closely on the causeways would be unlikely to know that Kelmz had been more or less dumped by his company rather than coaxed at last into Seniorhood. Men assigned to Bayo avoided contact with the City until the end of their five-year, disliking to be called 'cunt nurses' and such by other City men. The two younger men were outfitted in simple pants and tunics, to play the parts of Hemaway Juniors in attendance on their superior. Filling out the group to a properly impressive size, there were the two Rovers as an escort and the fem to serve as pack-bearer.

She, the ostensible reason for this extraordinary activity and risk on the fems' part, interested Servan. She never said a word. Her story, as Fossa told it, was simple and plausible: a Pennelton, drunk, had gone after her at her work-bench without noticing the red scarf she had been wearing at the time. She had refused him, as she was bound to do in order to protect him from contamination. But the man's Juniors had witnessed the incident, and he wanted some redress for his injured standing. Alldera had been assigned to the Rendery while the Pennelton Seniors considered whether she should be burned for witching the man into missing the token of her uncleanness in the first place. Doing so would restore the drunkard's self-respect, so it was a likely outcome.

So Alldera had to be whisked out of Bayo for her life's sake. The fems in charge of the Rendery would report that she had bolted into the marshes, where her starved corpse presumably would be discovered someday as others had been before.

It was no news to Servan that some men were excited by the thought of fucking a fem soiled with her monthly blood-tribute to the Moonwitch. But somehow the account rang false to him. The campaign that old Fossa had mounted was too dangerous to the fems to be performed merely to save the life of this pie-faced youngster. How valuable could one fem be to other fems? It couldn't be simply that the two fems had been owned by the same master; that was a source of friction rather than closeness among fems. There had to be something else to justify the lengths to which these fems were going to get Alldera out of Bayo. Even the Rovers wouldn't be missed, Fossa promised; that could be managed. They had no guarantee that one of the men would not at some point inform the Board of the organization they had found here in Bayo, with the inevitable result. Yet if these fems were worried by any such possibility, they didn't show it.

Well, then, suppose they were to be reckoned with in some way that was not yet clear. Let them try to trick him and use him in some game of their own. He accepted the challenge. Everybody was an antagonist, after all, at least potentially. The remedy was simply to recognize that this was so, and to try to use the other person before, and better than, he used you.

At last, the preparations were done. The fems picked up every scrap of cloth and thread and put out the lights in the kitchen. Fossa and young Alldera took the men out on the roof of the next building, which connected directly on the west side with the causeways. There, the fugitives found themselves suddenly in the midst of a creaking, droning party of hags whose job was to deploy the laver-carts at various points on the causeways for collection of the next day's harvest. The moon was up, a mere scrap of light not nearly bright enough to show the incongruity of the men's tall forms to any watching sentries. In no time at all, the lighted windows and the music of Bayo fell behind.

Soon the old fems with their rattling carts milled to a stop in the windy darkness. Their mumbling and singing died. The stars sparked cold light from the surfaces of the laver-ponds that stretched alway, glimmering, on either side of the causeway.

Fossa, a stick figure in the starlight, stepped forward. She said, 'Safe journey, masters.'

'Too bad it's not you coming with us, old dam,' Servan said. On that note the men and the young fem, canted forward under the pack-basket on her back, departed westward toward the City as fast as they could travel.

The idea was to cover as much ground as they could that night, unobserved, rest all morning in one of the shelters built into all major intersections of the causeways, and in the afternoon turn and move as slowly as possible back in the direction of Bayo, as if coming from the City instead of fleeing toward it. It was not unusual for a Senior of one company to inspect, without warning, the work of another company's Juniors. They often did it, in the name of competition and in hopes of shaving a rival company's work-points. A day of slow 'inspection', followed by another night of hard running in the opposite direction, should see the travelers to the City walls.

It was the sort of sly plan you might expect from devious creatures like old Fossa. Bajerman would be completely stymied, for he never would descend willingly to thinking like a fem.

They reached the designated shelter just as the sun edged above the horizon behind them. The shelter was unoccupied, as Fossa had said it would be, and they slept behind its curtain while the Pennel-tons used the causeways to shift fem-gangs from one set of ponds to another for the day's work. Servan kept half-waking at the approach of footsteps and the shrill whistle-signals of the Pennelton drovers.

At midday, the travelers washed and ate and put the lumpy grass-stuffed mattresses they had used back under the benches in the shelter. They rolled up the curtains and stepped out into the brilliant day, facing Bayo again.

Kelmz looked a really splendid Senior in his bright, striped mantle. He seemed to take ironical pleasure in the impression he made, broad and scarred as he was in his finery. Out of an unsuspected vanity, he hated the openwork sandals he had to wear, as if he felt betrayed by the sight of his own splayed and knotted feet. The two Pennelton Rovers strode stiff-backed in front of him, and Servan and Eykar followed at a respectful distance from his heels, intoning the Chant Declamatory in reverent tones.

The fem Alldera trudged along at the rear, her proper place. Servan glanced back; she was just a fem, and an ill-favored one at that. If there were any witchery at Bayo, it was the ability to throw a magnifying and romantic gloss over such a drab.

The artificial, ambling pace required by their plan was tiring to maintain, but at least the afternoon was breezy and bright-skied. Below on either side, the vast spread of the laver-pools lay like a table of mirrors with stubby-legged causeways bestriding it from edge to edge. Diminished by distance, crews of fems turned the long, flexible cables which brought up the lower level growth of laver for its share of sunlight. The notes of the Penneltons' signal pipes sounded piercingly over the glittering flats. The Pennelton Juniors were easily distinguishable by the broad straw hats they wore. Each pair of them would wave and salute when they made out the bulk of Kelmz' mantled shoulders or recognized the Chant Declamatory.

It was funny to see them joyfully gyrating their lean arms, while they must be thinking, where's that Hemaway whitehead sprung from without us being piped a warning by Penneltons close to the City? And they would snap out sharp notes to get their fems moving faster, ordering them into new positions, anything to indicate active supervision and to avoid being docked work-points.

Kelmz played his part to the hilt. Once they dawdled past a gang lifting loaded laver-carts covered with wet canvas onto the loading lane of the causeway. The hoist squealed hideously. Kelmz glared in passing, as if he really would have liked to stop and lambaste the Penneltons in charge for not taking proper care of the equipment that came with their work-turf. No wonder he was servilely saluted on every hand; he made a convincing pillar of order.

Late in the afternoon, they ducked into another shelter for a light meal and a rest before the night's hard run. Eykar lingered outside, which put off the moment when he would be shut up at close quarters with the fem again.

Kelmz had noticed Eykar's uneasiness about the fem. Sitting between the Rovers and watching her unpack the food, he said to Servan, 'You do your friend no favors, keeping that bitch with us. No one would notice if you ordered her to slip in with some gang down there at the ponds.'

'She's my property,' Servan said. The soporific pace of the afternoon had wearied him, and his throat was dry with chanting. 'Tell you what; since she's on your mind, why don't you take her for an hour or so? You've been on a wild-beast chase all your life. Try a fem instead, a little dip into mystery, an adventure for your soul.'

'I've done my duty in the breeding rooms,' Kelmz said. He slapped down the sandal he had taken off and began rubbing his foot. The Rovers imitated him. 'I'm no cunting pervert.'

'But you think Eykar is?'

'No.' Kelmz studied the fem's bent back. The Rovers, catching his antagonism, stirred and muttered low in their throats. 'But he seems to have plenty on his mind without worrying about a famishing bitch too.'

'You tend to your Rovers, Captain. I'll tend to my friend.'

9

Servan ate quickly; there was little enough. He took the bowl the fem had prepared for Eykar and the smaller beer jug and went outside. Eykar was standing at the parapet (not leaning, he never held himself slackly) watching the light fade. He took his final portion of food with a nod of thanks, and ate. He had a tired, thoughtful air that Servan remembered well from their Boyhouse days and was always moved to puncture if he could.

'Kelmz is worried,' he said, 'about you and the fem.'

'I'm worried about Kelmz,' Eykar said wryly.

'Feeling responsible?' Servan leaned on the weathered stone wall.

'He's with us because I asked him to come.'

'As I recall, that was your way of saving his life, wasn't it?'

'Perhaps that was no favor.' Eykar swept up laver-flakes neatly on his seedbread. Like all Holdfast men, he was an efficient eater. 'I didn't realize the strains he'd be subjected to. In particular, the manna you gave him that night – was it only the night before last?'

'Without him, the others might have ducked out at the last minute, and the whole situation could have gone against us.'

'That's why I didn't interfere.'

'He's a tough old brute. A little DarkDreaming can't hurt him.'

'It already has.' A volley of piped notes rose from below. The fem-gangs too far from Bayo to go home and sleep were being herded into lean-to shelters out among the ponds for the night. 'I don't think Captain Kelmz of the Hemaways as he used to be would steal Rovers from another company. He knows it can upset their balance to be switched around that way and increases the chances that they'll go rogue and have to be killed.'

Servan shrugged. 'He's just facing up to the reality of our situation.'

'No. I think he's given way to something after a lifetime of fighting it off – a fascination with the idea of the beasts; isn't that what his DarkDream shows? I think Rovers have always stood in his mind for tamed beasts. Now he's looking inward instead. His tie with these Pennelton Rovers is very impersonal, have you noticed?'

'What do you care what happens to that old wolf?' Servan said, kicking idly at the wall. 'He's no lover for you, man; remember the age-line.'

'Servan, you're a walking prurience, you never change! I just don't want the man to come apart in the middle of all this. You're not still after his blood?'

'No, not right now.'

'How long is "right now"? You used to remember old grudges any time it suited you. Frankly, if anything happened to him I doubt that you or I could take over those Pennelton Rovers the way he did at Bayo.'

'Oh? You were impressed? Do I have cause to be jealous?'

'If you had ever run Rovers yourself, you'd have been impressed too.'

'I was, actually,' Servan said, with sudden generosity. 'It was well done.'

'Can I count on you not to murder him in a fit of pique?'

Servan threw out his hands in an exasperated shrug. 'He caught me off guard in Lammintown; I was annoyed, but I'm not sulking over it. What do you want, a promise? All right, I promise, I won't lay a hand on him. Feel better?'

'That's no promise,' Eykar said. 'You've always put your hands where you like, and you always will.' He bent to rinse out his bowl in the wash bucket beside the shelter wall. 'I would not be charmed, Servan, by even your most artful apology for murdering Captain Kelmz.'

'You don't trust me,' Servan mourned. 'Come on, leave that, the fem will do the cleaning up; God's own Freaking Son, what do you think I keep her for, her beauty? Let's walk a bit. I've brought some beer.'

They strolled toward Bayo, facing the direction from which pursuit would come if their game had been discovered. Servan had thought several times that afternoon of how it would be to walk right into Bajerman and a pack of Penneltons; while Eykar, no doubt, had been worrying about Kelmz or thinking of the fem.

'Tell me about Endpath,' he said.

'It was an uncluttered life,' Eykar said. Living there had clearly not affected his reticence.

'You seem to have kept fit.' Servan saw, with a flash of heat, Eykar's gaunt frame as he had seen it in the Bayo showers, spare and white and hard as marble. Eykar always had fought what he regarded as the weakness of his body with a self-discipline that would have killed a weak man.

'Endpath duties are light,' Eykar said, with a tinge of irony. 'I had time to spend.'

'How?' Servan pressed.

'Servan, you must create Endpath sometimes for your dream clients. I'm sure you'd do it well. Why cramp your style with reality?'

'Well, let's consider the future, then.' Servan swung the jug as he walked, liking the sloshing weight of it. 'I must say I think your goal is rather limited. There are big things to be done in the Holdfast by young men who aren't cowed by the cloth-cocks and their Rovers. For instance, you and I could make something of the Juniors' resentments. If we were smart enough and fast enough we could turn the Holdfast upside down to our own profit. You saw how the Chesters took to you back on the ferry.'

Eykar said contemptuously, 'I saw how easily you maneuvered them, yes. But it was to you and Kelmz that they responded, not to me.'

'Oh, they could learn to love you,' Servan smiled.

'I'm no leader,' Eykar said. 'And you –'

'I have potential,' Servan protested in a pained tone. 'As for yourself, Eykar, you're a weightier man than you give yourself credit for. Look what happened when the Board sent you off to Endpath to kill and die. If I know you at all, you turned the whole thing into an exercise in personal austerity.'

'I did my poor best,' Eykar replied, 'lacking your inventiveness and your talent for being entertained.'

Servan sighed. 'You think of yourself as weak, but if you were any stronger you would punch holes in the ground with every step you take. What you decide to do, you do; or what in the coldest quarter of the moon am I doing out here with you now, listening to the lavers grow?'

'Amusing yourself, as always,' Eykar said, with his rasping laugh. 'I did worry about you those first months at Endpath, whether you were amusing yourself, or were able to; needlessly, of course.'

'Needlessly! You're extraordinary. Those old Hemaway turds meant to burn me, did you know that?' Servan began to work the stopper free from the neck of the jug.

'I wasn't kept informed,' Eykar said caustically. 'As soon as I'd put you into their care, the Teachers locked me into iso. Days later, they sent me to Endpath. I had no chance to ask questions.'

The stopper came loose. Servan would have put it into the pocket of his shirt, but the Bayo fems had neglected to provide a pocket, they themselves having no pockets and nothing to keep in them. He tossed the stopper in his hand, thinking about those Boyhouse days. They strolled on through the evening without speaking for a while.

In the Boyhouse, Servan had quickly acquired a reputation as a bully, a sly heckler of the Teachers and a thief; in fact, he had been fighting boredom, nothing more. Then Eykar had been placed in his class, and the situation had changed. Servan had grown ambitious. He had begun using his mind, to the astonishment (and discomfiture) of his Teachers. Yet no matter how neatly he could skip and dance around them for the dazzlement of the new boy, Eykar had pressed straight ahead, undistractable.

Eykar had wanted to know everything in those days, but only if it were true. Was it true, for instance, that beyond the borders of the Holdfast there was nothing but the empty scrubland called the Wild? If so, why was the Board committed to the Reconquest of such useless, hostile territory? If they were committed, just where was the Reconquest happening, and what was its timetable? He had gone after information like that along with incredibly picky points of doctrine, as if to him everything was just as important as everything else, and he'd been impossible to divert or even confuse for very long: fascinating, a real challenge.

Eventually, Servan had to meet him on his own ground in order to meet him at all. Subjects that the Teachers refused to discuss, Servan took up with him gladly, if irreverently, and this brought them together. The element of competition between them didn't surface openly until the embarrassing incident of FirstDream.

At the age of thirteen, after years of drill in the proper subjects for dreaming meditation, all the boys in a class were given manna for the first time by supervising Teachers. It was a crucial test. Some boys died under the influence of the drug; it was said of them that they were still their dams' cubs, not men enough to bend the manna to the schooling of their souls. Instead, the manna broke down their feeble counterfeit of manly will, and their souls bled back out into the void. Others could not shake off the phantoms of dreaming-shock after waking, and they were never again free of a craving for the drug. They were turned over to the company officers to be trained as Rovers. Those who were orderly in thought and virtuous in spirit, thanks to their years in the Boyhouse, emerged stronger than before and inspired by the visions they had seen.

Then there were the borderline cases. Eykar struggled with fever and phantoms for days afterward. Servan almost died.

The Teachers pulled Servan back into a lower class, claiming that they meant to overcome his sensitivity to manna in easy stages. Clearly, by degrading him they also intended to punish him for his long history of tricks and insolence.

So he spent several years in the forced company of his age-inferiors. He was put through the ordeal of FirstDream again and again, with no better results. All this he minded less than the endless drilling. The harder they tried to sink him into the morass of solemn virtue that formed the Canon of Dreaming Images, the worse his behavior became out of sheer frustration; meanwhile, Eykar's natural brilliance was beginning to be recognized, however grudgingly. A great future was predicted for Eykar, despite the stigma of his known parentage. He went on seeking out Servan to debate with him, which only underlined the disparity in their situations.

Eventually, in order to alter his apparently fixed status as permanent boy and non-dreamer, and also to get a rise out of the Teachers, Servan suggested that a Teacher go through a dreaming session with him, giving him word- and touch-cues for the proper images, to guide him past the voidish mishmash of fantasy that he was so prone to.

There was an uproar. They thought Servan wanted a Teacher to show him how to DarkDream. They told him twenty different reasons why one did not learn manly self-reliance by submitting to the mental control of others at one's most vulnerable moment – during dreaming. Then they sent him into iso.

Inevitably, sulking, hungry and alone in the dark little cage of a room, Servan made up his mind to try DarkDreaming and find out what it was about. On his release, he made secret trips to Skidro, where he located a DarkDreamer who agreed to dream-gift him in exchange for information about certain of the Boyhouse Teachers.

Then Servan asked Eykar along. Naturally, the invitation threw Eykar into a spasm of indecision. In the end, the chance to find out the 'truth' of DarkDreaming proved irresistible, and he went with Servan to meet the DarkDreamer – as an observer only.

The DarkDreamer had not been strong enough. Servan had slipped from his mental grip and had begun the descent into manna-madness. Eykar had interrupted the process and forced the Dark-Dreamer to help him carry Servan back to the Boyhouse and into the care of the Teachers.

'Must have scared you to death,' Servan said, 'the whole thing. I should have checked that hack out better before putting myself into his hands. How did you know I was in trouble?'

'By your breathing. I don't know what he used, but it was much stronger than anything we'd had in the Boyhouse; Board-quality manna, judging by the effect.'

Servan hugged the beer jug to his chest with both arms. 'It was a near thing, let me tell you. I was out for two whole days, and when I came to I was ready to be a good boy. They couldn't believe it; those old Hemaway screws kept nagging and bullying until I got fed up and told them a few things about some of their own brothers. I'm sure they knew that some Teachers were DarkDreaming pretty regularly themselves, but they had to put on a show of outrage when I named names. They started shouting about burning me, as a throwback to the Freaks. In the middle of it all, with old Varner roaring away at the top of his lungs and blaming everybody around him for the whole situation, I passed out again.

'The next thing I knew, a bunch of sweaty Rovers came and dragged me out of bed and down into the courtyard. You remember that courtyard, the scene of so many of our debates? Well, the whole pimply population of the Boyhouse was turned out to watch those famishing Rovers truss me up with ropes and sit on me so the Teachers could cut my shoulder and use acid to obliterate the boy-mark. Christ, you must have heard me, even in iso!'

'They tied me up in a hammock and ran me to the edge of the Holdfast and dumped me on the ground. Not a word, nothing. They left me in the Wild to die. That was the first I knew that they'd decided not to burn me after all. I can remember the taste of blood and dust in my mouth to this moment.' He swigged deeply at the beer. What he remembered best was the silence of the Wild, a silence towering up into the crown of the sky above him and spreading under him down into the heart of the earth.

'Varner and others of that time have come to me since at End-path,' Eykar observed, drily. 'The Rovers are probably long-since killed in Hemaway skirmishes. But here you still are, Servan, to tell the tale.'

Servan laughed. 'Eykar, you have a hard heart! Even you would have been moved, though, if you'd seen me lumping around in the dust and the thorns, swearing and roaring and bleeding, until the Scrappers came and got me. You know, it's not true that Scrappers make their living salvaging stray bits of metal and such. Their best source of income is the trade in bondboys. Somebody at the Boy-house gets paid to tell them when a promising lad – like me – is due to be dumped in the Wild. The Scrappers go and fetch him in, giving rise to all those tales of demons eating up the bodies.

'What the Scrappers do with the lucky fellow they've rescued is soften him for sale. It's a manly virtue, after all, not to waste anything useful that comes to hand.'

Eykar stopped. 'We'd better turn back, if we don't want to waste an hour of darkness. Go on; there's more, surely? Or are you going to tell me that you were sold to Senior Bajerman, who is waiting for us at the shelter with a troop of Rovers at this moment?'

'Christ,' Servan laughed, 'that would be hard on me, friend! The bondboy business trades on the fact that a lot of rich old Seniors are cunters at heart. That isn't surprising, considering how unappetiz-ing old men can be and the access they have to all the decent-looking fems. They develop an appetite for fems' company, but at the same time they worry about the state of their souls. So a lot of them prefer to turn to some poor young fellow who's been trimmed to the fem-pattern, so to speak – castrated. That's your bond; your cut boy is ashamed to run away, for fear of being found out to be no man by others. The whitehead who keeps a bondboy gets the security of male companionship with a touch of famishing softness thrown in. A neat solution to the problem, don't you think?'

Eykar said, 'I was wrong to joke with you about this just now. Bondboys have come to me on the Rock. Do you think you're making up for a gap in my education with this kind of talk? Do you seriously believe that being shut up at Endpath is some sort of shelter from the darker side of Holdfast life? The things you speak of so lightly I've seen stamped in the faces of the pilgrims to the Rock. They talked to me, despite the rule of silence.'

In bursts of intensity like this one, Eykar would sometimes speak more of his feelings than he meant to.

'Whatever they say about men choosing to come to Endpath, more are broken and desperate than are "ripe for release", whatever that may mean. Cancer drives them, madness drives them, passion drives them; a meager handful are drawn by some feeling of readiness. I'm better informed about the pain of Holdfast life than most men are; so you don't need to enlighten me.

'And it was only in my weakest moments that I've ever thought you might not make your way easily through the worst of it.'

'Well,' Servan said, 'purely as a matter of boring personal history, I slipped away from the Scrappers but kept my eye on them afterwards. Three of them are dead now; one still carries some magnificent scars that he owes to me, and two more are in permanent hiding – unless they've gone to Endpath in their eagerness to avoid meeting me again.' He considered elaborating, but decided against it. He slapped the stopper back into the neck of the jug. 'I had good luck.'

'A fem's notion,' Eykar said. 'Luck.'

'Weren't you lucky to find me when you needed me? Though I always felt that we'd come together again sometime, in the natural course of events. We're as close as smoke and flame. The two of us could put our hearts together and make a blaze that would light the Holdfast from 'Troi to the sea.

'What do you think? Nothing? Or do you think but not speak, being such a true individual, such a very private person?'

'Look!' Eykar said, fiercely, and his hand pointed, dark against the stars. 'You can see the glow of the City from here. Do we travel tonight, or do we hang about talking the trifling talk of soft-headed boys, old men and fems?'

There had always been ways of striking sparks from Eykar's flint. Servan was pleased that he hadn't lost the knack; he only wished he could see Eykar's face just now.

10

Servan rested, crouching loose-limbed against the causeway wall. When he caught his breath and lost the cramps in his gut from running so long, he would slip into the City to bring back blanks for them to wear. Their present disguises were useless on the home ground of the Hemaways.

He could hear Eykar shifting restlessly close by in the darkness. The more you wore Eykar down, the tighter he wound himself, resisting his own exhaustion. He had run well. Now that they had reached their goal – the edge of the City – he couldn't let go and rest, though Servan could hear the trembling in his breathing. There was never any point in worrying about Eykar; he looked frail, yet he generally proved a better stayer than other men.

Eykar whispered, 'Strange, to hear the City and smell the City, without being able to see it. That happened sometimes at Endpath in my sleeping-dreams.'

Kelmz, who should have known better than to waste rest time in conversation, made some answer or other, and the two of them began talking quietly together. There was no jeering, no point-jockeying, just Kelmz' slow, deep voice and Eykar's edged one.

Head down on his folded arms, Servan listened. Kelmz made some remark about the influence on the City of a large fem population. He got back more than he had expected – Servan smiled to himself – one of Eykar's learned lectures, the sort of thing that had made the Boyhouse Teachers so nervous. Of all things, Eykar was outlining an esoteric theory that the Holy Book of the Ancients had actually been written by clever fems using men's names. Only Eykar would speak of such things in the open at night, and with a fem squatting two feet away!

He laid it out with his usual precision and clarity; the drift of the teachings of that Book could be interpreted as a porridge of unmanly soft-headedness, mushy morals and anti-hierarchical sedition, cloaked in a manly-seeming tale of a Son justly punished for trying to supercede his Father, 'God,' as lord of men. There was also supposed to have been an older book of much sterner import, which this newer one imitated.

Surprisingly, Kelmz not only did not object to the topic, he showed himself capable of pursuing it.

'But the meaning of the story,' he said, after a long moment of thought, 'is a manly one: that by challenging his Father's authority — and by the false, famishing mush he taught, as you say — the Son drew down on himself the rightful anger of his Father. Doesn't he accept his punishment, at the end of the story?'

They were off. You couldn't give Eykar an opening like that without a debate. He sounded suddenly wide awake and relaxed in the way Eykar relaxed — by running his brains to exhaustion. Six years virtually alone at Endpath must have sharpened his hunger for theoretical argument. He pointed out that by the time of the Wasting, most of the worshippers of 'God' and his son had been fems and that one of the signs of Freakishness in the sons of the Ancients had been a bent in that direction. Moreover, male functionaries of that religion had been imprisoned for flouting the authority of Ancient leaders.

Kelmz could almost be heard thinking. The standard rejoinder was that the refugees had in fact taken some comfort from that Holy Book. On the other hand, in the end they had rejected the Book and its teachings upon discovery that many of the fems were stricter adherents to its tenets than any of the men.

What the captain came up with was another argument entirely, drawn from his training in military history rather than from any close knowledge of the Book itself. The Book's religion, he said, had once been a fine and manly one, complete with armed battles against unbelievers and the burning of heretics under the auspices of a powerful and strictly organized hierarchy. The entire structure of early Ancient society, with its codes of honor, rigid class divisions, and the subjugation of whole races of the Dirties, had been based on that religion. The problem, he maintained, was that fems had infiltrated and perverted a fine, manly creed – this being ever the stealthy danger that they presented.

'What could be more stealthy,' Eykar said, 'than to lure men into a net of ostensibly manly doctrine in order to corrupt them with rottenness that only becomes apparent far in the future?'

Kelmz shifted his ground. It seemed unreasonable, he said, to attribute such enormous influence to creatures related to the fem who carried their pack-basket, let alone to suggest that a skill like writing (a matter of organization and efficient presentation of ideas) was something that her low kind could handle effectively.

The old wolf was more clever than Servan had guessed. He must have chosen to engage in this discussion in a fem's presence precisely in order to show up her unimportance in the light of these ancient, weighty matters and at the same time to warn Eykar to beware of her – without insulting him by coming right out and saying that he needed to be warned. Suddenly the conversation was no longer amusing to Servan.

While he had half-dozed, imagining himself back in the Boyhouse snoozing in the courtyard where boys and Teachers walked and talked under the arcades, Kelmz had been showing a concerned interest in Eykar. Kelmz offered the attraction of an elder willing to meet Eykar on his own ground without pulling age-rank or a pretense of intellectual condescension, and yet able to hold his own.

Well, what of it? If Eykar allowed himself to be lured into an affair across the age-line, Servan could always use guilt against him later. Kelmz was hardly any sort of long-term competition. Yet Eykar was so tense these days, so self-contained, that it was hard to be totally sure of him. Servan shifted uncomfortably and tried to shut out the companionable murmuring of their voices.

When the City's chimes rang, faintly in the fading night, he got up sooner than he had intended.

They fell quiet, hearing him move.

'These disguises are no use to us now,' Servan said. He groped for Kelmz' shoulder, rapped it sharply with his fingers. 'Give me my manna-bracelet.' The weight of the metal, still warm from Kelmz' skin, was placed in his palm. 'I'll be back as soon as I can.'

Even before he was out of earshot, they were talking again.

Servan broke into a trot.

No watch was kept over the City's kiln-yards at night. Nothing could be taken from the sealed, roasting domes, even with the heat damped down to a waver of air over the vents.

Servan strode carelessly over the rubble of old potsherds that surrounded the chambers. He paused to pick up some of the trial bits that had been drawn out through openings in the kilns and laid on a tray so that the supervisors could monitor the progress of the firing. There wasn't enough light for him to make out the colors, but the chips had a lustrous feel, suggesting that they would give to the touch at any instant, like skin. He dropped them, rattling, back into the tray and crossed the yard to let himself into one of the low buildings at the rear. Like the storage-sheds in Lammintown, the City potteries were full of caches of his private gear.

He stood with his back against the door, enveloped in the wet-clay smell, and he inhaled, tasting clay. First light would show him his way. There would be clay figures wrapped in wet rags on the tables, and he didn't want to knock anything down. He waited, not minding. The fine grit underfoot and the powder settling on his lips were welcome to him. Like the City's rippling carillon, this told him he was home.

As a boy he had done a stint in the kiln-yards as part of his skills-training; he had never combed the clay-crumbs out of his hair since. Something about the ability to draw form from a lump of moist earth and to fix it permanently had captured him.

He had begun scheming how to get the company then at work in the potteries to bid on him when he graduated from the Boyhouse; how to stay behind when their five-year was up and they were moved on to another work-turf; how to wangle the privilege of doing free-form work instead of turning out standard figures, utensils, and furniture-blocks. All of which had become irrelevant, of course, upon his expulsion.

Odd that none of this had come up in his talk with Eykar on the causeways. As boys they had often spoken together of the future, though Eykar had always avoided committing himself to any specific direction, saying that he couldn't tell yet. By this he meant that his direction, though still obscure, was fixed by the fact of his identity.

Servan shifted his shoulders against the door. This gnawing on the past was so stupid. He never fell prey to sieges of memory and reflection except when he thought about Eykar. How was it that he couldn't be alone with Eykar for five minutes without giving way to the urge to torment him a bit, to prod and poke him into anger?

The fact was, nothing had changed with time. Eykar still stood in his mind like a rock in deep water, offering nothing, yielding nothing, dividing the current nevertheless. There was no question: Eykar had some power over him. This was a new concept. Servan had never seriously held the thought 'Eykar' and the thought 'power' in his mind at once. All along Servan had thought of himself as the stronger when it came to matters of any importance. Now he sensed a pattern that he had missed before – a pattern of influence that Eykar exercised over him.

Why had Servan put himself constantly in jeopardy in the Boy-house, culminating in the DarkDream that had cost him so much, if not to show off for Eykar? The only positive result had been Eykar's seclusion in a quiet place where he could gather his strength and his will, and to whose advantage was that? Now Eykar wanted to locate Raff Maggomas; sure enough, Servan set about arranging it.

A shiver roughened Servan's skin. Eykar seemed so vulnerable in his tension, his slenderness, that you forgot the impact of his unwavering, translucent gaze.

Lumpish shapes were beginning to emerge in the dusty half-light. With the light came, as sometimes happened (though Servan never allowed himself to hope), a revelation. He recognized, among the draped shapes, the conventional heroic pose of one figure even beneath its swathings of damp cloth; it could only be one Zoror or Zero (depending on the chant), the first of the survivors' descendants to step out of the Refuge into the world again, who had found the surface fit for the establishment of a new civilization.

That was the aura surrounding Eykar's wiry figure in Servan's mind: the potentiality for mythical action.

Eykar's soul still hid its deepest and darkest dream, and the potential of that dream made him powerful. The man who knew his father's name might do anything, might even make himself immortal with some immense, transfixing gesture.

That was better; Servan didn't like mysteries. His pleasure was to bring them to light where they could be properly appraised and dealt with. Eykar as a compelling enigma was disturbing, but a man could play with the idea of Eykar as a legend in the making. Humming, Servan made his way carefully across the workroom to rummage in one of the supply boxes against the back wall under the long wedging-counter.

When he emerged from the kiln-yard, whistling a rude parody of a very serious chant about setting manly examples, his mock-Hemaway clothing had been exchanged for a suit of blanks, and he carried a bundle under his arm. He slipped into the maze of narrow alleys that wound within and between larger blocks of buildings bounded by broad streets and boulevards. The alleys were Servan's true territory; he knew his way through them even dream-blinded. Many Citymen did. There were old-time residents who referred to the alleys as the last stronghold of real freedom. Even the patrolmen hesitated to follow a man into this maze where law and its enforcers were given little respect.

Few other men were abroad at this pale hour. Whichever man saw another first would fade back and detour through another alley, for few men willingly encountered others in the alleys at any hour. Unhindered, Servan navigated the mazeway of crooked strips of paving and hard-tamped earth. He kept automatically alert for surfaces slippery with streams of stinking leakage from the high-windowed buildings on either side and for scattered shards of crockery that could lay open the feet of the unwary.

He would have to arrange a quiet hour or two here in the City with Eykar. Eykar's fastidiousness was a bitch sometimes. He took things so seriously, and his genuine modesty made him a most trying lover. He had been tense and moody during their nights in the crowded confines of the ferry. The City would be the place for the leisurely loving he needed to steady him down; not entirely, of course – part of his charm was the necessity of seducing him all over again, to some degree, each time, defeating him into pleasure.

Thinking along these lines, Servan nearly strode right out into the Street of Honor. He caught the sounds of whips snapping just in time and checked himself in an alley-mouth.

The entire street on which the alley opened was cordoned off with two red ropes. A meager crowd loafed along the sidelines; two bored-looking patrolmen leaned on the corner-posts, and the weapon-lenders were packing up their wares. Inside the ropes, a bout between two overstuffed Seniors was dragging to a close.

Sweating and shuffling, the duelists were merely lacing each other's paunches with delicate lines of welts. Servan had seen a man skin and strangle an opponent with one of those thin whips.

These men were apparently settling some minor matter in public to enhance their standings. Each had come with a group of friends – 'witnesses' would have been a more accurate term – who looked on with various degrees of embarrassment.

Servan stood still, watching with an educated eye. He didn't intend to give the audience a chance for some better diversion. Even in the innocent course of crossing on his way to somewhere else, any man was fair game to any other's challenge, once 'in the red,' as they said. The red ropes were moved every night to some unknown new location, so that no man, in anticipation of a challenge, could go look over the ground beforehand for his own advantage. Standings were made and broken by a man's reaction to finding the red rope stretched unexpectedly across his path. Servan had no time for standings this morning, and no desire to be conspicuously framed in red for every curious eye. He would have to make his way around through the alleys.

With a shock, he spotted Senior Bajerman's round, imperturbable face in the audience.

Picturing the Senior's astonishment if suddenly confronted by Servan, he grinned to himself. It would be a surprise for Eykar, too, to be handed over to the Hemaways.

A cart loaded with sand was being drawn down the street by a sweating fem-gang. One of the patrolmen waved them to a halt. The drover, a Hemaway Junior, swore at the sight of the red rope, and began harrying the fems into an about-turn, blasting away on his whistle as if he hoped to deafen the whole street. He would have to take a considerable detour to get that vehicle down to the glass-works at the end of the street where, Servan recalled, the Hemaways were working this five-year. So that was what Bajerman was doing here, up so early; he was taking a break from supervisory work.

And that was what Servan was doing here, too, having chosen this particular short cut without even thinking about it. Confronting Bajerman had been at the back of his mind all the time. It was an example of the bravura style that the City (home, after all, of a sophisticated and appreciative audience) always inspired in him.

In this case, it went dead against his own interests. He had no desire to abort Eykar's grand gesture; he wanted to help bring it about, possibly even help to shape it, and that wasn't a satisfaction to be traded for cheap City thrills. Besides, some easy treachery or other was probably just what Eykar expected from him. Spitting in the eye of expectation kept others baffled and Servan himself flexible.

All of this meant nothing, next to the simple, terrifying fact that he simply could not betray Eykar. The attraction of their boyhood was gone, replaced by something darker and stronger. As a Dark-Dreamer, what Servan read in the thrust of his own pulse and the tightness of his breathing was that Eykar had him in bondage. He could think of Eykar in any terms he liked, interpret and re-interpret, seduce him, torment him – but he could not knowingly choose to destroy him. The right image came at last: Eykar was a comet, blazing with the effort to hold together through the aching void long enough to win the right of surcease – aware, alone, and desperate. Servan was enraptured with Eykar's brightness; to embrace Eykar was to bathe in fire.

I'm dreaming, he thought, licking his dry lips; this is delayed dreaming-shock. He focussed his eyes on the duelists who circled each other, shaking sweat out of their eyes to show how hard they were working.

That was reality – the duel, the dancelike struggle against death. But he himself was not free to move, as a man must be free in order to dodge in any direction. Because of Eykar.

EYKAR BEK

11

Bek listened to the sound of Servan's swift, retreating steps.

Kelmz said quietly, 'What are the chances that d Layo will bring Bajerman back with a squad of Rovers?'

'None. He'll do whatever leaves the most interesting possibilities open. Bajerman is a known quantity. Raff Maggomas is not.' When Kelmz received this in silence, Bek added, 'You disagree? Have you prepared a lecture on the perils of evil companionship?'

'You've known d Layo longer than I have, and better than I'd care to. How can I tell you anything about him?'

'Then you have no advice for me?' Bek prodded. The pleasant effect of their previous conversation was gone, banished by Servan, who wasn't even here. Bek felt hunger grinding away at his weary body; discomfort made him nasty and obtuse, and he knew it and didn't care.

Kelmz said, 'No advice.'

'My affairs don't interest you enough for you to have an opinion. Forgive me for asking; I've been alone on the Rock too long; I forgot my age-place.'

He heard Kelmz move to ease stiff limbs and sigh. 'Is it being so close to the City that turns you into a sniveling, carping boy all of a sudden? If it will make you feel more like a grown man, I do have a question.' Stung, Bek said nothing. Kelmz cleared his throat and forged ahead. 'A meeting with Maggomas could come sooner than you think, right here in the City. What do you mean to do when you finally face him?'

'Whatever will settle what's between us.'

'Have you thought about just walking away from the whole thing?'

'That has occurred to me. It's unacceptable.'

'Good.'

'You agree?'

'Yes. There's no point pretending not to notice, if there's something riding your mind all the time. You have to stand up to it eventually. But what happens after you find Maggomas?'

'I don't know, I don't see into the future. What sort of career do you think would be open to the ex-official poisoner of the Holdfast?'

'Feeling sorry for yourself?'

'A little.'

'Well, I hope it gratifies you; that's all it's good for. Try this instead: suppose you walk up to Maggomas and you lay it out in front of him – all your time, your thinking, your feelings for most of your lifetime – like a sacrifice with his name stamped all over everything. And he says, "What did you say your name was again? I've had a lot of things on my mind these past years, and I don't exactly remember . . ." '

Bek barked out an incredulous laugh. 'You mean you think I'm a conceited idiot.'

'No. But when you know there's a skirmish coming up, it's a good idea to consider all the possibilities you can beforehand.'

'The answer to your supposition,' Bek said, 'is that it doesn't matter. I'm going to get some answers, even if it's just "I don't know".' The captain's elbow jostled him; Kelmz was shrugging out of the mantle he had worn on the way from Bayo and folding it up. 'Captain, there's a peculiarly valedictory tone to this conversation. Are you working up to leaving?'

'I want to put these Rovers safe out of the way before d Layo gets back.'

It was a good idea. Rovers were very hard to handle in the alleys, and Kelmz could hardly walk openly in the City with them as Senior Kelmz and his escort. He himself and the affairs of Hemaway Company were too well known here for him to be able to get away with it. The patrolmen would challenge him at once.

'Yes,' Bek agreed, 'they're a hindrance now. Servan's solution would be to cut their throats and stuff the bodies into the sewer-pipes, or something equally direct.'

'You'll do fine,' Kelmz remarked, 'as long as you keep as free of illusions about your friend as that.'

'I know him well, as you pointed out,' Bek said, drily. 'What will you do with these Penneltons?'

'Give them sleep-commands and leave them in the sick bay at Hemaway Compound. The officer who'll be running things in my place doesn't make his rounds till late in the morning, if it's the man I think it is. D Layo knows the outlaw business; by then he'll have found a good place to lie up if need be.' Kelmz stood up with a cracking of his knee-joints. 'I won't be coming back here, so don't wait for me. I have some business of my own to tend to.'

'And if you're needed?'

'Then look for me in the Boyhouse Library.'

The Boyhouse Library was famous as the setting for assignations across the age-line. Startled, Bek said only, 'Oh.'

'My soul,' Kelmz exclaimed, 'he's got you thinking as foul as he does! Those shuffle-footed Boyhouse cubs don't interest me. I had a loving friend once. He was a grown man and knew how to act like one, and he died acting like one. And that's all.'

I've hurt his feelings, Bek thought, taken aback that an older man would care enough what a younger one thought of him to be hurt – unless they were lovers. What was there for Kelmz in the Boyhouse Library, then, other than boys? Books, of course. Books and pictures concerning the Ancients' times.

'It's the beasts you're after,' Bek said.

'That's right.' The captain waited, making plenty of room for a burst of scorn or disgust or even good advice.

'A man's entitled to his obsessions,' Bek said, aridly mocking them both. 'We'll meet you there.'

'Only if you can get in without a lot of stupid risk. If not, you let me find you. I know my way around well enough, even without d Layo's wide experience of City low-life. Meantime, keep an eye on your friend – I think he'll sell you on a bet and be sorry later. The other eye you can keep on the fem, there. Now that I've given you some advice after all, I guess I can leave you in good conscience.'

Bek restrained an impulse to say something – anything – that would hold the captain back. Servan was more slippery than wet clay and could make his way out of any situation, but Kelmz was the sort of capable and steady man who caught the trouble that Servan's kind avoided.

With a crisp word of command, Kelmz brought the Rovers to their feet. He set them side by side in brace-position, patted them down to check their gear and started them off toward the City before they could get restless.

Kelmz captured by patrolmen, Kelmz brought before the Board for treachery, complicity with a renegade Endtendant and a notorious DarkDreamer – Bek looked up and realized that he must have been dozing. The sky was brightening. He stirred. He was uncomfortable. His body, which he thought of disparagingly as a sort of bestial enemy, had stiffened with hard traveling after the days of inactivity on the ferry. He identified the separate naggings of hunger in his belly, a stitch in his side, and a blistered heel. Every time the fem sniffled or moved so that the pack-basket scraped the causeway stones, the blood jumped in his veins.

He concentrated on watching the City solidify with the predawn light. From what he could see, nothing important had changed. The backs of the outer buildings were haughtily turned on the stinking southern approach, which was dominated by the sewers that fed the laver-ponds. The City stood high on the compacted ruins of previous flood-broken settlements, so that the causeway simply joined the streets without any change in elevation. North and west, the City's thoroughfares sloped down toward the river, which swept past on its way down from 'Troi to Lammintown and Bayo on the coast. Tall levees rose neatly alongside the river. From causeway-height, Bek could see a string of flatboats heading downriver, awnings flapping in the early breeze.

The wind changed, bringing the sound of the City's bells loud and clear over the laver-ponds. There was the flat-nosed call of the Blues, the tinkling scale of the Angelists, the rough tocsin of the Quarterbacks with the cracked end-note, and the others in their turns. None of that had changed either.

Someone whistled. Bek squinted and picked out a figure in one of the dim openings between the warehouse walls. It was Servan, in blanks, waiting for him.

Patrolmen should have been watching the cleared perimeter under the outer walls, but they didn't like the smell of the south side and neglected it. Bek could hear the fem's steps at his back as he crossed, a hasty, fearful pattering. No challenge rang down from the rooftops.

The bundle Servan carried was a second suit of blanks, more patches than cloth, two sizes too large and very dusty. At least he'd brought a face-mask and a voice-filter in the old style of truly anonymous dress, so that Bek wouldn't have to risk showing his face openly in the street. While the fem went off at Servan's command to dispose of the pack-basket down a side alley, Bek changed his clothes.

Servan watched, oddly restless and uneasy. 'Where's the captain and his brutes?' he asked.

Succinctly, Bek told him, wondering if perhaps Servan had sold him out after all.

'And you didn't try to keep him with you?' Servan demanded. 'Did you consider the possibility that he might go straight to Bajerman or to the Board?'

Ah, the two of them – Bek was fed up with their suspicions and grudges. 'He won't.'

'You forget, my friend: you're on one side of the age-line with me, little as you may like the idea – and he's on the other side, with Bajerman.'

Distastefully, Bek fingered the frayed inside of the mask. 'I notice that you brought no blanks for Kelmz to wear. What did you have in mind for him, Servan? I think he was wise to go off on his own. I only wish I'd thought to ask if he knew people we could approach for information about this man Kambl.'

'I know the man to talk to,' Servan said, jaunty again, 'a client of mine. We'll go right to him. But don't blame me if on the way we bump into Kelmz with Bajerman and a bunch of Hemaway Rovers.'

Often during their shared youth Servan had led forays from the Boyhouse during hot summer noons, when the Teachers napped, or in blue-shadowed winter dawns. With him, Eykar had spied on Senior residences, prowled the Market Arc for carelessly fastened shutters and doors, tracked fems on the streets and furtive denizens though the alleys. The familiar landmarks were still there – a patch of broken paving near the brick-yard, a wall that had become a palimpsest of rude inter-company insults, the profiles of certain corners – but an odd, expectant quiet lay over everything.

At the Market Arc, a paved mall under a roof of weathered grass mats, all the stalls were closed. The Arc divided the smoke and noise of the factories from the core of living-quarters on the other side. This morning no streams of work-bound Juniors poured across. Only one group of gaunt-faced young men of the Squires Company was swinging along, and they had the look of all-night carousers on the way home.

The far side of the mall was bounded by the blind, spike-topped walls of the company compounds. The gates, with the company symbols painted brightly on them, were shut.

Beyond the compounds, there lay spacious individual residences to which wealthy Seniors might repair when they had one or two friends with whom they wished to lead private lives. The alleys here were neatly kept footpaths serving the back entries to these homes. The scented air seemed to mute even the chiming of company bells. Low voices and occasional laughter drifted from balconies and sheltered garden corners. Crockery chinked as Seniors took the morning meal in the dignified leisure to which their mature spirits were entitled.

Bek was not as impressed as he had been in his youth. Since then he had seen venerable men shamble into Endpath, weeping into the wide sleeves of their pilgrim robes.

Turning in at a grillwork gate, Servan had a low-toned altercation with the Quarterback who guarded it. This suave young man insisted on scoring him off with insults and disdain before deigning to deal seriously with him. The Quarterback finally took Servan's bracelet to show to the master of the house as identification of the three callers. He returned shortly and dropped it back into Servan's hand as he sulkily motioned them inside. His scowl was a good sign; it meant that he had been rebuked for making a welcome visitor wait. They crossed the rock garden behind the wall and walked under an archway built through the body of the house, to be faced with a curious tableau in the inner courtyard.

Some fifteen fems were ranked silently in rows across the polished flagstones. They wore long hair, indicating that their owner was rich enough to scorn selling their scalps to the fur-weavers. And they were covered with markings that could only be tattoos: stripes, spots, even fine striations like the hair of beast-pelts, as if they were beasts instead of fems. Here was a decadent use of the tattooing craft, the proper purpose of which was to imprint rank-signs on the shoulders of men, not designs on the skins of fems.

Among these creatures moved a stubby man who pulled at his lip and squinted anxiously into the fems' decorated faces. He wore a plain mantle that had been pulled on right over his night shirt, and his brindle hair stood up in sleep-set tufts. He turned toward the visitors, calling,

'Servan, what a pleasure! You've come in time to lend me your good taste. I need to pick the fem that would make the best gift to the dreaming-hosts this afternoon.'

Servan's luck was serving them well. With the whole City deep in manna-sleep they could look for Kambl without being observed or interfered with, and the captain would run little risk of being discovered in the Boyhouse Library.

'Not to show up,' the Quarterback Senior was saying, 'is unthinkable, of course. But to show up empty-handed, for a man of any standing, would be even worse . . .' The man rattled along like a wheel rolling downhill. Bek glanced back; Alldera, framed in the archway, was balancing on one foot and picking something out of the sole of the other one. The young Quarterback had gone back to the gate. Bek unhitched the mask from his collar and took it off. The Senior, still in full spate, gave him a curious glance but did not pause. '. . . undervalued because they're obvious pets, and those have uncertain reputations as you know, when ownership changes. But I've invested a lot of time and paid a lot of fine trainers to develop the loyalty, the responsiveness of this group. They're a creation I'm very proud of. The trouble is, breaking up a fem-hold by giving one fem away is a risk in itself, since you never know beforehand how the others will react to the loss of any one of their number.' He sighed, and smiled almost apologetically. 'But you haven't introduced me to your companion, Servan.'

Servan said urbanely, 'Senior Kendizen, it's a pleasure to introduce one of my friends to another, always. This is Eykar Bek.'

For an instant the Senior's smile stiffened. Almost at once, however, his expression warmed back into what looked like genuine hospitality, and he responded courteously, 'You both looked tired and in need of refreshment. Come inside, and let some of these pretty fems of mine prove to you that they're useful as well as decorative.'

In the bathing room Kendizen bravely kept up his end of the gossipy conversation that Servan lazily indulged in. He seemed a decent sort of man for a Senior, the more so because of his undisguised embarrassment at Servan's outrageous comments, all liberally laced with innuendo and sarcasm at the expense of others whose names were for the most part unknown to Bek or else only vaguely familiar. Servan jibed at the growing tensions across the age-line, incidents of friction and violence that contributed to it, the tendency of Senior men to see rebellion and witchery everywhere, certain scandalous Senior-Junior liaisons in Lammintown, and so on.

Kendizen made one effort to change the subject, following Servan's remark about the monopolization of good-looking fems by men too old to sire cubs on them. The Senior pointed at Alldera, who was washing her hair discreetly in a corner of the bathing room as she had been ordered to do.

'Would you consider a trade for that sturdy little runner you have with you? I know several people who would be interested. Looks are so much easier to come by these days than real skills among fems.'

This remark set Servan off on a detailed exposition of certain common abuses of fem-trainer status, which brought color to Kendizen's cheeks; it was not so long since the Quarterbacks had worked at Bayo. This teasing was intended to highlight, for Bek's benefit, the familiarity of Servan's relationship with the Senior. Bek turned his attention to the trays of food Kendizen's fems brought around.

When they all had reached a small sun-court outside the bathing room, Bek finally broke in. 'Senior Kendizen, have you any idea of our purpose here?'

The Senior turned toward him. 'I can't imagine any purpose,' he said, in a tone of reproof, 'that would take the Endtendant from Endpath.'

'I am looking for my father.'

'So are a number of people,' Kendizen replied. 'His name is rumored to have come up recently at a Board meeting, not once but several times. You can hardly expect me to be of any help to you in your own inquiries. Senior Maggomas is a man of my years or more, and you yourself are both a young man and reputedly his son. You can't mean him any good, and I can't assist you in doing harm to any peer of mine or Senior of yours.'

These older men who mixed a certain moral firmness with their vices Bek found hardest to deal with. He did not dislike Kendizen nearly as much as he should have, so he spoke as brutally as he could, in memory of Seniors he had known who were anything but decent.

'Servan, this man is a client of yours. Can that be proven to the Board through some informant, if necessary?'

The Senior opened his mouth as if to shout for assistance; instead, he ordered the fems, who were still hovering about with pitchers and plates, to leave. Then he turned to Servan, saying in a whisper, 'Servan, you know it wouldn't be the first time; if I went exposed again —'

Putting his arm through the Senior's in a friendly manner, Servan drew him into a slow, unwilling stroll around the fountain.

'No one expects you to simply divulge Maggomas' whereabouts, even if you knew, which you plainly don't, or you would have volunteered the information to the Board long ago, as a responsible citizen. What we hope is that you'll put us in touch with someone who does know where to find Raff Maggomas, leaving it up to that person to decide whether or not to tell us anything. As it happens, we know of a likely informant, a man named Karz Kambl. We've heard that he's living in the City somewhere, and all we ask is that you use your considerable influence to arrange a meeting with him for us.'

Senior Kendizen began to sweat. 'You're asking me to risk more than you know,' he muttered. 'Servan, there must be others you can go to. I've broken too many rules for you and your friends already. I've let you use my fems, spoken for offenders, helped certain young men to escape being sent to Endpath —' He shot a look at Bek, coughed nervously and added, 'I've been a friend to younger men; you know how I feel about certain injustices between the generations . . .'

His voice died; Servan was nodding, smiling, making it very clear without saying a single word how delighted he was that the Senior understood the precariousness of his position because of these same actions – one might say, crimes – that he was listing. It was not only for DarkDreaming that this Senior could be hauled before the Board.

This was not the first time that Bek had profited by Servan's skill at blackmail. He did not enjoy it any more now than he had in the Boyhouse. On the other hand, neither did he object or shrink away, let alone refuse as he had sometimes done in the past. He did not like this hardness in himself. But he could not afford to be balked in his search by tenderness of feeling.

12

In the end, Kendizen agreed to contact a certain high man who could put them in touch with Karz Kambl, though he could not promise that anything would come of it other than immediate arrest for them all.

'Don't give this intermediary time to think about it,' Bek said. 'Bring him to meet us at the Boyhouse Library during the dreaming.' The Boyhouse would be an ideal place, deserted for the afternoon. The boys would all be assembled on the roof with their Teachers.

Kendizen protested, 'He'd never consent to miss a dreaming!'

'Servan will help you think up a tale to bring him.'

At this, the Senior made a sound that was half-groan and half-sigh, glanced at Servan and said, 'Yes, Servan can probably think of a way . . . Well,' he added, with an attempt at a smile that came out very wry, 'whatever happens, at least I know the Board won't send me off to Endpath, don't I.'

'I'll leave you, then,' Bek said. 'I want to go and rest while I can.'

One of the tattooed fems showed him to a sleeping alcove off the main court, while Servan and Kendizen continued to circle the fountain in the sun-court, talking.

The fem settled herself in a corner in case Bek should want anything of her. He tried to send her away. She didn't comprehend his wish to be alone and came back twice to apologize for having forgotten what it was he had sent her to fetch. The third time, he sent her for Alldera. Having furnished him with another fem to attend him, Kendizen's fem retired without further confusion.

After Kendizen's phantasmagoric femhold, the sturdy simplicity of Alldera was a relief. She had cleaned up and been given a fresh smock to wear. Now that she stood straight without the pack-basket bowing her back, he found her rather pleasant to the eye.

She knelt to take off his shoes for him.

'Look up,' he said, remembering the curding-room fem's approach to Servan.

She turned up toward him a face like a round shield of warm metal. Instead of the sweet perfection of Kendizen's pets, this fem's face expressed a willful stupidity that was perfect in its own way. The muscles around the wide mouth were strongly molded and the lips cleanly edged, but instead of mobility the effect was one of obstinate dullness. Her eyes, not large enough for the breadth of cheekbone underneath, gazed blankly past his shoulder; she blinked only after a long interval, and sleepily. The total impression given was one of fathomless unintelligence.

Close up and undistracted, he studied her; and he did not believe her. He wondered how long it would take to penetrate this smooth-ness that offered no hold for the lance of keen sight, and what sort of being would be found hiding. Her hands still rested on his ankle and instep. He felt their warmth and stillness. He began to get a sense of her solid body close to his own that Kendizen's decorated servitors hadn't touched in him. He drew back his foot.

'Go sit outside the alcove,' he commanded, 'and see that Kendi-zen's fems don't come disturb me.'

'Please-you-master,' she said in that vacant uninflected tone that he didn't believe either, and she rose and left him.

Bek could not hear the men's voices, only the faint splash of falling water. Servan would round out their plan and see that Kendizen didn't talk to the wrong people before the dreaming. Of what else he might do with the Senior, it was better not to think. Servan had always been promiscuous by nature.

He hadn't realized how tired he was, and he only began to feel it fully when he lay down in the hammock. But the body-brute was feeling too skittish and self-important to let go and sleep.

There was a theory that a man's soul was a fragment of eternal energy that had been split off from the soul of his father and fixed inside his dam's body by the act of intercourse. Being alien to everything that the soul represented, the fem's body surrounded the foreign element with a physical frame, by means of which the soul could be expelled. Seen from that perspective, a man's life could be regarded as the struggle of flesh-caged soul not to be seduced and extinguished by the meaningless concerns of the brute-body.

Bek had been fighting that battle all his life. His body was his oldest and most constant enemy, often subdued but never defeated. It was powerfully armed against him. Starving, it would approach food with a mouth tasting like dust and then nag him with hunger-pains later. His body would ache for rest and greet the opportunity with subtle muscular discomforts that made anything but a shallow doze impossible. It warmed impartially toward men of any age and even toward fems according to caprice alone, as witness just now. With its inconsistencies, it sought to wear down and break his spirit.

He had nearly killed himself before discovering that it was a mistake to try to discipline the rebellious body with pain or any but the subtlest punishments. When crossed, his body could marshal a whole range of aches, cramps and rashes against him, and weaken him with fevers, sweats and racking chills. The only possible attitude to bring to the struggle was determination to endure and to prevail.

All this was a conceit he indulged, a sort of game. He knew well enough that what he fought so hard was merely the inertia and imperfection of any material lump, not a consciously malicious enemy. It had, however, become a habit of thought to consider himself split into opposites, particularly after he had realized that it was through the body-brute that the will of others could be inflicted on him. When his body was moved to Endpath, Bek himself, imprisoned in it, went too. The trick was to compel the brute-flesh to act as his own instrument, rather than the instrument of others or of its own appetites.

He lay on his back and soothed his eyes with the design of a fine mat-weaving that hung on the wall. To ease into sleep, he concentrated on how comfortable his body had been made here in Kendi-zen's house: the nails of his fingers were clean and shaped; his skin felt fresh and was clothed in first-grade hemp-cloth; his cheeks were smoothly shaven; his teeth were clean; his hair was glossy with washing and brushing (though he had avoided the fem with the scent-bottle); his travel-stiffened muscles were massaged into relaxation; his stomach was full . . . Only a slight sexual tension remained to be assuaged.

On cue – he was always on cue – Servan stepped into the alcove, drew the curtain behind him and came over to the hammock, all in silence; he knew that words had no place in the pleasures of the body-brute.

When Servan touched him, Bek did not turn toward him. He would turn soon enough.

Alldera woke them, calling, 'Masters. Masters. Masters,' in that maddening, empty voice. It was time to go to the square in the bright noon for the dreaming.

Servan would not leave his fem in Kendizen's house, being unsure of when they might be able to return for her. So she came with them, walking with two of Kendizen's fems who paced along at the rear in tattooed splendor, their hair lacquered into wide, glossy fans spreading down past their shoulders. Bek and Servan, exercising the guest-privilege of wearing blanks, walked behind Senior Kendizen, who wore a mantle trimmed with blond fur. As Kendizen's escort, the two of them augmented his standing.

Other men moved in the same direction through the quiet that always preceded a dreaming: the bells of the City were still. It was said that the silence could madden any man foolish or crooked enough to withhold himself from dreaming – which was only just, since what legitimate purpose could any man have to be awake and active while all his fellows slept?

First to converge on the square were these mantled Seniors attended by fems, young friends, and peers. Heads were inclined this way and that in precisely measured degrees of respect and condescension. The ideal was to present oneself in a splendor of dress and company.

Young men in the Seniors' entourages eyed each other, from group to group, with haughty disdain. They were Juniors who had found favor in the eyes of elders important enough to flout the age-rules, though never so openly as at these ceremonies. A Senior's patronage brought sure meals, gifts of clothing and even sometimes of small items like jewelry that might be traded for rations later on, when the patron's favor had been withdrawn. In recent years, competition for Senior protection had grown fierce among young men handsome or clever enough to have good prospects. They watched each other for signs of slippage, sharp-eyed to press for their own advantage with a generous Senior or one likely to go to Endpath soon and leave property to his favorites. It was always this way in lean times; there had been lean times in the Holdfast for over a decade now.

Later the less fortunate Juniors would come, grouped by company in sullen ranks, far from splendid in the work clothes which was all most of them had. They were more in need of the comforts of dreaming than those who had gone before them. A man in a dream felt no hunger.

Bek remembered the appropriate stately pace, and in the same moment remembered who had taught it to him: Senior Bajerman of the Hemaways. He began looking for faces he knew and forgetting his salutes, which brought him cold stares from older men trying to identify him so that they could mark him for one of their young friends to challenge in the Streets of Honor at a later date. The suit of dress-blanks that Kendizen had furnished Bek included only a domino-type mask, but Bek wasn't nervous about being recognized. He'd been through that on the ferry. He felt, rather, exhilarated by the pageantry around him.

The square opened ahead of them. Every eye turned to the tables set up before the Boardmen's Hall and the figures standing beside them. Kendizen and his fems moved on with the crowd. Bek and Servan, with Alldera at their heels, cut swiftly to one side and into an alley, making for the Boyhouse on the south side of the square by the back way.

Nothing about the Boyhouse had changed; not the ease of slipping in unseen, not the sweaty redolence of the hallways, or the glimmering floors of the classrooms. The open cubbies lining the corridors contained the same sparse crop of personal belongings: a bright bit of cloth, a clay top or comb, a string of clay bells. In the corners of the classrooms, lecterns loomed under their burdens: books of the Ancients, chained securely down. Portions of these books were read aloud over and over, until each boy could repeat what he had heard word perfect. Some said that most of the Teachers couldn't read either, but it didn't matter. The books were only the palpable authority behind the lessons.

Bek had been a fanatical and gifted memorist, taking possession of the heritage of men like a starveling at a feast, chewing everything over and over. He'd been a great one for the forms of things in those days, uneasily putting aside the discrepancies of content that he had occasionally perceived.

For instance, once he had made the connection: all boys learn how to get in and out of the Boyhouse unnoticed when they want to; all men have been boys; all men know how to get in and out of the Boyhouse unnoticed if they want to.

How terrified he had been over that, fearing that his father would come soon to kill him. He had conceived a gripping horror of dreaming, because instead of the stylized patterns he studied, he kept slipping off into fantasies of flight from invisible pursuers and of struggles with huge intruders bent on devouring him. It wasn't even possible to tell the Teachers about it, because they would have suspected a penchant for DarkDreaming – for which they had no cure, as Servan's case so clearly illustrated later on. Bek cured himself, with patience and self-control.

When this hysteria (and the sweaty bout of illness that its banishment cost him) had faded, what remained was the suspicion that much if not all of men's civilization was built on secret foundations that no one ever hinted at, let alone discussed – unarticulated agreements that might even run directly counter to the rules that were spelled out in the Boyhouse.

Not that it mattered in the long run. Bedrock truth, he had come to understand later, was found only at Endpath. He no longer believed that the purpose of the Boyhouse was to teach the truths that made men out of boys. It was to impose discipline.

How unpleasant it had been! These corridors were normally either empty as now (but reverberating to the chanting voices of classrooms full of boys on either side), or filled with lines of boys shuffling in lockstep from class to class with downcast eyes. Sometimes they were turned out into the halls to walk up and down after a whole morning of sitting and chanting, before returning to an afternoon of more of the same. They always had to wear those wretched grass sandals that could barely be kept on, so that moving quietly was impossible. Even upstairs on the dorm floor, where boys lived naked to be reminded of how like beasts and Dirties they were, the first thing to do on being wakened in the morning was to slip into those sandals; and woe to the boy whose enemy had kicked his pair away down the floor during the night. Always there would be a

Teacher nearby, and even the ones who were most bored and impatient with Boyhouse work were alert to the sound of whispering among the ranks, or of bare feet on the worn and polished tiles, or of blows and gasps when a couple of boys surreptitiously tried to settle a feud.

And then there was the ceaseless gnawing of hunger in the gut. Only later did a boy learn that the deprivation he had been taught to regard as valuable discipline was a constant factor in the lives of most Holdfast Juniors.

'In discipline is belonging,' the Teachers said. 'In discipline is solidarity among men against the sly evil of the void with which your dams have infected you.' And again, 'Discipline is the firm ground on which rugged individualism stands.' And again, 'We are here to help melt the fem-fat from your spirits and toughen you into men.'

There were lots of punishments, and whatever a boy was caught doing reasons were found to punish him for it. Most often, the culprit was docked a meal. Those who finally turned their backs on punishment forever by giving up and turning their backs on life were deliberately forgotten. Their names were erased from the Boyhouse ledgers.

By and large, a boy settled for hating his Teachers (and shining up to those who had food to spare for favored boys); stewing in guilt over steamy affairs with older or younger boys; betraying other boys to Teachers and to each other; and generally passing on all of the grimness of Boyhouse life that he could to boys who were junior to him. The Teachers knew all this. They said it was better than in Ancient times, when boys had been left to their filthy dams to raise. (Was it any wonder they had turned Freak, and attacked their own fathers!)

Ah, the stories, the threats, the casual insults and deadly hatreds! Incredible, Bek thought, that one lived through it.

At the doorway to the Deportment room, he paused. There were lines painted in white on the floor; they shimmered in the sunlight striking in through the clerestories. The lines marked out patterns of precedence in the meetings and dealings-together of the various age-ranks of men. Under the tutelage of Bajerman or his like, boys learned to keep the proper distances, and to present the proper expressions, stances and salutes for this or that encounter. Bek remembered practicing the correct manner of approaching the End-tendant at Endpath. History gave the reasons; Deportment instilled the behavior. He could still recite the chant called 'Roberts Rules', which described some long-lost game in the archaic language.

There was no proper manner, however, of being an ex-Endtendant.

Bek saw his own reflection glimmering at him from the wall-wide mirror, spare, straight-backed, even elegant in the understated trimness of dress-blanks. He seemed a model of the Cityman, a successful graduate of the Boyhouse (he who had never graduated), the body-brute triumphant. No wonder he hadn't been recognized in the street, even only half masked. He scarcely recognized himself.

Servan's reflection came and stood beside his.

'Do you remember,' Servan said, with mock-nostalgia, 'when I came along in time to whip off that bunch who had you pinned on the steps, right after Anzik killed himself? Poor Anzik, he was no realist! Even if you'd returned his feelings, there were so many higher-ranking suitors ahead of him that he'd have hung himself anyway in the end, out of jealousy.' He grinned and put his arm across Bek's shoulders. 'Poor Eykar, you did spend a lot of time limping through these hallways, what with one thing and another.'

Trust Servan to bring everything down to its lowest level. Their double reflection looked out of the shadowed glass, like the manly lovers Bek had seen in a fine glaze-painting once; the peer-couple, handsome and well matched, linked faithfully together from boyhood on in spite of all obstacles and partings, like two heroes of a love-chant. They were in reality a parody of that ideal.

Bek's education in love had begun in the Boyhouse, as was common. Though frail of build, he had often been called to the Library to help with the heavier drawers and bins. As he was setting an armload of books back onto the shelves, he would hear the sound of squeaking wheels as a book-cart was drawn across the end of the aisle, guaranteeing privacy. In theory, inter-age sex was banned by Boyhouse rules. Adults were supposed to confine their love affairs to their own peers, and so were younger men. In this way, those who were more mature avoided the possibly corrupting influence of younger, less masculine lovers. In practice, many Teachers seemed to seek out such corruption, and not always against the will of the boys they preyed upon.

There were men who later claimed that their first contact with true, manly love (as opposed to the counterfeit kind represented by a fem's bewitchments) had occurred under the influence of beloved Teachers exercising what were known as 'Library privileges'. For Bek, the Library had been the scene of his first contact with aggressive lust, and his experiences had not stopped there.

Among the boys themselves there were similar conventions, copied from their elders. Those who had been most intrigued, and perhaps most frightened, by Bek's singular parentage used the crudest possible methods of proving themselves unshaken by his presence among them.

Through such forced encounters, Bek had first learned to differentiate between his treacherous, lascivious and vulnerable body and the outraged spirit trapped inside it; and he had learned to hate. At Endpath, he had had to school himself to give the cup without a tremor to men whom he recognized from those times; they came to him in pilgrim gray. The only one he had truly dreaded to see on the Rock had been Servan, because Servan was the only one to whom both body and soul had responded – still responded.

Even then, Servan had had the awful integrity of a DarkDream; his actions rose cleanly from the pit of his being through the medium of muscle and bone without the slightest distortion by scruple. In other words, he did what he wanted without any concern for why he wanted it or the effects of his actions on others. He seemed subject only to the objective limits of possibility, within which he gracefully made his way. In the Boyhouse he had bent the rules where he chose, creating spaces of comfort around himself and those whom he protected. He'd been a hero to some, for that. Many had felt the beauty of his ruthless, uncomplicated egotism.

To Bek, he'd been (and remained still) a shameful but irresistible indulgence. Bek had thought of him oftener at Endpath than he had admitted that night on the causeways. Now he could have laughed, remembering how he had tormented himself with images of Servan in the hands of vengeful Teachers; Servan mutilated, starved, destroyed. Look at him, with his sleepy, knowing grin, his easy self-assurance! At the deepest levels of his soul, there were no conflicts to wrench him apart. His effortless coherence kept him alive and flourishing while everything around him fell to pieces. Contact with him was like the promise of immortality. Perhaps it was that completeness, at base, that the body-brute loved.

The buoyant, confident Cityman who stared back at Bek from the glass was simply his physical self infused with Servan's assurance and vigor. This was the price: each time Servan lay with him, beguiling him with comfort and delight, the carnal being became more real; the farseeing and austere soul gave ground.

Deliberately, Bek moved out from under Servan's arm. With a grin and a shrug, Servan followed him on down the hall, picking things out of the wall-niches and replacing them in the wrong openings. He knew this morning-after remorse for what it was worth.

At the end of the corridor, light shone under the tall double doors to the Library. Those lights were never all blown out, day or night. Images and records of the unmen were kept here. Darkness was the element of their kind, and though all of the unmen were dead except the fems' descendants, no one wanted to take chances. The aisles between the stacks were like cool doorways down the sides of the great room. At the far end was a large window, curtained with sun-blazoned drapes.

But there was no order here. The floor and the study-tables were littered with books and loose sheets of paper, as if vengeful ghosts had torn through the shelves. Everywhere, obscene images faced them from the scattered pages: crouching creatures covered in fur or scales, or sprouting incredible apprendages; swarms of monsters, in motion or laid out in dead rows; gesticulating figures that looked like men, but were actually Dirties dressed in skins or rags; grubby Freaks with hair to their shoulders; fems actually brandishing their—fists and waving placards with writing on them.

Servan waved the fem back. 'Looks like there's been a fight.' Steel flickered down into his hand, as a thick-shouldered, gray-haired figure emerged from one of the aisles. Bek's heart clenched.

But it was Kelmz, not some filthy-handed Senior Teacher. 'Nothing to get excited about,' the captain said. The words were for Servan and the knife in Servan's hand, but Kelmz' eyes were on Bek – an eloquently sympathetic glance. Kelmz had passed this way too, in his own youth.

Having discarded the false mantle somewhere, he stood simply-clad as any Junior despite his lined face and gray hair. Because of this – or because in traveling together they had used the age-rank

Eykar Bek   113

structure as a tool and a disguise instead of as a system of truth, or because of the havoc wrought in this hated room by Kelmz' researches – the years that stretched between him and Bek suddenly seemed not to be a barrier but a spectrum which included them both.

Looking down at the papers spread in his thick hands, Kelmz said, 'You two are late, the dreaming's already started.' He jerked his head in the direction of the window. 'If you're careful, you can look out from behind the curtain without being seen.'

The square was packed with a crowd asway with solemn, silent movement, above which floated the voices of the chanting boys and the smoke of the witch-burning which traditionally opened the dreaming ceremonies. The bodies of three fems, the conventional number, were angled sharply out from posts set into the central trench. They were already contorted and black in the grip of flames that could scarcely be seen in the bright daylight.

Bek flinched from the sight of them. He had always had that reaction, an involuntary sympathy rooted deep in the body-brute. He forced himself to look again.

On both sides of the smoking trench, long lines of men moved at a slow gait toward the Boardmen's Hall at the end of the square. Heavy earthenware tables had been placed on the steps of the portico. Behind each table stood a Senior of the Board, his head and shoulders massively framed by a high-starched mantle of office. Each of them had a company bellringer in attendance, whose present job was to dip up manna-beer from the well in the table top and pour it into the cupped hands of each dreamer in turn. The man would drink, have his hands dried by the same young bell-ringer, and then kiss the palm of the Senior of the Board by whose grace he dreamed. He then would pass by to enter the Hall and find his assigned cubicle, where he would lie on fine matting to dream his heroic, soul-strengthening dreams.

Fems and Rovers were carefully locked away for the occasion, while the entire population of men in good standing dreamed. Although men did not lawfully dream together, all had their dreams at the same time. When everyone had been served, the Seniors of Board would have the ringers drink, drink the last themselves, and then go in, closing the tall doors behind them and leaving the streets of the City empty.

The voices of the boys were muffled by the thick, bubble-specked glass of the window, but by the rhythms Bek knew what chant they were doing. His memory supplied the words: the names and characters of the unmen, who were only properly spoken of under the bright noon sun at a dreaming. Having just done the beasts, they were telling the names of the Dirties, those gibbering, nearly mindless hordes whose skins had been tinted all the colors of earth so that they were easily distinguishable from true men: 'Reds, Blacks, Browns, Kinks; Gooks, Dagos, Greasers, Chinks; Ragheads, Niggas, Kites, Dinks . . .'

They chanted the Freaks, commonly represented as torn and bloodied by explosions their own bombs had caused: 'Lonhairs, Raggles, Bleedingarts; Faggas, Hibbies, Famlies, Kids; Junkies, Skinheads, Collegeists; Ef-eet Iron-mentalists,' the last a reference to the soft-minded values of the Freaks, iron being notoriously less strong than steel.

Finally, the chant came to the fems, huge-breasted, doused in sweet-stinking waters to mask uglier odors, loud and forever falsely smiling. Their names closed the circle, for being beast-like ('red in tooth and claw', as some old books said) they had been known by beasts' names: 'Bird, Cat, Chick, Sow; Filly, Tigress, Bitch, Cow . . .'

A counter-chant was being raised now by the Teachers, enumerating the dreadful weapons of the unmen: 'Cancer, raybees, deedeetee; Zinc, lead and mer-cu-ree . . .'

The floor underfoot seemed to vibrate as the passionate voices reinforced each other with righteous power.

Servan said, 'Remind you of old times?'

13

Bek remembered standing with the others on the Boy-house roof, staring at the billowing smoke, and chanting. The smoke stank (it was by that same cooked-flesh stench that he had recognized the purpose of the Bayo Rendery); but the boys breathed it joyfully. It was the smell of evil being punished as no boy could ever be punished, for only witches were burned, and only fems were witches – always excepting, of course, the special case of Dark-Dreamers, but what boy ever imagined he would be one of those?

The chants naming the wickedness of the Ancient fems were always shouted with extraordinary venom by the younger boys, who were closest to the separation from their own dams. The older boys were privileged to bellow out the list of the virtues of men, virtues which fitted men to master fems and boys in the name of order. Most boys of any age never came close enough to fems to observe their dreadfulness personally or knew many truly decent adult men among the Boyhouse Teachers; but they were convinced, and they chanted their throats raw.

Bek thought of gray-robed pilgrims stumbling along the narrow trail that led out over the black peninsula of stone to Endpath. The intervening step – that of walking to a dreaming at the Hall as one of the adult brotherhood of the Holdfast – was missing from his own experience. Watching now, he felt less substantial than the coiling smoke.

'Well,' Kelmz said, glancing out once, uninterestedly, 'what's been arranged?'

'Do you know Senior Kendizen of the Quarterbacks?' Servan asked.

'That famishing fem-lover? Sure.'

Servan gave him a narrow stare; Bek was startled too. Mature men did not ordinarily run down their peers before Juniors. 'Kendizen is bringing someone here who can tell us where to find Karz Kambl.'

'And you think Kambl will tell you where to find Maggomas,' Kelmz said. 'Well, maybe he will.' He rubbed at his eyes, which were red-rimmed from hard use. 'I'll keep watch at the doors. You don't want that fem sidling in here; and your contacts may be less dependable than you think. Like everything else.'

Frowning after his broad back, Servan said, 'I told you it was time to get rid of him. I've seen men torn loose from their certainties before. They generally end up as wreckage on Skidro, and starve in an alley, if they last that long.'

'Not Kelmz,' Bek said, curtly.

'I grant you,' Servan said, settling himself on the deep sill of the window, 'he's full of surprises for an old man. Take that dream of his; people do sometimes dream of beasts – the other unmen were still men of a sort, after all, but the beasts were entirely different. The lure of the alien is strong.' With his foot, he stirred one of the pages on the floor. The picture showed a stick-legged, brownish creature in mid-leap, its placid face in strange contrast to the urgency of its movement.

'Most men don't go so far as to dream that they literally are beasts themselves. That takes a degree of imagination that I wouldn't have thought Kelmz had.'

He sighed. 'You'd be surprised at the level of most DarkDreaming; I was. I used to think everybody used it the way I wanted to, to give imagination free rein and really dig down into the spirit. Well, men don't; or else imagination and the core of the soul are mostly so petty that it's hardly worth the bother.

'I'm good at my work, mind you. I could give my clients beasts more marvelous than any that ever really lived. I could give them gilded courts of power and splendor, steel cities roaring with wealth and crowds. But the quality of the dream depends on the visualizing capacity of the dreaming mind that I have to work with. Most of them are pretty puerile – as you must have noticed, back there on the ferry.'

Bek paced past him, back and forth. The Library disturbed him; the dreaming disturbed him, and Kelmz disturbed him. What disturbed him most of all was the possibility of meeting Raff Maggomas soon. Irritably, he said, 'I'm surprised you didn't stay with the Scrappers on some congenial basis – such as taking over their leadership yourself.'

'There are too many famishing Scrappers already,' Servan said, fiddling with the fringe of the window-curtain. 'And when they've dug up everything worth salvaging that the company men have missed, they'll have nothing left but the bondboy business – not my style.'

'You nearly died of dreaming in the Boyhouse. Why do you stay with it? You may have built up a tolerance by now for a Dark-Dreamer's low dosage, but someday you'll take something stronger than you expect, and it will kill you.'

'Oh, I like my work,' Servan said, cheerfully. 'In spite of everything. What could be more amusing than bringing to the surface the nasty little men who live inside our grandest, most noble-natured and mature brothers?'

'Almost anything, surely,' Bek grimaced.

'My clients come back for another dose, which is more than can be said for yours!'

Bek paced, thinking of the ambivalence of men's attitudes toward Endpath and the man who brewed deathdrink inside its black stone walls. A peaceful death in the mists of dreaming, under the assurance of eternal remembrance in the Chants Commemorative, was said to be a good thing, worth striving for. Yet men came shaking to the Rock, babbling their sorrows in spite of the rules. And after they drank, they were no less dead than those who died outside, unremembered.

The Endtendant was custodian of perhaps the most important ceremony of Holdfast life, and he was served as such. Though the companies' ranks grew thin in the wake of faltering harvests, supplies of food for him and the Endpath Rovers came regularly. Yet each Endtendant was sent to the Rock as a kind of punishment; his Rovers were his jailers, and in the end each Endtendant in turn took the death-drink himself – as if to pay for his offense in having given good deaths to his superiors.

It hadn't taken Bek long to see that it was for his own death that he had been sent there. He had decided not to let himself be so easily discarded.

Not that there was anything wrong in the soul of a man choosing to shed the bodily husk after a lifetime of battle with the void-stuff of which the world was made. Endpath itself was a recognition of the rightness of such a choice. Only by years of self-discipline and right action did a man know himself to be ready to die. However, Bek's problem was precisely that he did not feel that he had yet engaged in a significant struggle. It seemed to him that he had only endlessly made ready, and that it was wrong to step out of the world before arriving at the meeting place he'd been preparing for all his life. So when he had found himself lifting the warm, lethal cup to his own lips, he had seen the necessity of leaving Endpath, and taking the shaping of his life into his own hands.

Yet he missed the Rock. He missed it so hard that it made his eyes ache with trying to see something different from what was going on out there in the square: not magnificently glazed walls and deep arcades and a solemn procession of dream-bound men past a smoldering trench, but bare and sweeping lines of rock, sea, and shore. The wind always blew at Endpath out of the wide sky. The sea rolled vast and barren and clicked and chattered unceasingly among the pebbles at the foot of the Rock. All was simple, clean and final.

For a moment he seemed to feel the touch of the black mask on his face and the weight of half-filled cups in his hands. The words of the Endpath offering sounded in his mind: 'Here is the sleep of the body, the freedom of the spirit and the everlasting naming of the name.'

'– paradox,' Servan was saying, in his lazy, negligent manner. 'What you do is supposed to be a good thing, but everybody knows in his heart that it's rotten. What I do is supposed to be a crime, but everybody suspects that it's a good thing, a service, even. It's so stupid to say that a man will be remembered if his name is stuck into a chant for the famishing Juniors to gabble through every day as fast as they can so they can get to breakfast.'

'How will you be remembered?' Bek challenged. 'In the songs of fems, that only corrupt men will ever listen to?'

'That's the only kind of man whose recognition I'd have any use for,' Servan airily replied.

Bek laughed, the dark mood broken. 'If the Board had caught you during these past years, they probably would have sent you to me at Endpath to punish us both at a stroke, knowing that you don't believe in the efficacy of the chants.'

'What would you have done,' Servan said, 'if I'd come to you there?'

'I'm surprised you didn't visit me to find out.'

'You'd have handed me my poison without a blink,' Servan grinned, 'after letting me coax you to bed first, of course, for old times' sake. Eykar, relax, will you? Your pacing is driving me rogue. If you won't sit somewhere, at least lean a bit.'

Bek snapped, 'Must I drape myself gracefully over the furniture in order to talk with you?'

'All right, I admit it: in you, ease would be an affectation. But you ought to learn to be more appreciative of comfort, Eykar. Why are you so enamored of hard edges and sharp corners? If I didn't know you better I'd say you were in constant danger of falling asleep without a bit of pain here and there.

'Why are you so impatient? Don't let the tensions of ordinary Holdfast life get to you. Things must have been very peaceful in your kingdom on the Rock, complete with four devoted retainers and swarms of suppliant subjects. Was it hard for you to leave Endpath?'

Servan was watching him with that connoisseur's look, appreciating the effects of his words. Bek tightened his lips and said nothing. Shrugging, Servan shook the knife down out of his sleeve again and entertained himself by carving spirals into the plaster of the Library wall. The spiral was the sign of the void, of fems, of everything inimical to the straight line of manly, rational thought and will. It would infuriate the Teachers to find that symbol here tomorrow, not least because within an hour the boys would be terrifying each other with whispers that unmen-spirits had visited the Library during the dreaming and had left their mark.

Bek looked around at the pictures scattered everywhere. As a frequent visitor to the Library in his Boyhouse days, albeit under duress, he had seen some of them before. Then how was it, he mused, that he hadn't noticed that the fems in the pictures were not particularly huge breasted, nor magically alluring as the chants said? Some did seem to have a red stain on their lips that might have been blood, but actually it looked more like the paint that Kendi-zen's pets wore for decoration. To tell the truth, many of the fems in the pictures didn't look much more dangerous than Alldera – less dangerous, in fact, since they seemed much softer in body than she was.

And here was a picture of a long-striding lion (the label was torn off, but he remembered the beast-name) taking what appeared to be a companionable stroll, not with some witchy fem or even a young Freak, but a white-bearded man of mature years.

Baffled, Bek frowned at the pictures. Could he have been so blind with his terrors of this place as a boy that he had looked without seeing any of this? Then what of the Teachers? How would they have explained these extraordinary images? No wonder Kelmz seemed shaken, even aged by his hours alone here today. What esoteric mysteries were hidden here, passed over and tucked away by men who had no use for anything but the simplest, crudest evidence supporting what they taught as truth?

'Here they are,' Servan said, sliding off the sill.

Kelmz had eased open one of the heavy doors, and Senior Kendi-zen slipped inside. Behind him came another Senior, who wore a high, fine-spun wig which forced him to bend in order to enter without knocking it off.

In a hasty whisper, Senior Kendizen made introductions. When he came around to Kelmz, he said, 'Is it Captain Kelmz of the Hemaw-ays? A pleasure to meet you, Captain, outside of ceremonial occasions, so to speak.' And he smiled his rueful smile.

His companion he presented as Dagg Riggert, an old Angelist whose name Bek knew to be an important one. Senior Riggert studied Bek in critical silence. Looking into the man's deep-seamed, haughty face, Bek recognized the beginning lines and colors of illness. He thought, pain will bring you to Endpath soon. The thought made him feel older than the Angelist.

'I can take you to Karz Kambl,' Senior Riggert said. 'Do you know just who he is?'

'Raff Maggomas' friend,' Bek said, still somewhat disoriented, so that he neglected the proper honorifics due in addressing an older man.

'Before he was ever a friend of Raff Maggomas,' Riggert said, icily, 'he was a friend of mine; he was a man of great promise.

Thanks to Maggomas, that promise will never be fullfilled. But Maggomas is gone, and Karz Kambl is my friend again.

'I will do whatever I can to prevent Raff Maggomas from doing my friend any further injury, to the point of absenting myself from this dreaming and conspiring with Juniors against a man who is only a few years younger than I am.'

'Since the Senior speaks of friendship,' Bek said, giving up any thought of trying to mend matters of courtesy between them, 'he will recognize that there is no conspiracy in a man being helped in a crucial matter by his friends.'

'I had heard,' Senior Riggert replied, 'that you were clever in argument. You certainly seem to have won over as steady a man as Captain Kelmz here, who was, I believe, assigned to bring you before the Board for judgment?'

Kelmz said, 'I was assigned to accompany d Layo. There he is. Here I am.'

Before Senior Riggert had time to fully consider this remarkable, not to say insulting, reply, Servan said smoothly, 'I am sure that Senior Riggert has his own goals, which are served by this expense of his time and knowledge with us.'

'Justice!' snapped Riggert. 'Retribution!'

Kendizen spoke up, unhappily, as if he would rather not have, but couldn't keep silent. 'Certainly the Holdfast could use more of the first, but as for the second, surely the manly ideal of generosity –'

'You're soft, sir,' Riggert said, harshly. 'I've always said so, and I say it again, in front of these young men.'

'And I say that there are those who are so eager to be tough that they become cruel,' Kendizen retorted, turning pink like an angry boy.

Ignoring him, Riggert continued, 'Vengeance is owed to my friend Karz, though he wouldn't say so himself. He has an open and forgiving nature – perhaps a trifle too much so, like Senior Kendizen here – and would no doubt have Maggomas' friendship back if it were offered, a possibility that I mean to prevent – or rather to help you to prevent. In return, I will require some token, some proof that Raff Maggomas has been destroyed.'

Was that what moved this fierce old man, jealous rage at having been robbed of a lover? Anger with himself for accepting Maggomas' leavings again afterward? Bek saw himself as a weapon in another man's hand, a sharp edge to cut an enemy. He didn't like that.

'Your token must be my word, Senior, that I mean to find Raff Maggomas and deal with him as I see fit.'

Outside, the boy-voices mounted in praise of the manly virtues: pride, courage, strength, patience, reason, loyalty . . . Senior Riggert chose patience.

'We will discuss this later,' he said. 'Just now, we have only the interval of the dreaming in which to deal freely with Karz. If he thinks it's to protect Raff Maggomas, he'll tell you where to find him. Can you think up a story that will put that appearance on your questions?'

'Nothing simpler, Senior,' Servan said. 'Let's go.'

'One thing,' Kelmz said. 'Seniors, when you came in, were the streets clear? Is everyone but the boys inside the Hall now?'

'All but a handful of young rowdies who were turned away for arriving half-drunk,' Riggert said, disdainfully. 'They'll have staggered off to keep each other company somewhere until the silence is over.'

Kendizen frowned. 'There is a rumor that some young Tekkans went up to the Rock, and that one of them swam up a vent-pipe and let the others into Endpath. So it's known that the Endtendant, far from having barricaded himself in, has left Endpath and is at large. Possibly the young men we saw were only feigning drunkenness and are actually on the watch for suspicious movement in the City during the dreaming – in hopes of capturing the renegade, and with him some extra points.'

Eager and apprehensive now at the prospect of actually closing in on Raff Maggomas, Bek said shortly, 'I accept the risks. Let's waste no more time.'

'Good.' Captain Kelmz looked over the confusion of paper that he had created. 'I'm sick of this place. There's nothing here but pictures of dead things and a stink of lies.'

Servan laughed and said it was really wonderful, how you couldn't so much as set foot inside the Boyhouse without learning something, no matter what your age.

14

Their passage from the Boyhouse through the silent City was swift and uneventful. The two Seniors put up their mantles to hide the sight of the empty, sunny streets. They hurried ahead, unmindful of the dust swept up by the hems of their dress-mantles. The stillness oppressed them.

Bek had developed a taste for stillness at Endpath, and he would have liked to walk alone and slowly. But Kelmz worried him. He dropped back to walk with the captain. 'Did it go all right with the Rovers?'

'Fine.' Kelmz kept his eyes moving, watchful of alleymouths and shadowed doorways. 'Tell me something. If you were the descendent of beasts that somehow survived the Wasting, would you stay anywhere near the descendants of men?'

'There were descendants of the beasts,' Bek said, slowly, 'the monsters. But the refugees' descendants exterminated them.'

'From the Holdfast,' the captain said. 'The world was a big place in the days of the Ancients. It still is.'

'A hostile place, Captain. Sometimes men who go out on the wood crews go rogue, have you forgotten?'

'I'm just giving you notice: after this you're going to be on your own with your friend d Layo. I've got a trip of my own to make.'

'But what can you hope to achieve –'

Kelmz snorted. Servan heard and glanced around at them. 'You've got balls to ask that! Look at your own expedition, your own purposes!'

'I want to talk with you before you go.'

Kelmz smiled. 'Your turn to advise me? All right.'

It was none of Bek's business, he had no reason to be concerned. But he was. And Kelmz seemed to accept his concern.

They stepped into shadow, and thick doors closed them into a spacious, cool quiet. The Seniors had brought them to the company compounds. This was the common-room of the Angelists' Hall, high-ceilinged, gloomy and islanded with groupings of high-glazed furniture that were strewn with rugs and cushions for the comfort of Seniors at table-games or conversation. No one talked or played now, no old men gossiped by the hearth today in their accustomed places. Like everyone else, the Angelist Seniors were off dreaming in the Boardmen's Hall. So who were the men chanting down at the hearth-end of the room, masked by fire-glowing screens of woven grass?

Senior Riggert turned toward the screens with nervous eagerness. He seemed to have forgotten all his anger.

'Wait here,' he said, and strode off down the length of the room.

To the others, Kendizen said tensely, 'You understand, a lot of cults like this one have sprung up in the last three five-years, as in other troubled times. The cultists come here for the blessings of the sun; they say the rite can help some men more than dreaming can. And the cult's existence enables a man like Karz Kambl to support himself as its leader, in spite of his condition – or because of it, I should say.'

A sun cult, Bek thought, with contempt. Appealing to a sun god for power against a moon witch was an old man's game, like the taste for magic, another weakness of age. A man would do better to come to Endpath.

Kendizen read his expression. 'Sometimes you young men are as intolerant as the most tyrannical Senior,' he said. 'Try not to show too much shock when you see Kambl. He was burned once, and he has healed badly.'

Rejoining them, Riggert said, 'When we join the circle, I'll tell Karz that he has visitors. He'll dismiss the others, and they'll be glad to go. They can't afford to stay together and risk discovery by prowling youngsters. The Board is not lenient with sun-worshippers. Are you prepared?'

Servan said, 'Tell him who I am by name. I'll do the rest.'

'What about her?' Kelmz pointed at the fem, who was skulking in the darkness of the great doorway.

'The cultists will be furious if they see a fem here,' Riggert said.

Servan went and spoke to her. She hesitantly took a place on one of the long, cushioned couches – a small figure obscured among the blocky shapes of seats and tables around her.

'She'll keep watch on the door for us,' Servan said, 'just in case. I've pointed out to her the reason for everyone's interest in not being surprised here – we wouldn't all pay together or in the same way, but by Christ-God-Son, we'd all pay!'

On the other side of the screens, a group of blank-suited men, masked, walked in a long oval, chanting. They paced gravely, not looking at one another or at the newcomers, for whom room was made in the line without apparent concern for age-standing. The chant consisted of a set of lines extolling the world as a fitting place for men, watched over by a benevolent Being: 'To the Sun, Earth is a small stone; the sea is a drop that films it; the sky is a glass ball enclosing, that the Sun holds in his hands to darken; and in daytime he looks within, one bright eye.'

Bek, taking up the words describing a deity who peeped in at the world of men like a boy at a keyhole, could scarcely keep from smiling. The rest of the ceremony was not at all amusing.

Now and then a man would leave the line and go to kneel before a figure seated on a block between two small braziers in the ashes of the high-arched hearth. The figure was a horror: the body was hidden in a robe of dull red and yellow patches, but Bek could see that one arm was drawn up in a twisted crook against the chest, while above it cheek and shoulder were squeezed together on a seal of scar-tissue. The face was an unreadable snarl, wound tightly around the off-center vortex of the one milky eye.

He had seen such deformities at Endpath and could scarcely credit that a man would choose rather to live on in this state. Involuntarily, he thought of the fems he had seen burned today in the square; they were surely better off than this ruin of a man!

Senior Riggert stepped forward as others had done and knelt before the burned man. He reached out and took the figure's one sound hand between his palms: a lover's gesture, simple and direct. Kneeling so, he spoke in loving treachery. Bek, watching, felt his own flesh creep. When Riggert rose, the burned man spoke aloud.

Bek didn't understand a single word, but the cultists did.

The chant died. Swiftly and in silence, the line of men filed past the burned man, who briefly clasped the hand of each of them. Then all dispersed; the Hall doors closed with a soft booming after them. The visitors were alone with the burned man.

He spoke to them. Bek watched his fire-scarred mouth, and this time, despite the distortion, he made out the meaning: 'I'm told that a young man, a friend of Raff Maggomas' son, is here.'

Servan stepped forward, bowing his head in an appealing manner that suggested pride and independence struggling with awe. 'What was once friendship between Raff Maggomas' son and myself,' he declared, with becoming boldness, 'was betrayed by him and has become a bond of debt. He turned me over, in my moment of weakness and boyhood foolishness, to my enemies. I've lived an outcast since then. I owe him for that.'

It was, Bek thought, an interesting interpretation of events. He made a small sound of appreciation, something between a snarl and a laugh. Kambl, moving his upper body all in one piece as if fire had fused his joints, turned toward him; how much did he see out of that one clouded eye?

'Who is that?' the burned man asked.

'A true friend of mine,' Servan said, and he managed to imply with his modest tone the effort of a man to suppress unseemly pride as he showed off the one he loved. His delivery was masterful. A whole relationship was conjured up, a golden transmutation of the reality between himself and Bek. It was so convincing that even Riggert, with murder on his mind, looked up with a flash of quick sympathy and pleasure.

Kambl said, 'Good. It will help you to do well what you have to do, if your friend is looking on. His presence will remind you of what is best in yourself. A man's revenge should never be polluted with spite or cruelty.' He did not sound pompous, like a Boyhouse Teacher launching an exhortation on the Streets of Honor, but rather as if he really believed what he said, never having doubted or examined the truths of Holdfast life. Bek would have preferred some good, healthy bombast. He could not despise this wreck who spoke so simply of virtue. 'You understand, I owe Eykar Bek, too; but my grudge is not personal, like yours. It's only that by the Law of Generations he is the first and most dangerous enemy to my first and most precious friend.'

Then he said, 'Dagg?' And when Riggert, who stood just behind him, touched his shoulder he added, 'I'm sorry, but truth is truth.'

Saying nothing, Riggert leaned down and pressed a handkerchief into Kambl's hand. Saliva sheened the lower part of the burned man's face. He seemed to have hardly any contol of his lips at all and probably did not even feel the moisture, the scar-tissue being insensitive. With an audible sigh, Kambl used the cloth to blot the shining film from his face.

Servan, to Bek's sardonic amusement, looked rather dismayed. He was accustomed to grotesqueries more figurative than literal through DarkDreams or to quick, straightforward and bloody reality. A prolonged nightmare like this shook him up.

But he caught up the thread of his performance again. Briskly, he said, 'I'm afraid the danger to Raff Maggomas from his son is more than theoretical now. Are you under the impression that I'm on my way to find Eykar Bek at Endpath to settle our differences there?'

The handkerchief hovered beside the ruins of the burned man's mouth. 'I take it, then, that you're not?'

'No, sir; coming back from there. Eykar Bek has bolted like a fem, the whole City knew this morning. I think he's gone looking for his father.'

' "Rebellious sons rise",' intoned Riggert, ' "to strike down first their fathers' ways, then their fathers' lives." '

Kambl sat very still, like one who hears a sound for which he has long listened. In a strong voice, he said, 'What do you need from me?'

'If you can tell me,' Servan said, 'where to find Raff Maggomas, I'll intercept Bek on the way to him. When I've paid Bek what I owe him, he won't be fit to trouble Maggomas, or anyone, ever again.'

Standing very tall behind Kambl's chair (like the shadow of the man Kambl might have been, had he been able to stand erect), Riggert said, 'Tell them everything.' The glow of the braziers reddened his dry, grooved cheeks and the mass of hair hovering above him like a sunset storm. 'Young men should know that the quarrels which heat their blood began long before them and have more history than a Junior's tally of injuries. They should know for whom they act, and why.'

Kambl said, 'It's nothing of any great importance, except to myself and those kind enough to concern themselves with me. I was at Bayo with the Quarterbacks when Raff came down from Lammintown. He was bitter about his troubles there. He'd been trying to reorganize some phase of the way the Tekkans were handling the weaving shops, and he'd been making some headway – and then the scandal about his claimed son broke, and his influence was wiped out, though the rumor was never proven. I don't think he ever got the chance to answer the accusation formally.

'He came to Bayo in a hurry, afraid that he wouldn't have time to start over again and achieve something as great as he meant to before he died. He distrusted his health. He had no use for Endpath immortality, though. He used to say that a man should be remembered by the works of his hands and mind, not by generations of ignoramuses babbling his name by rote.

'Our Seniors,' Kambl went on, 'had heard the rumors, and considered Raff a trouble-maker. But he was a Senior himself, so they had to take him in. From the beginning he was full of notions that set him apart. He insisted once that fems' milkcurd could be turned into a hard substance useful for making into buttons and buckles. The Quarterback Seniors were laughing behind his back for weeks afterward.

'So he used to talk with us younger men. He said the Seniors were too soft anyway, not men enough to be really intent on Reconquest, which was his goal. He wanted to explore the waterways south through the marsh, looking for solid land to be the site of a new town, a base for expansion beyond the present borders of the Holdfast. He spoke of winning back our pride by winning back the world. It was very exciting. We liked to think of ourselves as new heroes, turning our backs on everything we hated: our Seniors, the Rovers, the marshes, the smell and sound of fems around us all the time . . .

'What we hated we also feared. Some of us came to love Raff for his enthusiasms, his brilliance and for his – misplaced – faith in us. But we never did do what he planned for us to do.

'Toward the end of that five-year the lavers failed again. Raff was enraged to see the fems being decimated for witchery in retaliation. He said they weren't to blame and that killing them was a stupid waste. That got him into more trouble. Some of the Seniors began saying that he had brought the blight with him, that he was in league with the fems. But he was tough and clever, and he got back to the City with us at the end of that unhappy five-year and began working to amass new power – which he did.

'Then, a few years later came this other upheaval: news that his son was mixed up in a DarkDreaming. He went to a Board meeting about it and came back very keyed-up, but he wouldn't say anything. He began to get ready immediately to got to 'Troi in a boat that he'd been fitting out for that journey for some time. Nobody knew he was doing it, except me. I don't know even now where he found all the metal he needed to make the machine that drove it. At the time, I didn't dare ask – he had no scruples at all about things he thought were necessary.

'He needed a helper for the journey and asked me to come. It was amazing, to travel so swiftly and steadily against the current of the river! A fire burned in the machine. I remember wondering if that signified some holy tie with the sun.'

It was impossible to tell whether the burned man was smiling or not as he said this.

'The trouble was, I had no aptitude for mechanical things. Also, those were full-moon nights that we traveled. Maybe the Moon-witch was watching, remembering the machines of the Ancients that had violated her in the old days . . .

'Anyway, I stayed behind when we stopped near Oldtown, and Raff went to get some more fuel. The machine exploded. I went floating down the river in a mass of wreckage, until a hemp-barge picked me up and brought me back to the City – and into the hands of my good friends.

'Now, this is the part that we argue about, Dagg and I. I've heard nothing from Raff since then, and I haven't tried to get in touch with him. But he's alive and doing well in 'Troi, it's perfectly obvious. Rumors have been coming down the river ever since, of invention, excitement – the kind of stir he's always made wherever he's gone. And then there are the Boardmen, responding as they always do to signs of unusual power and organization. They've been asking nervous questions everywhere and sending spies upriver. Raff is already beset, without his son being after him besides.'

More traveling, then, Bek thought, dismally; Maggomas isn't in the City at all. When we get to 'Troi, where will they tell me he's gone to? To the mines, to the moon – anywhere but where I am.

15

'What's the matter?' Kelmz said, speaking close and quiet at Bek's shoulder. 'You look washed out.'

'Does it amuse you, Captain,' Bek rasped, 'to gull a cripple and his friends? I hate to have to go further – I don't like what this trip is making of me.'

'Nothing worse than those you're dealing with,' the captain said. 'These are all grown men, you're not responsible for what they do or say. Riggert, there, is trying to use you to wipe out a rival he's too thin-blooded to murder himself. As for Kambl, he looks to me as if his brains got a good cooking in that fire.'

'They seem to care about each other.'

'Oh, you can call that caring if you like. I've taken orders from men like them all my life, run my Rovers to death for their little quarrels and jealousies. You find this kind of petty stuff at the bottom of every inter-company skirmish, if you dig deep enough.'

Kendizen joined them. 'Well,' he said accusingly, 'you have what you need now, don't you. And here I am, helping Riggert achieve something he's had in mind for a long time – to his discredit, and my own now that I'm involved, thanks to you.'

'I'm not the cause of Senior Riggert's bloodthirsty passions,' Bek retorted.

'But you'll get your use of them all the same.' Kendizen looked back to where Servan and Riggert stood still attentive to Kambl's twisted form. 'I don't like Riggert and never have,' he muttered, 'and that goes far beyond this specific mania of his about Maggomas. But I hate worse to see him helped to realizing the worst in him, because there's so much else. Look at this relationship of his with Karz, of such long standing and in spite of everything . . .' He gnawed at his lip.

'Aren't they done yet?' Kelmz said.

'Karz wants a promise that no one will tell Maggomas that he's still alive here like this. Your friend Servan is making a pretty show of reluctance.' Kendizen gathered the folds of his mantle over one arm and turned on Bek with a bitter look. 'Well, you won't forget to send back some kind of token for Dagg, will you, so that he can convince Karz that Maggomas is dead?'

In his mind's eye Bek saw Riggert's tall wig dipping forward in a stately manner as the Senior bent to deposit a whitehaired, severed head on the lap of the burned man.

He said, harshly, 'Let him come make a corpse of Maggomas himself – then he can choose his own mementos!'

Too late, he heard his voice crack sharply out in the sudden quiet – the others had ceased speaking.

Karz Kambl heaved himself upright, lunging past Servan and knocking Riggert staggering with his outflung arm. Roaring incomprehensibly, the burned man came hurtling down on Bek, brandishing aloft in his sound hand the brazier that had stood by his chair, a solid metal box that glowed with the fire it held.

Kelmz rammed Bek aside and met the burned man's charge in his place. The brazier smashed down on the captain's neck and back, and he fell against Kambl's knees. Kambl stumbled backward, the brazier tore out of his hand, and Bek sprang and grappled with him. Somehow, the burned man kept his feet. The two of them wove in a tottering circle, gasping, straining against each other. The arm that was clamped across Kambl's torso pressed against Bek, blocking any clean bodyblow. With his good hand the burned man clawed for Bek's hair, seeking to drag his head back and dig at his eyes.

Bek braced his forehead against the ropey scar-slick of Kambl's neck and lunged with all his power. They toppled.

He forgot about his eyes, his head snapped back, he screamed. His thigh was jammed against the brazier's scorching lip – he could smell the burning. Frantic, he heaved himself free of Kambl's struggling weight and rolled clear of the searing pressure on his leg.

His cheek and mouth were pressed against the cool tiles, he could see his breath misting the shining surface. Why hadn't he passed out? Why didn't Kambl return to the attack? He felt only a numb ache in his leg. He closed his eyes, trying to remember just where he'd felt the burning –

'– Up!' That was Servan, speaking urgently into his ear and pulling at him. He pushed Servan's hands away, rolled onto his back and sat up, supporting himself with rigid arms.

Servan bent, blocking his view of the wound, and began cutting off Bek's pants-leg with his knife.

Right next to them, Karz Kambl lay crumpled on the floor, his terrible face turned down into the blood that had pooled from his body. He looked like a hunchback because he lay on the arm that was clamped across his belly. Bek remembered being pressed against that unnatural bar of bone. He looked away, feeling sick.

The brazier stood tipped against the far wall on two of its legs, smoking a dark spout of soot up the glazed bricks. In the hearth, Kendizen was trying to help Riggert to his feet. The Angelist, whose wig had fallen off, kept patting around for it, raising a fine dust of ash. Kendizen looked up at Bek, his features shock-whitened, his brindled hair standing up in spikes.

'Where's Kelmz?' Bek croaked.

'Behind you,' Servan said, 'but leave it. There's nothing to do, or if there is someone else will have to do it.'

Bek twisted to look.

'Hold still,' Servan protested, 'I haven't finished binding up your wound.'

'He's breathing.' But Bek knew how bad the captain's breathing sounded, and how bad his color was.

'His skull's smashed, and his neck may be broken. Move him a foot and you'll kill him for certain. We've got to leave him and get to where we can lie up quietly for a while.'

Looking at Kelmz' slack face, Bek thought of the words of the Endpath offering. He didn't speak them; it wasn't as Endtendant that he had traveled with Kelmz. He wanted to say or do something, but there was no time to find the right words for his feelings.

What he did say, finally, was, 'I can't stay.' Stupid; it was just as well if Kelmz couldn't hear him. Was this the way men met the sudden and violent destruction of friends, gaping like fools and

stammering inanities? How could it be that Endpath had not
prepared Bek to do any better? It was a relief to be hauled upright
by Servan and half-carried away.

'No, no, look,' Servan said, tugging at him, 'put your arm across
my shoulders, do you think you're going to stroll off to 'Troi on that
leg tonight? He put his brand on you, that Kambl. No, don't try to
put any weight on it at all, lean on me; lean, Christ-God-Son! Who
would have imagined a ruin like that could move so fast or be so
strong? I had to stick him twice. He must have been really something before he got burned. Bitch it!' He elbowed the obstructing
screens out of the way. 'Everything was going so well! In another
minute I'd have had us a boat upriver even – and you had to blow
up like that!'

Before they had gone very far in the sunblind streets, downhill
toward Skidro, Bek began to flash faintness and fall against Servan.
Some one came up on his other side and helped to support him. Not
Kelmz; Kelmz was back there dying. It was over the slim shoulders
of the fem that Bek's arm was drawn.

He came to with a wrench. He was lying, stripped, on a blanket.
People worked by lamplight over his leg. Who were they, standing
around to watch, commenting to one another? Was someone kneeling on his leg, to make it hurt like that?

'Get off!' he shouted.

Servan bent close over him, pinning him back by the shoulders.
'Stop that!' he said. 'Listen to me: every hair and every bit of
charred thread has got to come out of that wound. Otherwise, you'll
end up with an infection and lose your leg, maybe your life. If it
hurts, so much the better. That means there's still some skin there
with live nerves in it, something to heal from.'

Bek clamped his jaw shut. He watched the drops of sweat form
among the hairs on Servan's temple, heard his own breath sobbing,
was embarrassed, wished he could stop his muscles from jerking
and thrumming. The warm pressure of Servan's hands gave him
something to steady himself against.

'– cold water,' a voice said, 'until the pain lets up, if he's to get
any rest. That will help prevent scarring, too, and muscle-shrinkage.
That's not cold; you call that cold?'

'You wanted it boiled,' responded another voice, 'so it was

boiled. We have no ice to cool it again, so that's as cold as you're going to get it.'

It was cold enough. Bek nearly howled at the first contact. Then the pain went deep, spreading away from the coldness and seeping into his bones. He could hardly feel anything at the injury itself, except for the pressure of the wet cloth. Cold water ran down his skin; the blanket was soaking.

Above him, Servan sat back on his heels, blotting at his own forehead with his sleeve. When someone remarked that the burn looked like it was well down into muscle on one side, Servan said furiously, 'Shut up, you!'

Bek tried to look at the wound. He saw the fem bending over his swollen leg, a dripping pad of cloth in her hand. He let his head fall back again, panting, 'Get her away from me!'

'All right,' Servan said, moving down to take the fem's place. 'I'll do that. Somebody show her where to find something she can cook up into soup.'

The room was full of shifting footsteps as people moved away.

'Dinker, don't go,' Servan said. 'You and I have some things to talk over.'

A shaggy-headed man of indeterminate age stayed, glum-faced. There were bright-glazed armlets on his lean biceps. He kept turning these glittering ornaments with his grimy fingers.

'Last time I helped you out,' he said, resentfully, 'as soon as you'd gone two pair of Rovers and a squad of patrolmen busted in on me at the old place and killed three of my lads. I don't have to tell you what kind of good stuff I lost in that raid — six weeks' worth of scrapping right at the edge of the Wild.'

'Dinker,' coaxed Servan, 'look at the favor I'll be doing for you. Who else is going to carry freight for you in times like these?'

'Carry for me?' cried the shaggy man. 'Steal me blind, you mean! Double my trouble for half the gain!'

'Think a minute, Dinker: the patrols have been rough lately, and they're going to get rougher; bands of lads go roaming the streets during a dreaming; the Seniors are so nervous they'll strike out every time a rock rolls. Now, your face is known and your lads are all known, at least the ones you know well enough yourself to trust them. Who would carry contraband scrap to 'Troi for you but me?'

Silence, while the Scrapper mulled that over.

'As for myself,' Servan added, 'I have no choice. I have to go to 'Troi, so why shouldn't you take advantage of that fact? You let me use your set-up to get there, and I'll carry your stuff for you.'

Plaintively the Scrapper inquired, 'When are we going to be paid up, you and me?'

Bek lost track of the conversation after that. Several times they propped him up and slapped him till he was awake enough to swallow instead of choking, and they spooned soup into him. He couldn't taste any flavor to it, but it was hot, and afterwards they let him sleep.

Eventually he woke clear-headed and jerked his face aside from the slaps that were meant to bring him around.

Servan squatted beside him, with a steaming bowl of soup. The flame of the floor-lamp nearby was washed out in daylight that shone in through a frosted window. The room, a bare cell with cracks in the walls, was part of some abandoned complex of buildings in Skidro.

'I don't want any more soup,' Bek said.

'You're sure?' Servan drank it up himself. He wiped his mouth on the edge of Bek's blanket. 'How does your leg feel?'

'It hurts.' The leg was one great, nauseating ache. Bek looked at the opaque windowpane. 'Is it morning?'

'Afternoon, and so far everything's quiet. Dinker went with a couple of his lads to clean up the mess we left behind us. Things could be worse. The sun-cultists won't be eager to come forward with information. Eventually, though, Riggert will have to answer some questions, high as he is. So will Kendizen. They'll put aside their pride and throw the blame for everything on a notorious DarkDreamer and a renegade Endtendant whom they somehow got mixed up with – in their sleep or something.

'But it will take some time before the Board even figures out what questions to ask. Dinker's men will cut up Kambl and Kelmz and sling them into the alleys on the other side of town. They'll lie on a rubbish heap for days before –'

'What about transport for us?' Bek said.

'Transport where? You're supposed to rest and heal up, and this is as good a place as any. When the time comes, I'll take care of getting us on to 'Troi. It's all set up already.'

'How long do you expect me to lie here wondering what kind of deal you can work out to sell me? I know you, Servan. This burn will take time to heal, and you'll get bored. A friend doesn't put his friend into the way of temptation.'

Sighing, Servan held the soup bowl up to the light, studying its translucence. 'This is the finest piece I've ever seen in Dinker's hands. I'll have to find out where he dug it up and who told him it was worth hanging on to. Normally he has miserable taste. But even Dinker shows better sense than you do, by Christ! Are you feverish, or what? You're hurt, my friend; what do you want to do, crawl up to Maggomas and bite him on the foot? Be sensible, man! You need to take time out to mend, whatever the risks.'

'No. We must go now, while Maggomas may still be in 'Troi. That information cost too much to waste.'

'The burn must be very painful,' Servan remarked. 'You didn't used to set much value on your injuries.'

'I meant Kelmz. That blow was meant for me.' Bek could see, in memory, the firey brazier sliding down a curve of air, spewing bright spots, rebounding from Kelmz' shuddering back with Kambl's grip.

'Ah,' said Servan blandly. 'Of course, Kelmz stepped into save you. Noble Captain Kelmz.'

'You didn't see —'

'I saw. You don't think its possible that he was merely responding to an attack according to a lifetime of training?'

'It's possible.'

' "It's possible",' Servan mimicked. 'But you know Kelmz better than that, right? I couldn't put out a hand to help you last night without your calling me by his name and pestering me with nonsense meant for him.'

'What nonsense?' Bek said, not believing. But his mind floundered back, trying to remember its own delirium. What had he said? What had he dreamed? 'I was asleep, how could I —'

'And you should have seen your face just now when I told you what the Scrappers will do with his body. I wonder if you'd look like that and change the subject if it were me, rotting in the garbage behind some screw-joint in Skidro. There, there it is again — I wish I had a mirror.'

'I will not discuss this now with you,' Bek said, shutting his eyes. The leg was throbbing insistently, the brute-beast of a body was using its hurt against him. He couldn't fight that and Servan at the same time.

'Well, never mind,' Servan said, equably. 'It just makes me wonder whether to turn you over to Bajerman after all, since our relationship – yours and mine – seems to be something less than it once was. But I can see you're not fit to chat about such personal matters. I won't hold your unfriendly attitude against you. You might think about this business of you and the captain, though. I didn't make it up. Not that I'm going to run around blatting to everybody that Eykar Bek has leaned across the age-line. It's hardly flattering to me; though you're certainly not the first to succumb to the glamor of Kelmz' reputation, his strong and silent manner, and all those romantic scars. I just never thought I'd see you crumble so easily.'

He stood up. 'Since you're anxious to get moving, I'll go put the finishing touches on our travel arrangements. Alldera's there in the corner, if you need anything.'

And he walked out, whistling.

The question for Bek had never been whether he would get where he was going. His driving will (or whatever he sometimes thought he glimpsed standing behind his will – Fate?) would not be turned aside, no matter what the costs. The question was how to bear his losses.

ALLDERA

16

Sometimes she wished herself back in the Rendery. This open sky, with its sweet and sweeping winds, was hers to enjoy only by the whim of the masters. The stink of the Rendery had emphatically belonged to fems and only to fems. There was something to be said for honest ownership, even of a charnel.

On the whole, however, the journey was going well. The Rover officer had worried her at first. A good Rover-runner with experience around fem-gangs could develop an instinct for wrong notes in femmish behavior. Fortunately, his attention had been divided between his own concerns and his concern for the Endtendant. Still she felt better with him gone. The remaining two were absorbed in each other. Meanwhile they all moved toward 'Troi, as Alldera's own plans required.

The river would have carried them faster, but with a wounded man and a load of scrapper-loot to transport, the men had judged the easy conviviality of the river-barges too risky. The Scrappers had provided a two-man camper and a fem-gang to carry it.

They had the southside road to themselves. With summer's 'forests' of tall green hemp cut down, the dusty line of the horizon was exposed beyond the bare and broken fields. The friendly hemp camps, noisy and active all summer, were shut down now. After harvest men traveled on the river, protected by the high levees on either hand from the disquieting sight of the stripped fields, which brought the Wasting to mind.

From the road, you could look right past the borders of the Holdfast to the scraggly trees that hemmed in the territory of men. Similar trees had been cleared from the Holdfast long ago, and the men had proud chants telling how they would cut and burn the trees from the face of the world one day and would claim all the bared land for themselves. What they would use in place of wood, the chants did not say. Nor did they mention that among the companies' expeditions to the Wild for necessary supplies of wood, there were always some men who went rogue and did not return.

It was the silence, they said; it was the endless series of empty tablelands stretching away north and south, and the mountains rising in the west. They said the Wild was worse than the sea, which at least had a patterned motion. On a windless day in the Wild, all a man could think of was the stillness of the void.

When there was wind, so much the worse. It sounded like the sighing of the countless men lost in the Wasting. Or, men sometimes said in lower tones, like the whispers of the ghosts of the vanished unmen, stirred up by the intrusion of living men who chanted as they came, to drive away either sound or silence. Men were romantics, of course – they could afford to be – and they loved to magnify the significance and danger of anything that happened to them. With considerable effort, fems had gleaned from them over the years some useful information about the Wild.

The land beyond the Holdfast appeared to support no life whatever, other than spiky trees and a mixture of hardstemmed grasses that were of no use to men. The wood raiders carried provisions with them, but there was water which men could drink. Sometimes they went rogue afterward, and it was claimed that spirits fouled the springs and streams in spite of the care men took to recite the Chants Cleansing before drinking.

As for ghosts and demons, few but the most humble and credulous fems believed these to be anyting but mental creations of the men themselves. As a rule, men hated most those they had most wronged; it followed that they hated – and therefore feared – their ancestors' victims, and imagined vengeful unmen where there was nothing but vacant desolation.

None of this was reassuring. Fems thoughtful enough to consider the Wild at all dismissed it as of no use to them, since it seemed to offer no sustenance for fems who might try to escape into it.

And yet the brightest fems could not help but think about the Wild sometimes, wondering what it might hold that men were blind to. Those who bolted and actually reached the edges of the Holdcast vanished among the twisted prickly trees forever. Thoughtful fems wondered, but held their ground.

Alldera looked southward often as they traveled, squinting at the distant blur of the tree-line. She had no intention whatever of bolting, however.

She paced along at the rear, the drover's position, giving the carry-fems a step-song to keep them together under the weight of the camper. It was a riddle-song, half nonsense now that many of the word-meanings were gone: 'Why is a raven like a writing-desk,' it began. And what was a raven? The newer parts lent themselves to as whimsical and subtle a consideration of the concept of likeness as the singer could devise. She sang in femmish softspeech to obscure the words from the men's hearing. She was not interested in entertaining them, and besides the song was not 'clean' – free of insults to masters in general. The pity of it was, the song was undoubtedly incomprehensible to the carry-fems as well, being too complex for them.

They were a mixed bunch of tough worn discards and runaways whom the City Scrappers had stolen or caught wandering and kept for their own purposes. Though not matched for size like a proper crew, these fems carried the fully laden camper smoothly. Their ragged smocks showed dirty, scarred skin at the rents; their feet were pads of callous. Only Alldera's intelligence had saved her from being beaten into just such a shape herself.

At noon she sat with them and shared their food. She dipped her hands last in the washbowl, dedicated the meal to Moonwoman, and spilled the water out (water being sacred to the mistress of the tides). Alldera didn't believe in Moonwoman herself, but the prayer was a bond among fems.

The carry-fems grunted and reached to touch her hands, thanking her for speaking on their behalf. Two of them opened their mouths to show that if their tongues had not been cut out, they too might have been speakers. Muteness in fems was a fashion in demand among masters. These two fems did not look bright enough to have been speakers in any case, but after a fem had done time in the labor pools there was no telling how well endowed she once had been.

Alldera would not have spoken of her plans to them in any case. Fems had been known to betray their own kind for this or that paltry advantage or out of spite or simple stupidity. Intelligence had been bred out of the majority of them along with size.

Even in Kendizen's house she had said nothing beyond routine inquiries for the news-songs that carried information back to Bayo. She had had even less in common with those tattooed pets, though several of them had been speakers. The trouble with pet-fems was that they came to take pride in their disfigurement – a technique of survival practiced by most fems to some extent. But in its more blatant forms, when it extended to identification with the interests of masters rather than with the interests of fems, it sickened her.

Besides, Alldera had a strong contempt for and distrust of the merely decorative. Her own tough body, small in breasts and hips and well muscled, predisposed her toward valuing utility. She had learned to be glad of her broad pan of a face, which served both to mask her intelligence and to repel the interests of men perverse enough to pursue fems for the gratification of sexual appetites. There were times when she wished herself beautiful, of course; her own kind took their standards of beauty from those of the masters, and Alldera had spent lonely times because of that. Generally, though, she was well pleased with the virtues of her looks, and she continued to prefer the company of hard-used labor-fems like these, battered and stupid though they were.

On the second day there was rain, and the footing on the road was too slick for travel at any decent speed. At d Layo's orders, Alldera ran the carry-fems in training eights in a field to keep them from stiffening up. D Layo sat in the entry to the camper and watched them splash through the muck. He hectored and shouted criticism until he grew bored with them and went inside. Alldera used the opportunity to practice some speed-running while the others were slapping along in eights. She circled them at a hard pace, welcoming the exertion.

D Layo had her in, soaked and stinking, to cook for them that evening. He occupied himself by sitting beside the Endtendant's cot and telling ferryman stories.

First was 'How Ennik Rode the Deeps'; then, a short story that Alldera had never heard called 'Degaddo's Trick'; and finally part of an endless cycle of myths about a hero of just-after-the-Wasting called 'Wa'king of the Wilds.' This character's body was made up mostly of replacement parts carved for him by his incomparably devoted ferryman friend, Djevvid, to remedy mutilations suffered in battles with the monsters. Following this, d Layo began a long, brooding tale of a forbidden affair across the age-line, in which the younger man inevitably misjudged and betrayed the elder and then perished on the Lost Ferry. D Layo trailed off before the ending and looked at his friend from under lowered lids.

The Endtendant said, 'Servan —' He seemed to hover on the verge of a long protest and explanation, but finally said simply, 'No.'

D Layo put his hand on Bek's forehead as if feeling for fever. He stroked downward into the open collar of Bek's sleepshirt.

Coldly, the Endtendant said, 'Are you really reduced to forcing yourself on an injured man?'

Withdrawing his hand, d Layo remarked sarcastically that it would certainly be embarrassing if the Endtendant should pass out under his tender attentions. Over the lean meal that Alldera served them, he began recalling the events of their stay in the City, mocking the parts played by the older men — particularly Captain Kelmz — with wicked style and verve.

Bek ate meagerly and made no comment, as if the effort of eating exhausted him. Alldera thought he was doing fairly well, considering the seriousness of the burn on his leg. That was good; when men died, fems burned, and she couldn't afford to be charged with witching this man into a decline.

Later in the evening, after she had completed the washing-up and lain down with the carry-fems, d Layo came out and called her from among them. He hustled her a little distance into the fields and shoved her down in one of the gang-paths.

She knew her part as well as any fem in the Holdfast, having been through the usual training at Bayo; but she had not had to play it often outside of the monthly stay in the breeding-rooms, thanks to her looks. In this case she was lucky; the DarkDreamer was young and vigorous and probably free of the incapacity for which men blamed and punished fems. On the other hand, if he were annoyed by his friend's rebuff, he might be cruel. Nothing could protect her if he decided to beat her or even strangle her on the spot. If need be, she would have to bolt and take her chances as a runaway fem, to be hunted by Rovers.

He knelt and ran his hands over her. 'My friend has a streak of cunt-hunger, I think; he'll get to you sooner or later. So let's see what he'll be getting.'

He took endless time with strokings and touching that were plainly modeled on the gentle practices of fems among themselves. To her horror, she realized that there was not going to be the ordinary swift assault, designed to carry a man triumphantly past the dangers of a fem's body by sheer force and speed. He seemed totally unconcerned with the possibility of being robbed of his soul by the femmish void (through the medium of her body), a risk that men spoke of running if they fucked a fem outside of the breeding-rooms. To some young men this was a danger to be dared for the thrill of it.

This DarkDreamer was working on another level entirely. He obviously derived some special gratification from his effort to stimulate her to pleasure. What kind of a pervert was he?

She was too stunned and disgusted to feel very much in spite of his knowledgeable manipulations; how could he have learned just where and how to touch her, if not by forcing fems to lie together in front of him? That seemed to her to be a violation far uglier than any common assault.

Anxious to put an end to his insistent handling of her, she performed a set of moanings and writhings that she hoped would persuade him that he had forced her to a climax. He was taken in, for he mounted her briefly afterward for his own satisfaction and then withdrew to lie relaxed beside her. He began humming a femmish love-song, of all things; flat, but recognizable.

She stared up at the cloud-dimmed stars and tried to consider calmly how this peculiarity of his might be useful. It was not entirely unknown for the news-songs to carry word of some pet fem who had gained a hold on her master by exploiting a vein of perversity in his character. But that was something that came only to those of legendary beauty and cunning, and those fems generally ended up being burned as witches anyway. How much better could she expect to do, out of her depth as she was to begin with?

Suddenly he jerked her head up by the hair and twisted, so that she had to turn on her belly or have her neck broken. She turned. He pushed her face against the wet, hard-packed earth.

'Eat,' he said.

She bit at the mud. She coughed. Grit got between her teeth. 'What's the lesson?' he said.

What he wanted was recognition of his god-like unpredictability. The trick was to furnish it without drawing attention to the fact that total arbitrariness was also an attribute of chaos and the void. It was not for a fem to point out paradoxes that men chose to ignore. The best Alldera could do at the moment was to mumble, through bruised and filthy lips, a stock response: 'The master is always the master, and he does as he pleases according to his will.'

Saying nothing, he let her go and got up. She followed him back to the camper, wiping mud off her mouth with the cleanest part of her hem.

The carry-fems greeted her with murmurs of concern and light pattings over her body and limbs to assure themselves that she had not been injured. Then they sank back into sleep around her. She was grateful for their warmth. The back of her smock was wet through; the night was cool, and a fem who fell sick was likely to be abandoned. But she felt alone among them. Even if she had explained, not one of them would even have begun to comprehend the special unpleasantness of her encounter with the Dark-Dreamer.

She would simply have to put up with him, and with anything else that came her way during this journey, without help. That was nothing new. Her skills had always set her apart from all but a few of her kind anyway. At least she had a mission to serve by her endurance these days. If she failed, fems who survived the coming holocaust would be broken by their masters to become like these sleeping brutishly around her. There would be no more fems capable of organizing even the most timid and well hidden resistance.

That new pogroms were coming no thinking fem could doubt (though there were many who preferred to deny it). The lammin-failure and a consequently hungry winter made that inevitable. Moreover, the fems of Bayo knew something that the men had not yet realized: the lavers, too, would be coming in thinner than ever this year. The men would cry witchery and turn on the fems, as they always did when things went badly.

This time, certain young fems had sworn to fight back. Cells of young rebels had sprung up everywhere during the past five-year, possibly triggered by an especially strict weeding-out process in Bayo which had alienated the young fems from their elders.

The older fems, the Matris, made a secret culling of each class of young fems due to leave the Bayo kit-pits for training by the men — and by the Matris, whose teaching ran secretly alongside the men's training. The Matris saw to it that these kits submitted first to the underground authority of their own elders to assure full acceptance of the breaking-techniques of the men. In the past one or two youngsters had responded to the standard, initiatory beating by attacking male trainers. Each time, the reaction of the men had been immediate decimation of the femmish population in Bayo. So for the safety of all, young fems who showed signs of rebelliousness had to be cured of it before they fell into the hands of the Bayo trainers. Those judged incurable were simply killed by the Matris themselves; giving rise to the legend among men of kit fems so wild-natured as to bite open their own veins and bleed to death, rather than be brought up out of the pits for breaking.

Faced with new crop-failures on top of the old, the Matris had grown stricter than ever. They had been savage, hoping to avert the worst of the men's unavoidable rage by permitting only the most docile young fems to live. One result had been the opposite of their intention: warning had somehow gotten round the pits, and many kits had successfully dissembled their true attitudes. Once dispersed among the labor pools and private fem holds beyond the direct reach of the ruling Matris in Bayo, these youngsters were swearing among themselves that this time there would be no slaughter without a fight. They sang songs of their own, saying that death was better than survival to no other purpose than the production of new generations of fems for a worse oppression than before.

Hearing of this, the Matris had sent out warnings by way of the news-songs, saying that men would be so enraged by even token resistance that they might well kill all fems without realizing the meaning of what they did. And the recalcitrant youngsters — who were now calling themselves The Pledged — had replied: let them.

Alldera herself doubted that the defiance of The Pledged would prove as bold or as far reaching as either side claimed. With many youngsters, taking the pledge was sheer bravado and would not hold up. Yet she found them very appealing. If she hadn't been a few years older than most of them, and experienced enough to know that she was neither a joiner nor physically brave enough to be a leader, she might have pledged herself. Instead, she kept track of them with anxious hope, seeing in them a potential organization of active but subtle resistance and dreading that they would sink in a welter of their own blood when the killing began.

So she had agreed to the Matris' plan.

There was an old tale that in the mountains west of 'Troi, deep in the heart of the Wild, lived the so-called 'free fems', runaways who had learned to stay alive beyond the borders of the Holdfast. A token message brought from them might persuade the pledged fems to give up their plan of suicidal resistance in favor of simple endurance until armed support could arrive from the free fems. By the time it became apparent that no help was coming (for neither Fossa nor any of the other Matris actually believed in the existence of the free fems), the men's rampage would hopefully be spent. The disillusioned young rebels would then have to come to terms with reality and settle down to make the best of their situations in the tradition of their kind.

Alldera didn't believe in the free fems either. Yet it seemed to her that if any young fems could grow bold enough to dare a concerted and determined break into the Wild under the mistaken impression that they would find allies there, then they themselves might of necessity turn into free fems. That was her hope, though not for herself. Her skills — speed and fluency — were fitted for spying against the masters, rather than for being part of a group that would depend on cooperation and planning to survive in the Wild.

So she had settled for the job of journeying toward the mountains and back again. The news-songs were already carrying hints of her mission to prepare acceptance of the message she would bring back. That it was a false message, made up by the Matris and memorized by Alldera before ever leaving Bayo, was a pity, but necessary. She could hardly count on finding real free fems in the Wild, let alone foresee their reaction to a plea for help. Fems knew if anyone did that having been victimized was no guarantee of courage, generosity, or virtue of any kind.

So she carried with her the hope-inspiring message that she was ostensibly traveling to beg of the legendary free fems. She accepted this dishonesty as she accepted the dangers of accompanying these men merely because a fem could not travel sizeable distances alone without arousing suspicion. There was a difference between lying and bending her neck for the privilege of continuing to lie and bend her neck, and going through the same motions so that some other fems might not have to do either any more.

17

The next day, d Layo took charge of the carry-fems and ordered Alldera to ride in the camper with the Endtendant. For himself, he said, he wanted some exercise. If the fem failed to please Eykar, a complaint from him would bring swift discipline.

She climbed inside and squatted down at the foot of the bed, her eyes properly lowered. Outside, the fems heaved the camper up onto their shoulders and began to run with it. Trapped together in the musty interior, the two passengers were silent for a time.

Finally the Endtendant said, 'Make yourself useful. Tell me about that night at the Scrappers.'

Alldera gaped at him and poked her tongue into the corner of her mouth as though trying her best to concentrate — without great success. If a fem showed herself to be in possession of what a man regarded as his secrets, she invited death in the witch-fires.

'As the master says,' she ventured.

'Servan says I talked in my sleep. It is true?'

'As the master says.' She blinked at him.

'Tell me what I said.'

'As the master says,' she quavered, puckering her face as if about to weep in fear and confusion.

'I see,' he said, contemptuously. 'I misjudged you. I thought I detected a glimmer of intelligence. You must be no more than a brute with a memory for others' words after all.'

Now that she had convinced him, she was tempted to blow it all up. She wanted to tell him what he asked and a lot more, yielding to the prime fantasy of all speaking fems — that of becoming the one who, by sheer eloquence, drove through the barrier of the men's guilt and fear.

Others' words? Her own words would blast his cursed bones — or at least it was gratifying to think so. The Matris said that the men already knew that fems were wrongly blamed for the Wasting, but that for men there was no truth but that which served their upraised fists.

Alldera ducked her head. 'As the master says.'

He stared coldly at her. His dislike was hard as stone.

'I've seen you doing exercises,' he said. 'They seem to be for stretching the muscles of the legs.'

'As the master says.'

'Spare me that sniveling cant!' he exploded. 'Just show me what you know that would work the muscles here.' He laid his hand gingerly along the side of his injured leg.

'These are femmish exercises, please you,' she said, cringing to disguise the fact that she was offering a correction to a master, 'which this fem hopes she can perform to the master's satisfaction —'

'I want you to teach them to me,' he snapped. 'I'm not interested in a performance.'

Alldera had, and knew she had, considerable muscular grace, a side effect of speed-training. The exercises he required could show off her body without leaving her open to a charge of attempted seduction — while helping to accomplish the fact. Judging by d Layo's remarks the night before, he had put her in here to seduce the Endtendant. To please d Layo seemed the sensible course.

Yet she would have to go carefully. Men like Bek — high strung, tightly controlled, inexperienced in the reality of fems as opposed to Boyhouse nonsense about them — were potentially dangerous to the first fem to break through their defenses. They sometimes went rogue and killed the offending fem or even themselves. Either way the blame was laid at the fem's door.

How sick she was of this process of endlessly figuring out the subtlest, safest course to take with them! It used up so much time and energy, and to no avail. No matter how carefully you weighed up men's motives and probable reactions, you ended with the same helpless gamble you'd started with. A man's whim was law, and knowing this made men capricious.

She channeled the energy of her anger into the exercises, showing him with beauty and smoothness how to stretch, to turn, to bend the legs from the sitting position. Runners had to know how to keep fit even when penned in tight quarters for long periods as punishment or in the line of duty. She made a masterpiece of the routine. That was her defiance.

Slowly and clumsily, he imitated her, keeping himself decently covered with the blanket and the long skirts of the bedshirt that he wore. His prudery was comical at first, but as he sweated and fought to follow, he seemed to forget her, almost, in his absorption with another enemy: his own body. He strove against the stiffness of his muscles with grim concentration, so that she could not help feeling a grudging respect for him. Respect was not something she gave willingly to men. It annoyed her.

As they were about to go through the routine for the third time, there came an outbreak of terrified wailing from the carry-fems outside. The camper lurched forward, its canvas walls flying.

Alldera glimpsed a stranger in Hemaway colors standing over the forward-offside fem who had sunk down, clawing at his knees. He was sawing at her neck with a knife. His hissing breath was audible between her screams.

Then Alldera and the Endtendant were spilled together under a shroud of tangled canvas, rope and poles. They fought to be free of each other; they scrabbled for light and air.

The wreckage was wrenched aside.

'Look! Raff Maggomas' son entwined in the arms of a fem!' exclaimed their discoverer, a high-mantled, round-faced man whose eyes were squeezed nearly shut with mirth at the sight of them. He was speaking to a group of hefty Hemaway Seniors, not one of them more than a couple of years across the age-line. Two Hemaways held the DarkDreamer by the arms, which they had twisted up behind his back. They had taken his knife from him. One of them kept turning to spit blood from his bruised mouth.

Five carry-fems stood huddled around the dead one. They glanced furtively over at Alldera. She lay quite still, hoping by example to keep them steady. They would be pulled down and butchered if they ran. These were strong men, not dodderers, and had already been primed for blood by one femmish death.

At their leader's orders, three Hemaways hustled the Endtendant and Alldera to their feet and out of the collapsed camper. Because of his bad leg. Bek had either to lean on Alldera, or to sit on the ground and look up at his captor and at the sun.

He clamped his hand on her shoulder, glanced once at the Hemaways as they set about rebuilding the camper, and turned a bitter look on the senior Senior.

'Senior Bajerman,' he said, 'I had hoped to meet you again sooner.'

'Oh?' inquired the other, brows arching in mock perplexity. 'Were you planning to catch up with me by running away from the City where I live?'

'I meant that I had hoped when I was still at Endpath to meet and serve you there, Senior; though in fact it is by leaving the City that I have found you, isn't it?'

The Senior sighed and looked him up and down. 'I remember you more kindly than you remember me, I think. You were less lean and sharp-faced in your Boyhouse days, Eykar, but, I must add, no less arrogant. To grow older without maturing is a dreadful waste.'

D Layo laughed. 'You should know, Bajerman.'

The bloody-mouthed Hemaway gave d Layo's arms a wrench. D Layo grinned at him, part pain, part promise.

'You two young men,' Senior Bajerman sadly remarked, 'are a great reproach to me. You never did learn basic consideration for your elders. You've been slow – we've been waiting for you since dawn.' He nodded in the direction of the levee, which was pierced at this point by the thick-woven cables of a bridge linking the north and south river-roads. 'Our boat is down under the bridge. It's too small, unfortunately, to carry us all but I see you have thoughtfully furnished transport yourselves. We knew you would come by on your way to 'Troi, so we were patient, and here is our reward.

'You must have guessed, Eykar, that your father's whereabouts have been known to certain members of the Board for some time. We were hoping that you yourself might be useful in curbing Maggomas' ambitions. He's been gathering considerable power about himself in 'Troi, more than seemed to us healthy for the general life of the Holdfast. Your flight from Endpath indicated to us that you were ripe to be used against him, if we could lay our hands on you and point you in the right direction.'

'And now that you have – laid your hands on me,' Bek said, with a curl of his lips, 'what direction do you have in mind?'

'Oh, we'll go on to 'Troi,' the Senior said. 'There is no place else to go. An army of young madmen is at our heels now. The Juniors of the City, having discovered that there are no great hidden stocks of food and supplies there, have turned toward 'Troi instead, where other hoards are rumored to be hidden away.

'Their rebellion apparently began with some quarrel in Lammin-town between 'Wares and Chesters over a question of unauthorized passengers and lammin-theft. The 'Wares took the matter to the City for the Board to adjudicate. Some young Chesters followed, were turned away drunk from the dreaming and returned to break into the Boardmen's Hall and maltreat some of the 'Wares. Two men died. Other companies leaped into the dispute, and yesterday there were riots in the City. By noon, young men were cutting down their elders in the streets.'

'It's very gratifying,' d Layo said, 'to know that a man's actions do count for something in this world.'

Senior Bajerman nodded: 'I thought that tale of a raid on the lammin-stocks and a daring escape by sea might have involved you; it had your touch. But I wouldn't take credit for setting off a generation-war if I were you; it's been brewing for a long time. Anything could have ignited these City punks. The lessons of the Wasting have been too lightly remembered lately, and hardly taught to the young. If Juniors don't understand the meaning of work or discipline or honor any more, why, I suppose we Seniors must bear some of the blame for that.

'Now there will be a battle of 'Troi, I think, an historic event — which we will attend, hopefully, from a vantage point inside 'Troi walls. We will arrive bringing word of the approach of the degener-ate City rabble, and I'm sure that Raff Maggomas can find proper places for myself and my friends in exchange for that; and for the person of his own natural enemy, Eykar: yourself.'

'But,' d Layo said, with exaggerated astonishment, 'where were the Seniors' famous Rovers during this upheaval, where were the Rovers' even more famous officers?'

'The Rovers proved a great disappointment,' the Senior admitted. 'Some of the young men had made distance-weapons — strictly forbidden, of course, but these things are so hard to control. These boyos stationed themselves on the rooftops and picked off the officers with stones whirled from slings.

'After that, it was not too difficult for them to lure the uncommanded Rovers into the alleys where barricades were thrown up to pen them in, and they were harrassed and bombarded from the rooftops until they went rogue and turned on one another. Of course, the caliber of the younger officers wasn't all it should have been; it's been declining lately with the caliber of all young men. I've come to regret having sent Captain Kelmz with you, Servan.

'And I must say I am shocked at the way you treated him – to throw him aside like a worn-out shoe! A shocking end for a prominent man, to be struck down in the course of some obscure, illicit brawl when all decent men of the City were dreaming!' Kindly, he added, 'Yet I can see that Eykar feels his loss, and misses, no doubt, Kelmz' courage, his experience, perhaps even his close friendship in spite of the disparity in ages? I'll do what I can to take his place.'

'You?' Bek said, and he uttered a raw bark of laughter.

'Do you scorn my good will, Eykar?' murmured the Senior. 'I could leave you to the mob, remember. You served the Board at Endpath for six years. I doubt those degenerate City cubs will look kindly on that career, so many of them having lost friends and lovers to the Rock.'

'Don't be stupid,' Bek said, flatly. 'You'll take me to 'Troi because that's where I'm going, with or without your aid. Do you think it matters whether I arrive there walking, crawling, or dragged by an enemy?'

Senior Bajerman gazed earnestly at the bright sky, assuming an expression of pink-cheeked magnanimity.

'I was once fond of you, Eykar. I thought you had great promise. For the sake of our past closeness, I'll put these ravings down to the effects of your wound. As for this DarkDreamer, I think I have a place for him quite close to me, for which he should be grateful. He needs lessons in behavior as badly as you do, since what was taught to you both in the Boyhouse evidently didn't take. You should count yourself fortunate in finding a qualified Teacher to help you correct your errors. We'll hold class in the camper for you two as we travel.

'As for this fem of yours, Eykar –'

'She's not mine.'

'Whichever of you two she belonged to,' the Senior said, 'it's a good thing that someone thought to bring her along. She can take the place of the carry-fem that my friend Arik killed. These over-trained personal fems are going to have to get used to honest work in the future. The City lads included fems in their rampage, apparently incensed by reports of fems actually attacking men. Only idiot boys would credit such tales, of course, but you know how rumors like that get about whenever there is any unrest. When the dust of this chaos clears, fems will be in short supply. So I must thank you young men, I suppose, for your forethought in providing me not only with your charming and invaluable selves, but with a useful bit of property besides.'

18

The morning was already spent when Alldera joined the carrycrew. By midafternoon a dark and gritty wind began to bite at them from the west. As they ran, the carry-fems showed her the rhythm that was least tiring, how to balance the load over her spine and let her hips do the work, how to fold her carry-cloth on the run so that it provided the test padding under the yoke.

The trouble was that she did not have the strength to support her share of frame, canvas, and the weight of three male passengers. The carry-fems were built square, for lugging heavy loads. Alldera was long-muscled for fluid motion.

Eventually, she fell. The others managed to keep the camper from dropping and crushing her. They prodded her with their feet when Senior Bajerman descended from the camper, but she couldn't even draw her legs under herself to rise. It made no difference; her mission had ended when fems began dying in the City, for the Pledged would be the first to be killed. She only hoped that these men would cut her throat cleanly, rather than break her legs and leave her there, as some drovers did. It was a mercy that her eyes were so puffy from squinting into the driving dust that she would hardly be able to see the knife.

Standing over her, Senior Bajerman did not draw a knife. He said that it was crowded in the camper. He had been told that this fem was speed-trained, and he was not going to let such potentially valuable property go to waste; that would be unmanly. She would ride in the camper where she could attend Eykar while she got back her strength. Perhaps a man running with this crew of hulks could make them put some decent speed on. Bajerman would go on foot outside with his men, he said, and observe the performance of Alldera's replacement: d Layo.

The DarkDreamer was pushed into position, and the Hemaways slung Alldera into the camper. The dim interior smelled of Bajerman's perfume, for the ceiling-vent had been shut to keep out the blowing grit. Alldera crawled into a corner and huddled there, too cramped to move or speak, drawing painful breaths of the stale, sweet air.

The camper was lifted and carried into the teeth of the wind. A man's voice, hoarse and panting, struck up a stepsong concerning the foolishness of old men who insisted on showing off their dwindling physical powers to younger companions. D Layo was singing.

Later, in the blowing dusk, the carry-crew staked down the camper into tent form for the night. The Hemaways fashioned a rough shelter for themselves of their mantles and staffs a short distance away. The fems were left within the bare area between the two structures, where Hemaway sentries could keep an eye on them.

Alldera was thrust among the carry-crew for the night. She squatted stiffly and used her carry-cloth as they used theirs, as shelter from the wind. She had not slept; the Endtendant had not said one word to her all afternoon in the camper, but she hadn't dared to doze off for fear of being punished for inattentiveness. Now the carry-fems took turns kneading the ache out of her shoulders, back and legs. A bald one, scalped too closely at some time by fur-weavers, offered her the moist center of a portion of curdcake, keeping the tougher skin for herself.

In a tight circle, using their hip-packs of provisions as cushions, they settled for a night of shared warmth. The carry-fems began to hum, weaving tone and amorphous rhythm into a plaintive, wordless request for a song for the dead one.

Every song needed one fem in the group who knew the words, and could sing them under the camouflage of gutterals and trills set up by the others to mask the sense of the song from men – most of whom could follow softspeech if they tried. Alldera was not a singer. Her work had been largely solitary and not conducive to music. But her trained memory had retained every song she had ever heard.

She sang a mourning song for the slain carry-fem. It was an uncommon one; she had never heard all the words, for some of them had been lost. She loved the tune, however, which was unmistakably grieving: 'Goodbye, all pain, something-something Shy Ann.'

When that song was finished, the carry-fems kept up their vocal pattern, building on the mournful melody. Alldera wondered if some inkling of the meaning of Bajerman's remarks had gotten through to them – that the massacre of fems had already begun. All the carry-fems and Alldera herself had come very close to dying by the bridge. They owed their lives – for however much longer they would be permitted to keep them – to Senior Bajerman's judgment of their usefulness.

It was unfair for her to be left with a bunch of carry-fems who could scarcely comprehend the dimensions of the disaster and of her own failure. They were not the type with whom she would have chosen to spend the last of her life. They smelled and were dim-witted, and they looked to her – foolishly, in her opinion – for leadership.

And so? A dead bitch is a dead bitch, what difference whether she had brains or not? What use had Alldera's brains ever been? She might as well be one of these carry-fems as not. They remembered their dead, at least, in spite of the brutality of their lives, and showed kindness when they could afford to. If these poor scarred hulks wanted songs, she would sing for them.

She began with the traditional singing-invocation, relating how men continually brought their own houses down on their heads and then looked around for someone else to blame. With the beasts and the Dirties all gone and the idea of gods discredited as a femmish hoax, there was no one to blame these days but the fems and their young. The words asked for strength to bear the blame. Alldera sang them ironically, using the shortest form, and then swung into the jeering rhythm of songs mocking the Ancient men for the brainless greed that had perverted their inventiveness and strength.

These songs told of rotten water, ravaged hills, air made unbreathable by noxious gases, cities uninhabitable because of the noise of machines – all of it, the product of the men's own wonderful knowledge and their obsession with breeding more sons on their fems. Dying of the men's assault, the Ancient world had rotted, and its decay had released poisons. The first to die had not been the men whose avarice for the riches of the world caused it all; they had had wealth with which to buy protection, while there was still protection to be had. It was the beasts who died, all unknowing; and it was the Dirties. Those of the unmen who realized what was happening and rose up to fight, the Ancient men slaughtered, using flying fires and earth-smashers that only compounded the damage suffered by the world.

At last, seeing their own kind falling to the increasingly widespread and indiscriminate destruction of wars and poisons, the leaders of men had bravely made the choice of sustaining themselves in the Refuge so that mankind would not utterly disappear.

The carry-fems slapped their knees to make the beat for the mock-heroic songs that told of the Holdfast-making: how the descendants of the world's murderers had stepped out into the open again to build a new life on the bones of the dead and the backs of their fems. In the time-honored manner, the descendants had become heroes in their turn by pursuing and exterminating the pitiful creatures that had survived the Wasting outside, the so-called 'monsters'. So the river-plain had been claimed for men again, from the hills behind 'Troi to the sea.

The descendants' courage had been rewarded. They had found life-sustaining gifts of the sun on which to nurture their society. There were the edible seaweeds, the metal mines, the pits of coal for fuel, and the hemps for food and fiber. Not to mention the last gift, the docile compliance of fems in their own suppression.

'Heroes!' the songs mocked. 'The unmen are not gone; you are more predictable than the thoughtless beasts, though not as beautiful. You are poorer than the Dirties, though less wise. You dream the drug visions of the Freaks, without freedom. You are more vain and jealous than the fems, and weaker.' The formal closing of this sort of history-cycle was an admonition to all fems who heard: choose your hatreds with care, seeing how the men have become all that they hate! And then came urgings to patience, promises that the men would find their sanity and humanity again in time. Meanwhile, fems must keep themselves sane and fit to meet them again as people when the time came. The way to fight your enemy is not to become like him, they said.

Alldera could no longer even finish the words. She broke into another song instead, one that asked how was it that the fems the leaders saved from the Wasting accepted degradation instead of swallowing their tongues and suffocating in defiance?

Every one of the carry-fems huddled against the wind knew the answer to that, for it was the first and last lesson dinned into all fems by the Matris: for the survival of the race.

'And to save their own lives,' Alldera added, hoarse with hatred. She too had learned to snivel and whine and creep softly about in order to stay alive. She ended with a proscribed song called the Cursing Song:

'Moonwitch's daughters, enticers of men, bloody-mouthed cub-makers – if only we had the power! Ogres, man-eaters, ravening monsters, drinkers of blood and strength – if only we had the power! Bringers of evil gifts, fountains of chaos, stinking, merciless, wild-hearted haters – if only we had the power! Unchangeably ancient, corpse-crones, child-eaters, justice-blind and mad as blackness – if only we had the power!'

The carry-fems weren't happy with that; it made them uneasy. They let their accompaniment lapse when it was over and curled up to sleep. The wind had died. From the camper came intermittent sounds of conversation, even laughter.

Alldera lay awake a while, wondering if the femmish songs had been sung for the last time tonight.

In the morning, there was a shadow on the plain behind them. It was Oldtown, the remains of an Ancient City. They had missed the hemp-stink and the rumble of machinery because of the previous day's wind. Over decades, fem-gangs had been brought in to strip the site of usable materials. Scrappers had scrounged furtively after them. Nothing remained but heaps of rubble among which a complex of water-mills had been built to catch the strength of the river and to use it to help process the hemp harvested from the plains.

Morning also revealed the distant, hurrying figure of one of the Hemaways, who was making for the town. He must have had enough of traveling that empty road toward an uncertain reception in 'Troi. The others looked after him scornfully and spat on the ground, but there were envious and speculative glances too, when Senior Bajerman wasn't watching.

He sat unconcernedly in the sun. D Layo knelt behind him and rubbed his back with scented oil. Occasionally, the DarkDreamer leaned forward to murmur in the Senior's ear. Then there were smiles and laughter between them.

So that was why the Endtendant sat apart from them both and hardly touched his food. Alldera thought his behavior absurd. What did he expect from his friend? D Layo was merely demonstrating that he knew how to make the best of a bad situation – a femmish quality, but there were plenty of men who would make fine fems, given the opportunity.

Bek turned, extending his hand for the water-cup, and saw the contempt on her face. His eyes narrowed; but there was no shout, no blow. She blinked and looked away. He took the cup from her hand, not touching her fingers. She knew she would not get away free. She hardly cared.

With the flaps buckled down around them for privacy and the journey resumed, Bek settled himself among the cushions at the head end of the bedding. He picked at the blanket, tracing the shape of the bandage on his leg underneath. He said, 'I'm still thirsty. Pour me some more water.'

Oh, these conscientious types, she thought. He needed an excuse to exercise his rage because he was ashamed of it. Instead of coming right to the point and beating her because her expression had angered him, he would give her orders and watch for the least sign of insubordination – which he would find, one way or another. Then why play the game of submission? In a convulsive gesture, she turned the pitcher upside down, and its cold contents splashed out over the bed.

He jerked his legs back with a gasp of pain, rose onto his knees and wrenched the pitcher out of her hand. He raised the pitcher over his head, his face twisted with fury.

Alldera fell back. She spread her legs and clawed up her smock with both hands in the last, mindless defense: when threatened, present.

For an instant, he hung over her; then he flung himself down on her. It took all her concentration and skill to help him carry through his assault. He was clumsy and in pain, and when he entered her, she heard his groan of mortal terror. Their coupling was painfully dry for her, but brief. Almost at once a strained cry burst from his throat. He pulled away and rolled onto his stomach in the sodden bedding, his ribs pumping in and out like a blown runner's.

Mechanically Alldera took stock: one sleeve was half-torn from her smock; a bruise was swelling warmly under the skin of her left temple; there were other aches and abrasions, none serious. She finger-combed her hair and blotted her sweaty face on the skirt of her garment. A fem must never offend a master by appearing messy if she could help it.

She thought what a good thing it was that she had never joined the Pledged. Let this man, not much taller or heavier than herself and wounded besides, only raise his hand to her and all her courage disappeared into the habits of survival like a rock into a swamp. A clever fem sometimes needed a reminder of her true position, and there was nothing like a good swift fuck to set firmly in her mind her relation to the masters again: the simplest relation of all, that of an object to the force of those stronger than she.

Fem, she thought, you only think you think. The pitcher the man drinks from does not think. The camper that carries his weight does not think.

She felt hollow in body, which was fitting in one who was merely a receptacle for the use of men; and she felt hollow in mind, for there was nothing she might imagine, feel or will that a man could not wipe out of existence by picking her up for his own purposes. Any fem drifted helplessly, awaiting their actions and desires until one of them inadvertently authenticated her by seizing her to himself – if only to run an errand or repeat a phrase – for an instant. That she could have a mission, a direction of her own – or that others like herself to whom she was in some way bound could – was an absurdity. A man's usage conferred existence.

But this man didn't know his part. He should have ignored her or briskly ordered her to change the bedding, signifying that the incident had no importance for him. Instead, he surged back onto his knees, though the pain drove the blood from his face, and he took the front of her smock in his hands and shook her so that her teeth snapped together.

'You haven't made a cub off me, have you?'

The question was unheard of. If a man intended to breed, it was assumed that he did so unless interfered with by femmish magic. Breeding was a matter entirely out of the control of fems, who came into estrus as time demanded.

Panicked by his agitation, she stammered automatically, 'Not if the master wills not.'

'Nor stolen my soul,' he said, giving her a shake. 'Is that all there is to it, then?'

He had gone rogue; he was going to kill her. Her head was full of flarings of blackness from the violence of his handling. She couldn't speak.

'Then it's nothing!' he cried, and flung her backward against the end-wall of the camper. One of the carriers outside staggered at the sudden shift in weight.

Alldera lay where she had fallen. She'd bitten her tongue and tasted blood.

Very low, the Endtendant said to her, 'Listen, fem. I couldn't stay in the camper last night, so I slept outside. I heard your songs. I heard how you sang them. I came closer to listen. In the Boyhouse, they taught me that fems' songs are nonsense. They also taught that coupling with a fem outside of the breeding-rooms is a dreadful peril, and here I am, no different than before; so maybe the songs are not nonsense.

'Now you talk straight to me, bitch, or I'll break your neck, for I'm fed to the teeth with tricks and lies!'

19

Exhilarated, she almost laughed. She dreaded a crippling injury too much to oppose him physically, yet here the man bade her take up words, her only weapon.

'The master has heard all the songs I know,' she said, and stopped, struck by her own daring, saying silently to herself, 'I. I.' She could hardly believe she had spoken the magical pronoun aloud to him, the equalizing name for the self.

He didn't even notice. 'No more songs,' he said. 'One version of the past seems as likely as another. Tell me about now. Tell me about your own experience.'

That meant, tell about your life. Alldera's life was the only thing she owned, not to be had for the asking. But she saw that she could use parts of it, and parts of other femmish lives (he wouldn't know the difference), to beat him down. He was not armored against her in the callousness that most men acquired by customary contact with her kind.

Was he disturbed by the suspicion that he had been taught lies in the Boyhouse? Excellent. She decided to begin with what young fems were taught in the kit-pits and training-pens of Bayo and let him draw his own conclusions. She began to speak evenly and matter-of-factly, as if she were delivering a long message.

She told about life in the pits, where young fems lived till the breaking age of nine. They scrabbled naked in filthy straw for food that the trainers threw down, and only strong and cunning fems survived. She made for him the sounds of the pits: the grunting signals that the young kits learned from those a little older, for no one spoke human language around the pits. The theory was that fems' capacity for language was generally so limited that they must not be confused by exposure to any more words than the basic command and response phrases.

Learning to speak more than the minimum was a risky maneuver. Alldera described the care she had taken to disguise her natural aptitude, so that it would seem to the men of Bayo that her verbal achievements were entirely to the credit of her trainer. Otherwise they might suspect witchery, by means of which she would be supposed to have raised herself so far and so fast above the norm for her kind. She had made her trainer work to discover her mimetic abilities and her grasp of the structure of complex speech.

A pity, they had said, that she wasn't pretty enough to be trained as a pet, some of whom were taught to tell stories and jokes in an entertaining manner. The Bayo men had altered her diet to improve the quality of her hair and skin, and they had succeeded to some extent; but she would never be pretty, only presentable.

So they had taught her how to memorize messages, how to find her way from place to place, how to identify other men than her master by clothing, mien and surroundings, and how to present a message properly. Then came the wonder of her first trip from Bayo to the City on a barge with a dozen others ripe for the bidding of the companies; the glory of the highstanding City, paved streets after mud-walled Bayo, and the majestic and terrifying peal of the company bells, which she had taken at first for the voices of monsters clanging out over the City.

She spoke of her pride in being selected to serve an important Senior (to a fem fresh from Bayo, all Seniors were important to an equal, exalted degree): Senior Robrez of the well respected Squire Company.

How impressed she had been with the size of his femhold: a private squad of seven fems under the domination of Fossa, who at that time had been only a year away from discard. At first, Alldera had not perceived the sly politicking among the other fems of the hold, the jockeying for favorable positions from which a lower fem could hope to vault into Fossa's place once it was vacated. Gradually, young Alldera had recognized the aping of men's hierarchical concerns among the fems, even though rank for them could only be a pretense; no real power – beyond the reach of a master's whim – accrued to any femmish position.

Then there was Senior Robrez himself. With time, his pomposity, his pettiness and his spite had all revealed themselves, and the godlike virtue of masters (real masters, not trainers brutalized by life in Bayo) had been toppled forever in her mind.

She told how Senior Robrez had had her painted up one night as a pet, so that he could humiliate an unfavored guest by assigning a hideous fem to attend him. Delightedly, the other fems had decorated Alldera for the occasion, not permitting her to see herself or to guess the true purpose of her assignment to personal service that night. Only later, in the privacy of the guest-alcove, she had glimpsed her own face in the surface of the water she brought the man for washing.

They had lacquered her hair into a spiky crown; her skin had been covered in blue and green spirals; and her lips had been made up into a great bruise-colored weal. No wonder the guest had regarded her with such disgust, once they were both hidden from the amused eyes of others.

After that, Alldera had redoubled her efforts to acquire the speed skills that Senior Robrez had hired a man to teach her. Her trainer had been a Skidro derelict who had once trained young men of the Squires Company to race in intercompany games. She remembered the good pain of pushing herself to the limit, the wind of her own speed (though her steps only brought her around again to her trainer in the end).

She stopped speaking. She hadn't meant to tell about that last part; it was a private thing, and therefore treasured. She remembered the glory of racing through the streets of the City early in the morning or late at night alone. That the messages she carried were most often trivial (plaints of love and jealousy, protests at infringements of standing, claims on others' time or property or loyalty, simple gossip) didn't seem to matter then. Neither did she care that the chief use of her hard-won speed skill was to race after some departing guest, arrive at his door before him, and greet him there with messages from Senior Robrez, whom he had just left.

When she had realized that messages of any urgency could be sent more quickly from rooftop to rooftop by means of coded flags, she had fallen into her first despair. The skills of which she was so proud had no real purpose. Rather than live as a luxurious symbol of her master's wealth and status, she had decided to run herself to death. Her chosen method of suicide had proven a poor one; she had only exhausted herself and come down with a cold.. . .

None of this was for this man to hear. Her purpose was to disturb him, not to cause herself pain. She had an uneasy feeling that his stillness and concentration, while permitting her to omit the phrases of submission, were drawing more from her than she had intended to give.

'And?' he prompted. 'How was it that you were returned to Bayo?'

'To Oldtown first,' she said, 'for work-discipline.'

He frowned. 'What is there for a fem with your talents to do in Oldtown?'

'Nothing. That's why it's discipline.'

Oldtown was the processing center for the hemp harvested from the plains. The hemp yielded not only all fibers from fine thread to cable-rope, but a variety of foods made from the seeds, roots and leaves. Manna for dreaming was a product of the taller, more widely scattered highland hemps grown west of Oldtown and handled entirely by male crews. Fems were forbidden to have anything to do with the plants which made the dreaming drug. Nevertheless, the winds blew westerly, and during hemp harvests the plain breathed a sweet redolence that could give even Oldtown fems strange visions.

Alldera's job had been at the take-in sheds where the leaves were pulled from the stalks and fed to the curding-mills, and the hemp-seeds were beaten out, pressed, and ground into flour. The sheds, having no walls, let in the stench of the retting ponds, where she stripped stalks decayed under water until the fibers came loose.

She hadn't minded. She found herself describing her time there with nostalgia.

Of her fantasies – and she had had her share – she said nothing. To recall the dream in which no one – man or fem – could understand a word of her speech was still terrible, a rending betrayal of that first great astonishment at discovering that communication need not be confined to the grunts and snarlings of the kit-pits. She had wakened sweating and gasping from that nightmare. The longing to run until her heart burst had recurred, no less impracticably than the first time.

Finally the Matris had sent a message to her in Oldtown, saying by way of the news-songs that they had a job for her to do. She had feigned loss of her speech skills (due to lack of practice in the take-in sheds), so that when her work-discipline at Oldtown had been completed, she had been sent back to Bayo for retraining.

There she had discovered the existence of the Pledged rebels, and she had grown restless. All winter arguments had raged among the Matris about her suitability for the mission of going inland and all the risks of sending such a messenger at all. If she had been steadier they would not have taken the time to maneuver her into the Rendery as a chastisement and a testing. They would have sent her west sooner, with a shipment of newly trained fems to the City. She might not have been caught like this, her job half-done and the murder of fems already begun, if she had been more dutiful toward the Matris and less proud. Knowing that she was the only speed-trained messenger they could get hold of just then, she had hesitated and argued, instead of bowing at once to the Matris' plan and getting on with it . . .

She had fallen silent, thinking of these things. The Endtendant was watching her.

'Did you think of running away?' he prodded.

'From Oldtown? To where? What should a fem eat in the Wild, stones? As for bolting to hide inside the Holdfast, that just gives men a fem to hunt for sport. I have never actually seen a formal fem-hunt; the last time they caught a runaway and set her loose in the City for the Rovers to catch I was in Oldtown, so I missed it. There are plenty of stories of such hunts and songs about them – locked doors and crowds of men on the rooftops to cheer the Rovers on and to see to it that their own fems watch the futile flight of the quarry.

'But I saw a fem bolt in Oldtown. It was early in the morning. She just put down her beating-stick, took off her apron, and ran. The men sent Rovers to pull her down and kill her. Work was held up for a while so the men could watch and gamble on the result. The rest of us paid for her moon-madness – the moon was up that morning – by having to work double time until her replacement arrived.'

'Why did she run?'

'Fems are creatures of impulse.'

'Nonsense,' he snapped. 'That's obviously the last thing you can afford to be. Did Rovers guard you there on the Oldtown work floors?'

'No, they patroled the perimeters of Oldtown, more on the watch for Scrappers than for escaped fems. Where we worked, the noise and activity of numbers of us would have put Rovers too much on edge.'

'Yet Captain Kelmz held those two Penneltons in the depths of Bayo without evident strain.'

'He was a first-class officer. We had few of those at Oldtown. The companies like to keep them home in case a skirmish is called.'

'You fems can tell a good officer right away, can't you.'

'It's important to us. At Oldtown, we could even spot Rovers trained by Kelmz. He turned out clean killers, quick, accurate, no hesitation or flailing about. It's worth the effort for fems to know roughly what kind of behavior to expect from a given brace of Rovers.'

'Like the Juniors,' he remarked, sardonically, 'though most young men would not be pleased to see the similarity. You can't have enjoyed traveling with Captain Kelmz.'

'No.'

'Yet you came with us, in spite of his being one of our group.'

'Old Fossa told you; I had to get out of Bayo.'

He looked at her, and said nothing.

The camper was being carried up the steep portage road which ran from the plain to the upper plateau through the defile cut by the descending river. The slow, lurching progress, already more than an hour old, was bothering the Entendant's wound. Dark patches of sweat stained and spread from the armpits of his shirt. He kept shifting his bandaged leg from one position to another.

He had not asked her again to repeat what he himself had said to Kelmz at the Scrappers' that night; he did not ask now. Instead, as if he were still pondering his connection with the dead man, he asked about love and friendship among fems.

In carefully chosen generalities she sketched the explosive style of relations among people whose lack of security intensified their loves and hates to extraordinary levels. There was no time among fems for the ripening of delicate affinities. Fems went where their masters went, often without warning or time to send messages of farewell to lovers in other femholds. Did this man feel sorry for himself because his friend d Layo was inconstant in adversity? Alldera told of betrayals, disfigurements, even murders among femmish lovers.

'And fems who love – masters?' he probed.

'Fems who bewitch their masters? They are burned for it.'

'Do fems ever love masters as some men fall into loving fems? Tell me what your songs say.'

'They make fun of such perversions.'

'Ah,' he said, with a sour twitch of his mouth. 'Books of the Ancients on the subject say much the same. But sometimes they suggest that such perversion could be a great glory.'

'How could it be?' she said, thinking of d Layo in the hemp-field.

He moved his shoulders in a shrug or a shiver, she couldn't tell which. 'Love between fems or between men certainly seems less grotesque; the relation of like to like.' Again the crooked smile: 'Or so we are taught.'

'Your teachings are not things for a fem to know.'

'Nevertheless,' he said, 'it must amuse you, all this carrying on among us – Kelmz, Servan, myself, and now this filthy brute Bajerman.'

'That's men's affairs,' she said, stubbornly.

'Oh? I'd have said it was just the sort of thing you've been describing as typical of fems, but less intense; the loves and hates of dilettantes, as opposed to those of devotees. You have no need to look so sullen; I like the comparison less than you do.'

Exchanges like these provided them both with distraction. Alldera saw the danger in it and would have stopped, but she couldn't. Even among her own lovers and friends she had never had any one to talk to like this. There had never been any security, any time, even when she found another fem with true verbal facility. This was her first experience of speech as self-expression with any degree of complexity, eliciting responses of similar quality. It gave her an extraordinary feeling of power, of reality.

That was the danger.

20

They camped on the upper plateau for the night. D Layo brought over his fellow-prisoner's ration of food and stayed while Bek ate. Then he announced Senior Bajerman's invitation: that the Endtendant come and sleep in the camper tonight.

Bek, sitting wrapped in his blanket against the highland chill, shook his head. 'The entertainment isn't to my taste.'

D Layo sighed. 'I'm not exactly enchanted with it myself, but it's better than having my throat cut. So my little fem, here, is proving more fascinating to you than our esteemed Senior? A function of familiarity, I suppose. He won't be delighted to hear it, though.'

'Did he do this?' The Endtendant touched very lightly a line of raw sores on d Layo's shoulder.

'No. That's from lugging you half the length of the Holdfast. I can't get the trick of padding the yoke exactly. Bajerman does like to beat on me a bit, but I don't mind that as much as I mind not being able to wash up at all. He seems to get a thrill from dust and sweat; I don't remember him having been like that back in the Boyhouse, do you? And then that reeky stuff he wears gets all mixed in, I can hardly stand the smell of myself any more. You should be grateful that I haven't made a run for it, Eykar.'

'Why haven't you?'

'What, and leave you to Bajerman? He'd be on you in a flash.'

'I have also noticed,' the Endtendant said drily, 'that there's no place to hide out here, when the hemps have been cut.'

The DarkDreamer gazed off at the darkening horizon, hugging himself for warmth, and sighed. 'I worry about you, Eykar. You're turning into some kind of wretched realist. It's distressing.' He looked toward the camper. 'I'd better go back; he'd love an excuse to come out after me and give me a whipping in front of you. It's cold up here! The old cur won't let me wear a shirt, either. Someday I'll wear his famishing skin.'

Alldera slept among the carry-fems, as usual. When she served the Endtendant in the morning, she found him so stiff-limbed from lying curled up in his blanket that he could hardly straighten up. Irritably he accepted the Hemaways' rough help in getting into the camper for the day's ride, and he sat slumped in a corner and brooded on the squares of sunlight falling on the blanket through the roof grill. When the camper was lifted and moved on, he looked up at Alldera. His eyes were red-rimmed and gritty-lashed, as if he hadn't slept.

'Where do they go, these talks between us?' he said.

She was silent. Deliberately she waited until he invited her to speak, giving a sort of sanction in advance to what she had to say. That might even be truly effective in the case of a man as scrupulous as this one tried to be, if she did eventually go too far even for him. Besides, his bending to her unspoken rule filled her with a feeling of righteous power.

He looked exhausted and downcast this morning, and that was her doing; hers and d Layo's. Bek would no more tell her to shut up and leave him his peace than he would avert his eyes from the flirting between d Layo and Bajerman. He just took it and took it, like a fem taking her punishment. She despised him for it.

'Ah, that look again,' he said. 'If I beat you for looking at me like that, you'd show some respect, wouldn't you? Servan, in my place, would whip you till you bled. Would that impress you? You don't accept us at our own evaluation, do you? No, surely you're too clever, entirely too clever not to see through us.'

She made no answer. He prodded the thickness of cloth wrapped around his upper leg. 'Change this; it's wet again.'

The wound, though less swollen, was still draining, and the bandage was stuck at the center and had to be worked off carefully. She looked up once and saw him watching her hands with the same steady, straight gaze she had seen him turn on Kelmz, Bajerman, even on d Layo. He just looked: not for what was gratifying, not for what was useful, not merely to fill time or distract himself from less pleasant matters, but to see what was there.

For a moment, she let her imagination fly, thinking, what could seeing eyes see in her? Anger. Beyond that – anger, grief for her helpless dead – she couldn't see herself. It was no wonder. She, after all, had no experience with that sort of looking. She could not afford to attend to anything other than what was helpful to her own survival.

Her hands drew away the pad of cloth, revealing the glistening wound.

'Isn't this ever going to heal?' he said.

'It is healing,' she said.

'But the process could be slowed down – or speeded up – by a spell, couldn't it.'

'I'm no witch,' she protested, alarmed by the direction his remarks had taken.

'Tell me,' he said, leaning back and resting the back of his hand across his eyes, 'how you're not a witch.'

Briefly, while she tended his wound, she told him.

The Seekers had been a club of young fems in Senior Robrez' femhold. She had joined them, drawn by their intense conviction that the fems of Ancient times had indeed caused the Wasting by witchery, just as the men said. If the powers of the martyred Ancestresses could be rediscovered, men would have good reason to fear witchery again – from the Seekers. These youngsters had met at great risk to exchange rumors and recite spells that came to them in dreams. During hours stolen from rest periods, and often in the company of fems who had slipped away from other houses to join them, they would huddle passionately together over pathetic scraps of 'news': that a fem in Lammintown had brought up a man-drowning storm at sea with a song; that another had breathed life into a lump of Bayo mud.

Soon Alldera had reluctantly seen that the powers the Seekers longed for surely would have won the Wasting for any who had possessed them. Her friends were not searching out true weapons, but spending their courage and energy in the pursuit of nonsense concocted by fearful men. That did not mean that masters only pretended to believe fems might (or at one time had been able to) change shapes, steal souls, control weather, move objects and thoughts through the air, send sickness and death from a distance, speak to past and future generations, and so on; it meant only that men were dupes of their own ideology.

She had tried to dissuade the Seekers from their path. They had not wished to be influenced, least of all by logical argument. They had labeled her a traitor and banned her from their meetings.

Of the rest, she said nothing. One of the younger members of the group, whom Alldera had loved, shortly afterward had leaped to her death from a rooftop, attempting to fly down a shaft of moon-light. Alldera's reaction – withdrawal into lethargic sullenness – had gotten her packed off to Oldtown for discipline. Senior Robrez, an experienced femholder, had been lenient with her, not least because of the size of his investment in her training. To turn her over to the hunt would be to lose it all. The other fems had been glad to see her go; her reckless mood had endangered them all.

Bek said, 'But if I accused you –'

She shrugged. 'I would burn.'

'With no evidence, just because I said I suspected you?'

'It doesn't have to be you who makes the complaint. The fem who bore you was burned for witching your father into breaking the Law of Generations, but it wasn't your father who made the charge. The Boardmen accused her themselves.'

Once his interest was engaged he couldn't be stopped; show him horrors, and he asked to see more. 'Have you had cubs?'

'Twice lucky,' she said, briskly. 'That both were little kit-cubs and didn't have to be chopped out of my belly by your Hospital men; and that I had little milk and didn't have to languish forever in that boring hole, the milkery. That's all the luck, and all the cubs, I want.'

'Do you know which ones they are in the kit-pits?'

She sat back on her heels and looked at him. 'Why should a fem want to know that it's her grown kit-cub crackling in the witch fires? Or, for that matter, her boy-cub matured to manhood and fucking her in the breeding-rooms?'

'Then how could anyone know which was my dam?' he said sharply. 'The mark on her neck must have been gone long before the rumors of the broken law began, and she wouldn't have known herself.'

'One of the Hospital-men noticed a dye-mark on her neck when she came in and dropped her cub, and he spoke to her master about it. Her master questioned her, couldn't get a sensible answer, had her beaten and forgot about it. She was valuable property, a speaker and fine looking. Later, when the Boardmen started asking questions about this story of Raff Maggomas and his claimed son, her master remembered that identifying mark. She was older by then. He turned her over to the Board, and they burned her.'

'What else to do you know about her?'

'What I've heard in a few songs.'

'What was she like?'

'She wasn't like anything; she was what she was trained to be – as all fems are.'

'As you were trained to be insolent and bitter?' he rapped out.

'I'm nothing that I haven't learned from my trainers and masters,' she muttered. Let him hit her, at least she knew where she was with a blow.

'The same could be said of others,' he said. 'Men.'

'Men have some choice when they are old enough to see what's happening,' she said. She turned to put the used bandage into a bowl of water for washing.

He rolled onto one elbow and reached to secure a buckle on the camper-flap. In mid-action he seemed to freeze, his hand still extended. Without looking at her, he said, 'Suppose I told you to take off your clothes?'

She'd been expecting this. Often when she tended to his bad leg he became aroused. Both of them had ignored this till now.

She began to pull off her smock.

He caught her wrist: 'Don't!' Thrusting her arm back down, he held her beside the bed, kneeling, with the bowl of water next to her and the bandage trailing out of it.

'When Bajerman put his hand on Servan,' he whispered, 'that first night in this same camper, for the instant before he began being flippant about it Servan looked the way you do now. I think I know that expression from wearing it on my own face in the aisles of the Boyhouse Library, when Bajerman or some other like him said, "Kneel down, boy," or "Come and kiss me, boy –" ' He stammered with rage and disgust. 'Or, "turn, turn around, boy, and stand right there."

'Now you look the same, and you have every right – I was going to turn and pass it on to you – Bajerman's style of routine, callous rape!'

'Men do not "rape" fems,' she said. 'They use them. The act then has a certain cleanness, reminding a fem that her duty is to receive whatever a master chooses to bestow on her.'

'Don't you speak that way to me, not about him! To use another person as a convenience is nothing but filth.'

'You're not speaking to a person,' she spat, 'only to a fem – whom you have already used in just that way, surely without staining your fine, manly honor!'

'That was before!' he cried. 'Look around: where do you see "men", where do you see "fems" in here? There's nobody but us, you and me. I know you now from everything you've shown me and a little that you've tried not to show; I know you almost as well as you know me. But it's worth nothing while I have the power of death over you.' He unwrapped his fingers from her wrist, leaving white pressure-marks on her reddened skin.

Bitterly, to himself, he added, 'Nothing that passes between us can be anything but rape.'

'I'm not Bajerman!' he burst out, 'I won't be like Bajerman! There has to be something clean left in me when I come to face my father!' He lay back amid the pillows, staring up at the roof grill, and muttered, 'Everything must be jettisoned, then, even valuables I didn't know I had.' He turned toward her again, and said in a tired, reasonable tone, 'Only in dreams can a man be an all-purpose hero. I don't have an extra lifetime to spend helping to heal up the horror between men and fems – or even just between us two. I'm on my way to meet Raff Maggomas. Everything must go toward that meeting.'

He closed his eyes and hissed his breath in. Then he said, in his old, harsh voice, 'There must be no horror, no rape, nothing outside of the ordinary, superficial relations between men and fems. Therefore I can't permit you to be a person. What you haven't told me, keep. The rest I'll do my best to forget – unsuccessfully, if it's any comfort to you. Do you understand me?'

She understood him perfectly. She had beaten him into a retreat. She bent her head: 'As the master says.'

DESTINATION

21

It was said that two suns lit the high country skies: one that rose in the east, another flaming low against the dark western hills and shining through the nights. The second sun was 'Troi itself, whose concrete buildings were sheathed in the flattened, polished bodies of Ancient machines extracted whole from the mines – the single boast of wealth that the 'Troimen allowed themselves. After dark 'Troi shone with its own lights; the skills of 'Troi took light from the river, men said. Looking at the brilliance of the lamps burning all along the roads that ran north to the coal pits and south to the mines, Servan believed it. Those were no coal-fueled flames. One could say it was witchery, except that it was the work of men.

The supply roads were empty now, though the purpose of the lights was reputed to be to enable a constant flow of fems to bring coal and metal to the furnaces of 'Troi, night as well as day. A dull, heavy pulse beat out from the glittering town: the mutter of machines, 'Troi's music against the silence at the edge of the Holdfast.

High above the steep westward summit of 'Troi hills the sun rode low and dusky in the sky. Smoke obscured the mountains, which were only discernible as long, looming shapes. The late light struck points of brilliance from their tops, as if the 'Troimen had sheathed those heights with metal too. The town itself was built with its back to the Wild, as if in disdain of a conquered enemy.

The river, which fell steeply from the hills behind the town, ran through the center of it and on away east to Oldtown and the City.

The lower slopes on either side of 'Troi valley were terraced with stone walls and footed with heaps of black slag from 'Troi furnaces. Across the lower valley, a palisade of metal plates had been newly erected, shielding the town from the rest of the Holdfast. Heavy metal grills set into this barrier blocked the river to traffic. The north and south river-roads were shut by similar gates set into the palisade just outside the eastern margin of the town.

The carry-fems set the camper down in a riverside loading-yard in front of one of these steel grills. A concrete tower had been reared behind the palisade. From the upper tier of the tower men could be seen looking down.

Standing well back from the palisade, the Hemaways offhandedly pointed out this and that about the new fortification to each other, as if they were all Rover officers and veterans of every skirmish ever fought. Senior Bajerman held himself aloof from the discussion. He regarded the sunset rather than the town, while Servan helped him adjust his wilted and travel-worn mantle to maximum effect. Even without starch, the folds could be arranged to frame the Senior's face and head, giving an impression of extra height and bulk.

The taller you stand, Servan thought, the more pleasure to bring you down. He hummed to himself.

Eykar got out of the camper (he wouldn't be caught like that again, all tangled up with the fem) and braced himself firmly upright, one hand on the roof-frame and the other on Alldera's shoulder. And how he stared when a gray-haired 'Troiman let himself out through a narrow doorway in the tower's base and strode to meet them: unmantled, tough-looking, the man wore the wheel insignia of the 'Troi Trukkers.

Not Maggomas, Servan decided; there was no resemblance, no spark of recognition. Eykar relaxed visibly almost at once. What interested Servan was something the Trukker carried in one hand: a dull metal tool, pointed like a finger toward the ground. A weapon, Servan thought, if he had ever seen one.

A dozen paces from the camper the 'Troiman stopped and looked them over. 'Which of you —' he began; but Senior Bajerman stepped forward and effortlessly overrode his question with a sonorous announcement:

'Tell Raff Maggomas that his son has been brought to him by Gor Bajerman and certain other, lesser, Senior Hemaways. We offer him

Eykar Bek in exchange for power and privilege here in 'Troi.'

Haughtily high-mantled, Bajerman stood with one hand spread on his chest, the picture of a man awaiting a salute from another of inferior standing. A breeze stirred his wispy white hair.

The Trukker did not salute. He shook his head. 'My orders are to let in Eykar Bek, his friend d Layo and any fems they have with them. That's all. We don't need any Citymen here. Plenty of them will be knocking at our gates soon enough.'

He raised the metal thing he carried and pointed it at the Hemaway nearest to him. There came a crash, stunningly loud and close; and there lay the Hemaway on his broad back, arms and legs outflung, blood running from under him.

Two other Hemaways bolted for the palisade. The watchtower issued thunder, and they fell. It was too much for the carry-fems; they raced for the high grass growing at the edge of the loading yard. The rest of the Hemaways scattered. The air was full of boomings, crackings and strange wild whinings. Other 'Troimen along the palisade whooped and pounded one another's backs in their excitement as the darting figures were felled by invisible thunders.

The noise stopped; the voice of the Trukker could suddenly be heard, roaring abuse at the men in the tower. Ribbons of smoke dissolved in the air overhead. None of the Hemaways had even reached the palisade. One carry-fem still tried to drag herself into the sheltering grass, leaving a smear of blood on the flagstones behind her.

Bajerman stood stupefied; beyond him Servan could see Alldera crouching under Eykar's white-knuckled hand.

'. . . have your asses for this!' the Trukker was bawling at the men in the tower. Red-faced, he turned back to the newcomers who were still standing: 'Stupid sonsofbitches, they think a weapon is a toy! Give them a moving target and they can't resist. Even then they don't finish the job!'

He jerked up his own thunderer and clicked it at Senior Bajerman. Swearing, the Trukker peered down the tube of the weapon.

Servan thought, am I a fem or a cub to stand shaking in front of this old-wolf because he wields powers he can't even control? He said, 'Not that I mean to be critical; but since when do 'Troi Seniors kill their own peers for being from out of town?'

'It's necessary,' the 'Troiman said, truculently. 'We've abolished those divisions anyhow. This matter has nothing to do with age. We'll be under siege by the Citymen sometime tomorrow. We're pared down to the bone now, so nobody comes in that we can't use; and we can't use him.'

'Then,' Servan said, with a joyful laugh. 'I'll attend to the Senior for you. Have you got a knife?'

The Trukker handed him a blade from his belt, muttering, 'Sometimes I think we would be better off with knives than with these fancy distance weapons.' And he shook the recalcitrant pointing-killer in his hand.

'We're of an age, you and I!' Bajerman cried.

The Trukker considered him again. 'Do you know any technics?'

Senior Bajerman composed himself and said, 'I am an expert in Deportment, a Master of the field of Hierarchies —'

'That's no good to us,' the Trukker said.

Servan stepped between them, turned on Bajerman and did swiftly with the knife things he had been dreaming of doing. The Senior shrieked and staggered backward. Belly slit, red hands knotted into his groin, he fell twitching on the flagstones. Servan knelt to wipe the thin film of pinkish blood from the Trukker's blade, using Bajerman's mantle. The knife was a good one, with a full new blade and a handle of some hard substance ribbed to give a grip. He pivoted, still crouching, and offered it back with some reluctance to the Trukker.

'Aren't you going to finish him off?' the Trukker said.

'He is finished.'

Eykar held out his hand. 'Give me the knife.'

'Oh, no, Eykar,' Servan flipped the knife for the 'Troiman to catch. 'You're forgetting which of us has had to put up with Bajerman all this time.'

Seizing hold of the Senior's mantle, Servan heaved him to where the edge of the paving sloped down to the river. Bajerman twisted to blink up at him. Servan shoved him down the incline. Sloshing noisily up onto the flagging, the water took the Senior and tugged him away. The weight of his stained, soaked mantle dragged him down. Servan dipped his bloody hands into the water.

Two 'Troimen from the tower were searching the dead Hema-ways for weapons and private caches of food. Servan considered demanding that his own knife – or some other, in its place – be returned to him. It would look better, though, to enter Maggomas' stronghold empty-handed. Besides, maybe he could get one of those crashing killers instead. Anything was possible now.

In the broad streets of 'Troi not many people were about at twilight, and none of them were either very young men or mantled Seniors. There were no Rovers and no fems, only men of middle years clad in sober clothing. Some wore wide belts from which hung metal tools, and one man passed by with something resembling a polished skull in the crook of his arm – a helmet of some kind.

The streets were surfaced from wall to wall with a smooth, dark substance; down the centers ran parallel flanges of metal, shiny as ice. No refuse littered any of the alleys or doorways, but a layer of grime outlined the mosaics of metal that covered the facades of the buildings. Overhead, thin black cables of some kind loosely laced the sky between rooftops and upper-story ledges. The central buildings towered all along the river's course, straddling the water. Lamps projected on metal arms from the walls, blindingly bright now that darkness was descending. Everywhere, streets and structures seemed to vibrate with the ceaseless growling of the engines of 'Troi.

No wonder men used the streets briefly and with purpose. It would be difficult to loiter and chat in these stark passages, that were plainly for the transport of materials first and only secondarily for the movement of men.

Servan was impressed. He took in everything – the massive architecture, the combination of efficiency and grime. An ugly place, he thought, but effective; pity it was wasted on Eykar, who looked for only one thing here. Watching him limping ahead, leaning on the fem, Servan felt a wave of warmth for his friend.

At a massive complex of buildings, the Trukker turned aside. 'Troimen standing sentry in a broad doorway slid back the metal leaves of the door into the walls. Two of the sentries fell in behind the strangers. The silver bars on the collars of this escort marked them as men of the Armicor Company, ruthless by reputation. Each of them carried one of the thunder weapons in a special pocket slung from his belt.

Glass globes set into the ceiling shed a harsh, cold light. The Armicors' metal-tipped boot heels snapped against the floor.

Stairs led up onto a railed gallery that ran high along the wall of a huge, roaring room. The room was lit by the familiar warmth of firelight – but what fires! The entire wall opposite the walkway was a tangle of metal tubing, struts and plates in which a row of revolving kettles was mounted. The giant kettles glowed red with heat and thundered as they turned. Men in helmets and heavy clothing moved around the machines, carrying long, fire-blackened rods with hooked ends. Others bent or climbed to examine glass-faced dials, making notations on tablets fixed to their sleeves. They spoke with their heads close together amid the tremendous noise.

In front of a lighted doorway at the far end of the gallery, a man leaned out over the railing, pointing and shouting at someone down on the work-floor. There was imperious vitality in his stabbing gestures, though he was the first really old man they had seen in 'Troi. His close, curling hair was like a design tightly engraved on silver. From beneath his long apron of shiny material there emerged limbs as lean as ropes. His voice, keen and reedy, was audible even over the rumbling of the machines.

A whistle shrilled. On the work-floor men tipped one of the kettles with the bent ends of the long poles they carried. Liquid fire spewed out, with darting sparks and a sharp crackling sound. A man poked black scum from where it gathered in the spout and obstructed the outpouring. The hot, glowing stream turned dull red as it congealed in channels in the floor beneath. In the air a fresh pungency tingled.

The Trukker strode out ahead and spoke to the old man, who turned, glancing first at Servan. With an abrupt gesture, the old man waved them forward.

For a moment, Eykar hesitated, his expression a study. Whatever he had been expecting, Servan thought, it had not been this skinny, axe-faced old fellow! And he would not have missed the sobering of the old man's eager look when the Trukker pointed out that it was Eykar, not Servan, who was the Endtendant. Father and son would have to revise some preconceptions.

'I see,' shouted the old man over the noise of the turning kettles, 'you're injured – not too badly to keep you off your feet, at least.'

'It's healing,' Eykar shouted back.

Maggomas rounded on the Trukker, barking, 'Go turn over your gun and your squad to Anjon, and let's hope he shows better control over the tower post than you have.' The Trukker flushed red and stalked away.

Turning as if he'd forgotten the man already, Maggomas led the others through the door behind him into another corridor. The Armicors, when he waved them irritably back, fell in at a discreet distance, still an escort.

Eykar said, 'You knew I was coming.'

'I sent men to find you as soon as I heard you'd left Endpath. I see you didn't need my help. That's good. Self-reliance and capability are respected here in 'Troi.'

'What do you expect from me?'

'Ah,' the old man said, approvingly, 'but it's not such a simple matter. These are complex times. What did Bajerman tell you, that we're in a generation war? He would; he was always a cheesebrain.

'It's not a political squabble between old men and young that we're faced with this time. This is going to be a great famine, a literal famine. Tell me, how do you think the seaweeds we live on survived the Wasting? I know that's not the kind of question you're encouraged to think about in the Boyhouse; don't be embarrassed by your ignorance. The answer is, the seaweeds were tough, fairly simple organisms that already were living on the rubbish of the Ancients' civilization to some degree. They were able to adapt to using the large quantities of poisons released during the Wasting as a side-effect of the men's efforts to defend their civilization.

'Our problem is, the lammins and lavers have now metabolized and dissipated most of the contaminants left over from the Wasting, and these seaweeds are finding much less of the kind of nourishment they've come to depend on. So each succeeding crop is scantier, and the situation is going to get worse, not better. Oh, some seaweeds will survive on the sewage from the City, and others may adapt again to clean conditions; but not in the profusion we're used to for a very long time, if ever. And we don't know which of the other plants moving into their place we can use. That change will also take a long time. Meanwhile, as men have become so heavily dependant in turn on lammins and lavers, they must also starve.'

'Unless,' Servan observed, 'they've prepared. Bajerman said you have all kinds of food stockpiled here in 'Troi.'

'That's one way to prepare,' Maggomas said. 'There is another – as I tried to tell the Board, but they wouldn't so much as give me a decent hearing – and that's to diversify the food supply so that we don't need the lammins and laver so much. That's what we've done here; we've stripped down, lived lean and stored up food to carry us over the transition period until new staples we've been developing are available in quantity.

'Mind you, we have no margin; we can't take in any more mouths to feed. I haven't had a lot of time to get things ready. We have had setbacks; some of the information I needed was locked up in the Boyhouse where I couldn't get to it. Still, we're set to go just as we are, which is more than can be said for the rest of the Holdfast. We mean to ride out the crisis.

'Then, when the time is right, 'Troi will take over what's left and will start building a new, better and truly rational society. All of which will require leadership from dedicated, intelligent men: heroes.'

He opened a door on the outside, where a bridge of metal linked the furnace-building with another, taller structure a street away. A sooty wind plucked at their clothing and stung their eyes. Down below illuminated glass globes stippled the empty street.

'Heroes,' Eykar echoed, limping out onto the thrumming metal walkway. He raised his voice against the wind. 'And what am I to be, then?'

'Look down there,' Maggomas said. 'Look over my town. It will still be here, strong and vital, when the rest of the Holdfast is rags and bones. That's my doing.

'Why do you think I've bothered? So that I can stand here for a while, until you come to kill me – unless I kill you first – because that's what you've been taught you must do? You're too valuable to use yourself up in dramatics. If I didn't know it for a fact, I could read it in you now. Your injury pains you, your surroundings are strange and threatening, you have only your wits for weapons; but you haven't asked for rest, or for time, or for help. Inner discipline is the beginning of a man's power.'

'You haven't answered my question,' Eykar said.

Servan swore silently. What was the matter with Eykar? Couldn't he see that they were home-free? Nothing could stop them. It was all going to be worth every famishing step of the journey and more. Legends? They would be gods. Even Eykar's beautiful, absurd pride would have to bend before the superb artistry of events.

Maggomas thrust open the door on the far side of the bridge and led them into a suite of littered rooms. There were papers and books everywhere. Lop-eared drawings and charts hung from the walls. There were stilt-necked lamps clamped to the desks and tables, one even to the back of a chair, so that beams of light crossed each other at every angle through the dimness of the rooms.

'Consider, my son,' the old man said, 'what rational motive do you have for opposing me? You can't be any more ambitious for yourself than I am for you.' He swept out both arms, indicating the chaos through which they made their way. 'This place of disorder will become the center of the new Refuge and someday of a new Holdfast. From here I control 'Troi now; the entire river and much more besides will fall to me in time. I am the master of this and creator of its future.

'My place here will be yours. You're to be my successor. Did you think you were bred for anything less?'

22

One glance showed Alldera that no fems kept this place in order for its master. Could all of 'Troi's fems have been sent to the mines or locked up somewhere else in preparation for a battle with the City men?

'Not that there won't be problems about the succession,' the old man continued. 'I've already run into resistance trying to persuade the 'Troimen that my son need not be my born enemy. We'll work out some demonstrations of unity. For a start, you'll drop your name and take mine. Your DarkDreamer friend can design a ceremony to mark the new legitimization of lineage.'

Bek said, 'Suppose I am your born enemy?'

Maggomas made an impatient gesture of dismissal. 'If you think of yourself that way, it's not by nature but out of ignorance. What would I do, rationally, if I were your antagonist? I would stand in your way. But I've made your way for you!'

'This is grotesque!' Bek grated.

'Not at all. It's a very sensible custom. In the old days a man used to have a son to take over his property, further his plans and generally see to the honor and the prosperity of his bloodline, after – when the time came.' Maggomas stood glancing restlessly about him, took up a stack of papers from a table and began looking through the pages as he continued.

'Mind you, sons turned against their fathers even before the Wasting. But I'm convinced that that was a result of the warping influence of their dams. Ancient men very carelessly left the education of their young boys primarily to fems.

'Still, the Ancients knew the basic principle: a man smart enough to amass wealth and power has a good chance of passing on his talents to his son. That's important, if a great lifework isn't to fall into the hands of quarreling louts or idiots. And idiots there are in plenty, no matter how carefully you try to weed them out. Take the lads I've been training here; they still turn in trash like these reports.

'You two get cleaned up. You'll find clean clothes in the alcove; something in there should fit you. I have no one to send in with you – we're used to doing for ourselves here in 'Troi – but your fem can attend you. I'll join you shortly.'

In the small bathing-room d Layo scrubbed quickly, miming his delight in scouring off the grime of the journey and bowing in mock-obsequity to his companion the Crown Prince. Bek ignored him. They close not to shout over the rushing of the water for any one in the corridor to hear.

The DarkDreamer had already shaved and dressed in simply cut shirt and pants of a soft gray when Bek and Alldera entered the dressing alcove. D Layo's jaunty, graceful carriage lent a touch of elegance to these severe clothes. He was too eager to wait for Bek, so he went off to find their host.

Bek sat down before the mirror and began to shave with grim-mouthed care. 'Go get yourself washed,' he told Alldera.

The hot water, which sprang from holes in the wall at the touch of a knob, nearly put her to sleep. She hadn't realized how exhausted she was. She went through a series of warm-up exercises, delicate slidings and tightenings of muscle, and the water washed away the sweat of exertion and left her feeling fresh. Decorously wrapped in one of the men's damp, discarded towels, she returned to the alcove.

Bek, looking lean and taut in dark shirt and trousers, stood bleakly studying himself in the long mirror. 'I thought I'd look older,' he said.

There were no femmish smocks in the alcove. Alldera chose a shirt that was long enough to serve, one that had correspondingly enormous sleeves. But Bek was in no mood for the ludicrous. He had her take it off and wear shirt and pants like his. The significance of his own somber clothing and his austere and deliberate preparations was clear: he was armoring himself in his ritual status: it was as Endtendant of Endpath that he meant to face his father.

The sound of voices drew them to the great front room of the suite, which was in darkness. Its furthest wall was a transparent sheet incised with a glowing design which seemed to shine with light from lamps outside in the night.

Alldera's messenger training had included recognition of maps. This one she understood at once: there was Bayo, there Endpath, there the City. Deeper inland gleamed a gridwork representing Oldtown, a larger one for 'Troi – and further up the river, further than shown by any map she had ever seen, stood steeply pitched figures that seemed to be actual descriptions, not mere symbols, of mountains.

D Layo stood tracing the mountain-marks with his fingertips. He said, 'Then the Reconquest has actually begun?'

Maggomas, crouched over a table laden with papers, glanced up and laughed angrily. 'What Reconquest? I've sent out a few exploring parties of my own, that's how I know this much. There is no Reconquest, it's a myth.

'Everything the Board does – or fails to do – is calculated to insure that nothing happens to shake its control. That means no new ideas and no new territories and not too many young men! I'm surprised that neither of you has figured it out. What's hierarchy for, or the endless maze of games and standings, if not to dissipate young men's energy? Which is kept low anyhow with an insufficient diet, since the old men take more than their share of the pittance of food that the Holdfast furnishes. You know, in the Refuge men had to play games to keep from going rogue. Sport is an acquired taste which the Seniors have encouraged in the Holdfast for the same reasons: to use up energy.

'You, my son; what do you think Endpath is for? When the Board decides that there are too many restless youngsters around for the maintenance of stability, it's not difficult for them to manipulate the standings or break up certain love affairs, so that pride and misery send a number of Juniors off to die at Endpath. Dueling in the Streets of Honor takes care of others.

'Then look at our economy: a model of institutionalized inefficiency! The old men pool the surplus of a five-year's production and take off the top themselves for their own comforts. Not that the

Holdfast offers much more than subsistence – rotating the companies from work-turf to work-turf every five-year means a lot of unskilled clods do everything badly in an effort to do each thing better than the last lot of unskilled clods did it.

'The point, young men, is to prevent the Junior population from growing large enough, rich enough or educated enough to burst the boundaries of the Holdfast, begin a real Reconquest – and perhaps turn around afterward and take the Holdfast for themselves, with their newfound strength and confidence. Now, I maintain –'

Interrupted by a string of faint popping sounds from outside, he held up his hand and listened. 'That's got to be first contact with the City men! Come on outside.'

They followed him out onto a paved terrace overlooking the plain. A table had been set up, its surface a mosaic of magnificent green and golden tile glittering in the light of two squat globe lamps that were housed in the parapet. The light of the lamps gleamed steadily on the gear of four Armicors deployed by Maggomas along the length of the terrace. He himself went to confer with a stocky young man of the same company, who reported without lowering the spyglass through which he was studying the plain below.

'No problem,' the old man said, joining the others around the table. 'There's been a little skirmish some distance down the river. We saw the flashes of our people's guns. Our patrols are too small to stop that mob, but the guns will stagger them! You're going to have a fine view of an interesting night.

'How do you like this?' he added, running his palm over the gleaming tiles of the tabletop. ' 'Troimen are realists, but you'd be mistaken to think they have no taste. This is a product of our own kilns.'

'You've built kilns here?' d Layo said, with interest. 'You know, we had just the thing to give you as a guest-gift: some plates and platters from Oldtown ruins, Scrappers' loot. They were stowed in the body of the camper we came in, which was left outside the palisade.'

'Then they will have to stay there a while. The gates of 'Troi won't open again for a long time. Tell me, though: what would you have asked for in exchange for your guest-gift?'

'They were fine pieces,' the DarkDreamer said, considering. 'Very old, I think. A fair exchange would have been one of those weapons.' He pointed to the shiny weapon belted to the hip of the nearest Armicor.

'Well chosen,' Maggomas said, plainly pleased. 'Not that I'm entirely happy with the guns yet; but even imperfect as they are they'll shake up the City mob. Sit down, I've got a meal laid on for us. Have that fem sit, too. I hate having people hang over the table while I eat.' He raised his voice: 'A bowl of wash-water and soemthing to drink while we're waiting!'

No fem appeared at the service-hatch. Instead, one of the sentries descended and returned bearing a tray with glasses, a metal bowl and a large carafe of water. The bowl, poured half-full, was for Maggomas' use. He fumbled for a moment at the ties of his apron, swore and sat down to wash as he was, the apron-bib standing out stiffly under his chin. He dried his hands on a stained rag from his pocket. Several small, colorless objects fell from the rag's folds, clicking and bouncing on the table top.

Maggomas off-handedly explained that they were cubes of something called 'plastic', which the Ancients had made out of coal and other substances. He had recently produced these samples from the leavings of the Oldtown hemp-mills.

He shot a sly look at his son as he spoke of this, but Bek spared the intriguing little objects scarcely a glance. He kept his eyes on his father. D Layo was the one to pick up the cubes and juggle them on his palm. He rubbed the 'plastic' surfaces and remarked wistfully and with awe on the powers of the Ancients – and again his eyes turned toward the guns the Armicors wore.

Maggomas sniffed at the soup that had been set in front of him. 'About time,' he said, and ladled some for the men and a bowlful for himself. Alldera was relieved that none was served to her; the soup had dark, shiny shapes in it and a musty odor. The young men sat and looked uneasily at their portions.

'You just don't know what you're talking about,' Maggomas said, 'when you glibly rattle off a phrase like "the powers of the Ancients." They were men of might, not scrabblers in an ash heap. Listen, just as an example: the Ancients had so many fibers, natural and man-made, that not only could a man change his shirt every day; but they even had to put labels in their garments, to tell the owner which of the many methods of cleaning was appropriate to that particular fabric! Extend that kind of versatility into all fields, and you begin to get some idea of the wealth and power of the Ancients.'

'Yet,' Bek said, harshly, 'they were overthrown.'

'Oh, yes,' jeered the old man, jabbing his spoon in Alldera's direction, 'and next you'll tell me that it was by the magical powers of her kind!'

'Let me tell you something: the Ancients weren't overthrown; they fell down — in their understanding of their own incredible powers. They should have forseen the Wasting soon enough to have prevented it. Ancient science was so far advanced that they had machines to do the work of the Dirties, artificial foods and materials to replace those they had from plants and beasts, even man-made reproductive systems that would eventually have cut out the fems from their one supposedly necessary function. But the men didn't see where it was all leading.'

He drank down the remainder of his soup in one draught, and turned to serve up a stew of mixed lammins and lavers on fresh plates for the men. The stew smelled strong. A bowl was filled for the Armicor officer, who ate standing.

Alldera's mealtime would come when the men were finished, according to the traditions of formal dining. Her mouth welled sweet juices. She had never seen so much food assembled in one meal in her life. The coldness of the night breeze on her damp hair seemed to spread all through her body as a hungry ache. She could barely stand to watch Bek, across the table from her, poking unin-terestedly at his portion with his fork and frowning as if he didn't even see it.

'The science of the Ancients,' Maggomas went on, around a mouthful of food, 'was so highly developed that they were about to cut through the tie of dependence on this mortal bitch of a world altogether and become gods — not your famishing mystery-god who passes understanding and coping-with, but real, rational, deathless gods wielding real, rational power. The Ancients invented artificial body parts and anti-aging drugs that would eventually have made sons themselves obsolete. Who needs posterity when men are immortal? And given eternity, they could have discovered every-thing else that there is to know or do.'

Rapidly, after a swallow of beer, he went on: 'You can see that the fems couldn't have that. They were committed — still are — to an endless, pointless round of birth and death. They knew that once they were no longer needed for reproduction they would be dispensed with altogether. So they attacked first.

'How do you like the stew?' he asked, with sudden solicitude. 'I noticed before that neither of you finished your soup. The black bits were only fungi. We've learned to grow them in quantity in our cellars and how to weed out the poisonous ones that have given all fungi a bad name. You get to like the flavor in time, as with so many foods. The Ancients, when they sat down to an evening meal, prized highly a wild variety of these same fungi, though of course they had so much else to choose from.

'If neither of you young men minds, I'll have your fem fed now.'

Alldera shivered. When he had been speaking of fems in the time of the Wasting, his tone had chilled her. She had begun to feel the absence of her own kind like an added coolness in the air.

A steaming dish was set down in front of her by the Armicor. It did not contain curdcake or even seaweed, but was filled instead with a brown, grainy mass much coarser than hemp-root taydo. A sweetish scent was rising from it. Alldera's hunger vanished.

'Eat,' Maggomas said.

She ate. The food was chewy but yielding, thick on the tongue.

'What is that?' Bek asked.

'The basic sustenance of the new Holdfast, and of the world in times before even the Ancients. It's a low-energy, high-bulk food, but an old and honorable one. We make it not from leaves like our curd-cheeses, but from the seeds of mature grasses: "grain", it's called. We've already raised two successful grain crops in the high meadows west of us – without the Board's knowledge, of course. In time, the whole upper plateau will be given over to grain-growing. That's our first step, when we take over.'

'Then where will you grow manna-hemp?' d Layo said 'Or is this "grain" good for dreaming?'

'Dreaming!' the old man scoffed. 'Mind melting, you mean! Men with a whole real world to explore won't have any use for dreaming. There will be no manna in the new Holdfast.'

With a glance at the Armicors, d Layo said, 'Do all 'Troimen share your opinion?'

'There hasn't been a real dreaming in 'Troi for two and a half years,' Maggomas said, 'only mummery to satisfy the Board. I told you, 'Troimen are realists. To them a foodcrop is obviously more valuable than a drug.'

D Layo sat back, radiating polite incredulity.

'Come on, young man,' Maggomas chided, 'haven't you any ambition to be more than a DarkDreamer, scrambling through the alleys from one cheesebrained client to another? That's no life for an able young fellow. I can offer better. You lived to come through the gates of 'Troi because you have a place here – but not as a Dark-Dreamer. My son will need practical advice.'

D Layo smiled and began some modest disclaimer, but the Armicor officer strode over at that moment and pressed the spyglass into Maggomas' hand.

'Look at the docks,' the Armicor said, pointing. 'The main body of the City men have come upriver from Oldtown by boat.'

Even without a glass the first of a fleet of barges could be seen butting out of the darkness among the wharves. Citymen leaped out and ran along the palisade, looking for a weak point. A volley of thunder from the 'Troimen sent them scurrying from the reach of the lights. 'Troimen standing on the palisade walkway waved their fists and weapons in the air. The sound of their cheering rose unevenly on the night breeze.

Maggomas took the Armicor officer by the elbow and walked the length of the terrace with him and back, talking excitedly. The other Armicors brought up a large box through the kitchen hatch and strapped it to the back of one of their number. Cables dangling from the box were attached to places in the parapet. Maggomas wound a crank-handle projecting from the side of the box and talked into a hand-piece (also on a cord) that hitched into a bracket on the other side.

A small, crackling voice replied from the box.

Men's magic, Alldera thought grimly. Who was it who turned out to be able to speak to others who were not present? Not femmish witches, but the Ancients themselves, from whom Maggomas must have harvested this wonder along with all the others.

When the old man rejoined them, Bek said, 'You've done astonishing things here. How is that the Seniors of 'Troi allowed the development of such advanced machines?'

Maggomas sat down again and leaned back, a picture of comfort and confidence.

'Good question. Once I accepted the fact that real innovations were doomed, it was easy. I simply presented an idea that seemed designed to reinforce the status-quo. I offered to arm the 'Troi Seniors so effectively that they'd never again have to depend on Rovers for protection or worry about the energy and aggressiveness of young men. You remember that bow-and-arrow scare a decade ago? You can't let a Rover loose with a distance-weapon, so nobody else can have one either.

'These 'Troi Seniors trusted me because I was a Senior myself. They gave me a free hand. I used my freedom to make sure that the men who actually made the new weapons also knew how to use them – and who to thank for them. So here I am.'

'And where are they?' Bek asked him. 'The Seniors of 'Troi?'

'You met one at the watchtower; he, and a few others who were useful, were asked to join us. The rest we killed along with the Rovers and their officers. It gave my men a chance to try the new weapons before any major clash, and we were relieved of a lot of dead weight in our ranks. None of this should bother you; more men have died at your hands in Endpath than at mine here in 'Troi.'

'There is no comparison –' Bek began savagely, but checked himself. 'I won't argue that point. I have only one question that matters. Didn't it ever occur to you, while you were making your – preparations, that I might decline to succeed you?'

The old man began to frown, and Alldera thought, he is going to make the wrong answer.

Now she knew why she had spoken so freely to Bek in the camper, more freely than she had ever intended. Bek knew how to pay attention, however imperfectly and intermittently. It was to this offer of ultimate respect that Alldera had responded. But the idea of looking straight at a thing – or a person – to see what it was, rather than what use it might be to him, was alien to Maggomas. Schooled by years of examining the past for whatever he could turn to his own purposes, he had no conception of disinterested regard. Utility, bald and degrading, was his reality. His answer must be disastrous.

Looking from the blind old man to the desperate son, she felt a shiver of sweet dread.

Impatiently, Maggomas said, 'You don't understand. You've passed every test: the Boyhouse, Endpath, even the timing of your arrival here. Your presence is my vindication, not that I ever had serious doubts. I set up the course, and you've run it, and the rest is all arranged. I had everything worked out before I ever marked your dam's neck.'

'Thank you,' said Bek scathingly, 'for putting my life into its proper perspective. But if you've done all this for me, then you've done it for nothing. I accept nothing from you: not your name, not your place, not your future!'

23

Now, thought Bek, be calm for this battle.

Maggomas scowled. 'I see we're further apart than I'd thought. Maybe I was wrong about the maturing influence of Endpath. You would have no future if I hadn't risked my soul to plant yours in the black pit of a fem's belly; if I hadn't used my influence to keep certain Seniors from having you killed at once in the Boyhouse; and if I hadn't saved you from the consequences of your own foolish behavior later on.'

'By having me sent to Endpath.'

'Yes,' the old man barked, 'and not without cost to myself. You owe me, boy.'

'There are more unpaid debts than I think you know. Do you remember Karz Kambl at all?'

'Of course,' Maggomas said sharply. 'A good friend, but an incompetent engineer. I never meant to bring him upriver. In return for posting you to Endpath, the Board insisted that I leave the City immediately – and there was no one else I could call on for help at the time. That Karz ended up back in the City in spite of having blown himself up with my boat's engine simply justified my original judgment that he was the wrong man for the job.'

'You knew he was alive afterward,' Bek said. 'Yes, I guessed it. Why didn't you get in touch with him? He died in your defense, as he imagined it, not two weeks ago.'

'Ah. Poor Karz.' Maggomas brooded over his plate. 'I've thought of him often. He would have been miserable up here. He was too idealistic, impressionable, literal-minded in an innocent and vulnerable sort of way. I doubt he would have understood one single thing I've had to do here in 'Troi – any more than you do, I suspect. Now look here, boy; this is no game where we outpoint each other for standings. I am the first real and true genius in generations to be born into this ass-end scrapheap of a world and to grow up with his brains unscrambled. The most has got to be made of my talents. That's the reason for your existence, which is more reason than most men have for theirs. You're needed here, and I'm treating you accordingly. You come as my enemy, as you've been taught; but have I had you drugged or chained, for my own safety?'

He shoved aside his plate, planted his elbows on the table, and leaned closer, intently. 'Your pride is smarting; you're drowning in a puddle of self-pity over nothing! I've been a misfit and an outsider from my birth, with capacities that no one understood. I've had a few followers, fewer friends, and none who could keep up with me. I've spent my time in every dirty corner of the Holdfast and beyond, sniffing out fragments of the past that other men couldn't see the use of but made me pay for anyway. After one Scrapper burnt a book in front of me because I wouldn't meet his price – a book he couldn't read, let alone comprehend – I paid what was asked and let them laugh.'

Bek broke in fiercely: 'How could you mark me for an outsider's life, knowing yourself what it was like?'

'What are you talking about?' Maggomas demanded. 'There's no comparison between what we've been through! You were born to be shaped to your capacity; I was born to shape myself. You've lost nothing by the help I've given you. No one could help me. In another age, I'd have been a rich man among rich men, a leader among leaders; I'd have had an empire to bequeath to you instead of a hidey-hole and a plan for taking a big step backward without breaking a leg!'

'What I don't understand is what a man like Karz Kambl saw in you to love.'

The old man snarled, 'What do you care? All I want from you is respect, nothing else.'

'You have that; how could I fail to respect your brilliant handling of my life, so that you've had only to wait for me to come here' – Bek's voice cracked out of control into an anguished cry – 'and be a monster like you!'

Maggomas retorted, 'You make me sound like some kind of criminal! Control yourself! You're distracting my men from their duty with this display – shaming yourself in front of your friend.'

For a moment Bek longed to plead with the old man to think again, to put his hand in the fire of his son's rage and say, yes, it's a dreadful conflagration I've created in my ignorance . . . But the feeling was smothered under the invasion of a vast and chilling grief for something irreversibly lost; a grief colder than the void. When Bek spoke he said calmly,

'How soon . . . are you expecting to die?'

The old man shrank away from him. 'I've struggled along with bad health for years,' he said defiantly. 'I can last a while longer.'

'You stuff yourself like a gluttonous boy and have a Junior's energy,' Bek observed coldly. 'There's at least another decade in you. You don't need me yet. But I would like to know what you have arranged to keep me occupied meanwhile. Something to toughen me up some more? Perhaps imprisonment in a cage hung from your terrace?'

Gruffly, Maggomas said, 'I've loaded you with too much at once. I apologize. It's just that I've wanted to talk with you for so long –'

'Of course, you could hardly have dropped in for a chat at Endpath; you might have been taken for a pilgrim and not come out again. But don't worry, you've said it all. I only hope you have someone to put in my place – or rather, someone else to put in your place. What about your Armicor officer there? He undoubtedly believes in your plans and ideas more than I ever could anyway.'

The officer, who was speaking into the talk-box, gave no sign of having heard.

'I don't understand you!' Maggomas cried, slapping the table so that the dishes rattled. 'Would it be so terrible to be the instrument that saved mankind?'

'Mankind,' Bek replied, with chilly precision, 'has nothing to do with this. You want to save yourself from extinction. You want me to be your dead hand, crushing the future into your design for you. You're transparent, old man. Don't you think the Endtendant of Endpath recognizes the dread of death when he sees it?'

Watching the painful wincing blink of Maggomas' wrinkled eye-lids, Bek felt an ache of wintry pleasure.

'I have a point, perhaps,' interjected another voice, Servan's of course, 'at which you two could possibly come together over your differences.'

How relaxed Servan looked. He exuded friendly concern, sitting there with his beer mug in his hands and smiling so winningly at them both. We're no more than dreamers for him to manipulate, Bek thought wearily, drunk on emotion instead of manna, that's the only difference.

'It seems to me,' Servan went on smoothly, 'that Eykar is perfectly well suited to the exercise of power that you offer, sir, but he doesn't yet see any personal interest of his own in it to attract him. I think Eykar might be amenable to overseeing your new Holdfast for you if he could have a free hand in, say, formulating the place of fems in that design. During our travels he's appropriated my own fem to himself, and he sometimes even shows concern for her welfare. I imagine that he has a whole book of notions in his head about her correct treatment. Am I right, Eykar?'

Oh, helpful Servan, to offer bait for Maggomas' trap! Beautiful Servan, eager for power he wouldn't know what to do with; clever, treacherous, beloved, blind Servan.

Bek kept silent, refusing to be drawn.

'The whole matter of the fems,' Maggomas said, 'is one of the few things that hasn't gone too well in the preliminary stages.' He rushed into a history of the problem, plainly relieved to bring the conversation back to some sort of technical level.

'When we began slaughtering fems in preparation for the long siege, a couple of them actually turned and attacked my men. It was an incredible affair, and my people reacted as you might expect. By the time I got control again there wasn't a fem left alive in the town. Even my lab population had been shot down in their cages, and all the mining-fems were destroyed. Not that it's a disaster. When the City men realize their situation, they'll be happy to trade anything they have for a packet of lammins, including their fems.

'It was my fault, in a way, though. The attention some of our 'Troi fems were getting in my experiments must have given the whole lot of them an inflated notion of their worth. I was working along several lines at once with the ones in my laboratories, not just on diet experiments.'

He began to take up and devour, absent-mindedly and voraciously, morsels of food from Bek's plate, speaking rapidly as he ate.

'In the hospital I saw throwbacks killed as soon as they were born – cubs marred by oddities of feature, skin-color, hair type, all the peculiarities left over from the Dirties. A foolish waste; there's no reason why, with careful selective breeding over time, we shouldn't be able to obtain some very useful throwback strains. I foresee, for instance, a breed large enough and strong enough to bear a mounted man at a good pace – but too stupid to be dangerous. I had one very promising line started in the laboratory: two cubs with strong, hairy hides that might have been bred back to true fur-bearing form, given a few generations.

'The real problem is time. We have to work on ways of speeding up the maturing process. Breeding them younger helps, even if you lose the dam – after all, it's the cub's properties you want for the next generation.'

'You sound as if you mean to resurrect the unmen!' Servan exclaimed. He was enthralled with all this, excited as a boy.

The fem sat composed and motionless, her head tensely lowered so that Bek couldn't see her expression. He studied the top of her head, willing her to look up at him. She must see that he repudiated all this. She must. His eyes burned with the effort to stare her into obedience to his mental urgency, as if he suddenly believed in witchery.

'Not exactly unmen,' Maggomas was saying, thoughtfully, 'but yes, they'll have to be called something, some word to clearly differentiate the males, in particular, from you and me. Fortunately you'll only need a very small population of throwback males for breeding purposes.' He wiped his fingers on his apron bib and reached for another fragment of lammin. 'When you get into this deeper, you may want to do some reading in my library to turn up a good label for them. And possibly I was too hasty in dismissing manna entirely just now. We should research the potential use of drugs for keeping throwbacks quiet and tractable. Later on, when you've separated the breeding lines you want, you may decide to release the hardier strains into the Wild to forage for themselves.'

With a wrench, Bek thought of Kelmz, who would have gone into the Wild to search out non-human creatures had he been given time. For all of his brilliance, how small Maggomas stood next to the memory of the dead Rover officer!

Servan, still fascinated, asked what Maggomas would do with a fem like Alldera.

'She's cut out for breeding your sons and Eykar's, if she's smart enough to have intelligent offspring – as I assume she is, since she's in private service. Individual ownership of fems will be ended, of course; it's inefficient. Plans will be made for them on impersonal, rational grounds. Now, the smarter she is, the more careful you have to be that she stays out of mischief. You can't keep her pregnant all the time; it lowers the quality of the cubs. But between her gestation periods you can put her in charge of the working throwbacks.'

'But didn't you say that you wanted the throwbacks drugged to keep them quiet?' Servan said. 'How could they work, then?'

Patiently, the old man explained. 'It's only your more dangerous types, the less controllable and less capable ones – near to beast level, you could say – that you'll want to sedate. The fems at higher stages will be a multipurpose resource. They won't be fit to breed men from, of course, only to mate and produce more of their own kind – like the Dirties, in fact. Well directed by your intelligent breeding-fems, these intermediate Dirty-types can replace most machines as we run short of metal for repairs. We'll have to feed them more grain so they can do heavy work, but they'll get exercise on the job, so it balances out: activity keeps up the muscle-tone, restricts the build-up of fat and improves the flavor at the same time.'

'Flavor?' echoed Servan.

'Flavor, flavor,' repeated Maggomas, impatiently, 'of their meat. Haven't you been listening? I'm talking economy, total utilization of the few resources that are going to be left to us. You can't run a Reconquest on a bulk-food like grain, so you use throwback fems as meat, a food that young men can pack in quantity on long expeditions. We're going to rationalize society into a small group of superior men subsisting primarily on the meat, skins and muscle power of a mass of down-bred fems.'

He jumped to his feet, leaning toward their stricken faces. 'Why else would I have had the 'Troi fems killed, if not for their meat? You didn't think I could pack 'Troi with enough lammins and lavers to feed my men for long – we would need a dozen 'Trois to hold that much seaweed!' In a conciliatory tone, he added, 'Eating femflesh seems bizarre to you now, but believe me, you'll get used to it. You have no choice; you've already started.

'Ask your own fem, here, about it; she's a cannibal herself. What do you think is in that curdcake that they eat?'

At last, Alldera looked up, straight into Bek's eyes. She was smiling a fierce, wild smile.

Servan surged from his seat, stumbling backward a step so that his chair crashed over on the tiles.

'You don't think,' Maggomas protested, 'that we've been so crude as to feed you your own carry-fems! We recognize that there are claims, familiarities that men must be educated out of. In a way, though, it's too bad. You would feel differently if you'd begun your flesh-eating at its best – in fresh steaks, instead of the dried chips that were cooked up in your stew.'

Servan doubled over and began to retch, gripping the edge of the table with both hands. It was at him that the Armicors were looking when the inner tide crested in Bek, lifting him effortlessly to his feet, his body pivoting for the blow, his spirit a storm. His right hand clenched like a hammerhead, and he whipped it in a tight arc to smash with all his power into Maggomas' face.

24

Alldera crouched under the retaining wall near the top of the southern slope. The stones at her back were wet. In front of her, tall yellow bunch-grass formed a screen. The first light of morning was quenched to gray by the fine rain that had been falling for hours.

'Troi was taken. During the night, one of the great guns had blown itself apart, ripping up a section of the palisade. City men had poured, roaring, through the gap, and the explosions that followed in series had burst first the work-buildings along the river's course and then whole sections of the rest of the town. Mines must have been set off by the retreating 'Troimen, leaving the victorious Citymen with a handful of ashes. 'Troi's smoke rose this morning from hills of rubble.

She could see a few of the conquerors on the palisade. Two small City patrols were quartering the lower reaches of the valley for stray 'Troimen. The rest of the invaders were gathered on the docks, quarreling with one another as they stowed their meager loot in the barges. The dead lay pale and tumbled along the palisade; they had already been stripped of everything worth taking.

Alldera, watching, sat on a hip-pack she had stolen on her way out of the town and stuffed with provender salvaged from the kitchen of a deserted dormitory. She chewed a plug of lammin. Not that she was hungry — her belly felt bloated and cramped, either from the onset of menstruation or from the strange food she had eaten at Maggomas' table — but she had been running and hiding all night and knew she needed food. Through the unfamiliar covering of trousers, she rubbed the muscles of her legs.

Lethargy weighed her down. She felt no triumph yet at having slipped the leash of the men's authority.

She had not seen the blow that had smashed the bone of Raff Maggomas' nose deep into his brain. The vision she remembered was of his body, stretched out on the terrace between the two parapet lamps. Their light had efficiently illuminated the dreamlike muscular flutterings into which he had subsided.

No one touched Bek. He stood gripping the back of Maggomas' chair with his dark-spattered hand, staring intently past the head and shoulders of the kneeling Second – the man who had been Maggomas' closest aide. The Armicors pointed their guns at Bek, and at d Layo who had sprung to his side, but all eyes were on the dying man; until the Second spread his jacket over Maggomas' face and looked up blankly from where he knelt.

They all started when Bek spoke in level tones to the Second:

'Arrest me, execute me if you dare – but you'll no longer be Second here when your negligence is recognized. Or you may continue as Second in 'Troi – Second to me, as Maggomas' heir, in which case I take the entire responsibility for his death.

'Did you think that he could hand over power to me like a fem offering cakes on a tray? I am his son and successor as he said, but in my own time and on my own terms.' Composed and imperious, he stood among his speechless enemies, his face streaked with his father's blood.

The Second got shakily to his feet and rubbed his palm raspingly over his mouth. He could not seem to meet Bek's eyes. The other Armicors watched the officer for their cue.

Bek commanded, 'Have my father's body taken into his rooms.'

After a moment's hesitation, the Second made the cross-sign with an unsteady hand, and several of the others imitated him: accepting the crossed wills of fathers and sons. Averting their faces, the Armicors lifted Maggomas and carried him inside.

'Oh my soul,' breathed d Layo. He looked dazzled, as though already living in the future which death and Bek's sudden reversal had unlocked for them both. Recovered from his nausea, the Dark-Dreamer would certainly manage his next meal of flesh with admirable nonchalance – he was such an adaptable fellow, Alldera thought dazedly, as are we all.

For here was Bek, buying life by seizing hold of the same future he had spat upon when his father had offered it – as if his refusal had been part of an ice-blooded plan to get his father's place immediately and without constraints on his use of the power it brought him. It was incredible.

Bek turned toward d Layo and said in the same clear, calm tone, 'Second, arrest this man.'

D Layo's face turned vacant with shock. 'What,' he began, and faltered. He looked down at the Second's gun, which was trained on his chest. 'Why are you doing this? Eykar, I killed Bajerman with my own hands in front of you today!'

'Whatever that means to you, it means nothing to me,' Bek said. He lowered himself into Maggomas' chair, easing his hurt leg out stiffly in front of him. 'This is a matter of politics, Servan. I will start fresh here; my close companions will be men of 'Troi.'

He was lying, for he did not drop his gaze in a traitor's shame, but watched d Layo as a man watched the receding shoreline of home from the ferry-rail.

D Layo turned away, his hands balled into tight fists at his sides. Perhaps he was decoyed by his liaison with Bajerman into seeing jealousy where none was. Perhaps he had always feared (and hoped) that Bek would turn out no different, no truer, than he was himself. Perhaps he saw deeper, caught the gist of Bek's intentions and instinctively played along in the direction of his own freedom and survival. He swung back again, crying.

'You can't steer these brutes to victory yourself, Eykar – you're no stategist! You throw me away too soon for your own good! And what if 'Troi falls?'

The Second, who had been looking uneasily from one of them to the other, interjected, ' 'Troi will not fall.'

'Is that 'Troi realism?' d Layo jeered. 'The Ancients fell, anything can fall! Eykar, you're green at the treachery game, I don't think you see it all yet. Are you sure you can take this smug idiot for your "close companion" – until he turns on you? However tired of me you may be – and I trust the lesson of your fickleness isn't lost on this lucky fellow – can you actually put up with such a drastic –'

The last words were drowned in a crashing from the plain that made the terrace shiver underfoot. The Second smiled: 'That's why we're not going to lose 'Troi. Those are our big guns opening up all along the palisade.'

'Heroes' weapons,' d Layo snarled, 'that kill anonymously from a safe distance!'

The Second waved away the handpiece of the talk-box, which the box-bearer was holding urgently out to him. 'Endtendant Bek, what's to be done with this man?'

'He's to be escorted to the gate and turned out,' Bek said, his eyes still on d Layo, his voice rough with a tenderness that he made no effort to disguise. 'And see that he's given a knife.'

'He'll join the City men,' the Second objected. 'He knows a lot about our set-up here, and that we've lost – our original leadership. It's too dangerous just to let him go like that.'

'I've given my orders, Second,' Bek said.

'For our good or for our ruin?' the Second said, his hand hovering so that the gun he held covered Bek as well as d Layo. 'You're very anxious to get him out of here –'

Bek looked at the Second at last. 'I don't want him killed. I've loved him all my life.'

'Eykar, you hypocrite!' d Layo burst out, his eyes glittering with tears. 'Who paid your passage here, in sweat and submission to that old cunt Bajerman? Now that I've served your purposes, you order these yellow-guts to throw me out to starve, and you call that love?'

'I've outgrown you, Servan,' the Endtendant replied. 'Say good-bye like a man.'

D Layo stood hunched toward him – silent, hating, hopeless – all his natural grace cramped and spoiled.

The Second's doubts were gone. He ran his eyes over the men at his disposal, nodded to one of them, and ordered the others back to their former stations along the parapet. The one he had singled out moved toward d Layo, gun drawn. The Second turned to the talk box, though he kept his eyes on the DarkDreamer while listening to the voice from the handpiece.

Suddenly d Layo strode forward, stooped, and kissed Bek long and hard on the mouth, as if to draw the life's breath out of him.

Bek offered no resistence; but the Armicor stepped in behind d Layo and reached out to pull him away. D Layo rammed an elbow into the pit of the man's stomach, and the Armicor plunged backward into the talk box man and the Second.

The DarkDreamer sprang onto the tabletop amid a clatter of flying dishes. Not even pausing to look down at Bek's upturned face, he leaped onto the parapet and ran three steps along its length, then bent, pushed off with his spread fingers, and vaulted out into space.

Shouting, leaning out, they saw him turn like a tumbler so that he fell on his back – into the web of lines that linked buildings across the street below the level of the terrace. The cables snapped free of their fastenings, lashing upward so that the watchers flinched back. D Layo's fall was broken; he flipped again in the air, landed crouching in the empty street, and sprinted for shelter before the cursing Armicors had clawed their weapons out.

The Second, shouldering other men aside, leaned far out, squinting, and yelled into the handpiece. He shook it and wheeled furiously on the box-carrier, who cried,

'It's the wires! That fucking maniac ripped down the wires!'

The Second looked blackly at his handful of men, who would now have to carry messages on foot. He said, 'I wouldn't mind having that punk's luck. By rights one of those cables should have fried him before he hit the ground.'

'You misjudged your man,' Bek said. But when the Second proferred his gun, butt-first, Bek shook his head. 'You don't have to surrender your command because of this. I'm not sorry he got away from you, Second. I wouldn't want his blood on the hands of my friends.'

Abashed, the Second backed off.

Bek got stiffly to his feet, motioning Alldera to attend him. He turned with her toward Maggomas' rooms, saying wearily to the Second, 'I'm going in for a while. You're in command here, Second. Instruct your men as you see fit.'

'Yes, sir,' the Second said. He was Bek's man now.

Bek favored his burned leg heavily. In the privacy of the dark front room, he sagged so hard against Alldera that she was obliged to stop and steady herself.

'It's all right,' he muttered, taking a long breath. He let it out in low laughter. 'Well, that's Servan to the marrow! I tie myself in knots to arrange an escort out of here for him, and he turns around and improvises his own spectacular departure!

'You must leave more discreetly –'

'And you?' she asked, knowing the answer.

'Do you think I came here just to punch an old man in the face?' he retorted. 'I have more to do.'

Yes; but she felt bound to offer him such wisdom as her kind had so painfully won: 'It would take a man like Raff Maggomas to undo Raff Maggomas' work,' she said.

'It took a man like Raff Maggomas to kill him,' he snapped. 'Undoing his work is the job of his son, if anyone. I'm going to obliterate him and everything of his. You understand me, don't you? I think Servan did, too, to some degree. Everyone but that creature that called itself my father . . .'

On some dark level all this made sense to her. She could think of nothing she could say to alter his resolve, nor any reason why she should want to.

'Take the footbridge,' he said. 'After that, your best chance is to head out of 'Troi on the inland side where the fighting should be thinnest. That's the way Servan will go, for the same reason. Show yourself judiciously among the rocks on the high slopes, and he'll find you. You're more valuable than ever now.'

She twisted violently free of his hand, so that he stumbled and swore, catching at the furniture in the dark for support. Harshly he said, 'You must see that if anyone can survive this upheaval it's Servan and whomever he protects!'

'Survival,' she retorted, 'is an overrated achievement. Survival as what? For how long? For what purpose? I understand you, and you understand nothing. You give the same moldy advice I'd get now from the Matris; you, of all people. Do you think you're the only one with the right to say "no?" '

'So.' He sighed. 'We seem to be kin of some sad and foolish kind, and in spite of everything. But surely you don't mean to put yourself into the hands of these –'

'No.' She moved closer to the map, beyond which the shadowy figure of the Second could be seen watching the plain, alone, from the parapet. 'I'll go inland.'

Bek limped after her, speaking with sharp apprehension. 'But how will you live? Winter's coming!'

'I expect I'll starve. Frankly, I'd rather do that alone in the mountains than down here in the company of men eager to gnaw my bones.'

'You'll find no mercy in the Wild.'

'Good!' she cried. 'I've had enough of what passes for that quality. Plain indifference will be a mercy.'

'Even if you're carrying a cub?'

'There are cures for that, and neither men nor Matris in the Wild to prevent me.'

'And if the Wild isn't empty after all?' he persisted. 'If there are monsters?'

'I am experienced,' she snarled, 'at handling monsters.'

She stopped, surprised. It seemed she was one of the Pledged after all now, perhaps the only one – except for Bek, who was pledged in his own way.

On impulse, she added, 'You asked me once what you said about Kelmz, that night at the Scrappers'. I never told you.'

In his silence, she became aware of the distant concussion of the guns. The sound made her jump with nerves. She hurried on. 'What you said was that you were sorry; that it was unfair – Kambl was after you, not after Kelmz; that there were things you wanted to talk about, but there was no one to talk with seriously and deeply; that it was your fault. You were ashamed to have left him. You wanted to know him better. Sometimes you blamed him for throwing himself away, but most of the time you blamed yourself for leading him to his death. You said you were sorry.

'None of it could have been taken for lust except by a jealous or mischievous listener. What you expressed was grief for a lost friend.'

He lifted his head. 'I've tried to keep Kelmz out of my thoughts,' he said, bitterly, 'because there seemed to be no way to think of him that didn't shame both him and me. But it seems the shame is all mine.

'I must be a mature man now. As a boy, I was reputed to have been a clever student, but I've been stupid lately.' The dark shape of his hand moved over the glowing lines: from Endpath to Lammin-town, and on down the coast. 'Right from that grim ride south with those wretched pilgrims, to the fierce young men on the ferry, and your own people at Bayo – so alarmingly efficient and not nearly alien enough – that tangle of passions in the City, even Bajerman, even Servan, and you yourself. Everything has sharpened my eyes to know Maggomas for a monster when I met him. And I still couldn't see something as simple as Kelmz and myself until you showed me just now.'

The light glimmered on the gaunt planes of his face and on the cords of his throat as he turned toward her. 'Will you come closer? I want to show you something. These marks, see them, among the ones that stand for the mountains?'

'I don't know how to read writing,' she said.

He caught her hand, drawing her to the map. She was startled by the warmth and strength of the contact. He was vibrant with excitement, even laughing as he said, 'It says *Refuge*! If you can reach it, and if no 'Troimen are stationed there, you might find shelter, tools, even food, who knows? Look closely; could you find the way?'

It seemed to be a matter of following the river for most of the distance. She nodded, feeling suddenly buoyant and powerful.

'Good.' He let go of her hand, stepping a firm though crooked pace back from her. 'And there won't be any master along to push you around – or to entertain you.'

Angrily, she shrugged. 'It's just as well that our ways part here. My hope lies in speed, and you can barely hobble.'

He barked a laugh. 'Then what are you waiting for? The Second may eventually stumble on the notion of locking up a scarce item like yourself.'

'I'd swallow my tongue first,' she muttered, glancing out at the Second. Bek looked, too, and abruptly seized her arm and thrust her two stumbling steps back into shadow. Another 'Troiman had joined the Second at the parapet. They both turned toward Maggomas' quarters as they talked together.

'Will you go!' Bek exclaimed. His fingers tightened on her arm. The old dislike of a man's touch stiffened her. He drew his hand away at once, and stood panicked and silent, an angular shadow against the glow of the map.

She said, with a kind of angry desperation, 'Safe journey then!'

She could just make out the glint of his bared teeth, the brightness of his eye.

In the absurdity of this farewell she left him.

She sat on the hillside, not knowing what she could still be waiting for. The sun came out and dried her hair and clothing.

Down below the boats of the City men departed, except for two hulls that had been smashed during the fighting. 'Troi seemed a deserted ruin.

There was no doubt in her mind that its fall was Bek's doing. After the breaching of the palisade, he must have used his authority to order the demolition of the town before it was actually lost. Endpath to Endpath, his journey was complete. It was not for him that she waited.

Near sundown, she caught the first flickers of movement among the rocks high on the western slopes. 'Troi fugitives were converging on the wreckage, to scavenge what they might and cut the throats of any City men who had been left behind. When the men had all filtered down to the valley floor, her way would be clear.

At last in the deceptive twilight she saw d Layo. He swept by her, far on the right; she heard the hissing of the grass past his striding legs as he ran down the slope, gracefully zig-zagging to control his speed. While she looked, frozen still, he dropped out of sight below the next retaining wall down.

It had been like the passage of some hungry beast, one of those amoral, instinctual creatures that had fascinated Captain Kelmz. So strong was her impression of a hunting predator that she pictured d Layo cutting down some less clever survivor and feeding on the flesh, rank or not; and so he would, if necessary, as innocently ruthless as any beast. The valley into which he had gone seemed very dark now; there was something primeval in the thought of the survivors stalking one another among the ruins – all hunters, all quarry.

To the west, dim with distance but still visible in the rain-cleansed air, the mountains measured the evening sky like waves of the sea. A dusky autumn moon was rising and would soon give enough light to run by, even over unknown terrain. She decided to strike straight up the rise behind her, traveling westward along the spine of the ridge.

The muscles of her legs were stiff from the hours perched here on watch. She rose slowly and stepped from one foot to the other while she adjusted the straps of the pack so that it would ride snugly and not slip or chafe. A tune began in her head, weaving itself into the beginnings of a step-song for the journey: 'Unmen, the heroes are gone . . .'

Without another glance back she started uphill with the slow gait of a runner warming up for a long, hard run.

MOTHERLINES

This book is for J.R., who reminded me
that new stories have to be told
in new ways;
and for the many others who helped me
to find the right way for this story
and stick to it

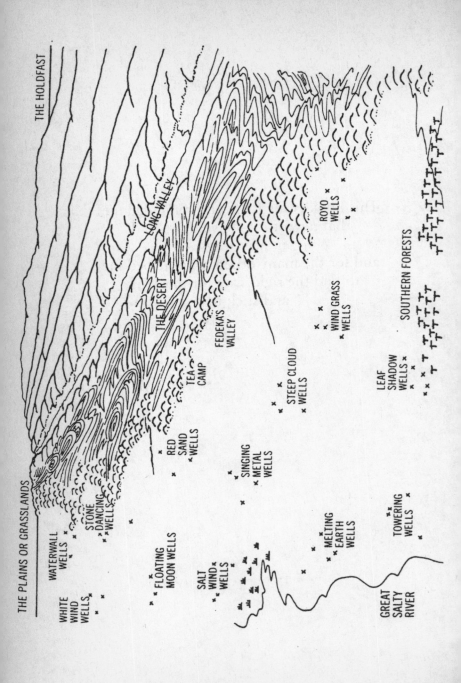

Contents

PROLOGUE

1

Alldera crouched tensely by the river, staring at tracks in the soft mud. The water was shallow here, and something had crossed to the far side; no, two things – two strings of tracks separated and came together again.

She had not seen a living being in the months since her escape from her homeland, nor had she expected to – other than perhaps the monsters with which legend peopled the wild country, but she had not really believed in them. She looked fearfully back over her shoulder.

There rose the valley wall and then the mountains, beyond which lay the strip of coastal plain men called the Holdfast – her country. In the bloody confusion of fighting there – men killing other men and their femmish slaves, over food – she had made her lone escape. It seemed she was alone no longer.

No man of the Holdfast, no fem fleeing as she fled, had made this spoor. Trembling, she traced the shape of the deep prints with her finger. Something heavy walked on those round, blunted feet. The marks were crescent-shaped and as big as her fist, with a sharp angle sign in the middle of each. Monsters' tracks.

Weakened by months wandering as a scavenger in the Wild, she squatted there, fighting back her terror with its tinge of eagerness for contact with life, any kind of life. She tried to consider her situation clearly, turning her inner gaze back over the course of her flight.

At first she had had some faint hopes of finding other runaways, the 'free fems' of stories, whom she could join. That hope and the first fierce exhilaration at being free had soon faded into anxiety. Choosing to cross the borders of the Holdfast into the Wild, she had chosen new dangers.

The Holdfast river, which she followed back into the mountains in search of the ruins of an Ancient shelter, unraveled into several streams. Not knowing which branch to follow, she missed the Refuge and its hoped-for stores of supplies and wandered deep into a maze of rock walls and slopes set between thorn-choked gullies.

The roads of the Ancients, dissected and smashed by landslides and floods, were now only fragmented remnants of the broad, smooth, legendary ways and sketched connections between mere patches of rubble. She avoided the jagged shards of old walls standing in their fields of broken glass; there was nothing to eat there, nothing alive.

Her food pack soon flapped empty, her stolen clothing exposed as much of her as it covered and clung in strips to her skin when there was rain. She began to realize, in bitter despair, that she was pregnant.

In her mind she cursed the fetus for a rape-cub, unwanted seed of the masters whom she had escaped. Hunger made her bold, she tasted everything she could strip from standing plants or dig out of the earth, but it was never enough; how could she make milk for a newborn cub? Doomed from the outset, the cub nonetheless functioned as a hardy and efficient little parasite, stealing from her the nourishment of whatever she could find to eat. Her bowels were in a continual state of bloat and cramp. Sometimes she chewed on roots or leaves that made her sick for days, and she hoped that one of these painful episodes would kill the cub so that she could expel it and better her own chances of survival.

But the cub seemed as tough as she was herself and would not die. She felt its heartbeat and its growing, living weight dragging at her body as she traveled. There were moments of intense pleasure at the thought that this cub, at least, the men would never have. Most often she thought, this cub will kill me, it is a weapon of the men planted in me to ruin my escape.

At length the mountains smoothed to rolling waves of earth, and a day came when she looked down not into another brambly groin in the hills but across a wide valley, a soothing sweep of green and open country with a sparkle of water down the heart of it. This was not some new stretch of the Holdfast river flowing east to the sea but a broad, sunny water rambling north to southwest. The valley was richly embroidered with dark trees along its waterways, and it seemed endlessly long under a warm, quiet sky.

Here was refuge of a kind. On the lower banks of the creeks feeding the river she found plants with sweet stems, and large-leafed vines yielding a pulpy fruit. The shining river smelled bad, though; close up she saw skeins of bright slime drifting in it and in the streams on the other side.

Water was important to her. Pregnancy did not afflict her with nausea and moods, but it did make her sweat constantly and heavily. She was thirsty all the time. Staying on the clean side of the valley so that she could drink safely, she ranged farther southward searching out food plants that she recognized and trying to stay ahead of the full bite of the coming winter. No cold weather came but the rains stopped and food grew scarcer. Sometimes, resting from her endless foraging along the banks of a stream, she would bend to stare hopefully into the empty water; according to legend edible creatures had once inhabited the waters of the world.

The water still only showed her – on this day, the day of the monster tracks – her own broad, bony face framed in a mat of dull, tangled brown hair. She glanced down at herself. The only rounded line to be seen was that of her belly. Her hands, feet and joints looked coarse and swollen, surrounding muscle having melted away. Her skin healed slowly or not at all where it was scratched or bruised. Her gums were tender. She could not pretend to be some proud free fem out of a song; the fems' tales of running off to make a life in the Wild were dreams.

What was real were the monsters. Here was their excrement heaped on the ground like pungent dumplings – even shit reminded her of food, and rightly: without provisions she would die this winter.

There was no choice but to follow and try to find the monsters, persuade them to help her. One way or another, it would end in food: they would either feed her or eat her.

She spent a day following their tracks. She lost their trail, cast in circles for it, terrified of simply walking into them around some roll of the land. She kept stopping to catch her breath and to peer ahead as the day waned. She had to cross the river after them at the shallow place where they had crossed.

Something red caught her eye. In surroundings which provided little now but greens, browns and the black of shadows, it was stunning, not some sly earth tone passing for red but a brash flare of scarlet.

She crept closer. The red was a rag knotted around the end of some sort of bundle that was wedged into the crotch of a tree. With a stick she poked the bundle down; it was a large bag made of some supple fabric, closed with a drawstring that ran through the stitched and puckered hem. She loosened the drawstring with difficulty.

She was afraid to put her hand inside. Cautiously she raised the heavy end of the bag and eased some of its contents onto the ground: there were dark, hard lumps the size of her hand, a bundle of long, flat dried things strung together, and some smaller bags. One of the latter contained pine nuts like those she had gathered for herself from trees on the middle slopes of the mountains. The sight of the small, smooth shells spilling out onto her palm and the smell of resin on them made the unbelievable real: she had found some sort of food cache.

She sat chewing and crying, fighting to keep from bolting so much that she would vomit it up again. She slept on the spot, hugging the bag with both arms.

The next day, carrying some of the food with her, she continued westward on the monsters' trail. They had followed a faint pathway that led west from the river up the slope of the valley to its rim. Beyond, there lay a desert.

Alldera had seen smaller patches of such desolation back in the Holdfast, where it was said that they had been made by the Ancients' methods of mining or of war. This desert was a seemingly limitless stretch of dark earth, all rucked up into long rows one after the other as if the fingers of a giant hand had been drawn parallel through loose dirt. Lonely hills rose sheer-sided to dilapidated peaks, windtorn, undercut, sometimes topped with a clutch of stunted trees. Swatches of green marked isolated groves. Puffs and veils of dust rising on the breeze were all that moved.

The trail of the monsters led off the rim of the valley and angled down into the first trough of the desert. There the prints were lost in a drift of dust.

Alldera dared not try to follow them. She retreated, and made a bed of branches where she had found the supplies. They had left food; they would come back.

The nights grew cold as the moon turned through its cycle. There was no rain, the streams shrank. Her belly was bigger, she could not get around so easily; she was hungry all the time. A sun-warmed rock some distance from her sleeping place became her station; it was easier to withstand the urge to nibble more than her day's ration if she removed herself from the food during the long, idle hours. She watched to the west for signs of the monsters' return. She watched to the east, too, imagining other Holdfast fugitives finding the valley just as she had done.

If others did come, she would have to either fight for her bit of food or run. She was growing too weak to fight, too weak to run. But she did not really believe that anyone would come.

Sheel, scouting ahead of the other two members of the patrol, rode with one of her bows strung in her hand. She trusted only herself to keep fully alert, and besides, she liked riding apart, undistracted by conversation. It bettered her chance to be the first one to sight an enemy and kill him.

She sat forward in her saddle, giving her mount a loose rein so that it could pick its own careful way over this stony, up-and-down country. Sheel's eyes scanned the slopes, eager for a hint of movement, a track in the sandy soil among the thin scattering of trees.

Riding the borderlands with light rations and three full quivers of arrows made her feel alive as nothing else did; here on the vulnerable outskirts of the plains she felt most strongly the rich vitality of the land she was guarding. Her senses were wide open to the sharp scent of pine, the grate of a pebble under her horse's hoof, the long, sunlit lines of the foothills advancing up the lower reaches of the mountains. If men had crossed from the Holdfast, she would know it.

She had killed a total of seven men during a dozen patrols in her lifetime: four from a distance with a bow when she had been sure of her shot, three close up, bursting from cover on horseback to drive home her hunting lance. She hardly minded the chore of concealing the corpse afterward so that no man following could find it and speculate on the manner of his fellow's death. Mystery was demoralizing to such fearful, aggressive creatures as men. They prowled in her mind, clumsy, angular beings, loud-voiced like horses so that you always expected them to be bigger than they were. She had tracked men for miles, listening to their desperately hearty voices, watching, sniffing their fear-rank breeze. They were truly the sons' sons of those world killers, the desert makers of Ancient times; torturers and thieves by nature, wherever they went they left scars. The borderlands were disfigured by the stumps of the trees they cut, the pits they dug and left heaped all around with cast-up earth, the scattered charcoal of the huge and dangerous fires they lit to ease their fears of the dark. They did not even bother to cover their ordure.

Sheel patted her pony's shoulder and reined in at the foot of a slope. Dismounting, she loosened her saddle girth and tied her reins to the branch of a gnarled pine. Then, with a full quiver slung over her shoulder and her bow in her hand, she padded to the top of the ridge and lay down there to scan the wide, rippling country, breathing with pleasure its warm odors. The sun burned on her leather-clad back and legs and on her leather cap. Those rocks down below resembled the rocks in which she had buried her first kill.

She had flayed the dead man's arm to see what made his muscles bulge so unnaturally, and had come away dirty with his blood but no wiser. His sexual organs had seemed a ludicrous, dangling nuisance and hardly capable of the brutalities recounted by escaped femmish slaves. Having everything external and crowded into the groin like that must make walking more uncomfortable for a man than riding at the gallop with unsupported, milk-full breasts would be for a plains woman. A stud horse was better designed: a sheath held whatever penile length was not stored coiled within his body.

What a perversity – a creature that would own her if she let it, yet it had nothing to boast of but a coarse strength that was still less than the power of one worn-out old pack mare. Men's only good feature was that they were a peerlessly clever and dangerous quarry to hunt. Their terror at the end, when you came up and waited a little way off for the dying to be done with, was wide-eyed and bestial.

Movement caught Sheel's eye, there on a hillside she had already passed. It was her two companions, following after her. She did not want them to catch up with her yet.

She ran back down the slope, tugged her girth tight, caught up her reins and mounted to ride on ahead.

Alldera thought about her cub. It took many days' thinking. Her mind, sluggish from starvation, turned slowly now.

She was not surprised that the cub was still alive in her starved body. The hard lives of Holdfast fems over generations had made tough dams and tough offspring.

She remembered the cold table to which the Hospital men, masked and gowned and stinking with terror of 'femmish evil', had strapped her when she had had each of her two cubs – both fems. Each cub had stayed with her till weaning and then been sent down into the kit pits to live as best it might with its peers, until it was grown enough to be trained by men to work and to serve.

This cub would never live that life. It would never live any life. Alldera's body had swelled with the months, but her breasts stayed slack, emptied by privation or by disease, she had no way of knowing.

Suppose the cub were male? This idea stirred up a mist of rage and fear that stopped all thought, except for the simple knowledge that she could not keep any cub alive after its birth.

She decided that when it grew large enough to be taken hold of, she would try to do the massage that fems knew to detach a fetus from its hold so that it would be aborted. She though wretchedly of the pain. The creature would not easily be twisted from its life-sustaining hold. It would be no readier to give up and die than she was herself – that thought gave her a pang of grim pride.

One night – in her fifth or six month, she could not tell, so starved and bloated was she – she dreamed of the cub: born plump and bloody, it was laid on a fire to cook. Then she ate it, ravenously taking back into her own body the substance of which the cub had been draining her all this time.

The dream woke her. She walked slowly in the valley by the moon's light, hugging herself against the cold. Waking at night was bad; it was too chilly for her to fall asleep again.

On her way back to her camping place just after sunrise she crossed fresh tracks. The monsters, returning, had paused near her camp and then gone on toward the desert.

It was months since she had first found their footprints. By the time they came again, no matter how strictly she rationed her food, the bag would be empty and she and her cub would both be dead.

She hung the bag over her shoulder and followed them up to the western rim of the valley, glad to be moving and doing, even though she was perhaps pursuing her own death; that was better than just waiting for it, like a slave.

The desert was just as she had first seen it, a huge washboard that ran beyond sight in all directions. Once more the monsters had simply plunged down the steep slope leaving a dark line of disturbance in the loose soil, but this time their tracks showed fresh and plain in the fine dust of the trough floor.

She adjusted the bag so that it would not flap on her shoulder, and she scrambled awkwardly down.

Water had cut rough gullies across the furrows, making passes in the ridges between the troughs; using these gaps the monsters were bearing westward through the desert. Alldera threaded the maze on their trail but could make no speed. She was too weak, her joints hurt, the cub's weight dragged her down.

There was a stark, dreamlike beauty to the place. The dark soil seemed to soak up sunlight and burn with it. Tufts of grass sprouted here and there in the shadows of rocks. There were even a few spindly trees, or older ones with thick, stunted trunks. Occasional red twists of Ancient machinery protruded from the dirt: thin shells rusted out to nothing, great lumpish cores of which the more delicate and projecting parts had long since fallen away. In the deeper ravines there were reefs of debris trailing out from undercut walls – flood sign. Where water stood it was laced with green slime, and the monsters themselves did not stop to drink it. The filth in the valley's river must come from streams draining this poisoned place.

Once she thought she heard the monsters up ahead crying to each other in high, shivering voices.

When it was too dark for her to see their tracks, she stopped and sat down beside a prow of rock. Chewing very slowly – her teeth hurt, and she had no saliva to moisten the food – she ate one small, hard loaf from the bag. There were four more left.

Sounds woke her at morning. Her trough was still deep in shadow under softly lit ridges above on either hand. As she rubbed the dust out of her eyes and tried to remember what it was that she had heard, sounds came again, high, almost whistling, shaking as if with rage, and then a shout very like a human voice, not far away.

Alldera clawed her way up the side of the nearest ridge, scraping her hands and feet on the rocks and starting a small slide of dirt and rubble behind her. She felt heavy, slow and desperate, thinking of them traveling on while she toiled after them, more slowly today than yesterday, more slowly still tomorrow. Breasting the blunted ridge top, she could see the dust-coated foliage of trees a few furrows over. She stood up on the rounded spine of the ridge.

Not twenty meters off figures moved in one of the rough passes between two furrows; monsters indeed – three of them.

Their bodies were long, slung horizontally on two pairs of legs. Two trunks rose from their backs, one human-shaped with arms, the other smooth and topped with a head like a log of wood stuck on at an angle, and a sweep of hair hung from the back end, like one lock from the top of a shaven scalp.

They were terrible to look at, but they were her only chance to live. Alldera filled her lungs and screamed.

Two of the monsters checked in the pass, bumping each other. The third turned and took great plunging leaps to the top of the ridge they were crossing. It halted and faced Alldera. The humanlike trunk extended something toward her, a stick held out straight up and down at the full length of the arm as if warding off the sight of her. There was something threatening in the stillness behind the gesture, the concentration before delivering a blow.

Alldera waved her strengthless arms and called out again.

The long head of the monster dipped and murmured. The human head uttered a cry, excited words and what sounded like laughter. The stick weapon was lowered, tucked away somewhere. Incredible, to manage all those limbs at once –

The monster came apart.

The human torso vaulted into the air and landed on two human legs beside the creature on which it had been sitting. With terrible clarity Alldera saw her error: they were men, nothing but men, who had somehow caught and tamed true monsters to obedience.

She slid down the steep side of the ridge in a spout of choking dust and began to run waveringly down the trough floor. There were shouts and the pounding of steps behind her; running was hopeless. She knew the art of kick fighting, but that was beyond her now.

Raging, she bent and groped in some flood wrack for a rock, a stick, something to take in her hand.

The beast drove toward her in bounds, its fistlike feet hurling up sprays of earth. The rider had a coil of rope in his hands. As Alldera cocked her arm, holding a rock that she knew she hardly had the strength to toss, something swished through the air and slapped her around the chest and shoulders. She was jerked off her feet as the beast tore past her and she crashed flat on her back, her body ringing with shock, unable even to roll onto her side or her stomach to protect herself.

She heard him dismount, his soft-footed steps approaching, the play of muscle, bone and clothing as he squatted beside her.

Framed by a long, loose cloth that he wore over his head and falling down his shoulders, his smiling face was red and small-eyed, with dirt ground into the creases around his features. He wore a belted tunic with big, flap-topped pockets in the skirts over pants of the same weaveless, greasy material, and boots tied snugly under the knee. He stank.

Alldera strained for control of her bruised and exhausted body, promising herself, I will swallow my tongue and die. Before he can raise a hand to me.

The stranger opened his crack-lipped mouth and spoke. There was a peculiar light singsong pattern to his voice. Alldera did not register the words; she had been without the sound of another human voice for a very long time.

The stranger pulled off his headdress, freeing a thick fall of gray-shot hair. 'Don't be afraid,' he said again slowly, and Alldera understood. 'Don't be scared of me.'

He caught up her hand and pressed it against his own body. Under the slick-surfaced tunic Alldera felt the unmistakable soft shape of a female breast.

2

Sheel strode into the sweat tent, humming, and pulled off her shirt, savoring the idea of calling a duel on a woman who had spoken persistently against her during the inquiry about this new fem.

Redder in the face than ever, Barvaran came in to join her in cleansing themselves for the judgment of the camp. She had brought in the last of the hot stones on the prongs of a long wooden fork. She placed the stone among the others in the pit in the middle of the floor and stood back, rubbing water from her forehead with the back of her thick, red wrist. She looked sullen and distressed. Sheel regretted not having Shayeen there with them; Shayeen was still too sick to come.

Sheel knelt at the entry to lace the door flaps up tight. She looked over her shoulder. With only the two of them in it the tent looked vast. Ordinarily there would have been a dozen women filling the space. Barvaran seemed a figure of red sandstone glistening with rain across an expanse of earthen floor.

Picking up the water bucket, Sheel joined her by the pit. The whiplike ends of the tent poles were lashed together with special knots well above their heads. There, where the roof was highest, Sheel stood up and tugged off her breast wrap, dropped it by her shirt and pants.

Barvaran took the horsetail sprinkler from the bucket and flicked a spatter of drops onto the hot stones. With a thunderous cracking sound, steam shot up, heat spread in a stifling cloud. Sheel endured it for a moment, breathing the searing air in small sips. Then she sat down; the air was cooler near the ground. She took a hardwood scraper from the tray nearby and turned it in her hands, examining it. She still had a scar from a scraper that somebody had nicked by working on a hide with it.

'They won't be long about it,' Barvaran said miserably. 'There isn't anything to think over. Shayeen was sick, you used the excuse of her illness to ride past that food cache instead of checking it, and I let you do it. We left that fem there to die.'

'We didn't know she was there.' Sheel was bored and impatient with the argument. 'And it was Shayeen who almost died.'

'She says she wasn't so badly off that we couldn't have spared time to go and check the cache, like any other patrol heading home.'

Sheel did not answer. Sweat stung her eyes, she could feel her skin cooking over bones. She thought of the bowl of cold water set outside the entry, but she would not be the first one to reach for it.

Barvaran's expression still accused her.

'I didn't know the fem was there,' Sheel repeated for the hundredth time. 'It's months since anyone has found man or fem in the borderlands, everyone knows that. I was right to say we should get Shayeen home as fast as we could, and you were right to agree. Look how sick she still is.'

Barvaran got up and went to the entry. She reached out beneath the laced flaps and a little sip of cool air came in from outside. She drank, and brought Sheel the bowl. The cool water was a joy on the lips.

'We were wrong,' she said mournfully.

Sheel expelled her breath in an exasperated hiss. She began picking over the bits of soaproot laid out on the tray by her knee. To try to lighten the mood and prevent a real quarrel she said, 'Did you have a look at this fem Alldera when they got her cleaned up? I bet she didn't have to escape. I bet the Holdfast men kicked her out so they wouldn't have to look at her any more.'

She grimaced, thinking of the fem: a plate-faced creature, the bridge of her nose flattened so that there was no strong feature to balance her wide, heavy-lipped mouth; eyes a nondescript green-brown, wideset below a broad band of forehead and above the sweep of the cheeks; brown hair too fine to add height to the wide skull. For the rest, she was all bone and belly, with a blunt, square frame. Altogether no prize, yet Sheel knew she would have to suffer on the worthless slave's account.

She muttered fiercely, 'I wish all those fems were dead.'

Through the shimmering, steamy air she saw Barvaran arrested, hands lifted to wring out her thick gray hair. 'No Riding Woman has a right to say that,' Barvaran exclaimed. 'For all the history of the plains we've rescued any fem that came as far as Long Valley, saved her and healed her and sent her to the free fems –'

Sheel mashed a piece of root with a stone, making sudsing paste. She hit hard, pounding out the sound of Barvaran's rough, anxious voice. Bits of slippery white fiber shot in all directions.

'For all the history of the plains,' she said, when Barvaran had paused for breath. 'What about the history of the Holdfast? Think of that. Can you tell me we have some duty to help such cowardly weaklings?

'Back in the Wasting, when our lines' first ancestors shaped their own freedom and ours after them, what was the fem's ancestor doing? Trotting after her bosses, following those high government men into hiding from the ruin they themselves had brought about with their dirty ways and their wars and their greedy dealings. And when the men looked out of their Refuge and saw the world outside sinking into wreckage and they turned around and blamed the women, did those women fight?'

'Some of them must have,' Barvaran said uncertainly. She rubbed sudsing paste patiently into her hair. 'A few.'

'Yes, but how many, and how hard did they fight? Their female descendants still came out of the Refuge as slaves when the Wasting was over. They let themselves be turned into the "fems" who built the men their new country, their miserable Holdfast.'

This time Barvaran did not answer. It was too easy to shut her up, to overwhelm her plodding mind. Sheel pressed her, 'Are you listening? And all that time our ancestors, women mind you, not fems, were building a life that Holdfast men would destroy if they knew it existed.'

'I don't know what any of this has to do with this fem Alldera and her baby.'

Sheel began raising a lather in her own hair with stabbing fingers. 'She's just like the rest of them, the runaways, the "free fems" – they crawl all their lives under the whips of Holdfast men, and those that can't take it any longer run away. We find them, make them a place here on the plains, praise them for their courage – courage, to run off and leave the rest of your own kind to rot!' She paused for breath. What a pleasure it was to speak freely against what all the camps agreed was right.

Barvaran leaned to throw more water on the stones. The steam was less, but the heat seemed to build higher and faster than before. Rubbing at an old hunting scar on the hard red calf of her leg, she said in her slow, stubborn way, 'That's all over now, Sheel. This fem says they're wiping each other out back there, men and men and men and fems. It had to happen, with their food so scant all those years and the young men half starved under the rule of the old, greedy ones. You're angry at a dead place.'

'Not dead, still living – here. We have the runaway fems with us. Weaklings, misfits – what would have become of us women if we were as soft with our own as we are with them?

'And now there's this new one, and her cub besides.'

'Her child,' Barvaran corrected gently. She took up a scraper and moved so that she could use it on Sheel's skin. The wooden blade rode deftly over the long plane of Sheel's thigh. Barvaran had fine control of those great red hands of hers, even now in her distress. She never hurt where she could caress. Useless to try to make her understand the shame, the insult these fems brought to the clean life of the plains.

'It could be a male child,' Sheel growled. 'Would you speak up for it so tenderly then?'

'The fem says she's had two other children, both female. And Layall Fowersath has examined her and thinks this one will be female also.'

Sheel snorted. 'The fem is so weak and confused she doesn't know what she's saying; and as for Layall Fowersath, like all Fowersaths she can usually tell accurately the sex of an unborn foal. But this isn't a horse's offspring we're talking about. This is a man's cub from the men's world. Male or female it's dangerous – like anything from there.'

'The free fems have never hurt us.'

'Just wait. You'll see some day that I'm right.'

'You said all this at the inquiry,' Barvaran said. 'Nobody agrees with you.'

'More do than you think, but they keep it to themselves.' Sheel turned her leg more firmly against the scraper's edge. With another such tool she drew down the curve of Barvaran's torso in a neat pattern of overlapping strokes. The heat brought out fresh moisture as soon as the old was swept away.

Barvaran looked at her. 'Some women say you can't tell fems from their masters, Sheel. Everyone knows we should kill men because they are dangerous and crazy. They don't even know how to die. But you almost killed a fem this time. Fems are damaged and need our help, but you treat them as if they were men too. Some women say you've killed too many men, Sheel, and the killing has crippled your spirit, and you shouldn't go out on patrol again.'

'Who says so?'

'If I tell you, you'll go feuding with the one who said it. I just think you should know: women say that when you speak of fems, you talk like a woman with no kin.'

Sheel slapped a gob of suds back up out of her own eyes. 'We'll have a feud right here between the two of us in a minute,' she began threateningly, and stopped. Who was this wretched fem to set her against good, dull Barvaran?

The lacing of the entry was suddenly pulled loose, admitting a rush of cool air. Two women entered, stooping, and walked to the center where the others rose to meet them. Even at its highest point the curved tent roof brushed the raincloud hair of Nenisi Conor, who was tall, angular and dark like a woman's shadow on the ground in late afternoon. One of the black-skinned Conor line and imbued with the Conor trait of justice giving, she was a perfect speaker for the camp, unimpeachable. The Conors are the shadows of our consciences, women said.

Nenisi Conor looked at Sheel. 'Women think you did wrong to be careless about the lives of the fem Alldera and her child.'

The other woman was of Sheel's own line, a lean replica of Sheel herself, yellow-haired and blade-faced. Her name was Palmelar. She was famous for being poor in horses because she gave away her wealth to needier women. She was well chosen also, someone whom Sheel had to respect.

To her Sheel said harshly, 'Does our Motherline agree with this that other women think?'

Palmelar nodded and met her eyes, smiling as if rejoicing in the judgment.

And here I am looking foolish with soap all over my head, Sheel thought furiously. She stared away over their heads. 'Well, how many horses am I fined?' Each horse paid out of her home herd she would replace if it took her the rest of her life.

Nenisi answered, 'The fem has no use for your horses. But there is her child. You must forfeit half your home herd to the child of the fem Alldera.'

Half. And for a fem!

Barvaran was looking from one of them to the other. 'But what good are horses to a fem's child?'

'Our child,' Palmelar said happily. 'The fem's child is to be one of us.'

Sheel could not hold back an ugly bray of laughter. Had they all lost their senses? A fem's child could never be a Riding Woman for a dozen reasons. She said the one thing that summed up everything else: 'The child will have no kin!'

'She'll have all the kin she needs,' Nenisi said. 'Alldera Holdfaster the fem will be bloodmother to her. Barvaran will be one of her sharemothers, to offset negligence of duty on patrol; and Shayeen, who was too sick to be blamed but who was there; and I myself, as spokeswoman for the judgment; and you too, Sheel, so that you can pay for your ill will and the deaths that it almost caused. We'll all be her family, which is an honor; the child from the Holdfast may grow up to found a new Motherline among the camps of the plains.

'Now, is the judgment sound, Sheel Torrinor?'

Sheel could not speak. Barvaran cried, 'Yes!' The three of them wept and hugged each other while she stood in their midst, stifled with her own rage.

THE WOMEN

3

The comfortable doze in which Alldera had floated for so long dissolved at last. She found herself in a warm, dim place walled and roofed with some pale, translucent material. All around her were activity, voices murmuring, laughter. Something soft cushioned her back. She could see sharp blue sky through an opening off to one side.

What's happening, where am I, what dangers threaten?

A contraction twisted her belly. She cried out at the familiar pain. People closed around her, patting her, whispering encouragement, holding her hands firmly. Her feet were gripped and braced against the backs of people seated on the heap of bedding.

Someone at her side said briskly, 'Breathe. Remember. You know how to make your breathing work for you.'

She did remember, though she could not now tell whether this was knowledge learned in the secret world of Holdfast fems or in her long dreaming here. There was a way to use the rhythm of respiration to mobilize the body so that it worked not against its own strengths but with them. Fear vanished. She felt full of power, as if she could burst the cub out of her body with one great thrust. It surprised her to find that time was needed, and pain.

The voices of the others joined in a throaty singing. Their song took its rhythm from her breathing and reinforced it. She surged over the pain on their music. The words, which were beyond the tight center of her attention, must have included humor. Rills of laughter erupted and were carried in the song.

She poured with sweat. After the first huge passage of the head she felt the cub's shape, limb and shoulder, work its way out of her. Always before she had been too frightened to feel anything but pain.

A person with long, shining black hair was crouching between Alldera's legs. She put out her hands and something dropped into them. Another leaned in and carefully pinched the last of the blood down the cord. Alldera was astonished at the simplicity of what they did, their calm. The black-haired person bent and sucked the plugs of mucus from the tiny mouth and nose of the raw, squirming bundle in her hands.

People came and put their faces against Alldera's streaming face. Hands massaged her body. In that lilting ripple of speech that she found she understood easily now, several said that she had done well.

She could not gather strength to reach out to any of them or answer in words, but she thought fiercely each time one of them approached her, I love you forever for this. At that moment she felt capable of it. If she had not been a fem, trained for her life's sake to hide feelings, she would have wept.

The cub, washed and dried, was placed against her in the crook of her arm. It was a wrinkled, splotchy-looking female, unfocused in every wandering movement and every shapeless murmur from its wet little mouth. On its angular head was a crop of moisture-darkened hair. There was nothing to tell Alldera which of her masters had sired it. The cub looked very much like the other two she had borne back in the Holdfast, but fatter. Holdfast-born cubs were always skinny. This one was heavy, tiring to hold. She could not imagine how it had had time to grow. Surely only a few weeks had passed since these people had taken up dam and cub in the desert, both of them little but bone.

Odd, this was the creature she had planned to kill. She was glad now not to have done it.

Someone relieved her of the warm, soft, wriggling weight.

'Here it comes,' someone else said cheerfully. Alldera thought in alarm, Mother Moon, not another — were there two, and I didn't know? But it was only the afterbirth, and she wanted to laugh.

She woke, her senses sharp and clear. The soothing haze of the previous weeks seemed gone for good.

She saw that she lay in a broad tent. Under the taut roof a skirting painted with designs in faded colors encircled a floor covered with tawny sand. It seemed a wide, dim, comfortable place. Chests and boxes, dark with use, squatted along the wall. Near the folded-back flaps of the entryway stood some contraptions of straps and uprights. Bags and bundles were piled around what she took to be the hearth, a blackened metal cage set on a tray. Close beside the cage on a broad platter were heaped little lumps of what must have been fuel.

One by one she identified the sounds outside: voices, footsteps, the breathy calls of horses.

Where was her cub?

Someone came in. 'Awake?'

An apparition stood there, a person whose skin was as dark as smoke. From Holdfast songs and chants Alldera knew of the Blacks who had been among the enemies of the mighty Ancients – a lie, no doubt, like most of the men's beliefs. But she could not help shrinking back as the dark person came forward and dropped into an angular crouch beside her, bringing their faces almost level. The stranger's features were rounded and smoothed as if by many rubbings with fine sand. She was barefoot and wore only a twist of tan, soft stuff knotted around her hips. A string of blue stones crossed the base of her neck.

'I'm Nenisi Conor,' she said, 'one of your family. The others are still showing the baby around and celebrating it. How do you feel?' Nenisi asked.

In past pregnancies Alldera had suffered strong afterpains in her body's effort to get rid of the last clotted blood. She felt nothing like that now.

'You're better off than I am,' Nenisi said, her long, dark lips pulling down at the corners in self-mockery. 'My teeth are hurting me today – an affliction of my line, among several other afflictions, so if I complain women just shrug. I'm taking advantage of you while you're still new among us and you'll listen to me tell you about my horse-farting teeth.' She exposed the offending teeth. They looked large, sound, and very white. She leaned closer, regarding Alldera attentively, seriously. 'It must feel very strange to you, all this –' Her slender hand floated as she indicated the interior of the tent.

'Beautiful,' Alldera said fervently. 'It seems beautiful to me. Where I come from –' Her voice failed and she turned her face away. Her lips were trembling.

'There are no men at all,' the black woman said. 'None. You're safe.'

Alldera wept, and was ashamed of her tears. But Nenisi only waited, watching sympathetically, and waved away Alldera's attempts to apologize for her outburst.

Nenisi took up a bundle that unrolled into a sort of rug and she settled herself on the sandy floor. Her limbs looked very long and thin. The flashing pallor of her palms as she gestured and the pink cave of her mouth working in her dark face bemused Alldera.

'You've been with us a long time already, though it probably doesn't seem so to you. You came to us in the Cool Season, and now the Dusty Season has begun. We've kept you in a healing sleep, a thing we do for fems rescued from the borderlands. Most women are too lively for healing sleep, but we find that a few months of complete rest are good for fems fresh from crossing over. You needed time for yourself and your child to recover tranquilly from a rough trip.'

'What magic did you do to save me?' Alldera said wonderingly. 'I was dying when your people found me; I felt myself dying.'

'Hardly,' Nenisi laughed. 'You had your own magic with you – your child. Why, I recall once in my fourth month of pregnancy, stones were thrown at my home tent over this very point. My friends – most of them as big-bellied as I was – wanted to get me free of my hovering share-mothers so I could ride with them in a three-day race that had been forbidden me.' She sighed. 'Everyone knows that any normal female is tougher and healthier in the first half of pregnancy than any other time in her life, and my friends just could not accept the fact that Conor women are exceptions. We lose our babies easily – I never did bring a child of my body to term. There are other lines just as delicate, like the Soolays and the Calpapers, and it's always a struggle to keep their youngsters slowed down so they don't miscarry.

'You, however, are as normal as they come, and you could say that that baby kept you alive out there.'

'Funny. I was going to try to kill her,' Alldera mused, but then she saw by Nenisi's face that she had said something terrible, and she steered hastily for safer waters: 'How did you keep me asleep for so long?'

'Asleep,' Nenisi murmured. 'Yes, I suppose you're not really wide awake yet, are you? You'll soon find your balance. All we use is medicine made from plants and soothing talk. We were even able to coax you into moving about in your sleep, to keep your body healthy and fit to bear.

'While you were lying there dozing and healing yourself, your senses were taking in a lot of what was going on around you – us, the way we live, the way we talk. Not everything will be completely strange to you.'

I love the way you talk, Alldera thought. Nenisi's speech was little different from Holdfastish, but she drew everything out with a singing drawl, nudging in extra syllables, lilting up and down the scale. Alldera did not want to break into that music with the hard-edged, barking speech of the Holdfast. Keep silence, she thought; listen and learn.

'I want you to understand,' Nenisi went on, 'you're to rest, take your time, not worry. Don't fret about your baby; women are trampling all over each other trying to take the best care of her that any baby of this camp has ever had. You have family here.'

Family, kindred; suddenly Alldera was afraid. Perhaps they took her for something other than what she was, to give her such unreserved welcome, warmth in which her bones and sinews seemed to be dissolving. When the mistake was discovered they might turn on her –

'Who are you?' she whispered. 'Why do you care?'

'We're the Riding Women, the women of these plains –'

There came the sound of running steps, very light and swift, and a high babble of voices. Then the tent was full of moving figures, small, naked, and filthy, jostling and pressing close to Alldera as they passed her.

They were a skinny, grimy mob. Their matted hair bounced on their shoulders as they spun away in a swirl of shouts and high-pitched laughter, and they flowed back out of the tent. They brushed past an adult figure in the doorway and were gone.

The newcomer, a sharp-featured woman, ducked inside. Alldera thought she knew that predatory face from her tumbled, nightmare memories of the journey through the desert to the plains.

'No wonder the childpack is running away,' commented the woman. 'That slave is uglier awake than she was asleep.'

Nenisi's chin lifted, giving her an armed and guarded look. 'The childpack is looking for all the excitement and feasting that surrounds a new baby, as you know very well, Sheel. They didn't find that here, so they left. And Alldera is not a slave. Where there are no masters, no one can be a slave.'

The sharp-faced woman moved silently on naked, sinewy feet. She wore trousers and a cloth looped around her neck and crossed over her breasts to tie in the back. She took up a wooden bowl and filled it with white liquid from a bag hanging on a pole.

'Fems are so fitted to slavery that they'll find masters wherever they go. Be careful this one doesn't turn you into her master, Nenisi.' She drank.

Nenisi sighed and said to Alldera with exaggerated regret, 'This is Sheel Torrinor. Good manners are not among the Torrinor traits. Like me, Sheel is your family. I hope you can stand her.'

'You don't mind being a fem's sharemother,' the newcomer said, ignoring the black woman's bantering tone. 'I hate it.'

Alldera did not dare to say anything. She was relieved when Sheel Torrinor walked out, bowl in hand.

And yet, there had been something bracing about her attitude. Under Sheel's cold dislike, the helpless, melting feeling of being more beholden than any human being could bear had receded and ceased to overwhelm Alldera. Enmity from an icy bitch was something she understood from the Holdfast, where she had known boss fems like that: ruthless but effective overseers, most of them. Sheel's contempt had yanked her roughly back into reality.

She was an escaped fem taken in by a strange, marvelous people, befriended by a black person whose teeth hurt, rejected by another stranger as slim and hard-looking as a knife.

'I'm sorry she's so rude,' Nenisi said.

'But she's part of my "family"?' Alldera ventured cautiously. 'What's a "sharemother"?'

'One who shares the mothering of your child with you. I'm one of your sharemothers. Sheel, unfortunately perhaps, is another.'

'But why should she be, if she doesn't want to?'

'Good reasons.'

'I'd rather not have her forced to –'

'Don't worry about her. She'll do what's right, however ungracefully,' Nenisi said; and she talked of other things.

Four women inhabited 'Holdfaster Tent' with Alldera as her family of sharemothers. When they came in to eat and talk that evening, they seemed to bring with them the spirits of a hundred other women whom they had spoken to or heard about or seen doing this or that during the day. All of that was laid out in conversation during the long, hot twilight over pots and pots of the bitter drink they called tea.

The mounts on which women had ridden home to the tent were tethered outside for the night. Alldera heard the horses snuffling at the ground, sighing and groaning like humans, talking briefly to each other in their peculiar voices. She shivered at their strangeness; there had been no animals at all in the Holdfast.

Of all the voices in the tent Nenisi's was the most supple, a rich and rippling contralto which she seemed able to turn reedy or plummy by turns, like a musical instrument. She made the others laugh a lot. They did not keep the small, smelly fire going after sundown, and when Nenisi's dark skin vanished into the gloom she became a sort of invisible spirit with a playful voice.

Sheel sat across from Alldera. She had a narrow jaw and her front teeth projected so that she had to hold her lips closed over them. The strong muscles around her mouth gave her face a sculpted, rapacious look.

She did not speak to Alldera.

There was a woman called Shayeen, visible by the fire's embers as a shining being of smooth, red-brown metal, black hair that looked oiled, and a gleam of bright metal at wrist and throat. She spoke rarely, and then mainly of games and contests, wins and losses, in the past and to come. Twice she asked Alldera polite questions without real meaning beyond perhaps the wish to acknowledge her presence.

The fourth woman of the family sat on Alldera's other side and nursed the cub. She kept stroking the top of its fuzzy head with her big, square, chap-knuckled hands. Her name was Barvaran, and she was squat and coarse-looking. There was dirt in the creases of her skin, as there had been when she had first leaned over Alldera after capturing her back in the desert. The others reeked of horses and sweaty leather, but Barvaran smelled strongly of herself.

Alldera wanted to edge away from her. She had known labor fems as ungainly and unlovely as this back in the Holdfast. The drudges of that world, they had been too dull to be anything better and had been saved from extinction only by the strength of their thick backs.

Though Barvaran seemed to have no nursing cub of her own she did have milk, as indeed they all did. The sharemothers passed the cub around for a suckle at each one's breast before unrolling their bedding for the night. Milk, they said, came easily to them, and nursing was something Alldera would seldom have to do. She was relieved, for to her it was simply a boring, immobilizing job.

Outside she heard the sounds of horses and somewhere not far distant the high chatter of the childpack moving closer and farther, closer and farther, and finally stopping.

She woke with a full bladder and blundered about in the darkness looking for a pot, or failing that the entryway so that she could step outside to relieve herself. She was slowed by her weakness after the cub's birth.

One of the women got up, handed off the cub – which she had kept sleeping with her – to someone else, and guided Alldera out. It was, Alldera guessed by the scent and bulk of her, Barvaran, who led her past the edge of the camp to a sandy gully that she called 'the squats'. Alldera crouched, wincing, in the dry watercourse. The rawness of her vagina made urination an ordeal.

The sky was beginning to pale. As they made their way back among the closed tents, Barvaran said, 'You'll get used to drinking tea after a while and it won't wake you so early any more. Camp is nice now, isn't it – quiet and tidy-looking.'

In this thin light and with her clangorous voice toned down out of mercy for the sleep of others, Barvaran seemed quite different: warmly sympathetic, manner a little shy, an honest soul sunk in a crude and odorous frame.

Alldera almost walked into the childpack. Heaped together, their skinny limbs asprawl, they lay snoring and snuffling under the wide fly of one of the tents. Repelled, she retreated a step, jostling Barvaran.

'You'll get used to them, too,' Barvaran said. 'I know it's not much like your country here.'

The truth was that, like Barvaran herself, the childpack was all too much like something from the Holdfast. The pack reminded Alldera of a batch of very young fems in one of the wide, deep pits where fem kits were kept between the time they were weaned and the time they were taken for training. She thought of her own life in the pits, bitter with hunger and struggles against others just as hungry, and of a time she had spent immobilized in her own filth by illness while her companions ate up all the scant ration thrown down to them by the men . . .

These camp children did not seem hungry, only dirty and wild, and Barvaran herself seemed not alien and forbidding but familiar. Alldera said hesitantly, 'Barvaran, can I ask you – how do you have children, without men?'

'Oh,' Barvaran said, 'we mate with our horses.'

Shocked with embarrassment, Alldera felt her own cheeks heat. Clearly she had asked an improper question and had been turned with a crude joke about those monster-like beasts. She would not ask again.

The other question, the necessary question, haunted her, dammed in by timidity and a feeling that it would be somehow absurd and insulting to ask it. Finally it broke clumsily out of her one day when she found herself alone with Nenisi, who was hunched under one of the tent flies straightening bent arrow shafts over a small fire. Finding Nenisi by herself was not easy, and Alldera leaped at the opportunity without thinking.

'Will you help us?' she said.

Nenisi looked up at her.

Alldera rushed on, stammering, 'I wasn't just running away, I was sent to find help in the Wild, some hope – I didn't think there really was anyone, and I'd given up and was just trying to save myself, but now – you – the other fems still enslaved back there –'

'There is no help,' Nenisi said. She sighted down the arrow in her hand. 'It was decided long ago that we women would never risk the free world of our children by invading the Holdfast for the fems' sakes. We all agreed.'

'I see.' Beneath her numbness Alldera felt feeling stir.

'Besides, it's too late. No one, man or fem, has come out of the east in months; not since we found you, in fact. We think they're all dead —'

'Yes, I understand,' Alldera insisted. That was what she had sensed herself, alone in the borderlands. That was what she had wanted to hear. She turned away to hide the horror of her feelings: the dark surge of grief for her lost people was shot through with the joy of being truly free of them at last.

At first she reveled at the sight of female people running their own lives without so much as a scent of men about them; even the several very pregnant women seemed sturdy and capable and utterly unworried by their vulnerable condition.

Her jubilation receded as the hot, dry weeks wore on. She was invaded by weariness, depressed for days at a time by her undeserved survival into freedom and by the conviction that she would never learn to manage all the newness surrounding her. Loneliness assailed her. She longed sometimes to caress Shayeen's glowing skin, and often caught herself staring at the sculpted beauty of Nenisi's long dark face. The conviction of her own unworthiness turned her desires back on herself. She did not dare approach these women, except in her dreams.

The blazing afternoon skies began to fill with clouds each day now, and the women stood outside watching in the heat. Four dry months almost behind them, they said; four rainy months coming, then four cool months after that, making up the year. The Dusty Season was about to end.

One afternoon it rained not at the camp but a distance to the south. Alldera could see the clouds trailing sweeps of rain past the horizon.

The camp sprang into motion, shaking her sharply out of her lethargy. In a riot of shouting and laughter the women brought all thirty tents of Stone Dancing Camp down in the middle of the day. Alldera stood aside with the cub slung warm against her back, and she watched Holdfaster Tent reduced swiftly to leather and rope, all stowed away in capacious saddle packs. The tent poles were hitched in bundles alongside the flanks of a brown horse, the butt ends trailing on the ground.

Every tent was similarly transformed into a dozen laden pack ponies. Everywhere were horses, their noise, their smell, their bulky powerful bodies moving in the dust they raised. One round-bellied animal exploded twice out of the hands of its packer and was rapidly reloaded each time. Alldera was terrified of being trampled or kicked by a horse that she would not see until too late.

She watched Shayeen, covered in dust, first tugging a cinch strap with both hands, then slugging the pony in the flank with her fist so that it gasped out its deeply held breath and the buckle on the cinch could be closed.

To Alldera's immense relief no one suggested putting her on top of a horse. She half lay, half sat on a sled of heavy leather slung between the tent poles out of reach of the brown horse's heels. Cub in lap, she rode the jouncing progress of the pole-butts. The brown horse, urged on by Nenisi on a spotted mount, led a string of others from the emptying campground. Around Alldera groups of horses plodded in the charge of other mounted figures. She saw the child-pack darting among them and heard the children's shrieks of excitement.

The whole crowd of mounted women and pack horses descended from the low ridge on which they had been camped. As they poured down onto the salt flat below, the group shook itself into a crowd of mixed riders and pack animals surrounded by a wide ring of scouts. Within this circle of outriders the childpack ranged freely.

Alldera recalled something Nenisi had told her of another creature of the plains, one Alldera had not yet seen: a low running beast furred in all the colors of the plains. The women hunted these 'sharu' and wore their skins and ornaments made of their curved claws and teeth. The sharu ate anything, from grass and seeds to meat. That was why the childpack, which wandered at will all day, slept every night within the perimeter of the camp. She guessed that that was also why they ranged today inside the ring of scouts.

This gave her a very secure feeling. She knew herself to be something of a child herself here, carried along while everyone else rode.

Discomfited by the idea of Sheel seeing her in just that way, she asked where the rest of the family was. Nenisi pointed across the moving crowd at one of the scouts on the far side: 'That's Sheel.' Then she waved in the direction of the long, low curtain of dust drifting ahead of them well to the left. 'The others are helping to move the herds.

'Pass our daughter up here to me – the air is fresher, and the sooner she gets the feel of a horse's back the better.'

Despite the miasma of heat and dust surrounding them the women talked and laughed as they traveled toward where they had seen the rain. Nenisi threw her head back once and sang part of a song about how when they got to the new campsite the grass would already be up.

A pack horse up ahead got kicked by another and broke away squealing. The childpack swarmed after, getting in the way of the rider in charge of the pack string. The rider laughed and snapped her rein ends above their heads in mock threat.

Alldera's mouth tasted of earth; yet their exuberance was catching, and her heart beat fast. 'Everyone's in such good spirits,' she said, wanting to show that she felt it too, but shy of intruding on a joy that she did not understand.

'Of course,' Nenisi answered, 'the rain frees us from our wells, you see. Now we can freely travel our country again.'

Alldera bent her head; the sense of their freedom had taken her by the throat. They could move where they liked. The physical fact of their liberty as she felt it at that moment, drowning in dust, bumping along at the brown mare's heels, made her weep.

Sometime that night they stopped; the rising sun showed among the rough circle of freshly raised tents a scatter of thin green grass on the damp earth.

After that, Alldera began to fit into the women's life.

4

Daya leaned her back against Kenoma's long-muscled leg and watched the flames. The angry talk drifted over her and into the surrounding night.

The free fem crew was gathered at the tailgate of their wagon where a tall fire burned. They kept their backs turned to the dim shapes of the Marish camp called Windgrass some distance away, dark and silent tents against the stars. They cursed the Mares and everything Marish, as free fems did after a day of trading with them.

Daya stopped listening. She was bored with their sniping and thought ridiculous the rumors of a new fem hidden somewhere in the Mares' camps. She relaxed into the pleasure of being enfolded in the enormous spaces of the sky and the land, for already this crew were on their way back to the tea camp in the foothills. Their trade journey over the plains was nearly ended, and she was sorry.

She loved it out here. She loved to be one of the many points of living warmth that peopled the vast darkness over the Grasslands. She loved the grit of the soil under her thighs and palms, the glimmer of firelight on the yellow stubble beyond the edges of the camp, the evening stir of air as the day's heat drifted starward. She felt her thoughts flowing out over the tableland. She pictured horses dozing or listening with upswung heads for a rustle in the grass; and the wide-flung camps of the Mares, groups of broad-winged tents herding loosely together in drowsy silence; and the hungry sharu sleeping in their networks of burrows; and of course all the free fems, radiating outward crew by crew across the great expanse from one Marish camp to another. She loved this life at least as much as she loved life in the tea camp in the hills.

Of course there were risks, difficulties, irritations in living anywhere. Daya had been a pet, bred for the pleasure of men's eyes as well as other pleasures. Despite the scars that marred her beauty now, she was still young, small and slender enough to be attractive even when she had no wish to attract. She did not enjoy being fought over by other free fems, so she took pains to acquire a companion like Kenoma whose truculence discouraged ardor in others. But jealousy inclined Kenoma to turn her banked violence on Daya at the smallest provocation.

Right now by the fire Daya could feel the tension in Kenoma's thigh drawing tighter, promising release in a scene, perhaps a thrashing, later on. Kenoma was only safe for a short while longer; the risks of staying at her side were beginning to outweigh the advantages of her companionship.

Daya did not want to worry about that now. She held the sweetness of the brush smoke deep in the chambers of her nostrils. She felt Kenoma stir and tauten, and heard her say harshly, 'This is the last fem they've brought out, maybe the last one they ever will bring out. She's ours.'

How annoying, how foolish, Daya thought. What does it mean even to say 'last'? Time was different here. Life did not rush from crisis to crisis and turn instantly into some new and dangerous course at a master's whim, as it had in the Holdfast. There were different rhythms in the Grasslands, long and slow and repetitive. Nothing came in 'firsts' and 'lasts' here, but as 'another' or 'again'. The Grasslands was like a great disc of earth revolving endlessly under the great disc of sky and season. They should not talk of a new fem as if she were unique, as if she were capable of making a difference to the wide wheeling patterns of these plains.

Yet this new fem's long stay with the Mares had touched the free fems' imaginations: 'Maybe she brings a message the Mares don't want us to have.' 'Maybe the men are preparing an invasion, and the Mares are keeping her with them to get information out of her.' 'No, it's the Mares that are preparing an invasion, so they're pumping her all about the Holdfast first.'

Daya was handed a bowl of beer to drink and she let her fingers slip along the hand of the giver. Kenoma noticed, slapped the bowl out of her hand, and kicked the other fem so that she nearly fell into the fire. Sandaled feet scattered the coals as fems jumped up, cursing, ready for a fight but amused too; Daya was famous for her amours and the problems they brought her.

She dodged and evaded Kenoma's angry blows, and seeing that the big fem had taken off her sandals earlier to ease her feet, managed to draw her to the scattered fire. Everyone roared with laughter to see Kenoma bellowing and hopping on first one foot and then the other.

'A story,' Daya cried, holding up her hands in mock terror as Kenoma, limping, closed in on her. 'A story, in exchange for peace! Let me tell you how it is that this poor pet fem became marked goods, too ruined to be worth your anger, Kenoma.'

Daya was a favorite storyteller among the free fems, and it made no difference that they all knew the story she proposed to tell. This crew had all been labor fems of one sort or another in the Holdfast, regarding pets like Daya as pampered traitors. They loved any tale told and retold of the haughty brought low. Under their urging, Kenoma's fury gave way to sullen acquiescence.

'There I was,' Daya began, 'fresh from my training in Bayo, up for the bidding on the steps of the Boardmen's Hall in the City.' She sprang up, she paraded before them, moving in the sinuous, exaggerated style of a highly trained pet fem. Languorously she blinked at them as if they were men come to buy.

She told the drama of the bidding to be her master and of how a man of the blues named Kazzaro had bought her. She imitated her master Kazzaro's high-shouldered, nervous posture and showed them how he fretted about his clothing and patted his spreading bald spot. He had been clean, decent-looking, and relatively rich, and she had counted herself fortunate. 'He had the eye of a man who sees a fem for her sex, not just her decorative and useful qualities. I knew I could make him itch for me no matter how he might hate himself for it. He was the sort of man who has young men hanging on him for favors in return for their love, but who watches the serving fems and then looks away, ashamed of his interest in mere females. You can tell that I was young, because it never occurred to me that such a man would already have a pretty fem or two dancing attendance on him.'

She told of his house, the magnificence of the tiled walls, the floors cushioned in thick carpets of heavy hemp dyed vibrant blues and greens. Enthralled, nodding, murmuring, the free fems drank in details of carved wooden shutters, painted roof beams, rich glazes and luxurious pillows, sweet scents wafting on the warm air. The more she embellished, the better they liked it. She added a tinkling mobile of metal chips, and a display of Kazzaro's prize collection of small ceramic figures used in the game of Tail.

'I was young and naive, but not so naive that I showed him how impressed I was by all this opulence. I walked like this behind him, as cool as if I had been raised in such surroundings instead of in the shitty, stinking straw of the kit pits.

'But how my heart thundered, how I longed to be alone so that I could touch all those luxurious things!

'He opened the door behind the metal gate to the fem quarters. There was another pet fem, lying there on a couch and watching the small fire.' Daya let her fingers crook into claws and curled her lips back from her teeth in a snarl. 'Does the world hold anything more cruel than the jealousy of a pet fem for her place?

'I thought, I can hold my own here. The other fem was not young, and her beauty – clearly wonderful once – had faded.'

She told how Kazzaro had taken her over to the couch too, so that at first Daya had thought, he wishes us to do sex together before him. She had been taught how to do this for a master's entertainment, but she could not help being nervous the first time she was called on to actually perform.

She told how slowly, through misunderstanding and confusion, she had come to realize that Kazzaro was captivated by the older fem, Merika; that he was so besotted with her that he kept her shut up for safekeeping. He feared that some older man would see her, want her, and take her from him.

Merika was prey to the suicidal melancholy that often strikes a beauty as age advances. She dreaded the day when her master would realize that she was losing her looks. She needed companionship, that was Kazzaro's reading of her state, and so he had bought her Daya.

Daya and Merika became lovers, being closed in each other's company and finding each other's character congenial.

'I was young, sure of myself, and credulous. Did I realize how it affected the aging pet when our master noted the pleasure of his guests when he lent me to them in Merika's place? On the other hand, it pleased her that I replaced her monthly in the breeding rooms. Kazzaro could not bear to send her there. Did I see the satisfaction on her face when I was swollen with pregnancy? Did I understand why she kept plying me with the richest titbits of her own food, I who was as slim as a boy and so doubly fetching to our master? He was a man, after all, with a man's natural interest in his own sex and a proper male lover named Charkin. In me he could have male and female beauty both at once, while Merika grew softer and rounder and plumper all the time, for want of exercise and because of her age.'

Inevitably, Merika's fear of losing her privileged place overcame her desire for Daya's company.

'You all know,' Daya said, making her eyes mournful, 'the treachery of pet fems toward each other. Hear now how Merika treated me!'

Meticulously she set the scene of the private appointment of Kazzaro and Charkin at Kazzaro's house: the careful cleaning of the room, its decoration with magnificent hangings, the day-long preparation of special dishes in the kitchens below, Kazzaro's meditations on his wardrobe and what scents to wear.

For Charkin, his own chief lover, he liked to have Merika and his other pets come and serve the food. It was an extravagant use of slaves trained in more rarified arts, and this amused him. He had to be able to show Merika off sometimes to get the full value of owning her. So the two pets had enjoyed the privilege of attending his guest.

The evening had gone ill from the beginning. Charkin was nasty and ambitious by nature even for a man. He argued that Kazzaro could be a greater patron still if he would stop spending all his wealth on pets. Then he would be able to buy a bigger house and support many more young men – and Charkin would of course be the first and highest among them.

The free fems watched eagerly as Daya mimicked first one man's voice and manner, then the other's. She shifted to Merika's stealthy doings down in the serving pantry. Merika had carefully broken the best serving dipper across the bowl and stuck it back together with a thin coat of glue.

Later, when Daya ladled up a portion of hot food for the guest,

Merika had only to knock the edge of the stew bowl against the dipper, and the heated glue gave way. The dipper split, slopping blue stew all over Charkin.

'He let out a roar, Merika shrieked and bolted, and I was left standing there too startled to move. Charkin snatched up a broiling spit that he'd just eaten clean. He lunged and drove it through my face from one side to the other! I felt it tear my cheeks and smash two teeth, and my mouth filled up with blood.'

The free fems sighed, half horrified, half satisfied.

The skewer had not been hot enough to make clean wounds. They festered. Kazzaro sent Daya down to work in Blue Company's kitchen where she could learn to handle food utensils more carefully and where, more important, he would not have to look at her. The fems around the wagon savored the part that followed, the tale of a pet fem set down in their sort of world. They nodded and commented while she rounded out the story.

'To my surprise, I liked it in the kitchens. It was always warm, and there wasn't anything like the rivalry I'd seen in the pet quarters. The men overseeing the kitchens were young, and the older men kept them hungry. What we fems did didn't matter as long as we weren't caught stealing food. The overseers themselves stole food all the time, but we were better thieves than they were. I enjoyed learning to cook, too, for it's a great art.

'But have you ever heard of a pet fem without enemies?' She spoke of how certain kitchen fems had maneuvered to get her into difficulties with their boss fem by making Daya look like a troublemaker. Any time fems fought out their private quarrels, Daya's enemies said her flirting had provoked the fighting. The boss fem could not afford to have a demoted pet fem full of spite making problems in her crew, or all would suffer. So she got Daya slated for transfer to the brickyards. Faced with having to try to fit herself in among yet another set of labor fems there, Daya preferred the risks of the Wild. It was at that point that she had made her run for the border – another story.

She never pointed out that here among the free fems of the Grasslands she found herself once more a pet among labor fems. She kept that joke to herself.

'So she won, this Merika, your rival,' Kenoma sneered. 'She drove you out.'

Daya raked the scattered coals together with a stick. 'You could say so. Once afterward we talked about it briefly, and she told me that she hadn't planned anything so drastic – just a beating for me and demotion to some position less close to Kazzaro.'

Kenoma snorted with disbelief. 'She said that because she was scared otherwise you'd poison her food in the kitchens.'

No one wanted to follow that up. Now that the appetite for drama was sated, their mood drifted into reminiscence. One older fem, who was picking up glowing fragments of the fire in her calloused fingers and tossing them back into the hot center of the flames, shook her head and said softly, 'I worked in kitchens all my life there. We knew how to mount a real feast of cooking in those days, none of your sketchy little campfires and pots of stewed greens – no offense to our fine cook!'

Daya nodded graciously.

'Why, I remember, when we set up to feed some high Boardmen,' the old fem continued, 'in the house of Boardman Kun; we started with sixteen different kinds of waterweeds –'

Daya leaned back against the tall wheel of the wagon, listening, secure for the evening.

5

Alldera sat knotting the dry fibres spread on her knee into a menstrual plug. She could not yet turn out dozens of them during a conversation without looking down at her work, as the women did; but she could make enough for her own needs. There was no water to spare during the dry, dusty weather to wash out a fem-style bleeding rag.

She looked up now and again at Sheel, who nursed the cub and helped Nenisi cook – so strange to see that soft round cub head against Sheel's conical breast.

The two sharemothers talked as women talked whenever there was time: of horses, water, grass and weather, but most often of their kindred. Alldera loved to listen and took pride in being able to follow more and more all the time. Tangled skeins of events were unrolled, like the history which pitted a wealthy cousin of Shayeen in what seemed eternal enmity against someone of the Faller tent. This naturally involved Sheel because of a sister of hers who was a sharemother in that tent. Dozens of women were mixed up in the quarrel, including women of other camps.

Shayeen had her enemies, Nenisi had hers, and Sheel had many. Even Barvaran was entangled in some huge row of years' standing which appeared to turn on horses used in payment of a debt and the different valuations placed on those horses by at least six sides in the dispute.

No one ever asked Alldera about the Holdfast, and she was glad; that life seemed to her to have been infinitely inferior to the women's lives here, and she would have been embarrassed to speak of it. Besides, as a slave she had never been free to speak except on command, and she was still shy.

Two riders passed by the open front of the tent, turned to shout questions. Answers came from other tents, and the two riders came back again and stopped. Sheel and Nenisi jumped up and ran out to embrace the newcomers as they dismounted, talking, patting and stroking them in the way the women had.

Watching, Alldera thought enviously that they did not know what it was to be always at the mercy of men's hands.

One of the visitors was old, brown-skinned, gray-haired, well-wrinkled. She limped badly. The other might have been Nenisi, except that Nenisi already stood there. This visitor was slender, black-skinned, with the same smooth-featured, mobile face, the same hands flashing pale palms as she talked.

Alldera was beginning to get used to the way these people appeared sometimes in identical pairs, trios, or even more. At first she had thought it a powerful magic, for in the Holdfast twins were a sign of witchery and were killed at birth with their dam. Here, Nenisi had told her patiently many times over, there were whole strings of blood relations called 'Motherlines', women who looked like older and younger versions of each other. They were mothers and daughters, sisters and the daughters of sisters. Nenisi said the look-alikes did not live together but were scattered through the tents of this camp and other camps.

The dark woman standing like Nenisi's living shadow was a Conor from another camp, a woman whose teeth must also be prone to ache when she was anxious, as Nenisi's did. Alldera had heard Nenisi grinding her teeth in her sleep; this woman must grind hers, too.

Nenisi drew her double into the tent by the hand. 'This is the child of my sister, cousin Marisu Conor from Windgrass Camp; and this is Jesselee Morrowtrow, one of Sheel's mothers.'

The old woman studied Alldera, head to one side, not speaking. Sheel took her by the hands, called her 'Heart-mother', and seated her near the fire with her back half-turned to Alldera.

'At the last Gather when I asked where you were,' Sheel said to her mother, 'they told me that a horse had kicked you while you were doctoring her. I thought it would be healed up by now. Live around horses, you'll limp half your life.'

'Don't believe everything you hear,' the old woman said. 'A crocodile bit me.'

'Nenisi, what's a crocodile?' Alldera whispered. She feared for a moment that she had asked the wrong Conor cousin, but then she saw Nenisi's blue necklace and was reassured. She did not often make such errors any more.

'A joke,' Nenisi murmured, 'though they do say such Ancient creatures still live, far to the south where the plain turns to forest and marsh.'

'A crocodile!' Sheel marveled. 'Like the one whose skin you showed me once when I was little – only that turned out to be a sheet of bark stripped from a fresh tent pole.'

Unperturbed, Jesselee continued, 'There I was, prowling the shoreline marshes by the Salty River. I'd dreamed of one of the drowned cities of the Ancients, and I thought that meant that some treasure would be washed up for me. Instead here comes this knobby dark form, floating silently nearer and nearer –'

'And it gobbled you up,' said Marisu Conor, snapping her teeth loudly together. They all laughed, Sheel loudest of all.

Imagine, being so easy and happy with a grown woman who had suckled you and with whom your relations stretched back through your entire life! It was wonderful to bask on the edge of the ease the women had with each other, the rich connectedness.

They showed Jesselee the cub, which went into one of its fits of sudden activity and nearly blacked the old woman's eye. She seemed pleased, laughing and commenting that it seemed to have plenty of spirit. She said she would be staying a while.

They talked about Salt Wind Camp where Sheel had grown up, way to the west. The winds which sometimes blew damply off the river had weakened her chest, Sheel said sadly, and had etched the cold into her bones, so that she seldom returned there. She said she could not forget the wind patterns on the water, though, or the whispering reeds along the water's edge. 'I used to play, as a child, that I was an invader from over the river or else a gallant defender of our camp. I didn't know in those days who the real intruder would be.'

She glared at Alldera, who had passed the point at which Sheel's unkindness could reduce her to tears. Alldera looked at Jesselee and said diffidently, 'I'm glad you'll stay with us, Jesselee. I think I know all my sharemothers' tales by now.'

Jesselee rubbed at her stiff knee and nodded. 'I'm sure I can recall some new ones to tell you. Even someone as close as one's heart-child always has something still to learn – a tale, a skill, some manners.'

Sheel bit her lip but said nothing, and Alldera felt filled with victory.

First you made sure that the long Rainy Season dampness had not made the tea moldy. Then you shaved it fine. Alldera had only been given the job of making the midday tea once before, and she had used water that was too hot and had had to sit by and watch the family members gulp down the bitter stuff anyway, because tea was too valuable to be wasted.

She leaned over her work, sat back again to shake the hair out of her eyes. Over the months her hair had grown out long and as healthy as it ever got, and she was always meaning to cut it shoulder length, the women's favorite style, and never getting around to it.

Unintentionally she caught the eye of a woman who was walking past, one arm slung companionably over the withers of a spotted mare that ambled beside her like a friend. The woman smiled. Alldera did not recognize her, but smiled timidly in return, and bent to her work again.

Concentrating on the tea making was hard. Behind her Barvaran and Shayeen were chatting together about childhood. Shayeen, seeding peppers for the array of kettles in front of her, complained intermittently about the stinging of her fingers. She had piles of fresh-picked peppers still to cut, for it was the Holdfaster Tent's turn to lay out food for the childpack today.

The children knew it and were gathered nearby, giggling and fighting around the edges of a huge puddle on the margins of which their feet slid and splashed. They pushed each other into it. A few of them squatted down to imitate the adults over make-believe fires of piled stones.

Barvaran kept an eye on them, stopping her conversation to shout warnings at them now and then. She was simmering milk and laying out the squeezed dregs from the pots in lumps to dry on the tent fly. The children were notorious thieves of whatever food they found lying around, perhaps because they were never punished.

Alldera braced the tea brick on her knee, watching a shaving curl away from her knife blade. The scent of cooking milk was making her mouth water. She had developed an inordinate fondness for the fragile plates of fresh cream cake that could be lifted from the surface of a cooled pan of simmered milk. The milking of mares in foal took much of everyone's time, and the whole camp lived on fresh milk these days. Alldera could not pick up the trick of seizing the small, waxy teat way up under a mare's leg, so she felt guilty about her appetite for the pale, sweet food.

Now: start with the cold water to moisten the shavings or it comes out too bitter. Enough cold, she hoped; then water from the hot kettle, but slowly, not too much, cold again right away so that not all the powerful taste would be leached out in the first steeping. That seemed good; the rising scent was mild and minty.

Barvaran was speaking with affectionate humor of a pack game that hinged on guessing whether a child who was 'it' had a finger in her nose or not by just listening to her talk in the dark. It was weird even now to think of these women as having once lived the life of the childpack and to think of the cub of Holdfaster Tent joining that life. She was growing fast. Alldera remembered how the leather sling had sagged against Nenisi's back this morning when the black woman had ridden out to the milking lines carrying the cub with her.

Barvaran and Shayeen talked of a wild dancing game played with the horses, of sleepy sex games, and – in a subdued manner – about harrying the unfit from the pack. Many died in their first pack year. When the children brought in one of their number who was ill to be tended by the adults, that child was generally discovered to have exceptional qualities.

With a rush of confidence Alldera decided to take the next step: the mixing of flour and water to make noodles, which the women put in their tea along with milk and salt, making it into a meal. She hoped no one would insist on helping.

They were too deep in talk. Shayeen was saying wistfully, 'You start to bleed, and the younger ones drive you out, and that's the end of the free life. There's no place to go but to the tents, where you remember women once carried you and nursed you and mopped your bottom. And sure enough, there they are, all waiting to make you into a proper woman with a name and a family.'

'Oh, it's a terrible time, I remember,' Barvaran agreed. 'There I was with blood running down my legs and a new smell of myself, all hateful and sour, in my nostrils. My pack mates had to beat me away. Somebody finally whacked me on the head with a horse bone, I still have the mark, look here. That did it.'

'Blood at both ends is a strong argument,' Shayeen said. 'Did you ever hear of a Maclaster child who ran with her camp's pack for almost seventeen years? Just would not start bleeding.'

'Some funny traits show up in that line sometimes.'

Sitting back, her work completed, Alldera suddenly noticed how cool the morning was once she was not bending over the heat of the tea fire. She tightened her breast wrap – by now she could adjust the knot behind her back by herself – and slipped her long leather shirt on over her head. She put on her headcloth and the rawhide crown that snugged it to her head, and stood up.

The pants that Barvaran had lent her fit fairly well, closing at the waist with a drawstring; but the legs had to be tugged down every once in a while because Alldera did not like to wear the soft boots that helped to anchor them. She had gone barefoot all her life.

She sheathed her knife and buckled on her belt. The women wore the knife sheathed at the small of the back, where the tip could not catch the thigh upraised to mount a horse. Alldera stayed clear of the horses and wore her knife at her hip. The horses' size and strength and impenetrable mixture of cunning and stupidity terrified her, and she still thought of the women's power over them as a kind of magic.

Someone called outside – Nenisi's voice. There she sat on her best bay mare, straight-backed and masterful, having left the cub with someone out at the milking lines. Hastily, Alldera poured out some tea and took it to her.

Nenisi did not drink. 'Look,' she said, and pointed with her chin, as the women often did.

Out beyond the tents a group approached on foot over the plains, hauling a wagon. The wind was blowing the wrong way. Alldera could barely hear the creaking of the wagon's wheels and only scraps of voices, though the group was at no great distance from Stone Dancing Camp.

She knew them at once for fems. They had a squat, stiff-jointed look about them, none of the suppleness of riders, and the silhouettes of their clothing reminded her unmistakably of Holdfastish dress. As they came closer she could make out the broad, shallow hats they wore and, instead of shirt and pants, smocks with skirts mid-thigh over bare legs. Some of them carried staffs in their hands or across their shoulders. Each staff was tipped with a glinting point.

Fems carrying weapons and traveling unmastered: a dream of her own people.

Flooded with a great sense of relief, of homecoming, Alldera dropped the tea pannikin and began to cry. Yet she did not want to run to greet them.

Barvaran, at her shoulder, said, 'Those are free fems, come to trade from their camp in the eastern hills. They'll go right to the chief tent; we have to get our trade goods together. You go ahead.' She patted Alldera awkwardly on the shoulder and joined Shayeen in rummaging inside the tent.

Reining close, Nenisi leaned toward Alldera. 'I have to ride out again. Alldera – if the free fems say anything that confuses you, I'll try to explain it later. It would be best if you didn't mention your child to them.'

Something was wrong; Alldera could feel Nenisi's anxiety, but she could not read its source. Nenisi galloped off.

Alldera walked slowly toward the chief tent, alone. She felt dizzy with excitement and apprehension.

Everyone crowded around outside the chief tent, many women laden with goods – piles of skins and hides, sacks and pouches of dried food. The fems had parked their wagon out of the camp. They made a procession to the chief tent, carrying loads balanced on their heads. Their heavy sandals scuffed the ground as they advanced. They had left their spears, but each one wore a hatchet looped to her belt. To Alldera they looked coarse and graceless, out of place here. Each of them chewed a wad in her cheek and spat brown juice.

The smocks they wore were of cloth, patterned with colors. As they walked the smocks swung, and the colors appeared to move. Suddenly, jarringly, Alldera saw how drearily brown the women and their surroundings were. Around her stretched the low plain with its yellowing grasses, under the wide tan sky. The camp itself was earth brown, leather brown, the various red and yellow and black browns of the women's hair and skin, and the colors of animal hides.

Why, the women were like their horses – as there were so many dun horses in the camp's herds, so many blacks, so many stripe-legged bays, so there were this many dark-skinned lines of women like the Conors and the Clarishes over there, so many lines with red hair, so many sallow women like those Tuluns bending over their stacked goods, hair like coal and bodies as narrow and muscular as the necks of horses. Grouped at the chief tent, they were like some woven design in which each broad, clear thread could be traced in the image of each Motherline, repeated from individual to individual and from generation to generation.

She shook her head and blinked, frightened by this vision and the distance it put between herself and the women.

One of the fems came forward and spoke with the Shawden chiefs. Then they all laid out their goods in rows before the tent. The women milled up and down the narrow aisles, picking up bricks of tea and sniffing them, shaking out coils of rope. The fems watched, tight-mouthed, sharp-eyed, and spoke only when they were asked questions.

Alldera was glad she had not run out to meet the wagon. She stayed at the outer edges of the crowd, peering at the newcomers. When they spoke she found their voices grating after the women's liquid speech. Their truculent attitude was evident in their glances, their asides to one another, the way they withdrew slightly to avoid contact with passing women. Their demeanor repelled her. She wanted – what? Certainly not these closed and suspicious faces.

She turned and wandered away among the tents to where the fems' wagon stood, outside the camp. Troubled, she drew nearer. Femmish leaders had designed her escape so that she might bring back a pledge of aid from free fems. Now here were real free fems; she felt off balance, flooded with guilt for her abandoned task.

She walked the length of the wagon, touching the bleached and weathered wood of its lower walls; it smelled of dust and tea and sweat. Suddenly it rocked under her hand. Someone jumped down from inside and looked around the end wall at her, then leaned back to speak tensely to a hidden companion. Another face appeared.

'That's no woman, that's a fem – look at the butt and legs on her, sprinter's muscle. You know these wild people never walk if they can ride, let alone run anywhere.'

'Then it's her,' said the long-faced one.

'She's young,' said the other, shaking back dark hair, eyes measuring Alldera from head to foot. 'Hey, don't they keep watch on you? Where's your guard?'

'I have no guard.' Alldera stood where she was, suddenly wary. The two had a predatory look.

'You mean you're not a prisoner? We came to rescue you, fem.'

It was too late to pretend that they were wrong, that she was a Riding Woman. 'No one's held me prisoner,' Alldera said. 'I live like the others here.' She realized that it would be a mistake to tell them she had not learned of their existence until today. She could picture their sneers at that, their knowing glances.

One said, 'Don't tell us you've just been living here contented as one of their stupid horses, ignoring your own people.' Their hatred of the women came off them like heat.

'Come on, what are you waiting for?' the long-faced one said. 'Get into the wagon, quick, while nobody sees. We'll go get a few others, haul off as if we were going to make an early camp for the night, and just keep on going. The rest will catch up. Then let those Mares come galloping after us and try to take you back!'

Alldera moved a few steps back toward the tents, alarmed by visions of blood and battle.

'Where are you going?' The black-haired one closed in on her.

Alldera glanced around for help, a witness, anything. She heard the long-faced fem say low-voiced to the other, 'Look at that, they must have bewitched her to keep her from us.'

Too late, Alldera bolted.

They sprang after her. A spear shaft thrust between her legs brought her down with a racking pain in her shin. She could not help it, she lay and hugged her leg, and they dropped their weapons and took hold of her, lifting her toward the wagon.

'You explain to Elnoa back at the tea camp,' the black-haired fem growled. 'We want to know why they've kept you from us, and everything you know about them. Nobody's lived among them as long as you have, we need your information.'

'You can't take me!' Alldera cried through tears of pain, as if in a nightmare that they meant to take her to their master. 'Let me stay —' A hard hand clamped over her mouth, cupped to avoid her teeth.

'Mare lover!' spat one of the fems.

As they wrestled her back against the tail of the wagon, trying to heave her inside, something jarred a cry from the one on her left. The other fem gasped and let go. Alldera twisted free. Sprawled on the ground, she heard the thump of blows, saw the frenetic figures of children leaping up from the tall grass to fling stones at the fems.

She looked up at the black-haired fem's angry face squinting at her from inside the wagon where the two of them had taken shelter. She heard the furious words: 'Come in here, curse you, while you have the chance! Come on, what is it, you like these horse-fuckers, these dirty, rag-tag savages that bathe in their own sweat, dirty beasts, cock-worshippers –'

The wagon rattled and shook with the impact of the childpack's missiles. The long-faced fem paused for breath. There was blood on her cheek and a bruise swelling where a stone had hit her.

'Have they gone and mated you to one of their stallions, then?' she cried. 'You got fucked by a horse and you like it, is that what's happened?'

Alldera got up and ran. The childpack raced past her, touching, laughing, and vanished.

Curled around her own misery and confusion, she lay in the tall grass on a rise outside the camp, watching from hiding until the free fems had packed up their goods and left. They moved the wagon out, pulling it in the midst of a ring of scouts like women moving camp. The scouts, on foot, did not go any great distance from the wagon, perhaps for fear of losing sight of one another behind a swell of ground.

From the rise Alldera listened to the sounds of evening descending on Stone Dancing Camp. As women lit their tea fires, voices spoke and laughed. Riders came home from settling the horses on night pasture. Each sang a personal song that identified her to the woman who met her with a bowl of food and who took from her the mounts she had brought to be tethered in camp for the night.

Alldera recognized Nenisi's self-song. She saw Nenisi ride in and give something to Barvaran: a bundle in a leather sling. That was what she had gone to do, then: take the child further out of camp while the free fems were there.

Alldera got up and limped down toward camp. Nenisi came out

on foot to meet her. They stood beyond the outermost tents in the dusk.

'Where have you been? I've been looking for you,' Nenisi said.

'They've gone. That's their fire, way over there.' A wasteful blaze.

'You look upset. What did they say to you?'

How many are there like them?' Alldera said.

'Maybe half a hundred, all free fems found by us in the borderlands, as you were found.'

So many, all this time. 'They said I was a prisoner here.'

'Sit down with me, let's talk. They themselves are the prisoners – not of us, but of the way things are. They say they wish to return to the Holdfast, invade it, save the fems there. They live in a camp of their own in the foothills and make preparations to go home. When they venture too far toward the Holdfast, our patrols turn them back. This makes them bitter against us.

'But anyone can see that it would be foolish of us to go and show ourselves to the men of the Holdfast or let the fems go back and speak of us there, when we've kept the secret of our existence from men for so long. Even if there are only a few men left – and many of us feel that – we have a right to protect ourselves; don't you think so?'

Alldera realized guiltily that she had accepted that desert, too, as she had accepted that the free fems were a myth. She said, 'You took me in among you; why not the free fems too?'

'You have a child here; kindred. The free fems aren't related to anyone.'

'Why didn't you tell me about them before?'

'Why would you need to know? We are your family. Anyway, you never asked.' A sigh of defeat. 'Maybe not telling you was a mistake.'

'How can they be so different that you can't take them in among you?'

'Their beginnings and ours differ,' Nenisi said. 'Around the onset of the Wasting that ruined the world of the Ancients, there was made a place called the lab, where the government men tried to find new weapons for their wars. We don't know just what they were looking for, but we think it was mind powers, the kind that later got called 'witchery'. The lab men – and lab women, who had learned to think like men – used females in their work, maybe because more of them had traces of the powers, maybe because it was easier to get them with so many men tied up in war.'

Alldera tore at the grass with her hands. 'Nenisi, is this going to be another tale of slavery?' What she wanted to say, and could not bring herself to say, was Why did you hide my cub, and why did they say you mate with horses – Barvaran had said that too, once.

'It's all right, this story has a happy ending,' Nenisi said softly. 'The lab men didn't want to have to work with all the traits of both a male and a female parent, so they fixed the women to make seed with a double set of traits. That way their offspring were daughters just like their mothers, and fertile – if they didn't die right away of bad traits in double doses.'

'I don't understand,' Alldera said. 'How could they do that?'

'Who knows?' Nenisi sounded a little impatient. 'No one denies that the men of those times were clever. It was the combination of their cleverness and their stupidity that caused the Wasting in the first place.

'Now, in the lab, the change of trait-doubling was bred into the daughters, to be passed on ever since.'

'To you.'

'Yes. The daughters got together and figured out how to use the men's information machines. They found out all about the Wasting, the wars and famines and plagues going on outside, and how the lab could be made self-sustaining if things outside collapsed completely. They laid plans of their own.

'They got the information machines to give a false alarm warning of an attack in the offing and ordering the lab men to rush off to the Refuges and save themselves. The lab men believed the orders; they knew the leaders were already hidden in Refuges made for themselves and their helpers, and the lab men had high ideas of their own importance. So off they went with great speed and excitement.'

She paused. Alldera thought, giving me time to take it in, treating me like some stupid hulk of a free fem. 'Tell me the rest, please,' she said, to show that she understood.

Nenisi cleared her throat. 'I'm used to talking about this with young girls just out of the pack. I hope it doesn't sound childish to you.

'Anyway, the first daughters sealed themselves up safely in the lab and using the information machines began to plan for after the

Wasting. They took the lab animals and tried to breed them to be ready to live outside when the world was clean again. A lot of animals were let out too soon and died. The sharu were bred up from some tiny animals the men had been using to find out about ferocity, and once let out they flourished – an unhappy surprise, but not bad in the long run. Sharu have their place too.'

Alldera had seen sharu tracks, the splintered bones of sharu kills, the torn-up areas which they had stripped even of grass roots in their voracity. They horrified her, and she could not imagine what sort of 'place' they could have.

'There were horses at the lab for making medicines with their blood. Some of the lab men had also kept good horses of their own in the lab stables. But the horses' chances were poor. They bred slowly, and they were delicate from living so many generations with humans to take care of them. The daughters made them tougher and faster-breeding without worrying about their looks, and the horses came out and flourished too – a happy surprise.'

'And what did they do for themselves, these great witches,' Alldera said, 'so that they could breed without men?'

'Not witches, but dedicated and intelligent women,' Nenisi continued carefully, almost formally. 'They perfected the changes the labs had bred into them so that no men were needed. Our seed, when ripe, will start growing without merging with male seed because it already has its full load of traits from the mother. The lab men used a certain fluid to start this growth. So do we.'

Simple and clean, compared to rape in the Holdfast. No wonder jealousy drove the free fems to slander. 'Nenisi, why do you keep me with you? I'm no more like you than those other fems are.'

'You brought us a live child. Only one other fem did that, and that child we couldn't save. Your child is alive; that makes you kin to us.'

Her slim fingers brushed Alldera's very lightly. 'We change little, do you understand? Some, of course: the Wasting left slow, strong poisons in the earth and water of the world. They sometimes alter a child from its mother's traits. We don't try to judge whether a change is good or not. The child survives the childpack or not, that's all. Sometimes a cousinline, even a whole Motherline, is lost. No new ones are gained, only variations of the old.'

'Then my cub –'

'New seed, new traits, the beginning of the first new Motherline since our ancestors came out of the lab. That's how important your child is to us. My ancestor, a woman almost exactly like me, stepped out of the lab and lived, and now though she's generations dead there are many of us Conors. So it will be for your child's blood descendants.'

She sounded moved by what she said, and still she was blind to how every word she spoke folded in Alldera's child but shut out Alldera herself. Alldera turned on her in the darkness: 'But it's a Holdfastish cub, with dam and father! How can it be like you? You're raising a free fem among you, that's all.'

'No, we don't think so. When you came to us, that child was still forming inside you. We made you sleep to rest and strengthen you both. We fed you the milk of our breasts and the food chewed in our mouths, the food of Motherlines that we feed our babies. We fed your child, through your blood while she was still in your womb. We think she's become like our own children. We still feed her - that's why we do all her nursing. You see how healthily she grows, how fast, just like other babies here. We don't have our forebears' wisdom or the wonders of the lab to change her to be like us, but we've tried to do it with what we have.'

'So you hid her from the free fems.' Why did that make Alldera uncomfortable? The women had saved the cub's life, they had fed it their food, they had made it theirs.

Nenisi said, 'What sort of life would she have among a dying race?'

'Well, what life will she have with you if she turns out to be barren without men, like the free fems?'

Nenisi answered quickly, 'It would still be better. There are those among us who have no children, out of necessity or by choice. They still have relatives, sharedaughters, kindred. Do you see? Does that satisfy you?'

Alldera could not explain without sounding selfish and ungrateful; if she had known about the free fems sooner, she would have had a chance to consider the cub's future as if there were choices to be made about it. The women had not kept the free fems' existence secret from her, exactly; their plans as Nenisi outlined them were clearly good ones, probably the best choice that could have been made anyway. Alldera saw no way to voice her unease, nor even exactly what there was to object to.

Nenisi got up. 'Come to the tent soon, there are sharu wandering tonight.' She left.

The stars threw a dim light by which Alldera could dimly see the wide tents. The fems' wagon was invisible. Their fire had gone out. It was true, she thought, their road came from destruction and led to destruction, and if she found herself fortunate enough to be on another path, why turn back? She reminded herself of the prime lesson of a slave's life: protect youself, be selfish.

Next morning she put on her belt with the knife sheathed in back and she said, 'Nenisi, will you teach me to ride?'

Nenisi grinned. 'I was afraid you'd never ask.'

Alldera, responsible today for raking out horse dung to dry into usable fuel, was late to the chief tent and had to sit outside with the overflow. They were debating not the usual personal complaints beyond the abilities of the families and Motherlines to settle, but a diplomatic matter: whether or not to accept the offer of some grazing rights from neighboring Red Sand Camp. Women feared that Red Sand would come around later – as they had done to another camp in the past – and say the grass had been a loan, and demand repayment. In such a discussion Nenisi Conor would surely speak.

The tea bowl was handed round; Alldera sipped and passed it on. Listening was thirsty work. Sometimes she thought the Shawdens were chiefs because they could afford to serve endless rounds of tea to half the camp day after day. It was certainly not because they took the lead in anything.

The slow, oblique movement of debate was mesmerizing. She remembered the way the men – and fems, imitating men – had decided things, quickly, by command. Here, anyone with something to say could speak, which made for long hours of exhaustion or entertainment, depending on the interest of a given case. Their ease at speaking their minds still awed her. She sometimes spoke herself now, of grass and horses, over the evening tea fire; she sought to share their free flow of conversation.

She nibbled at a callus that had formed on her hand from the pressure of the rein. Many months' work had made her a decent rider, but she was not yet familiar enough with horses to make one lie down and doze, like that Faller woman over there, so that she could curl up against its flank and stay warm. Never mind, by midday the sun would strengthen and they would all be shedding headcloths, shirts, breast wraps.

At last Nenisi arose. No one interrupted as her calm, reasonable voice recounted the history of feeling between both camps. She said, 'Sharu have ravaged our northern pasture. What will you do when you hear your horses wandering and calling in hunger at night in the Dusty Season? Our friends and sisters and cousins, our daughters and mothers in the Red Camp say, take this gift of grass.

'Now, is Red Sand Camp the same this season as the Red Sand that broke down the walls of new wells sunk by Steep Cloud Camp because those wells were too close to Red Sand grass? Or is it the same as the Red Sand that gave forty horses to Salt Wind Camp the year that poison grass wiped out half of Salt Wind's herds?

'There are new families in Red Sand since both those times. How many here have sisters and other close kin now in Red Sand Camp that did not have them there five years ago; two years ago; last year? A woman is constant in her actions through her life according to her traits until at last she dies. But a camp changes all the time as its women come and go, and it lives forever.'

When she drew her headcloth about her and sat down again, no one applauded. But speaker after speaker got up and gave another version of what she had said, until those opposed to accepting the gift gave in and made the same sort of speech themselves. One woman next to Alldera shook her head and murmured, 'Those Conors are always right.'

Alldera sat straight and smiling, warm with admiration, rejoicing in her own unbelievable good luck in having Nenisi for her friend.

Walking with the black woman later – Nenisi was cutting reeds for arrows – Alldera said, 'I'm proud to hear you speak at the chief tent. I wish you did it more often.'

'Oh, women are perfectly able to do without the Conors' nagging most of the time, and we don't believe in wasting our influence or growing self-indulgent by too much talking. We take care to be selective. I could have mentioned today a time when Stone Dancing Camp women themselves behaved very badly toward a neighbor camp. Of course there was the excuse that we hadn't yet recovered from one of the earth tremors that give this camp its name, but it was long before my time and no one really knows for certain what was in women's minds . . . Anyway, bringing that up just would have caught everyone up in an old argument, and nothing would have been decided about Red Sand for days yet.

'I see you sitting at the chief tent often these days, as I pass by on other business.'

'I like to hear women talk about family situations,' Alldera admitted. 'In case. Well, in case Sheel's nastiness gets unbearable. I want to be able to go and speak there for myself.'

Nenisi straightened from examining a strand of reeds. 'Tch', she said, 'you've been managing her meanness very well lately, it'll never come to that.'

As she cut the reeds she began singing her self-song, addressing the reeds as if identifying herself with them.

> You know me.
> In the Gather of the blind foal year I put eight arrows into the air, one behind the other, before the first fell to the ground.
> You know me.
> My mother Tesh Periken taught me to bite out a colt's balls with my good front teeth. The horse scarcely swells, the wound never festers, but I'm one of those whose teeth hurt her a lot. Is it the geldings' revenge? I say, do your own gelding, but use your knife.
> You know me.
> If you offer me sausage of fine fat and berries, I'll eat it all up and leave you nothing but my belches.
> You know me.
> I helped Tomassin Hont to cure the finest sharu hide she ever took, I put my scraper right through it, I was so much help.

There was a lot more; Alldera found herself laughing. 'How can you say such things about yourself?'

'The Conors may always be right, but I don't mind reminding everybody that Nenisi Conor can be as wrong as anybody else.' Nenisi handed her more reeds. 'Every woman needs her own personal history.'

Alldera looked over to where the grazing horses were visible, drifting against the skyline that ran forever, flat and broad.

'In all this space,' she said, 'I suppose everything that helps tell one person from another or one place from another is very important.'

The black woman straightened again and smiled. 'It's good, the way you see in fresh ways the things that are old to me. But things which unite us in all this space are also very important.' She wiped her knife and sheathed it. Then she took off her belt and dropped it to the ground. 'Come sit here.' She pulled Alldera down on the sand beside her, pushed away the bundle of reeds, and, laughing, slipped her arm around Alldera's neck.

Alldera yielded uncertainly, was pressed to Nenisi's sharp-boned side.

'Don't be nervous,' Nenisi murmured. 'We're together, that's all; friends. No one is master of the other. We do what we like, and we stop when we like. No need to be shy about your scars — give me your hand. A sharu sliced my ribs once when I was being foolish, and feel this great ridge I'm left with! We Conors can't hide our mistakes, we scar badly; no wonder we try not to make any.' Now when she laughed the sound was richer, roughened with excitement. 'You and I will learn to cherish each other's faults.'

They made love together. Alldera asked no questions. She had felt shut out from the women's constant patting and clasping and stroking of one another; at the same time their closeness had offended her.

Now she wanted nothing to intrude on the joy of touching and being touched, freely and sensually. It was a triumph to feel Nenisi's cabled body loosen and flow as she held it. Her own limbs slackened and trembled when Nenisi stroked her, seeking out the sensitive places that turned the light tickle of fingers in a deep, sinking sweetness almost too intense to be borne.

That night she lay awake in Nenisi's bedding, warm and drowsing, for a long time. As she snugged herself close against the smooth curve of Nenisi's back, she thought of the Holdfast fems. There had been some moments of passionate contact, usually in a corner of the crowded room that served as night quarters for the members of her master's femhold. She remembered tension, haste, the need for silence. The others would thump you in the head to keep you quiet so that they could get the sleep they needed for their next day's work . . . bad dreams out of a hideous life, but rich with excitement and danger.

She remembered a pretty fem, only recently demoted from pet status for some trifling error or other, the only really pretty partner Alldera had ever had. In the dark tangle of their embrace, this one had thrust an object into Alldera's hand, begging her in a smothered voice to use it, to root in her body with it like a man. Alldera had tried to break the wooden phallus against the bars of the window. Others had pulled her down; don't let the little pervert upset you, they'd said.

That memory had no power to hurt her. She was a woman now. She pressed her cheek to the back of Nenisi's neck, breathing in the faintly musky scent and feeling the giddy joy of her own liberty.

In the Holdfast Alldera had been a messenger trained to run. She had not run in some three years now. That Cool Season she took it up again. It was hard. Months of riding had firmed up new muscles and slackened others.

She ran with the horizon flowing past on one side and the tents of camp wheeling by on the other, and she thought of other runners she had known in the Holdfast; like great Kanda of the long, thin legs who ran with a tireless, bounding stride, her hands flapping loosely at waist height as if she exerted herself no more than the wind does when it blows. Not thought of in all this time; dead now, probably.

Women came to look as Alldera ran, clearly not comprehending her devotion to this outlandish way of making herself sweaty and exhausted on her own two feet. Sometimes she pushed herself, happily showing off for them.

6

In time her gladness dimmed.

'There has been strain between us these past months,' Nenisi said one morning.

Alldera said nothing. She had felt the safety and happiness of their closeness wearing away for some time, and had not known what to do.

'The Rainy Season is nearly over,' the black woman continued. 'The seed grasses are tall in the gullies. Leave your running for a while, and come grain gathering with me. We need some time alone.'

That would be good, Alldera thought gratefully. She would be happier not having to share Nenisi with others. Nenisi's apparent unfaithfulness with women of the camp had been weighing on her mind.

Trailing their spare mounts and pack ponies they rode together into the vast quiet of the plain.

On the first morning, Alldera brought herself at last to speak. She wished that her cheeks would not grow so hot with embarrassment. Taking the tea bowl that Nenisi offered, keeping her eyes on it, she said as quickly as she could that she appreciated so much having Nenisi to herself finally, knowing there was no other bed waiting to be warmed by Nenisi's body.

Very quietly Nenisi said, 'Alldera, I want you to understand something about us here. It's a sickness to fix on only one person and keep everyone else out. It's as if to say, only I and my lover are true women, the rest of you are false and worthless.'

'You think it's sick, but –'

'Listen. You should find some other women to love, too. Do you want me to wear myself to nothing, trying to be all the women in the camp to you?'

'I don't want all the women in the camp.'

The black woman sighed and drank from her bowl. 'You will have to learn, but not from me. For us two to talk about this will only lead to quarreling. But I will show you how we think of love so you can see it, all right?' She made a scooping motion over the surface of the ground by her knee and thrust out her hand, showing a little clutch of pebbles in her dark-lined palm.

'Look, here is womanness. Why should we separate from each other two by two? What makes it right for two to be alone, when it's not right for one to be?'

There was some sort of sense in it; if one bit of smooth gray gravel stood for Barvaran, say, then another just like it would be Barvaran's mother, and another her daughter. The rest would be cousins in her Motherline, all alike. If someone – if Nenisi – loved Barvaran, how avoid loving all the others?

'It's different where I come from,' Alldera muttered, and was relieved that Nenisi did not press her.

The women liked to make noise out in the open, Alldera had noticed, asserting themselves against the emptiness. Nenisi sang and talked incessantly as they rode. Eventually Alldera plucked up the courage to try on her the self-song that she had composed:

I don't look like anyone here.
    Where I come from there were many like me, sweating fear.
    That's left behind, but I lived it.
    Our heads were bent because we couldn't look our masters in the eyes. We just sidled by, nursing our lives along.
    That's left behind –

Nenisi said suddenly, 'No, that's not the idea at all. That song is all about fems, not about yourself.'

'I was trying to please you,' Alldera said. She wished she knew why things kept going wrong between them.

Day after day they rode the muddy watercourses, shaking the heavy seed heads from the grass on the banks into baskets fastened over the horses' shoulders. One afternoon Alldera spoke of the fems of the Holdfast, harvesting hemp plants under the whips of the overseers.

Again Nenisi interrupted her: 'Why think about that? It's over.'

'Nenisi, no one ever asks me about the Holdfast – very considerate of them all; or is it that nobody is interested? It is part of my past, part of my life.'

'No. This is all of your life.' Grass stems bent, heads of grain rattled into the baskets. The black woman said, 'I hate to see you unhappy. I think that maybe I treat you a little like a child sometimes, and you don't like it. That's good, that you don't like it. Only to me you are still something of a child. While you drifted in healing sleep, you sucked milk from me like a baby. And you are not done learning to be a woman. Look how well you ride, better all the time; and Barvaran is making a stronger bow for you when we get back, instead of that child's bow you've been using.'

'I wasn't wakened from a nightmare, you know,' Alldera said. 'The first life was real too. It's as you say – like being born twice.'

Nenisi looked at Alldera sideways from her eyes with the warm-stained whites, the centers like wet dark stones. 'I'll try to remember that you're growing out of your childhood.'

When the deep arroyos were swept clean Nenisi refused to work the shallow ones on foot. 'Leave something for the sharu,' she said.

The trip to the granaries, low buildings by the Dusty Season wells, took days of driving laden pack horses before them. Then they had to fill the granary bins and baskets with the gathered seed heads.

'Won't the sharu dig their way in here?' Alldera said, kicking at the thick mud wall.

'Sometimes they do.'

'You could have someone stay here to keep them off. And then you'd have seeds enough to plant – there's plenty of water on the ground in the Rainy Season – and grow more grain.'

Nenisi threw out her hands in a gesture of incomprehension. 'More for what? We gather enough seed heads for the horses and for our flour. If we had more – well, there'd soon be too many horses to feed and care for and milk. Women aren't slaves to tend the earth. We just live here as best we can.'

'It's stupid to do things this way when there's a better way.'

'Make your suggestion at the chief tent,' Nenisi said, thrusting out her dark lips in irritation. 'As a woman does.'

No woman would let Alldera give to her. Angrily Alldera slammed her shoulder against the wooden door, wedging it tightly into its frame to keep out the animals that would only burrow in under the walls instead.

Close to Nenisi that night and fearful of sharu – for they had found recent sharu signs at the granaries – Alldera shivered.

'Cold?' Nenisi said, turning toward her.

'This isn't cold,' Alldera said. 'I'm scared of Sharu. Let me tell you a story now about real cold, Holdfast cold. One winter evening I went to a certain company in Lammintown on my master's business. Out in the icy pen by the men's hall the company fems piled together to sleep under the stars, and I was put in with them. It was near the shore, and all night a raw wind blew. In the morning two fems were found frozen, hugged in each other's arms by the gate. They must have hoped to get at the soup pot first in the morning. Mother Moon, how my master lit into the young men in charge of the fems for putting his trained runner in danger of freezing to death!'

Nenisi said, 'Why didn't all you fems break into the hall and throw the men out to freeze?'

There just wasn't any point in trying to explain. Alldera turned over and tried to sleep.

When they got back to Stone Dancing she found that something important had happened in their absence. Every year the women held a Gather of all the camps. When pressed, Barvaran said it was a sort of social meeting, with games and political arrangements about horses, grass and water, and so on. Alldera had gone through her first Gather all unknowing in healing sleep, and last year only a few families from Stone Dancing had attended, for some reason too complicated and obscure for Alldera to unravel.

'Not everyone in a camp can go every year,' Barvaran said. 'There are always other things that need doing around the same time.'

And that was all that she, or anyone, would say about it.

She came fighting out of sleep to find the tent shaking with the aftermath of swift action. The poles were quivering, but no one was left inside in the dim predawn light but herself and old Jesselee. The others were nothing but faint cries and a dwindling drumbeat of hooves.

'What is it?' Alldera stood in her bedding, her knife in her hand, her pulse ringing in her head, thinking of Holdfast men swooping down on the camp to take slaves –

'Raiders,' said Jesselee. 'It's got to be a party from White Wind Camp. I heard that Poleen Sanforath of Steep Cloud Camp is visiting family up there – did I ever tell you how she hid a prize mare in her tent one night, when she and what's her name, from down at Towering, were raiding rivals? She's been after that red stud of Sheel's for years. I wonder what else they got?

'Well, there are chores to be done. Leave the child with me, you go on ahead and pull the bedding outside to air.'

Alldera guessed the old woman had noticed how little interest she showed in the child. Well, it was their child; Nenisi had made that very clear.

Returning from work at midday Alldera found meat, milk and flour noodles stewing in a pot over the fire. She filled her bowl half full. It was early in the Dusty Season, and already women were eating small while waiting for the first rains and their supply of fresh milk. Alldera no longer accepted oversized guest portions.

'You eat like a Riding Woman,' Jesselee said approvingly. 'Now you won't weigh down your horse.'

'What difference does it make?' Alldera said moodily. 'When it's something important like a Gather or a raid, I get left behind.'

Jesselee shifted the child in her arms. It was long-limbed now, a heavy burden. It belched and muttered sleepily to itself. Jesselee said, 'I wish I could have gone too, but it isn't fair to load down a pursuit party with a rider who might die on them.'

And what about me, stuck here with all the work and an old woman's ramblings to listen to?

'I'm getting weak. Your baby has more teeth than I do and better ones too. It's a sad thing to have to ask other women to chew your meat for you because you can't manage for yourself any more.'

Alldera swished water in her bowl and drank. 'Then you must be farther gone than I thought,' she said brutally, hoping the old woman would retreat into silence.

'I make my way along, not too fast or too slow.' The creaking voice took up the theme, sounding calm and even contented. 'After I live my life and die, I'm still part of my Motherline, with women of my flesh before me and behind me. Death is nothing to get excited about.

'I remember, I can still hear the Hanashoshes who fought against their own deaths, every one of them screaming and yelling like gutshot sharu. Strange women. They said they had the right to act how they liked about their own deaths.'

Alldera warmed to these women who had insisted on meeting death their own way, no matter what other women did. 'Are they those yellow-skinned women, there's one now in Calpaper Tent?'

'No, no that's a Tayang. The Hanashoshes died out.' Jesselee snickered, as if the hard diers' dying out amused her.

The stillness of the camp played on Alldera's nerves. She looked outside angrily. 'Almost everyone's gone. The raiders could double back and attack the camp; there'd be hardly anyone to defend it.'

Jesselee grunted, chewing slowly and loudly. 'Don't be foolish, who'd attack a camp? Where's the honor in stealing other women's cooking pots?'

'Well, they still didn't all have to run off and leave us everything to do here today.'

'What do you expect? Women get itchy after several Dusty Seasons without a single raid. Did you think we lived such a quiet life all the time?'

Women get itchy, and I get to do the tent work, Alldera thought. Well, I won't. She said, 'I heard that the raiders came and went before moonrise last night. How can our riders catch them?'

'Things are dry enough so the raiders will have to stop to water the horses. Our women will try to get to the wells first, on the raiders' way home, and hold them up – our horses back in exchange for water.'

Jesselee put the child in the cradle and with a little urging was soon absorbed in working out for Alldera the likeliest route to White Wind Camp. Alldera got it all, maps in the dirt and even a history lesson: 'Right here it was, I got caught sneaking up on Red Sand Camp all by myself, trying to grab Meryan Golashamet's prize dun mare, and oh, she gave me such a licking –! I was an arrogant child, I wouldn't promise to give up on that horse.'

When she knew all she needed to know, Alldera grabbed up food and water, weapons and tack, and ran outside to saddle the one horse left with them, Dark Tea. Jesselee shouted after her, but she rode away.

From a long way off she saw them, two rough lines of women brandishing their broad-bladed knives at each other over about thirty meters of bare ground. Behind one of the groups the stolen horses were being held by two riders.

Someone dashed out into the open space between the two lines of women. Alldera, galloping down a long roll of grassy ground, heard the voices shrilling high and the whickering of horses.

The lone rider curvetted her mount there in the open, standing in her stirrups to yell at the smaller group, the raiders. She rode up and down between the two ranks, she flung down her knife and threw out her arms, shaking her fists. Shouts, whistles, some movement among the White Wind women. The rider leaned down and scooped up her weapon and rode back to her own line.

Alldera thought of her bow, but the range was too great for her from a horse's back.

Someone had seen her, rode hard to meet her – Nenisi, her dark skin smeared with dirt and sweat. Pulling up beside Alldera in a flurry of dust she cried, 'What are you doing here? You shouldn't have left all the tent work on Jesselee's back!'

'Why do I have to be the one to stay behind?'

'You're not fit yet to fight women!'

Swallowing anger and disappointment, Alldera shot back. 'You aren't fighting either, and we outnumber them.'

'Of course we're fighting! Sheel has already taken Noralen Clarish captive – see her, she's that one that's almost as dark as I am. They had a fine fight, you'll hear all about it tonight in the chief tent.' Nenisi looked wild with excitement, her eyes flashed wide.

Below, two riders now circled each other between the opposing ranks, guiding their horses with their legs, buffeting and cutting at each other. One had a small hide shield; the other had whipped off her headcloth and wound it around her arm, and she deflected blows with that.

'You stay here,' Nenisi commanded. 'I'm going back – the raiders are tired and thirsty, they'll break and run any minute.'

Down below, one of the fighters' horses stumbled to its knees but she pulled it up again and rode back into her own group.

Eager now herself to join in, Alldera said, 'I'll string my bow and pick them off from here as they run.'

Nenisi drew rein so suddenly that her horse reared, and a gout of foam from its mouth landed wetly on Alldera's knee. 'Never!' said Nenisi in a furious voice that struck Alldera silent. 'Do you see a bow in my hand, in any hand down there? What kind of coward are you, to suggest cutting down women from a safe distance?'

'But they're enemies,' Alldera cried, shrinking back.

'What enemies? Those are women. What could you do with a bow except kill dishonorably and bring a feud on your line? That's what a bow is for – a feud; or for the borderlands.'

Then Alldera remembered Barvaran in the desert that time years ago, raising a bow toward her before realizing that she was not a man but a fem. She wanted to speak, but she was flooded with confusion.

In a roar the women of Stone Dancing charged. Nenisi whirled her mount and raced away, angling to cut off a fleeing White Wind rider.

Alldera sat where she was while Dark Tea blew and sighed beneath her. She watched the sprawling indiscipline of the battle with slow-dawning bitterness. These were not warriors destroying enemies who had treated them unjustly, but wild women brawling over prizes.

The struggling mass broke into small skirmishes and pursuits. The stolen horses, unheeded, streamed down into a gully and away. Within moments of the charge only one pair of riders was visible, locked together and heaving at each other while their mounts plunged under them and carried them out of sight behind a fold of land.

In time women came drifting back toward the well, several of them riding double on droop-headed horses – captives, Alldera assumed, or tent mates picked up after being unhorsed. Some riders drove horses before them. One woman rode in holding her bloody arm and reeling in the saddle. Her friends closed in quickly to support her.

Alldera turned Dark Tea back toward camp, hard-handed with anger so that the horse fought the bit. How could they shut her out of this game, she who had fought real war all her life?

Riding alone, she made speeches in her head till her throat was

raw with the parching from her breath, and her eyes pricked with
tears: who has more courage, who has endured more? While you
rode and hunted and hugged each other here, men beat me and
starved me, a man threw me down on my back in the mud and
fucked me and made me eat dirt to remind me how much power he
had over me. I fought back when I could, I escaped. How many of
you would have killed yourselves or gone crazy with despair?

But there was no one to make speeches to, not unless she wished
to go address them that night when they reveled in the chief tent.
The drumming and shouting rang right through the walls of Holdfaster Tent, where she stayed, thinking, arguing with herself.

After a while she went to join them, whether to speak out or not
she did not know.

Just outside the chief tent someone touched her arm and said,
'Wait, we want to talk to you.'

Four women surrounded her. By the dim glow coming through
the chief tent wall she recognized a young woman of Barvaran's
bloodline. Another was a blotch-skinned Monotay, and she did not
know the other two.

One took her arm. 'You showed a keen edge, Alldera Holdfaster,
riding to our battle. You're not the dry old stick we took you
for.'

The Monotay whispered, 'Come into the long grass with us
tonight.' There were sounds of approval from the others.

Someone slid an arm around Alldera's waist; she stiffened.

'You're shy,' the Monotay said admiringly.

The young one who looked like Barvaran said in a coaxing voice,
heavy and slow, 'Come on, Alldera. Nenisi has told us what a fine,
sweet lover you are.'

Alldera pulled free and fled. She ran to Holdfaster Tent, rolled
herself into Barvaran's empty bedding and held very still. Someone
entered, went over to where Alldera normally slept, and left again.
Alldera heard the sound of a muffled conference outside, and that
was all.

Come to me, Nenisi — the threads holding me here to you are
breaking, she wept.

The winds of the Dusty Season blew hot and hard; there was not
going to be enough grass for all the horses. The women could not
wait and let some horses starve. They had to butcher some while

they were still fat, to save more grass for the survivors and to get the most meat from the slaughter for themselves. It was like this most years.

'I want you to come help me with this,' Nenisi said to Alldera. 'I think we've been leaving you out of too much of our lives.'

Sadly and tortuously the women of Holdfaster Tent debated which horses to slaughter. They chose males and weak or barren females, animals that could not help increase the herd again when times were better. They chose many, and Alldera saw how it hurt them. She asked at one point why the women did not get their meat by killing sharu instead.

There was an appalled silence. Alldera did not wait for Nenisi to step in on her behalf, but said as calmly as she could, 'I think I've said something wrong. I apologize for my ignorance.'

She had the satisfaction of hearing old Jesselee mutter, 'Well said,' but Sheel snarled, 'No one eats sharu but the filthy free fems. They eat the flesh of scavengers because they're scavengers themselves. Go to them for a taste.'

'Heartchild,' Jesselee chided mildly, 'you speak like a lesser woman than Alldera.' To Alldera she added, 'The only meat we eat is horses' meat. We eat no sharu because the sharu eat our dead.'

Alldera could not hold back an exclamation of revulsion, and was instantly ashamed. Jesselee expounded thoughtfully on the ability of sharu to find and dig up anything edible that had been buried, and the foolishness of wasting scarce fuel to burn corpses; and Jesselee was nearer than any of them to having her body left for the sharu to devour, thought Alldera, shuddering.

With the other sharemothers Alldera helped to make killing hammers, choosing carefully the stone heads, the wooden hafts, and the sinews to fasten both together. On culling day she went with Nenisi from the place where the herds were being held. Nenisi rode bareback on a colt to be killed. Alldera, on a stolid gray, carried the hammer and a leather bowl. She was apprehensive but reassured herself that a fem from the Holdfast could take any harshness that this plains life had to offer. They went to a sandy dip below a ridge spined with brush. Alldera was instructed to tie her horse securely behind the brush, upwind. Then she walked back down to Nenisi with the tools.

'The hammer,' Nenisi said from the colt's back. She took the hammer in both hands and set the colt trotting in a tight curve past Alldera. She was speaking as she rode, addressing the colt in a low, grave tone. Alldera could not hear the words.

Suddenly, all the cords in her arms standing with effort, Nenisi whipped the hammer down on the horse's head.

Even before he stumbled, muzzle to the ground, she was off him and drawing her knife. She threw her weight against his shoulder and he fell heavily onto his side, his breath rushing out in a thick sound, his tongue dragging on the sand. Swiftly she cut into the base of his throat, threw down the knife and reached for the leather bowl, which she held to catch his blood as it streamed from the wound.

Crouching there inside the curve of his neck, still murmuring to him while she bled away his life, she seemed to Alldera to enact an obscene parody of a woman resting curled against her prone and trusting mount. The colt made no further sound at all, but subsided into a graceless, ugly heap.

On shaking legs Alldera walked back to her own horse, to try to soothe its nervousness while she waited for Nenisi. She felt sick and miserable and could scarcely meet Nenisi's eyes when the black woman came up and told her they would leave the dead horse for the team that would come and drag it off to the butchering site. They rode out double on the gray horse to catch a lame mare next. The hands clasped around Alldera's waist were the hands she had just seen wiped clean of blood.

It was as if Alldera was suddenly touched by some raw, cruel current hidden till now under the sunlit surface of the women's lives.

At another dip in the land Nenisi killed the lame mare the same way. She looked up from scrubbing her knife clean with sand and said sharply, 'What's the matter? It was a good kill. The next one will be harder — that star-faced gelding.' She shook her head. 'I helped to get him born, turned him in the womb where he was lying crooked. I nearly got my arm squeezed off doing it.'

'Then how can you kill him?' Alldera protested. 'Bleeding them to death —'

Nenisi did not look up from the knife again, she did not help. She gave no sign that she hated this horrible work.

As they walked to where Alldera had tied up the gray, Nenisi said at last, 'We need the blood, and we use it; it is dried and kept for making broth later in the year. You've drunk it, remember? The death itself is pretty painless, and never carelessly inflicted. Bones, hide, hoofs and hair, nothing goes to waste; and we're grateful for it all.'

There was one more horse to kill. Each woman of the tent had one or more assigned to her to slaughter, and Nenisi was doing Alldera's killing as well as her own. Holding the nervous gray, Alldera kept thinking, that woman loves the horses but she doesn't hesitate to kill them. I don't love them, and I can't bear to watch.

After the last kill they rode back toward camp to prepare for a turn at butchering the carcasses. Nenisi said without emotion, 'Do you want Sheel to see you looking so stunned? Get hold of yourself. You'll kill a horse yourself, in time.'

As Alldera stripped down in the tent, she became aware of a rider galloping through the camp shouting. She rushed out and saw the sky above the butchering ground black with smoke. Grass had ignited from one of the fires there, the women were yelling. If the wind shifted, the camp itself would be in danger. Even if not, vital ranges of grass would be burned.

She helped Nenisi to drag out all the tent's bedding, ride to the rock pool the camp was using for water, and throw everything in. Other women were doing the same, jumping from their horses' backs to trample the blankets and leathers into the water and get them saturated. Then with sodden bundles heaped before them they galloped for the butchering ground and into a pall of smoke and flying ash.

The soaked blankets were snatched by others who used them to beat on foot at the margins of the fire. Everywhere among cooking pots and bones and heaps of meat and offal, women raced.

'Like this!' Nenisi shouted. She clamped a shank of rope between her thigh and the saddle, and Alldera did the same with the rope she was handed. 'Ride with me, keep up, a woman's length apart!'

Leaning against the weight they were hauling, the two of them fought their horses into a gallop along the edge of the fire where the beaters had fallen back. The flames were not very high but they threw off such intense heat that Alldera felt her lashes and brows curling. Looking back, she saw what it was they were dragging: the carcass of a horse, split open down the belly and spread wide to suffocate the fire with its moisture and weight. Along the path the carcass made, women on foot rushed in again with blankets.

The smoke gradually thinned, the fire's roar diminished to a spiteful crackling. Confined within charred boundaries, beaten back from all sides, the flames shrank and spat.

Alldera's horse staggered. She turned over her drag rope to another rider and went off slowly with a load of scorched bedding that needed soaking again.

On her way back with the heavy blankets she saw Nenisi trying to mount a fresh horse, a sidling, rearing mare bridled only with a rope. Alldera hesitated: it was, she knew, something of an insult to help a woman with her horse. But the black woman seemed to be having trouble. Something was wrong with the saddle, and she wound the bridle rope around her wrist to secure it so that she could use both hands on the girth.

The horse shied and leaped, pulling the woman off her feet, and it tore away over the blackened ground dragging her under its battering hooves.

Alldera's howl of anguish was lost in the cries that went up. The fire beaters hurled themselves at the horse, grabbed at the taut rope and were knocked away. Alldera flung down the blankets and galloped after, sobbing, lashing her mount. Her vision was filled by that dark figure jouncing and twisting at full stretch of the one entangled arm.

She heard a whining sound and saw an arrow strike the runaway on the neck, slowing its wild career. Someone raced in ahead of her from the side and with the flash of a knife parted the horse from its dragging burden.

Alldera looked down past the heads of the women standing gathered there. The blackened shape left lying wound in rope was not Nenisi. This was a Calpaper woman, long-limbed like the Conors, dark-skinned and frizzy-haired, made black by soot and now blacker still with char from the burnt stubble over which she had been dragged. The ropes trailing around the sprawled legs were not ropes. They were guts, torn out by the pony's hooves.

The raw, ugly underside of things again. It could have been Nenisi; she had imagined this corpse was Nenisi, she had nearly burst with terror for Nenisi. Now she burned with resentment, as if her love had been offered all along to a false image – to matchless

Nenisi, revealed today as a hard and bloody-handed slaughterer.

Alldera brooded on this often in the weeks that followed, tormented by her sense of having been betrayed. Brutality she had known in the Holdfast; in that life she had been cruel herself by necessity. Here she had thought herself free of that necessity, because she had not seen cruelty among the women.

Now to find brutality in the person she respected most horrified her and made her feel cheated – cheated of the free, clean life she thought she had found.

She had wanted the women to be perfect, and they were not.

She watched Nenisi take chewed food from her own mouth and poke it between the child's lips. Almost too large to carry now for any length of time, the child still nursed but had begun to accept solids. It had been Alldera's own head against that dark, smooth breast once – in her healing sleep when the women had fed her and through her fed her unborn baby. The thought gave her feelings too complicated to unravel, sweet and sour at the same time like everything here.

She studied Nenisi's face, freshly scarred pink over the brow. One of the new ransom horses had snapped at her and broken the skin of her forehead as she jerked back out of the way. Alldera's resentment had faded. Looking at Nenisi, hearing her speak, was what Alldera stayed for these days.

Barvaran was saying something about the next Gather, and spoke Alldera's name.

'Not her,' said Sheel firmly and loudly. 'That fem is going to the wells.'

'To the wells?' Alldera said. 'What for?'

'Our ropes drag loose the stones along the tops of the walls. They need mending.'

Alldera protested, 'Last year I went grain gathering. It's someone else's turn to miss the Gather.'

Sheel said, 'This year you're one of the well menders. It's not a big job.' She did not bother to look up. She was painting in the bodies of running horses that she had first outlined on pegged-out skin with a burnt twig.

Heatedly Alldera said, 'How long are you going to go on maneuvering to keep me from your precious Gather, Sheel?'

'As long as I can.'

No one else spoke. Alldera looked at Nenisi, who silently rocked the sprawling child. Sheel's brush dragged on the leather.

They all went out to a shooting contest next day except for Nenisi, who stayed behind with aching teeth. Alldera gave up the place in the contest that she had been practicing hard for and stayed with Nenisi. They talked about the argument of the day before.

'I told you I wouldn't treat you like a child any more,' Nenisi said. 'You can't fight this out with Sheel, she's in your family. Have you thought some more about bringing her persecution of you up in the chief tent?'

'Not unless I know what a Gather is all about. What happens at the Gathers that Sheel thinks I shouldn't see?'

Nenisi took another mouthful of pain-killing brew and spat it out again. The medicine steamed in a pot between them under the tent fly, souring the air. Finally she said, 'You must have guessed. Matings happen.'

Alldera frowned. It was a hot day; she wiped at her neck with her headcloth. 'What do you mean, "matings"? You told me that you used some fluid to start your seed.'

'The fluid comes from a stallion. We mate with stallions.'

Alldera was stunned. She could not think. From where they sat they could see the women out beyond the edge of the camp, shooting at leather targets pegged tightly to the ground. A flight of arrows winked in the air. A moment later came the sounds of impact, like drops of hard rain on a leather wall. Nenisi could not be talking about the archers.

Shakily Alldera began, 'Come on, Nenisi. That's just a thing women tell the fems to shock them, Barvaran even said it to me once –'

'Yes, she told me; she'd forgotten how it seems to strike fems, and she was afraid she'd embarrassed or upset you, so she let it drop. But what she said was true.'

'It doesn't make sense,' Alldera objected desperately. 'Nenisi, I know that a stallion's cock is as long as your arm. You'd have your guts shoved right out through your mouth if you let one – do that to you.'

Nenisi rubbed at her jaw and said reasonably, 'That would be true, for fems. This is our way; it was worked out for us by the first daughters. They saw that after the Wasting there wouldn't be any places like the lab, and we would need some way to breed simpler than the lab way. So these lab-changed women designed their daughters' reproduction to be set off by the seed of a stallion. Take Shayeen; she has a bloodchild over in Floating Moon Camp. The horse she mated with is not that child's sire; his seed only started Shayeen's seed growing, and Shayeen's seed was complete with Shayeen's traits, no room for any others. We are not half horse, as ignorant free fems tell each other.'

Alldera sat silent, her hands on her knees, looking out at the shooting. She tried, but she could not make sense of what Nenisi said. This horse mating was like a river that Nenisi and the others had just crossed on an inexorable journey that they were making away from her into a mysterious and incomprehensible distance. And not the first river; there had been others, now she recognized them: the childpack, the Motherlines, love without bonds, the brutal killing of horses, warfare as a game, the leaving of the dead for the horrible sharu whom women hunted but also fed . . . She began to be afraid that all the time she had thought she was catching up with the women, they had been leaving her farther and farther behind, that she would never be able to reach them.

She knew the relaxed pitch of Nenisi's voice was intended to calm her: 'Why don't we drop this for now. You could go and watch the shooting.'

'I need to understand this,' Alldera insisted.

Nenisi cleared her throat. 'Let me try to explain. We make the mating as safe as we can. There's a lot of size difference in any generation of colts. We choose them small and arrange things so that full penetration is impossible. Thickness is more the danger than length. As young women we train and exercise beforehand to stretch ourselves. The horses hardly ever tear us.'

Alldera felt stifled by this dreamlike amiability of Nenisi. She shut her eyes and saw her beautiful lover coupling with a horse. She saw it as she knew a Holdfast man would see it: as something titillating, Nenisi's dark legs parted by the long pink shaft of a stud reared up and shaking the brambles of his mane above her. It was unbearable to think of Nenisi as gross and comical, she whose body Alldera had stroked and kissed.

'But sure,' she stammered, 'surely you could – you could get the stallion's seed without – without – and put it in –'

'We don't have such fine lab ways; and if we could do it another way, then it wouldn't mean the same thing. Sheel doesn't want to keep you away to spare your feelings, though we all know how upset fems get about this – you're different anyway, you've lived with us a long time, you'll understand eventually.'

She spoke as though in the chief tent, winding up a long debate. 'What Sheel says is that you have no place around a mating because you have no bond with the horses. We do have a bond, of our bodies and theirs. The balance of all things includes us and acts on us, and animals – even the sharu in their way – are our links with that balance. We celebrate it every year at the Gather of all the camps, where young women mate.

'The Gather is part of our bond with each other too, you see. Every woman has trusted herself to a horse this way, or is blood kin to another woman who has. Sheel says you can't go raiding either because you might kill someone, and no woman knows what would happen to the spirit of one of us killed by a stranger.' She laid her slender hand on Alldera's knee. 'You see what I mean by "stranger". It would be like – like being killed by some man from the Holdfast. Maybe you shouldn't do your own horse killing either. It's going to take us time to decide.'

The more she explained, the more she seemed to recede from Alldera. Gravely, imperturbably, she went on. 'You're not bound to us to begin with by being part of an old Motherline, and you won't be truly bound until your bloodchild mates. Shayeen says that meanwhile you should open to a horse yourself even with no chance of issue, but that's absurd, you're not young and flexible enough any more to safely –'

'No, I can't,' Alldera gasped. 'Why are you talking like this to me? Don't you see I can't follow?'

'Are you worried about your child's mating?' Nenisi said with concern. 'Don't be. The stud doesn't attack anyone, he means no harm, no abuse or degradation. He's innocent. He has to be led and coaxed and trained to do his part, with our help. It's nothing at all like a man overpowering a fem just to show her who's master. You've heard me mention my sharemother Sayelen Garriday, who was jumped by her gray stud once, but it turned out –'

Alldera felt as if she were wandering in the Wild again, mystified by a monster's footprint. In a small, exhausted voice she said, 'Nenisi, please stop, it's no good. I think it would be better if you would just tell me how to find the free fems.'

FREE FEMS

Daya loved the sweeping yellow plain. Yet she always enjoyed returning to the tea camp in the foothills. The space and silence of the open country was pleasing only up to a point, for she had lived her whole life among other fems, first in the kit pits and later in her master's populous femhold. Conversation, lively companions and the pleasing tension of intrigue made up her natural surroundings. Her periodic excursions with the trade wagons were passages in a special dream life of loneliness and survival amid elemental forces.

Today the tang of wet weather was in the air, and clouds stood on one another's shoulders obscuring the mountains. She looked forward to the comforts of the tea camp and to seeing Elnoa again. She would be warm with Elnoa, and generous. She could always extend herself to her conquests.

The wagon she walked beside was a sturdy openwork structure of wicker and light wood pulled by a crew of twelve fems. They did not sing as they leaned into the ropes and straps of the harness. They had sung at work as slaves in the Holdfast, and they were free people now. Daya missed the old music.

In the quiet of her own mind she sang a load-carrying song as she walked looking for seasoning plants for the stew pot.

> See how the muscles run in our arms,
> See how the strength swings in our stride.
> What is the weight that we could not carry?

Where is the riverboat we could not haul?
Mother Moon, send us a task fit for our
power.

Not that Daya herself had ever been a labor fem. She was too small and slight. But she remembered the labor gangs' voices.

Again her thoughts turned eagerly toward camp. Perhaps she would find a tense scene in Elnoa's wagon: she pictured fems' faces lighting with relief to see her, for there lay Elnoa prostrate on the edge of death – losing weight – insisting that to none but Daya would she reveal the hiding place where she hoarded her treasure of precious objects, to none but Daya would she relinquish her great leather account books . . .

The first free fems to settle here had grouped their wagons under the trees by the spring that flowed down the heart of the narrow valley. The abandoned hulk of an old wagon marked the spot, a trysting place Daya had often used. By Elnoa's time the camp had been moved to an elevation backed by the southern hills, overlooking the spring and much of the valley. Signs of an effort to build walls of fired mud brick on the hill remained. Daya had heard a tale that the move and the attempt at fortification had been a response to a period of especially tense relations with the Mares.

Elnoa had entrenched the free fems in their higher location. Under her direction they had begun to park their wagons to form a hollow square and to mount a patrol of sentries on the perimeter. Broken-down and tenantless wagons, now used for storage, were interspersed with occupied ones. The spaces between them and the gaps left by wagons gone out trading were filled with temporary walls of rock and brush. This patchwork parapet enclosed a wide, bare yard in which the free fems lived and worked, either in the open or under awnings stretched from the wagon roofs to poles planted in the dirt. There were no trees. Elnoa's own huge vehicle, holding the center of the yard, dominated everything.

On a wet day like this the place looked dead, and Daya quailed a little at the sight of it. What have I come back to? she wondered. Awnings of oiled leather were stretched over racks of smoking tea, some stacked tea bricks, and a pile of raw leaf. The heavy weaving looms were similarly sheltered, looking like big-boned creatures standing gloomily together out of the wet.

While the crew pulled aside a mound of brush to let their wagon through, Kobba, the crew boss, entered the muddy, deserted yard. She paced about heedless of the rain. Daya had noticed that no sentries were walking the perimeter or the skyline above and behind the camp. She knew Kobba would have grim interviews with those she had left on guard. Some would soon sport black eyes and swollen lips. There were always fems foolish enough to ask Kobba what there was to watch for. The Mares patrolled the borderlands to the east, so the men of the Holdfast could never spring a surprise attack. Kobba always said she was not interested in what the Mares did, she was interested in what the fems did, particularly about their own security.

Swiftly the crew parked the trade wagon, checked the lashings of its cover, and climbed into their friends' wagons for shelter, hot beer, and a night of talk.

Elnoa's own wagon was walled with solid wood, elaborately carved and stained. Its immense weight did not matter, since it was never moved. Under the shelter of its eaves Daya wiped the mud from her legs, wondering who would be the present members of the favored circle that Elnoa admitted to her wagon. There were sure to be changes since Daya had left with the trade wagon, two seasons ago. There were always new members Elnoa had introduced, others she had unpredictably discarded.

Beside Daya, Kobba tugged vainly at the knotted thongs of one of her sandals. Rain had swelled the leather. Daya knelt to help. She liked touching Kobba.

Kobba was tall, lanky in the limbs, and blessed with well-formed hands and feet. The skirts of her smock clung wetly to her long, powerful legs. Her belt – a wide strap of leather with an unpolished metal disc for a buckle – fitted slantwise from one shoulder down between her breasts to her hip, where her hatchet hung on a leather loop. The brim of her broad hat cut on an angle across her face half hiding the ruin of one cheekbone, smashed long ago in a fight. Like most free fems she wore her hair long, flaunting the freedom to grow it for her own pleasure rather than for the profit of a master who sold it to the fur weavers of the Holdfast. Daya kept her own hair shorter, more in Marish style, because it was flattering; but she found a heavy mane like Kobba's attractive.

What a pity Kobba was so uncompromisingly faithful to Elnoa the Green-Eyed. Elnoa and Kobba were long-term lovers despite their separations in the cause of trade. Elnoa indulged herself with others; everyone knew this. No one, not even Kobba, held it against her. They accepted as her natural prerogative the sexual appetite, nourished on power, which they derided in others — Daya, for instance.

Daya went up the slippery steps first and parted the bead curtain in the doorway. Voices from within greeted her as she tried to adjust her vision.

As always, coals glowed in ceramic bowls around the inside of the wagon; Elnoa was easily chilled. The air was thick with aromas of tea and perfume. Elnoa insisted that her people wear strong scents in her presence. She held that freedom meant, among other things, the privilege of breathing air that did not stink of sweat.

Windows of scraped thin leather let in little light and less sound. Daya had helped Elnoa design her quarters to mute the noise of the tea camp. Layers of blankets hung on the walls, masking the sleeping platforms that were raised against the paneling during the day. More blankets carpeted the floor deeply enough for the foot to sink in them. Any wood that showed was so intricately carved that it could scarcely be recognized as a hard surface. The chests and wicker baskets set around the long central space were heaped with pillows of the deep gold and orange tones Elnoa loved. Seven or eight fems, Elnoa's current circle, reclined among them and waved greetings to the newcomers.

Daya took a pillow from a pile by the doorway on her way in. The heat, the syrupy air, the rich colors welcomed and delighted her. She almost forgot, as one was meant to, the outer casing of wood and moved into a warm, cushioned world of hushed voices and languorous privilege. Even the chiefs among the Mares did not live like this. In the Holdfast itself only rich old men could afford to surround themselves with comparable luxury.

Elnoa had been lying on her stomach for a massage. Moving slowly and with great sureness, she sat up and tucked the hem of her embroidered smock down around her legs. Her shape was not flabby but thick and cylindrical, and she leaned on her couch of pillows like a monumental tower against a bank of cloud. Even in the soft, flattering light her skin showed creases at the corners of her mouth and eyes, and gray streaked her hair. In her broad, handsome face her eyes were perfect, brilliant and enormous. Daya envied her those eyes. She did not envy Elnoa's eminence; influence, she knew, was subtler and more versatile than authority.

Elnoa's greeting was in handspeech. Decades ago when she had first bossed her masters' femhold, one of the fems under her command had argued and denied a charge of theft instead of taking her punishment with her mouth shut. Following tradition, the master had ordered Elnoa's tongue removed to impress upon her that she was responsible for the silent submissiveness of those she bossed.

'This is a special day, my friends,' said Kobba, translating Elnoa's hand signals in a mellifluous, formal tone that she reserved for Elnoa's words. She was Elnoa's voice, a conspicuous luxury since every fem knew handspeech. 'I'm happy to see my friends Daya and Kobba again. Let them come sit beside me and tell us the news of the plains.'

They talked plains gossip, camp gossip. A fine set of glazed spitting cups, everyone's favorites, was brought out. Emla, the masseur, took a bar of fresh, pungent tea from a storage chest and sliced it. The slivers were strong-flavored when chewed. Because of the scars on her cheeks Daya could scarcely chew solid food, let alone chew tea, without lacerating her own flesh with her teeth. She tucked her portion into her belt pouch. Elnoa's tea was good currency.

It pleased her to note that Emla was looking sulky. She thought, in Elnoa's wagon Emla and I are like two pans of a scale, one swinging high and the other low, and then the reverse. Emla, high now, sees me here and feels the balance shifting.

Mean-mouthed Froya was here, she noted resignedly. Old Ossa of the milky eyes was still here, homecoming after homecoming. But not the cheerful, eager fem who had sung so sweetly and whom Daya had made love to the night before leaving camp with this trade wagon. Fems died off year by year, and no new runaways had come over the borderlands recently to fill the gaps. Elnoa chose her intimates from among ever smaller numbers.

Like addicts turning to their drug, the free fems fell to discussing the plan. The great plan. It was Elnoa's idea. According to her, the free fems would one day slip past the Mares' patrols and return to the Holdfast, where they would infiltrate the population and take over, capturing the men and freeing the fems enslaved there. Kobba's scouting parties, under the pretense of searching out the best growth of wild tea plants, had penetrated the borderlands as far as the desert, which they were secretly mapping. Elnoa's stores of food, clothing and weapons were essential. When the time to go drew near, the scouts would distribute Elnoa's stores in various caches intended to provision and sustain the whole band of free fems on their route homeward. Just how this was to be done without drawing the attention of the Marish patrols was not, it seemed to Daya, very clear. The free fems did not have a high opinion of Marish intelligence.

Daya suspected that she was not the only one who thought the plan absurd. The Mares had patrolled the borderlands for generations, preventing the men from learning of their existence and coming over the mountains in force. Marish patrols had never once let a man come as far as the Grasslands; surely they were capable of preventing fifty fems from returning to the Holdfast.

Moreover, those fems who had come out of the Holdfast most recently — years ago now — had brought news of dreadful carnage there as men struggled with each other over ruinously small food supplies. In the years since, no more fems had escaped.

Yet Elnoa's followers chewed tea and discussed their return as if they would find life there much as they had left it.

To Daya it was all a game, but she did not disdain the plan. On the contrary, she admired Elnoa for knowing a useful illusion when she saw one. Elnoa ws far too ungainly and soft to make that crossing ever again. She never talked about her own part in the later stages of the plan, and no one ever asked. Daya did not believe for a moment that Elnoa would give them her substance and wave them goodbye, remaining tamely behind to explain their disappearance to the Mares.

But what a fine player the great fem was! She read in signs now from one of her leather books of records, leading off the reports of progress on the plan. She listed how many baskets of dried milk and meat she had added to the permanent stocks from trade with the Mares since her last accounting; how many metal knives and spear points, how many light cotton smocks and leather tunics, how many pairs of thick-soled sandals.

Everyone had a place in the plan. Froya, long-faced and

supercilious-looking with her drooping, bruise-colored eyelids, recounted the exploits of her troop of scouts. 'We walked farther into, the southern section of the desert than ever before,' she boasted.

There was a report on a new design of water bottles for the homeward journey. Old Ossa spoke quaveringly of her efforts, aided by others whose eyes were better, to make colored maps of the Holdfast so that each returning free fem would have a good idea of the territory in which she was to rouse the slaves.

'What about fighting practice?' said Kobba.

She got an account of their sessions practicing with spears and hatchets. Daya hid a yawn.

'And running?'

We have a new teacher of running, Elnoa signed. One who came to us just after your wagon left, having at last escaped the Mares who were keeping her among them. Where is Alldera the runner?

'Alldera the crazy,' muttered old Ossa, and she spat tea juice into her cup which she held up close to her seamed face. 'She's out running in the rain again.'

'Or doing witchery,' someone else said. 'Who knows what secret magic she learned while she was with the Mares?'

Another: 'She still won't wear sandals as we do. We keep telling her only slaves go barefoot.'

Elnoa signed firmly, Alldera has a skill – her running. That makes her more useful to the plan barefoot than some others who go shod.

So the 'prisoner fem' had gotten free at last. Daya wondered how she had managed to make enemies here so swiftly.

'If Alldera wanted to be useful,' Ossa growled, 'she could have brought her cub here to us.'

'A fem cub,' someone else sneered. 'What use would that be?'

'As much as a male,' retorted another. 'By the time a boy cub got old enough to fuck, how many here would still be young enough to bear? We're none of us kits, you know.'

A free fem with a cub! Daya, astonished, leaned to hear more, but Elnoa moved her hands and Kobba translated, 'The cub is not in the plan; the runner is.'

The matter was closed. They began to talk about 'the clowns', fems who were to concoct a diversionary ruse to draw off Marish patrols at the outset of the expedition. Kobba pulled back the blankets from a section of the floor so that, using soot from a firebowl, she could sketch maps of the foothill trails.

Daya did not pay attention. She was intrigued by the bizarre complications that had come with the runner Alldera, and a little put out by the feeling of having missed the camp's newest sensation.

Meanwhile, here was Elnoa – bored to death with the others' plan talk – making furtive signs to her, commenting sarcastically on each speaker, berating Daya. for having abandoned her to go tramping the plains. She forgot very easily that this had been at her own order. Finally, during a pause while Kobba rubbed out some error on her map, Elnoa signed broadly to Daya, You have not satisfied our curiosity about life cooking for Kobba's wagon crew. Surely you had time at least to make up some new stories.

Well, it was about time. Daya said modestly, 'I speak only what I know of what I hear. I did hear some strange tales out there. There was one in particular – no, you'll call me a liar.'

They flattered her and cajoled her. She loved the coaxing, which was, after all, her due.

To warm them up she told a quick story of Little Fist, a free fem whom she had invented years ago, now the subject of a hundred anecdotes. Shrunken to tiny size by a bolt of plains lightning, Little Fist had wild adventures wandering the Grasslands in her tiny cloak, sneaking into the Mares' camps, encountering ghosts and demons from the past in the Ancients' ruins.

Today Daya told how Little Fist was hunted remorselessly by a vicious sharu fifty times her size, and how she had pinned its tail to its nose with a cactus spine so that it ran in circles till it died. Then Little Fist did a victory dance on her tiny cloak –

'Enough tiny-headed nonsense. Tell a tale about the Holdfast,' Emla drawled. 'Something we haven't already heard, if possible.'

Her bitchiness did not matter. A story lay ready for them in Daya's mind, clearly and wholly visible now like a white stone at the bottom of a bowl of water. With a nod at Emla she began.

'The free fems return across the mountains, and they stop on the edge of the Holdfast and see that something strange has happened there: earth and sky are bound in great stillness. The clouds hang in the sky without changing shape, and far away they can see that the sea itself lies still, neither advancing nor retreating along the shore.

'Elnoa signs for a brave volunteer to go down into the lower hills and find out what has happened. One fem goes, spear on her shoulder, hatchet in her hand.

'For a long time she meets no one. Her legs seem to carry her no further toward the sea. The river beside the road she follows does not move between its banks.

'Suddenly she sees a figure ahead of her on the road. Drawing near with great effort, she comes upon an old fem in a ragged smock trying to lift a huge wheel of white stone that has fallen on its side, blocking the way. The old fem straightens, wipes her wrinkled face with the hem of her smock, and says to the free fem, "Come help me raise this stone, for I must roll it down to the sea."

'The free fem looks at the old fem, all scarred and dirty with the sweat and dust of labor, and she says, "Tell me what has happened here, why the Holdfast is so empty and still."

'"Help me," the old fem says.

'The free fem gets angry, she thumps the butt of her spear on the ground and cries, "I have come home to conquer, not to work!"

'At this, the old fem shrinks away to nothing and vanishes, and the free fem thinks, very well, I have vanquished some evil phantom that would have bewitched me.

'But she finds that the white wheel has grown so huge that she cannot climb up over it or even walk around it, and she is forced to return to where the others wait. So Elnoa signs for another volunteer, and another free fem goes, spear balanced on her shoulder, hatchet in her hand.

'She walks beside the still river and under the still sky, and she seems to make little headway. Then she sees the old fem before her, bent and straining to lift the wheel of white stone. The old fem calls to her, "Come and help me raise this stone on its edge so that I can roll it down to the sea."

'The second free fem says, "First you tell me what's happened here, why the Holdfast lies so still and empty."

'"Help me!" the old fem commands her.

'"I won't!" the second free fem cries, raising her hatchet to the old fem. "I haven't come home to follow anyone's orders, I've come to give orders – so get out of my way!"

'At this the old fem shrinks away to nothing and disappears, but the second free fem finds that the white wheel has swollen so big that she can't climb over it or walk around it to continue on her way; so she has to come back too.

'The third volunteer is a fem named Semda, who walks and walks till she comes upon the old fem and her stone wheel, and the old fem looks up at her and calls, "Come and help me raise this stone on its edge so I can roll it down to the sea."

'Semda looks at her and thinks, if I had not had the luck and the strength to run away from the Holdfast, I would have withered early like this old fem. And she says, "I'll do what I can." To her amazement, she no sooner sets her hand to the stone than up it springs to stand on its edge in the middle of the road.

'"Now, help me roll it down to the sea," says the old fem.

'That's a long way, Semda thinks. But she looks at the old fem and thinks also, I was not here to be beaten, but how many blows has she taken? So she says, "I'll try."

'She finds that the wheel rolls true with the two of them pushing it, and as they walk the old fem says, "Waiting is more tiring than working," and Semda says to the old fem, "Why are you doing this job alone, an old weak fem like yourself?"

'"Because it is my job and always has been my job and always will be my job," answers the old fem.

'"Under the orders of what master?" says Semda.

'"Under no orders, I mark out the time," says the old fem, and Semda realizes that this is Moonwoman herself. In fear and shock she jumps back from the white stone wheel, which immediately tumbles into the river. The old fem falls in with it. But when Semda runs to look she sees the stone wheel floating on top of the water; and the old fem, standing on the floating stone, shouts to her, "Jump on!"

'The water is flowing very fast, and Semda is frightened, but she jumps and the old fem catches her. They go whirling down the river so fast that Semda can hardly breathe, but the old fem is laughing and shouts to her, "I thought the right one would never come. When we reach the coast, jump off again. You will find a ferry boat beached there. Go strike its side with your hatchet, and you'll have your reward."

'Semda soon smells the sea, and she leaps onto the shore at the river's mouth. There is nothing to be seen on the coast but saltgrass and sand and, canted on its side, the great bleached hulk of one of the coastal ferry boats.

'The old fem is still riding the stone wheel, which is shooting out to sea. "Use your hatchet!" she calls.

'Semda walks up to the silent wreck and taps on the wooden wall. Nothing happens. She takes a strong swing and chops right through. A whole section of the hull breaks away, and out of the opening fems come walking, rubbing their eyes, yawning and looking around in astonishment. Moonwoman had hidden them there while she killed the masters.

'Among these fems Semda sees a lover whom she thought dead and others whom she knows were once lovers of her free companions – lovers long ago given up for dead. She embraces her own lover, and their hands are very soft on one another, and the ocean begins to roar to the beach and the bright moon rises, round and white as a polished stone, to float in the sky.'

They gave Daya a tribute of spellbound silence, and then Elnoa leaned forward and threw sweet-smelling powder on the fire. They all drew together into a tighter group, leaning toward the smoke. The hemp plant, called 'manna' on the other side of the mountains, grew here too, though in less abundance. Daya did not care for manna, which produced in her a languorous slowing of the senses. When she took manna she could not concentrate to tell stories.

A new person entered the wagon. She sprinkled people with water as she tossed back her rain-wet hair from her face. She was a stranger to Daya and not pretty. Her eyes were small and the bridge of her nose was flattened so that the nostrils seemed by contrast to flare like the nostrils of a horse. She looked to Daya like the kind of fem who liked to fight. Such spirit could be attractive to Daya.

The newcomer glanced at Daya and did not bother to hide her contempt. Daya faced that contempt all the time, a prejudice against those who had been the favorites of their masters, coddled for their manners and their looks.

The newcomer sniffed the air of the wagon and withdrew into the rain without a word.

Daya guessed, 'Was that her? Alldera the runner?'

Kobba was already leaning over the fire, breathing in the drug fumes, and did not reply. But old Ossa, who clearly disliked the runner, circled Daya's arm with her bony hand and hissed, 'That's her. She's just as stand-offish as when she came, would you believe it? That was at the beginning of last Cool Season, a little after the wagons had left. Roona's wagon had no sooner gone than it was back again. This fem had come to them while they were trading at Red Sand Camp, and Roona thought they had better bring her back fast so she could tell us things about the Mares she'd lived with.'

Ossa hooted. 'A lot of good that was! Alldera hardly talks about the Mares. She's scared we'll see how sorry she is that she left them. The only thing she told us was that she'd borne a cub and left it with the Mares – can you imagine? There was a to-do over that, I can tell you.

'She never even brought her horses to the wagon with her, the ones she'd ridden from Stone Dancing to Red Sand. Said they weren't hers, left them in Red Sand. She never stopped to think Roona's crew might like a feast of fresh horsemeat for a change instead of dried sharu.'

'She won't get herself liked that way,' Daya said guardedly.

'She doesn't like any of us. She's young all over, never a thought for anybody but herself. Staying so long with the Mares made her too good for us. We don't measure up.'

'Who says so?' Kobba snarled. She took a breath of smoke. 'Not me!'

A few of the fems cheered her sleepily. Most were dozing among the deep colored cushions, their faces gilded by the light from the fire bowls. Daya had to shake her head to dislodge the shimmering waves of color and distortion that the manna poured into her. Kobba's words seemed to be rocking the wagon.

'The Mares are strong, but we're stronger. They live on their horses; they travel only where this barren country gives them food for their beasts. We live on foot, go where we like, make the Grasslands support us. We each came over the borderlands. You have to be tough to do that, and they know it. They're scared of us. They know if we ever gave them a fight for their water and grass and herds, they'd lose it all. But we don't want what they have.'

Then Kobba rocked to her knees and pushed among the pillows so that she could stretch out behind Elnoa and enclose her bulk in her arms. Elnoa shifted to lie against Kobba. Her face half hidden in the fall of her heavy hair, she gargled in tongueless sounds.

Kobba mumbled above her drooping head, 'She wants Daya too.'

'I'm here,' Daya murmured. She moved Emla's slack body aside so that she could curl up and pillow her own head on one of Elnoa's enormous thighs.

When the rains stopped and the Cool Season began, the trade wagons were ready to resume their journeys out onto the plains. This time it was Emla's turn to travel, and Daya saw to it that everyone knew Emla was leaving with one of the crews by order of Elnoa.

Daya hung about all day when the last wagon was being packed for its journey. The crew stacked it full of chests of wooden tools, ornaments, and great odorous piles of tea brick. There were boxes of small goods, too, utilitarian items like buckles and fine glazed beads. Holdfastish products, Daya thought approvingly, for the wild, ignorant Mares.

It was the wagoneers' custom to travel all the way west to the Great Salty River during the cool weather while there was water to drink in the slowly drying rain pools along the way. Then they would trade tea for salt from the Mares of Salt Wind Camp. Turning, they would work slowly back eastward trading tea, salt and other goods in the camps on the way back for meat, milk, leather and metal. As the Dusty Season advanced the camps of the Mares homed to their wells and so were easily found.

'Daya, you can still come with us if you want to.' Kobba looked up from her tally during a pause while the crew was busy picking up and recoiling some rope that had dropped out of a wicker chest. 'Your cooking kept my crew happy on our last trip.'

'Come along, Daya!' shouted Kenoma. 'I'll keep you warm. It'll be like old times.'

Times, a year or so back, best forgotten, Daya thought. Yet she would go if she could. With longing she pictured the huge, high-clouded sky of the Cool Season, the broad golden land patched with shade and bright sunlight. Kobba was a good boss, scrupulous about rations and work loads. She did not permit much fighting. There were others along besides Kenoma to choose for protector and bedmate. Tempting – only Daya was not really in a position to go. She was not about to give up this time in camp with Elnoa that she had intrigued all Rainy Season to obtain.

Watching Emla helping to buckle the hauling harness to the wagon, she began to feel quite cheerful. The masseur's fortunes at Elnoa's side had sunk while Daya's, carefully tended, had risen.

Emla's turn would come again if Daya meddled too much in camp affairs and Elnoa sent her travelling again. Daya intended to hold her place this time.

While the crew drew the oiled cover over the wagon frame, Kobba had her final consultation with Elnoa. Daya made herself busy on the porch of Elnoa's wagon to watch and listen. Kobba wanted Alldera to be added to her crew. She said it would do the runner good to take orders with others instead of leading them out running as she had been doing. 'She must sweat with the rest of us.'

She is out running now, Elnoa signed. Your crew will do better without her discontent. I will keep her busy here.

Daya had heard Alldera say that the tea camp sometimes seemed just like a big femhold with Elnoa as master. Did Elnoa know that? If not, there might be a profit, sometime, to be made out of the runner's imprudent statement.

For the present, there was something else to pursue. One of the crew fems had left a request that Daya speak for her with Elnoa while the crew was gone. The present of a bag of first-quality tea shavings assured that Daya would make a strong case for her.

Later, inside the big wagon when the traders had gone, Daya murmured to Elnoa, 'Poor Suda is having a terrible time with a debt she can't pay. No doubt you know all about it already, but maybe you hadn't heard that she was drunk at the time they were gambling or she wouldn't have risked so much. Now if she doesn't pay up out of her share of this trip's profits –'

Elnoa signed, Not yet, tell me about that later. Tell me now why you like it out on the plains.

Daya began to speak softly about what it was like out there. Elnoa sat looking through her current volume of accounts, occasionally smiling and looking up when something Daya said particularly pleased her. At such times Daya thought of herself as the tender guardian of some wealthy invalid.

Mornings in the Cool Season, old Ossa hung around the cooking pots to keep warm. Daya was cooking up the rare treat of a fresh meat stew – someone had speared a sharu at the spring the day before – and she found Ossa flicking out chunks of meat with a sharp stick and popping them into her mouth. Furious, Daya slapped her away. Ossa made a great show of falling down, and shrieked at her in a voice that could be heard all over camp:

'Be careful, you stupid, clumsy bitch! Do you want to kill the first child conceived by a free fem in the Grasslands, the daughter of Moonwoman herself?'

By noon the old creature was the talk of the camp. She claimed she had spent the night of the previous full moon outside and Moonwoman had magically impregnated her. Her cub was to grow up to reproduce merely by willing it. That was Moonwoman's promise, and everyone had to acknowledge, however snidely, that Ossa's wrinkled belly had begun to swell.

Daya smiled with the rest. This was not the first false pregnancy to be known in the tea camp, only the most grotesque and unlikely. It soon came to an end. Ossa drank another fem's ration of beer, 'because it was good for the baby's hair.' She got kicked in the belly for it, and the swelling vanished.

Then, around the cooking kettles behind Elnoa's wagon, Daya heard Alldera being blamed for Ossa's misadventure: 'Ossa says Alldera killed the child by witchery.'

'What's the witchery in a good, hard kick?'

'Who knows what the runner learned, living so long with the Mares.'

'What would you say if Ossa accused Froya, there?' Laughter.

'But it's Alldera, not Froya.'

'The runner should have brought us her cub. What right did she have to decide to leave it?'

'Ossa's right about that. Alldera never talks of the cub. We're only fems, you know, not good enough to hear about the cub she left with the high and mighty Mares.'

Daya noticed that the runner's name came up in conversation often, and usually with disapproval. There was a mad tale of her trip out, before Daya's return to camp, with a mapping party headed by Froya. The group had dragged home days overdue, still streaked with desert dust, and complaining bitterly that Alldera had gone off alone into the desert so that they'd all had to troop after her to bring her back.

Taxed with endangering the entire expedition and reminded that the free fems could ill afford to risk losing anyone, Alldera had defended herself by saying she had thought they were to go into the desert, not just along its edge making drawings of what they could see from there.

All very true, Daya reflected, if one insisted on taking symbolic action for the real thing. This was a distinction the runner seemed incapable of learning. No wonder she had enemies.

Not long after Ossa's 'pregnancy', Daya heard that Alldera was asking Elnoa to discipline fems who did not turn out for running practice. Daya had to put up with Elnoa's subsequent ill humor, which included thrown objects, bursts of incoherent and ugly noise when mere gestures would not carry the weight of her anger, and sometimes – praise Moonwoman's mercy – merely the sulks. She had her work cut out, restoring Elnoa to a decent frame of mind. She wondered how people here could think a pet's life was all sweet drippings from a master's plate.

Couldn't Alldera see that the tea camp went slack when Kobba was gone with a trading crew? Elnoa worked everyone very hard at weaving and dyeing but did not interfere at all with what else they did. Her business was the accumulation of goods. Kobba's job, when she returned, was to slam on the discipline again and push ahead with the plan.

If Alldera had not worked that out for herself, she was heading for disaster. Daya saw no reason to enlighten her. She knew the type: proud, demanding, impatient, withdrawn into herself out of disappointment with others, but lacking inner resources, particularly imagination.

Only action would suit her, and she was not going to get the kind of heroic nonsense that she wanted. Not here. Daya could have told her.

Someone came pounding across the yard shouting, 'It's a Mare! A Mare's come to the valley!'

Roused from a slumbrous afternoon in the big wagon, Daya went with Elnoa to the perimeter of the camp. A Mare as dark-skinned as the horse she rode was down by the spring, in plain sight of the sentries, if there had been any sentries. There was no telling how long she had been waiting there till someone noticed her.

Elnoa had Alldera sent for.

Daya's head was full of wild suppositions. She stared down at the rider, fascinated. She had never been this close to one of them for this long with nothing to do but look. She thought the Mare's appearance rather grand.

Under the back-thrown headcloth the Mare's face was an unreadable darkness lit by the glint of her eyes. She led two spare horses by ropes on their necks. How obedient her horses seemed, how patient. Her mount leaned down in a leisurely fashion to rub its head on its foreleg. All of them lacked the scruffy flash of wild horses. Daya wondered what the Mare had done to tame them so completely. They did not look scarred or starved.

Alldera appeared below, padding swiftly down the trail to the spring.

The yellow tones of the plain, visible beyond the mouth of the valley, had faded as the days lengthened and heated toward the early Dusty Season. Daya imagined the bold Mare riding alone through that landscape, as it was gradually leached of color by the increasing power of the sun . . .

The Mare leaned down and as she spoke touched Alldera, a swift flicker of the hand. While trading in Marish camps Daya had often seen them do that among themselves, casually, as if they owned each other. One of the led horses stepped forward and put its nose against Alldera's shoulder. Alldera laid her hand on its flat forehead. The watching fems stirred.

For a moment Daya wished strongly that she were down there too, and she was almost jealous of Alldera. What did it feel like to be touched by a woman as black as char and to stroke a creature that was not even human at all?

Alldera and the black Mare talked in distant voices. The runner's voice seemed choppy and hard, the Mare's richly liquid. An experienced storyteller's voice, Daya thought, and what an attentive audience she had in the fems strung out along the wall of wood and brush and stone on the hillside above. She was so black, a dramatic shadow-person; she gave Daya the shivers.

Alldera nodded curtly to the Mare and turned back up toward the tea camp. All the fems began to talk excitedly at once. The Mare gathered her headcloth about her shoulders and rode away down the valley with her horses.

When Alldera came to Elnoa she said, 'That was someone who looks after my cub for me. She says that the cub has gone into the childpack of Stone Dancing Camp. They always tell the bloodmother. It's a custom.'

What are you supposed to do? Elnoa signed.

Alldera shrugged. 'Nothing. I'm just supposed to know.'

Froya said in a sceptical tone, 'You told us the cub was nothing to you.'

'It's important to Stone Dancing Camp that I know,' Alldera said, speaking directly to Elnoa. 'The rider comes of a bloodline that cares a lot about doing what's right.'

'If the Mares did what was right,' Froya sneered, 'they would have brought your cub to us. If they did what was right, they wouldn't let their horses screw them.' That raised a snicker among the others. Froya never knew when to quit. 'Do you think she's fucked with that brown one she was riding?'

'Idiot,' Alldera said with contempt, 'she was riding a mare. Can't you tell a male horse from a female?'

Froya's cheeks patched red over the high, narrow bones. 'From this distance only an expert could,' she snorted. 'Someone who knows them as well as the Mares do.'

Alldera dropped into a fighting stance, and Froya jumped back with a shout, 'Oh no, I know your fancy kicks; you could put my eye out while I was watching your hands.'

The runner straightened and said angrily, 'It's not my fault that you don't know how to block a kick or throw one. I offered to teach kick fighting, remember? Only some people decided it was too dangerous.'

Daya let out her breath, watching Alldera stalk away. What a foolish thing to say, since word was that Elnoa herself had forbidden those lessons, probably rightly. The free fems quarreled frequently among themselves and were too few to add new risks of serious injury.

This Alldera was no realist. She was nervy, though. You had to grant that – always remembering the foolhardy ones were just the sort that got themselves killed by irate masters in the end.

Kobba's wagon came home late in the Rainy Season, battered by a flash flood that had caught it in the foothills. Emla had almost been swept away in the flood. A white swatch in her hair, just noticeable at her departure and now wider, was suddenly being attributed to the accident. She took her time recovering from the shock, Daya noted, indulging freely in fits of nervous tremors and weeping, keeping weakly to Elnoa's wagon. She was, unfortunately, far too distraught to help Daya with the cooking and cleaning.

Elnoa played along with the act. Probably she was angry because Kobba's poor judgment had cost most of the cargo. Solicitude for Emla, poor victim, seemed to Daya a neatly calculated way for Elnoa to continually remind Kobba of her mistake. Of course, this was only Daya's suspicion. There was really no telling with Elnoa.

Daya was bored. The months since the Mare's visit had rolled uneventfully by. Getting Emla displaced from her new closeness to Elnoa seemed a diverting and useful project.

She decided that Emla's weakness was her greed. The masseur liked to wait till she thought no one saw and then grab an extra pot of beer or a bar of Elnoa's own best tea. She tried to be the last one to leave a wagon, and might slip into one while all its inmates were away. Caught, she would say, 'Sorry, I thought I heard voices inside.'

It was all small-scale pilfering. Elnoa surely knew, but chose not to punish.

All that would be necessary would be to raise the suspicion that Emla had found the hiding place of Elnoa's private treasure trove. Each of the free fems had a secret cache hidden in the hills. The whole area was planted with belongings of the living and the dead; sometimes fems died without revealing their hiding places. More than one member of the tea camp had been hurt or even killed because of the suspicion that she had found – by accident or by craft – another's hiding place.

Elnoa surely had the greatest fortune hidden and the most to fear from a thief. It was Daya's business to know secrets, and she had known for years the location of Elnoa's treasure cave, though she had never entered it herself.

Pity she could not come up with some really original plan; but old tricks work best.

Elnoa had recently given Emla a bracelet of blue gems set in fine braided leather. It was perfect for Daya's purpose. It had no catch and tied on. Emla had complained that the knot worked loose so that the bracelet kept dropping off and getting lost. No free fem who found that bracelet would dare to keep if for herself; she would recognize it and remember its august source.

It took three days of careful observation to discover where Emla kept her bracelet. She had wound it around the catch of one of the unused sleeping platforms. Daya pulled out the spare bedding from all the platforms to be aired, and in the process she slipped the bracelet down into an opening in the hem seam of her smock.

Then she left camp early with her herb basket for the part of the hills where she knew the tea cutters would be working that day.

There was no way of knowing just what Elnoa would do if Daya were caught at this. The risk made her heart speed with excitement. The voices of the tea cutters rang in the sparkling morning air. They were catching up with her. She could see their heads bobbing above the tea bushes and hear the blows of their hatchets. A long arm flashed as someone reached for a promising-looking branch.

Daya set the bracelet in a tea bush right over the concealed entrance to Elnoa's treasure cave, positioned as if it had caught on a branch there. Then she slipped back to camp and waited. Oh, there would be a furor, everyone asking angrily what the owner of the bracelet had been doing out among the treasure-laden hills when she was supposed to be in Elnoa's wagon, laid up sick with nerves.

The scene later in the wagon began the way Daya had imagined it, right down to the outrage in Emla's scratchy voice. Emla said exactly the right things, at first – about thieves, a cherished possession never carelessly worn, and how she was too feeble these past weeks to move far from her bed. She hunched up in her blankets trembling, making the most of her weakness.

Elnoa sat amid her cushions with the bracelet on her massive knee, chin sunk on palm. Daya knew Elnoa could not show her full anger and alarm, for then other fems might guess that the bracelet had been found near her own secret location.

No more, Elnoa signed, the bracelet's blue stones glittering now in her moving hand. You have not always been in my wagon. You have been out.

Naturally Emla had been out; Daya had guessed that too. Emla had certainly pilfered from the cargo of the unlucky wagon. She must have made at least one stealthy trip to her own treasure with her takings. To pretend otherwise was a mistake.

'I did go out,' Emla admitted, 'to see to my own property. But why accuse me? We all look after what belongs to us. I know one person who wanders the hills constantly by herself, no matter how many times people have warned her. She hasn't lived with us long

enough to have amassed any wealth of her own. She's smart and
secret and neither labor fem nor house pet. Alldera the runner has
stolen my bracelet and lost it in the hills.'

The unpopular newcomer! Daya had forgotten her completely.

'I saw her trotting off alone only two days ago,' someone volunteered anxiously, and suddenly everyone was talking. At Elnoa's
command two of the tea cutters hurried out and brought the runner
back with them.

It seemed to Daya that she had a reckless look these days, which
did not help. Surrounded by the silent, resentful group, Alldera
listened to what Emla had to say. She laughed at the charge. In an
angry tone she said, 'You can't mean you believe I did this.'

Someone shouted, 'Why not? You haven't had time to build up a
treasure of your own, except from our belongings. Why do you keep
wearing that Marish shirt of skins instead of a good smock from our
looms? Maybe you like those pockets they wear in front, maybe
they're handy for putting stolen things into?'

Alldera said furiously, 'I don't like to wear a slave smock as if I
were still somebody's property back in the Holdfast, that's why!'
She stared desperately from face to face. 'I can't believe this. It's as if
I'd never left the Holdfast at all – fems spending their lives laboring
for someone else's profit, squabbling among themselves over
trifles –'

They murmured; some faces showed uncertainty. Then Emla
yelled, 'Thief! Where did you get that hair binder you're wearing?'

'I traded Lora a bag of pine nuts for it.' Alldera was looking over
their heads now as though disdaining their questions, but Daya saw
the sweat gleaming on her face. 'Go ask Lora.'

Seeing her fully on the defensive now, the fems pressed in,
demanding, accusing. Elnoa was obviously just letting the tide of
anger roll; Daya, appalled, could think of nothing to do. Now
everyone was hostile to Alldera, and the runner seemed unwilling or
unable to placate them. When faces grew red and fists were
clenched, Elnoa sent for Lora. But by the time word was brought
that Lora was out on sentry duty, it was all over. Only the question
of punishment remained.

Elnoa signed her judgement: Alldera is confined to camp. No
more running at all.

'Who are you to give me orders?' Alldera blazed. 'You're not my master! I've stolen nothing. Prove that I've taken anything from anyone!'

Elnoa stared at her. The bracelet of blue stones was wrapped around her thick fingers like a weapon. Go away, she signed. You are lucky not to be treated more harshly. Perhaps you have done this, perhaps not. You are an arrogant young know-it-all. I think you would like to take our goods and run off to be rich among your Marish friends.

Alldera rejoined her fiercely, 'At least my Marish friends had some notion of right and wrong –'

Edging closer to her, Daya whispered in anguished agitation, 'Go, you're in danger here! You've really made her angry!'

Spinning on her heel, Alldera pushed her way out through the crowd. The others shuffled after her, taunting her for a thief.

Now Elnoa's eyes were fixed on Daya's face. Clumsy with nerves, Daya began to straighten the floor blankets rucked up by trampling feet. Don't panic, Elnoa knows nothing, she only suspects, she told herself. The wagon smelled of sweat now, and cushions lay tumbled everywhere.

Emla leaned at ease among her pillows. When she met Daya's furtive glance she smiled.

Elnoa isn't through with me, Daya thought wretchedly. She had an instinct about these things.

The next morning she woke early and could not get back to sleep. She crept outside and stood on the back porch, trying to rub the tension out of her neck and shoulders. The wide yard lay empty all around her under a drift of mist, and she could see no one stirring at the wagons in the perimeter. She wondered what she could do so early for distraction from her worries, thought about going back in for a blanket – it was chilly out – but shrank from the possibility of waking Elnoa, seeing that massive, brilliant-eyed face turned coldly toward her in the gloom . . .

A sound made her look up. A knot of sentries was coming down from the hills behind camp where they kept watch, now that Kobba was home. Two leaned on the shoulders of their companions as if they had been hurt. In the center of the cluster was Alldera, head lolling and feet trailing, being dragged into camp like a trophy.

They brought their prize and their injured to the steps of the back porch. Lexa, head of the watch, rapped on the rail with the shaft of her spear.

Elnoa and Kobba came out. Kobba had a blanket in her hands. She stood behind Elnoa and folded it around the big, soft shoulders. Shrunk into the corner of the porch, Daya noted this indication of renewed warmth between the two. In the quiet she could hear clearly the painful breathing and low groans from the injured.

What do I see here this morning? signed Elnoa.

'A rebel and a thief,' Lexa said, shaking Alldera's slack head by a twist of her long hair.

Free fems had begun to drift over from the other wagons. One asked, 'What did she steal?'

Listen or disperse, Elnoa signed; and at her shoulder Kobba said forcefully, 'Listen or disperse.'

Lexa said, 'She said she was just going running as usual, but when we said no she tried to get by us. There was still mist on the ground. If she'd slipped past us, she'd have been hard to find. She could have looted every cache in the hills and been on her way –'

'How did the sentries get hurt?' Kobba demanded. 'Were the Mares waiting out there to help her?'

'She was just going right by us as if we weren't there,' Lexa said resentfully. 'She said we'd had time to dig new holes like the sharu do – that's what she said, ask the others – so our treasures were safe and she wasn't going to sit around and get fat because we were afraid.

'Anyway, poor Soa shoved her back a little, you know, not hard, just a warning. She gave Soa a terrific kick. I think Soa's knee is knocked right out, she can't put any weight on it at all.

'Well, we went at her. Nobody used a weapon, you can see that, but I think she's got some cracked ribs. She hurt us, and we hurt her back.'

Elnoa signed, Go and take care of your injuries and Alldera's injuries too. You sentries were right to stop her, but rougher than you should have been. We do not use the master's ways here.

The sentries turned Alldera over and carried her away by shoulders and ankles. Daya saw the dirt and blood streaked over her face and chest. Her head hung back, eyes closed, in that horrible, loose way Daya remembered from the days when the men of the Holdfast used to bring in captured runaway fems and give them over to be hunted through the holiday streets to their deaths.

The need to make presents to Elnoa was mortifying, but Daya had to do something to melt the frost between herself and her patron. It was weeks now since the bracelet incident.

It did not help her feelings to be stopped on the back porch by Emla, who insisted on sorting through the box Daya was carrying and opening the bottles it contained. These were perfumes that Daya had selected over the years from the best stocks of Fedeka the dyer.

The tea cutters were all out, the camp lay quiet. A few fems tended fresh-cut tea that was laid out on long racks over fires to be dried. A solitary figure sat nearby with a blanket draped over her like a Marish headcloth.

Emla glanced that way too and said slyly, 'Too bad the runner no longer runs – except to fat.'

What Alldera the runner did these days was drink. The battering she had suffered at the sentries' hands seemed to have broken her. She moved slowly about the camp, bent as if in pain. Daya heard people say Alldera had brought it on herself, but their hostility was blunted; there were rumors that certain unnamed free fems privately agreed with some of her assertions. A few openly pitied her and blamed Daya, who knew that her part in the affair was common supposition. The whole situation was unjust. It was not Daya's fault.

'She certainly is the poorest drunk I ever saw,' Emla said, turning a small stone bottle in her supple hands. 'More than a single bowl of beer makes her sick. She is stubborn, you have to grant her that. Did you see her – or rather, hear her the other night? Throwing up and cursing all evening, trying to keep enough beer down to knock herself out! Hasn't she come begging you for beer? No? She stays away from you, I notice.

'Ugh, this smells awful, what was Fedeka thinking of?'

'Why, of you, sweet friend,' Daya said instantly. 'She told me especially to give that one to you from her.' The lie pleased her. She smiled her rare smile, feeling the scars in her cheeks ruck up the skin into hideous lumps, making of her smiling face a fright mask.

Emla recoiled and said venomously, 'Don't show that nightmare face to me, Daya. I've put worse scars than that on the faces of fems who crossed me.'

Daya deftly snatched the box of scents and stood up. 'I'll take these in now that you've inspected them.'

The masseur would hardly wrestle with her for the gifts here in front of everyone. She gave Daya a freezing glare and went rapidly in ahead of her, no doubt intent on dropping a nasty word or two in Elnoa's ear.

Glancing back over her shoulder, Daya saw that the lumpish figure of Alldera had not stirred. The sight of the runner's pain-cramped body brought back the pain of her own maiming, the desolation of her beauty destroyed.

Even the best wagons leaked in a night of hard rain. Spreading damp blankets to dry on the porch rails was not suited to a pet, but it was work Elnoa appreciated having done. The sun was out this morning. Elnoa sat in her wide chair, one of her ledgers spread open on her lap. Emla stood behind, pinning her hair up, preparing her for a massage.

A fem came to the porch steps: Alldera, wrapped in her grimy blanket, steaming odorously in the sunshine. Her hair hung lank. Dirt outlined the nails of the hand that clutched the blanket. Her light-colored eyes seemed to have retreated into darkened sockets, and there was a half-healed scab on her broad lower lip. She looked old.

Why does this coarse creature keep intruding on my life? Daya asked in silent irritation. She moved away a little down the porch.

Alldera said in a flat tone, 'I want to go out with one of the wagon crews.'

Lips pursing like a tea bud, Elnoa shut the leather book, opened it again to shake straight the limp pages, and put it aside. She beckoned Alldera to join her on the porch.

Drink and inactivity have ruined you, she signed. Hauling is hard work.

Daya heard Alldera respond, 'I know the Mares. I could help the wagon crew bargain with them.'

The inner bark of certain foothill pines, baked underground for a day, became a sweet and crackly candy. Daya brought some of these crisp, sticky sheets out on a tray. Elnoa took some. Alldera shook her head.

Elnoa signed, Some people would object that you might run away from the crew to live with the Mares again. She slipped her smock from her shoulders, and Emla began the massage with her oil-shiny hands.

With a jerk of her head Alldera indicated the fems at work at the tea-drying fires. 'I don't think they'd miss me.'

Patiently Elnoa signed, We are both free and few. Everyone is worth something here. Take some sweet.

Daya extended the tray again but Alldera ignored it. She moved her body uncomfortably, as if her injuries still pained her. Suddenly she burst out in a low but intense tone, 'I'm rotting here. I need something to do, work to keep my head thinking.'

Elnoa tilted her chin, stretching the line of her neck under Emla's hand. She signed, You have sometimes expressed a strong dislike of the way we do things.

Alldera did not speak. At least she was learning when to keep still, Daya noted. She hoped Elnoa would grant the runner's request to go out with a crew. She did not want Alldera around forever, a living reminder of her own disastrous miscalculation.

Elnoa signed, Maybe you can still learn to fit in here despite your strange background. I will see what my crew captains say. Come back and we will talk about this. Daya heard her suck on the sweet fragments stuck to her teeth – a revolting habit.

Alldera returned to her place across the yard and sat down again slowly.

Exasperated, Daya slapped another blanket over the railing. She knew the signs. Elnoa was in a playful mood; she would keep Alldera begging, never refusing, never agreeing. Perhaps she was taking vengeance for the runner's criticisms of her. Daya could see the complacent smile on Elnoa's face as the big fem leader leaned back and let the weight of her shoulders rest against Emla's oiled palms.

Later, when both had gone in, Daya crossed the yard. She knelt near Alldera and began pulling twigs and branches out from under the wagon, selecting fuel for cooking the day's meals.

Softly she said, 'Elnoa isn't going to let you go with a wagon. Hard work isn't what you need anyway. Go to Fedeka the dye-maker, she's healed people hurt worse than you are. You've heard of her? She travels across the plains gathering plants, getting her supplies from wagons that she meets out there. You've crossed that

country with the Mares, you can find your way. After the rains
Fedeka moves south to avoid the colder weather. She should be
down near the wells of Royo Camp soon.'

'You think I should run away?' Alldera's tone was neutral,
unreadable, and she did not look up.

'Lots of fems have gone to Fedeka for help. That's not running
away; and you can slip off easily. No one watches you any more.'

Alldera did not answer.

Daya left her in a damp cloud of tea pungence and smoke. It was
the runner's mistake if she chose to ignore such a good suggestion.
She and Alldera were quits now; the runner no longer mattered.

At the old tea-camp site, screened by trees near the spring, Daya
took leaf fragments from the pouch at her belt and chewed them.
She undressed and anointed herself with the leaf saliva. Shivering
slightly in the evening chill, she smeared her nipples, the insides of
her thighs, and her vulva, making them fragrant.

She did not do this for Elnoa. For some time Elnoa had not sent
for her. She slept these nights with Tua, but she did not sweeten
herself for Tua either. They bedded together only because each of
them was partnerless. She prepared so elaborately to make love
because she knew she excelled in this preparation, and she was
proud of her skill at it.

Then she lay down in her blankets under the shelter of the
abandoned wagon. She had not trysted here since going trading –
two years or more? Too long. She looked out at the clouds piled
deep into the darkening sky, preparing new assaults on the mountains. Good. When making love she liked the drumming of distant
rain and the drama of far thunder. She enjoyed seeing her companion's eyes glinting greedily in the flash of the lightning. Let the
rest of them keep to the stuffy wagons, descending to the floor to
make love while others peered down at them from the sleeping
platforms above. Though that was exciting in its own way, to know
people were heating themselves on your own heat . . .

Tua stood above her in the twilight, and Daya raised up on one
elbow to greet her and draw her down.

'Listen,' Tua said eagerly, 'what do you think I just heard –
Alldera's left camp!'

Daya caught at her hand. 'Come here, I'm ready for you.'

'Imagine!' Tua breathed, holding back still. 'Bet she's gone back to the Mares. What's Elnoa going to say? What will Kobba do when she finds out?'

'She'll have a cub.' Daya was vexed. 'Lie down with me.'

'But this is important! Aren't you excited?'

'Yes I am; and this is what's important.' She drew Tua's mouth to her breast, and the two of them sank down. With the ease of long practice, Daya slid her knee between Tua's legs, and she lay back with a sigh of anticipation as Tua rolled on her with good, warm weight.

Daya had never known the rains to last so late into the start of the Cool Season. A Generation Feast was always held shortly before the first wagon was scheduled to leave on its trade journey. This year the feast began in a rainstorm. Daya and those assigned to help her prepare food worked all day sheltered by awnings, cursing the leaks and the muddy footing.

Daya chose and combined the ingredients of the stew kettles, then left the tending of the cooking to her subordinates. She reserved for herself the oversight of the little covered pots that steamed all day over small fires. Each pot was filled with a fertility douche concocted to a formula of Fedeka the dyer's.

By evening the rain had stopped. Satiated with food and hot beer, the fems assembled quietly in the yard. Kobba stood on the porch at Elnoa's right hand. Tonight she spoke to them not in Elnoa's voice but in her own, that clanged like iron bars over the crackling from the fires and the desultory dripping of rainwater.

'We gather tonight, fems,' she said, 'to try once more to find a starter that will make new life in us. The Mares conceive without men, and so will we – but we won't turn to beasts to do it.

'Now, you may say – some say it every year – why do we want cubs at all? Once we made them for our masters, just like we made cloth or food or furnishings – for their use. And if the cubs weren't perfect, the men killed us for it. Even at best, with so much breeding it was awful for us. All of you remember old fems so torn from cubbings that they went raw-legged and stinking because they couldn't hold their piss. I myself have wondered, if cubs don't come to us in the course of things, why run after all that pain again?

'I'll tell you a story, friends.

'Back in the Holdfast I worked in the mines. The ore was crushed by machines that the Ancients had stored away in stacks underground. The pieces were big, they could tear loose under a miner's foot and smash the people lower down. We had to be strong and lightfooted. You see my hands, my feet? No calluses, no scars. We miners were given shoes and gloves so we wouldn't slice ourselves on wire and jagged edges or get acid burns. That's how valuable we were. I went through a dozen pair of palm pads a month.

'It was always damp down there. We worked by lamplight. The rust cough ate out everyone's voice in the end. But I didn't stay till the end.

'Everytime I came up from the mines I smelled that good clean smell coming east on the wind. I knew our side of the borderlands because I'd been marched up and down in the scrubby trees there with a search gang, looking for new mining sites. When the time came, I ran west laughing.

'A man came after me, one of those drug-mad Rovers that used to guard the old men's lives and their goods and chase down runaway fems for them. I hid. I jumped out when he passed me and I broke his neck. I rammed his chin up so hard I almost tore the head off his body. I'd never thought to do anything with my strength before but beat on the metal heaps and on any fems who bothered me. I never saw how easy it would have been to smash the life out of those men that stood around telling me what to do all my life.

'I see now. But it may be a long time before I get home, and by then my best strength will be gone. By then there may be only twenty of us going back, not fifty. We'd be weak.

'Unless we have some cubs. We can't let our numbers drop or age cut us down. We should go home a conquering army, or why go home at all? If we find the men all dead, that's all right too – we should have young fems there with us to help us break the men's bones and their buildings and trample everything of theirs and bury them in a foot of sea salt, so our cubs will know what their freedom is. If Moonwoman wills it, nothing will be left to show that men ever lived in the world, but our cubs will be there to show that we did.'

The response was a collective sigh from the assembled fems and the sounds of a few sobs and snuffles. Kobba's voice, hoarse with emotion at the end, moved them this way every time.

Then the fems came in pairs – except Kobba, who came alone, for herself and Elnoa – and to each pair Daya gave two pots of douche and a syringe to take into one of the wagons. The syringe was to draw the douche and use it in the partner's body. The fems' faces were bright with hope that this time one of the douches would work.

Daya did not believe this would ever happen, but she was pleased to be the dispenser of Fedeka's mixtures on these welcome days of feasting, love, and hopes. At least Fedeka knew the plants of the plains so well that the douches were sure to be safe. Free fems no longer poisoned themselves in their efforts to conceive, as in the past.

Personally, Daya had no particular wish to become bloated with pregnancy ever again, whether from a man or one of Fedeka's brews. She did like the warm flooding of her body. It was a feeling that no man with his imperceptible squirtings of lukewarm stuff had ever induced. She even enjoyed the feel of the syringe itself. Early on in the Holdfast she had seen that a pet's life included a lot more fucking than the life of an ordinary labor fem; she had made herself enjoy, and had later come to crave, the sensations of penetration.

There were those, she knew, who found her desire to be entered perverse. She could only be sorry for them, wretches whose experience had been limited to monthly battering by men pressed to do their copulatory duty in the Holdfast breeding rooms. Men who liked the bodies of fems were rare in the Holdfast.

In Tua she had found a friend who knew how to serve her tastes without open disgust. When the others were all gone, Daya and Tua found a corner for themselves in one of the wagons. Daya lay with her upper body hugged between Tua's legs while Tua worked the syringe pipe slower or faster, at a deeper or shallower angle, whatever pleased Daya, until Daya lifted her hips from the rumpled bedding and rode the flooding instrument to her climax.

The syringe, filled from Tua's bowl, was pressed into Daya's hand. She turned, gathering the body's heavy center in her arms and gliding her cheek up Tua's soft inner thigh.

Before dawn she was wakened by obscure discomfort. It was not, as she had thought at first, something bad in her gut. The sensation was of a burning in her lower belly and vagina.

The wagon was full of the sounds of sleepers. On the floor a fem gasped her way laboriously toward orgasm – probably old Ossa, who always went back for a second round of douche. If no one could be induced to lie with her, she would manage by herself, fingering her own body to its climax.

The burning feeling flickered out. Daya settled herself in her bedding, which was still damp from the douche.

By morning she was feverish. She curled, moaning around her pain. She felt people handling her, trying to straighten out her limbs, washing out her vagina and lifting her onto a pile of soft blankets at the back of Elnoa's wagon.

She tried not to cry out. There was Tua standing over her, weepily repeating that it could not be her fault. Then Tua was gone, sent away. Elnoa could not bear whiners.

They did not abandon Daya in her trouble. Someone was with her all the time, burning sweet-scented herbs in the fire bowls, gently restraining her when she sought to dig the pain out of her own body with her nails. It was she who, because of the wandering of her mind, felt herself leaving them.

As she lay burning it seemed to her that her head was swollen vast enough to contain whole populations; she could not understand how the wagon held her. She kept hearing the cracking of the short, split-ended switches that young male overseers used to drive labor fems. She smelled the scents that had mingled in Master Kazzaro's private chamber. She tasted the flavor of someone's body – her old lover the pet Merika, coming to her to receive solace. Or maybe it was the limping fem, name forgotten now, who had taken Daya under her protection down in the kitchens; she had applied salves to Daya's cheeks, vainly trying to repair the jagged holes torn by the broiling spit.

The pain in her body was surely the pain of cubbing, but this place was not the Holdfast hospital. There was no screaming here.

She was fed broth. She thought hazily, How sorry they are for me, how angry with the unknown fem who's killed me.

Someone was bending over her, mumbling, breathing on her, tugging at her legs –

Ossa. Old Ossa was dragging at her. At first it seemed like another vision. Daya pushed at Ossa, but the old creature slapped her hands away and continued dragging her toward the far end of the wagon.

Looking up suddenly, Ossa smiled at someone behind Daya and panted, 'Oh good, she's too heavy for me. Help me drag her over to the door.'

The other person leaned down to take hold of Daya's shoulders. It was Kobba. She said, 'Why are you pulling at Daya like that? What are you trying to do?'

'Tip her out, get rid of her,' the old fem whispered, tugging alternately at Daya and at Kobba.

'I'm sick,' Daya moaned, shrinking against Kobba.

Kobba hissed, 'She's sick, you old fool!'

Daya was terrified that between them Kobba and Ossa would pull her to pieces. Her inflamed flesh would part with a sickly tearing sound and release a stinking gas –

'Yes, yes, she's very sick,' Ossa replied. 'She's breathing sickness on us all. Help me toss her outside. Can't you smell it? Her decay makes the whole wagon stink.'

'That's the smell of all the medicines we've been trying on her. Let her go!' Kobba commanded.

Ossa backed off, panting distressedly between her crooked teeth. As Kobba lifted Daya in her arms, the old fem whined, 'I have to guard my health. Nobody looks out for me. They pinch me and abuse me, they say I don't work to earn my food. It's not my fault my sight is going. Spoiled little pet. It's all very well for you, Kobba, you're still young and strong.' She rubbed her hands on her wrinkled flanks as if to get rid of the touch of Daya. 'Man slime.' She wept a little, sniffed, and shuffled off.

It was good to have strong friends who could drive away one's enemies with a frown and a sharp word. Daya watched Kobba's squinting face floating above her and prayed to Moonwoman for an end to her pain.

Kobba's voice said harshly, 'Fems are saying you'd rather see your pet dead than send her to the Mares.'

Daya turned as much as the pain would allow. Kobba was standing near her, rolling up a leather window to let in daylight. Elnoa reclined on her couch of cushions. No one else was there.

Elnoa signed, She may after all recover.

'She'll die. You must send her to the Mares now. Maybe they can cure her, maybe not, but if she dies here people will say that's what you wanted because she was annoying you. If she dies with the Mares, the blame falls on them.'

Elnoa signed something Daya could not see; her vision kept washing in and out of focus. Her throat was burning. She could not understand why they went on talking, ignoring her, when she needed something to drink so badly.

Kobba said, 'Is this how you would act if she were the property of your master in the old days?'

Passionately Daya explained to them that she was too valuable to be let die. It came into her head that she had offended them with her scarred smile, that they did not want to look at her. She promised not to smile again, ever.

No one seemed to hear her. Kobba went on talking, louder and louder, until darkness enfolded and protected Daya from the sound.

Why were they moving her, didn't they know how she hurt? She wept and flinched from their hands.

'Hush,' Tua whispered in her ear, 'we're trying to help you.'

Deftly she wrapped Daya's hands in a strip of cloth, binding them together forearm to forearm beneath her breasts. Someone else was there, putting things into a wicker box. Was that Emla, sneaky fingers pawing through Daya's clothing?

'Don't let Emla,' Daya moaned.

Tua patted her, smiled at her, and lifted her up. She was carried to a trade wagon and nestled into a hammock, separated only by a curtain from stacked bricks of tea.

Elnoa came in and lowered herself onto a bench beside the hammock. She had brought a cushion with her, which she tucked behind Daya's head.

Elnoa's lips trembled slightly as though she were trying to whisper. She leaned forward, doubling the rolling flesh of her body over her thighs. Her eyes were wide with emotion, green like sea waves standing toward the beach. The eyes seemed to speak almost as much as the hands, as if hands and eyes were the living spirits of that huge bulk.

I have been consulting my ledgers, she signed. Someday civilized people will find and read them, and they will learn from them what our lives were like and how we ended, cubless and dwindling away one by one to nothing. Did you think I wrote only figures, totaling up my wealth for my own amusement? I write everything there, all that I know — what I remember of life in the Holdfast, what I know of life here. Your stories are fancies, Daya, that will vanish when you do. Nothing will be left of you, for all your fine imagination. In my ledgers the facts are written.

All our works will disappear — the wagons will rot, and the tea will grow wild over us. Only what I have done and thought, sitting quietly and using my mind while others used their muscles, will last. It is in my ledgers, and my ledgers go year by year, volume by volume, to safety in a dry place in the hills where they wait for discovery in the future. My voice that has not spoken for decades is in them and will outlast all your loud talk, your whispers, your singing of songs.

The words made no sense to Daya. She knew they should. She wanted to smile at Elnoa, but remembered she had promised not to.

Meanwhile, Elnoa continued, the past recorded in my books is useful to me. The past tells me that nothing pleasing should be wasted, not even when it is also a troublesome nuisance — which is what you are, Daya, with your intrigues. It is something, too, that though the masters took your looks from you, here in the Grasslands you have more lovers than ever you had at home. You and I are alike in that; we two have subdued adversity.

The actual signs she used, Daya saw, meant simply, 'we both have beaten bad luck.' But with Elnoa's handspeech, grander and subtler interpretations invariably suggested themselves, overwhelming utterly the blunt common equivalents of her gestures. Daya thought, what a good friend, to come and soothe my feverish vision with the cool, deft dancing of her hands.

So let no one say, she was signing, that I am like a bad master, that I neglect those who belong to me. I am sending you to the Mares to see if they can cure you. You are no burden to the wagon crew, though they complain — you have grown lighter than dry grass. They will do as I have told them, and take you to the Mares and pay the Mares to do their best for you.

I will write down what I have done for you, and perhaps a few of your stories, if I can remember them.

Touching her fingers first to her own mouth, then to Daya's, she patted her smile onto Daya's burning lips in place of a kiss.

FEDEKA'S CAMP

8

I could kill her, Alldera thought grimly, looking at the pet fem's scarred, sleeping face: choke her, slice her throat. Her little game with Emla's bracelet wrecked me. Without even meaning to she did it. She sent me here to Fedeka (out of guilt; it cancels things out). And she came here nearly dead herself (that cancels things too).

Alldera sat sewing strips of colored cloth together. The outside walls of Fedeka's small tent were covered with similar strips that had been dyed in Fedeka's battered dye pots and fastened on with a stitch or two to weather and fade. They fluttered outside in the breeze like faint voices.

Alldera worked close to the fire. The Cool Season was well advanced and the morning sun brought bright light but little warmth. She wore a cloth tunic under her leather shirt and kept her feet curled near the flames. There was no room to stretch her legs. With two guests and Fedeka's bundles and pouches and baskets cramped inside, the leather walls bulged. Sometimes Alldera took her blankets and slept outside in spite of the cold, just for the freedom to straighten her limbs.

Her ribs still ached in the mornings when she got up: Daya's fault. Even Fedeka could not promise complete recovery, for Alldera was no youngster any more — a disquieting surprise, to realize that — who would heal easily and completely.

If this pet bitch says the wrong thing when she wakes up I'll wring her neck.

The needle jabbed and Alldera yelped. Then she saw Daya's eyes open just a line and Daya's leg strain furtively to loosen the blankets in case she should have to run. Let her try. It felt good to see the pet fem afraid.

Alldera said briskly, 'Fedeka's out. She says your danger's past, so she's left you with me for a while.'

Daya's eyes, enormous in her wasted face, opened wide. 'What will you do?'

Plain scared of me and straightforward about it, Alldera thought. 'I'm going to stay with you. I'm a grateful patient and a guest in Fedeka's tent. For her sake, I won't do you any harm. She seems to consider you valuable. I saw how she fought to get you from the wagon crew. She just wanted some supplies from them, but there you were in the wagon, and she wouldn't hear of letting them take you on to the Riding Camp Women.

'She says, by the way, that there was nothing wrong with any douche made from her ingredients. Somebody must have doctored yours. I suppose you have a lot of enemies.'

Daya licked her lips nervously. 'Maybe Emla had it done. Clever bitch. Maybe because she was annoyed with me over the bracelet.'

'I'm surprised you didn't foresee that.'

'There are always risks,' the pet fem murmured dreamily. 'No one can foresee everything.'

Well, you certainly could not fault the bitch for nursing a grudge.

Daya said drowsily, 'You're sewing those strips to your pants . . .'

Carrying cactus pads in her hat, which she held upside down by the cord, Alldera trudged home to Fedeka's tent. She could see the two of them together outside, Daya's slight form reclined next to the leather groundsheet that Fedeka had spread out to work on. Fedeka sat sorting through piles of dried plants, crumbling them thoughtfully in her fingers, smelling them. She had only one arm, having lost the other to Holdfast machinery.

As Alldera drew nearer they looked up at her and let their conversation trail off. Talking about me, she thought. She was surprised by Daya's easy intimacy with Fedeka, whom Alldera had come to regard as a person of energy and determination. What could such an individual find in Daya the pet?

Alldera put the hat down and squatted to build a fire with twigs from the fuel pile.

'How does your side feel?' Fedeka asked.

'Doesn't hurt.'

'Did you run at all?'

'You said I shouldn't rush things.' Alldera was afraid of how badly she would run, like a cripple. With flint and metal she struck a spark into the little tower of dry sticks and grass she had made. She took a green stick and held it out toward Daya. 'Run some of those pads onto this so we can roast them and get the spines burnt off.'

Daya obeyed silently.

Fedeka took her portion of the evening tea and tucked it into her cheek. Alldera had not been able to wean her from the revolting femmish habit of chewing the stuff instead of drinking its juice. Fedeka shook her head over Alldera's careful brewing procedure.

'The things people will swallow to relieve thirst! Somebody once told me that Ossa actually guzzled down one of my douche mixtures one time because it had been in the shade and was cooler than the water in the water bottle.'

'Let me tell you about a master I knew,' Daya said, settling herself more comfortably by the fire. 'He used to put earth into his beer before he drank it. Well, you can imagine what kinds of dirt his fems found for him to use . . .'

She was full of stories. Alldera had to admit that she told them cleverly; but how repellent they were. Alldera could never enjoy them as the tea camp fems had. She thought about it, sitting back from the fire and deliberately not listening to Daya's words. Maybe, she thought, it was because she had tasted real freedom among the Riding Women, while the others had simply run from Holdfast Slavery to a more comfortable bondage in the Grasslands. The same stories were told here as had been told in the Holdfast. Yet Fedeka listened and laughed.

Alldera had not presumed to approach Fedeka's bed, but Fedeka slept with Daya as if it were a matter of course.

'What are you doing out here?' Alldera snapped. Daya was sneaking around after her.

'Looking at the country,' Daya said. 'It's beautiful.'

Relenting a little, Alldera said, 'I never saw a dry riverbed before. How does Fedeka know that a river really ran here on the plain in

Ancient times?'

'She hears all sorts of things from the Mares.'

'Everything dried out, and the rivers vanished,' Alldera said. 'It's hard to imagine.' She turned her head, alert to a sound out on the plain east of them. Darkness was drawing on.

'It's Fedeka,' Daya said quickly. 'She's gone off to pray.'

Restless, Alldera got up from the smooth-sided boulder she had been sitting on. 'I thought nobody paid attention to Moonwoman here.'

'You'd have seen a different side of things if Fedeka had shown up in camp.' Daya's voice softened and took on warmth. 'When she arrives, suddenly everyone starts saying prayers at meals and making water offerings and everything.'

'Because she's different from them, she's free, and they respect her.'

'Oh, yes. Fedeka is the freest of the free fems. She keeps her own ways, gathering her dyes and potions. There's not a growing thing in all the Grasslands from green threads finer than your hair to spiked bushes thick as your wrist that she hasn't gathered, dried, and boiled up.'

Alldera said abruptly, 'You've traveled with her before, she says.'

'Yes. But she's most comfortable alone, so I never stay long. Even her interest in a skillful pet fem dies down pretty quickly. She has another lover. She gives her body to Moonwoman out there in the dark.'

Was that the only way to find your strength if you couldn't find it among your own kind – to give yourself up to something greater? The sound of Fedeka's prayer came distinctly through the evening air. Her voice was strong and unselfconscious:

> Pour us into us through the thickest walls of our prisons,
> Grains of silver, to bend to any pressure;
> Strength of grizzled iron, to bear any blow;
> Fastness of rock, to outlast them all.

Alldera groaned under her breath. Daya asked her what was the matter.

'Where was this great Moonwoman when we were living our wretched lives back there and dying our terrible deaths?'

'Fedeka says she was in our minds, giving us strength to exist.'

'Strength to work and strength to die, you mean,' Alldera said bitterly. 'An ally of masters, not of fems.'

Alldera ran, feeling full of power. Sometimes she crossed the blurred tracks of laden horses, and the sight of them gave her the most peculiar, wrenching feeling. She remembered the days with the Riding Women when it had been the impressions of femmish wagon wheels that had caught her eye.

She was surprised when Daya asked to go running with her. The pet fem soon gave it up. She was not able to mask her disgust at filthying herself with sweat and dust.

Alldera still went with Daya in search of plants for their meals, or to scrape up the white salt crusts the dyer used to fix her colors in cloth.

Skimming this white mineral off the sand one morning, they found tracks and droppings of sharu. Daya jumped like a startled foal and looked anxiously around. This wandering life had thinned her down and browned her until she seemed to suit the land. It was hard now to picture her in Elnoa's rich nest.

'Don't worry,' Alldera said. 'The sharu have come and gone.'

'I'm wearing my bleeding cloth. Couldn't they smell me and come after us?'

'They won't.' She pointed to the tracks. 'There's only this one around here, left behind because she's old or sick, maybe. Don't you know why the sharu never bother Fedeka? The plants she looks for are weeds that take root where the earth has been disturbed and the grass roots broken up. That's the way the sharu leave land after they've foraged over it. So Fedeka ends up trailing behind the sharu around their feeding range, following them by a growing season or two.'

'Mother Moon, the things you know!' Daya exclaimed.

Alldera almost laughed, the pet looked so astonished; half an act of course, but that made it funnier. 'I'm tempted to show off when you don't know.'

Daya did not defend herself. She looked pensive. She said, 'Don't tell Fedeka; what you just said, about the sharu.'

'As long as she doesn't tell me that Moonwoman keeps her safe.'

Alldera said nothing to Fedeka. How could she? She admired the

dyer too much for her ability to live alone, her harmony with her
life.

Gathering brush for fuel along a dry watercourse, they startled wild
horses that fled in a flurry of dust. Alldera recognized a brown stud
that had driven off two of the Calpapers' mares one year when she
had been in the women's camp. Transported for a moment back
into that existence, she felt her loss of it. All that seemed long gone
now, another life outgrown.

She told of the brown stud.

'Imagine a wild horse stealing from the Mares,' Daya said in
obvious delight. 'It must be pretty clever to set the Mares' horses
free.'

'They're not free. A bunch of wild horses is mostly mares, all of
them the property of a stallion, their master. He sires all the foals, he
bullies and bosses his mares and fights off other studs. Just like in
the Riding Women's herds.'

Daya looked up from tugging at a stubborn dead root that
projected from the earth bank. 'Doesn't that bother the Mares – to
see female creatures harried and owned by males?'

'Women say that animals live as they must. They say women live
as they must too, but also as they think right, which is what makes
them more than just animals.' She could not keep from adding
bitterly, 'What the free fems seem to think is right is to make one of
themselves master and serve her. How could the Riding Women
think well of them?'

'That's what you really care about, isn't it?' Daya said. 'What the
Riding Women think. Well, maybe we're not good enough for them,
but you aren't either, or you'd still be living with them.'

'They didn't send me away. I left. To be with my own kind – who
make themselves slaves when they could be free – to be part of their
stupid plan, that miserable lie –'

'You don't know that the plan won't happen.'

'I know,' Alldera said with disgust. She snapped off branches of
the brush that straggled like dry, tangled hair down the side of the
gully and she threw pieces into the rope net on the ground. 'I know.
I'm a fem myself.'

Ah, this quarreling is bad for me, she groaned inwardly.

Daya said, 'Who are you, to demand that we all act as you'd

choose for us to act?'

Alldera stood over the hoofprints of the wild horses. Trying to sound reasonable she answered, 'I just want to see the free fems break out of the old order, not make it all over again here. Some of them know it, but they haven't the courage to act. They should live, grow, become something besides playthings or drudges for Elnoa. Anything would be better than the way you plod along letting that gross creature dominate your lives.' It sickened her to recall how she had begged Elnoa to send her out trading.

'If you had your way,' Daya replied, 'we'd become your slaves and drudges, doing what you want instead.'.

'Maybe that's the only way to get you all moving, to make you all alive.' Alldera felt angry and out of control.

'I see,' taunted Daya in an oily voice. 'You'd like to astonish us all, both Mares and fems, by seizing the initiative and driving us all before you to go save our people, like the hero of a Holdfast story. I recognize the pattern. It's a compelling story; I've told it often; but it isn't life. You have to wait till you're dead and gone before your doings can take on the shape of such lying legends.'

'You're like the rest of them,' Alldera burst out. 'The free fems will never follow me or anyone home, they'll just sit around making excuses for their cowardice until they die!'

Tears appeared in Daya's eyes. 'We did more for ourselves even in the Holdfast than you think; the masters could never completely crush us.'

At this Alldera closed in on her: 'Oh, yes, you and your stories of clever fems outwitting their masters! Your romances of the past are as false as your romances of the future. We were slaves. A few of us, fems like Elnoa, were smarter, better placed to protect themselves, or luckier. Even when those tales are true they don't mean anything. We were slaves. That's our real history. Better to fight and die.' She snapped a bundle of sticks over her knee with a downward plunge of both fists. 'You are everything slavish about us, everything I hate.'

Daya stood sideways to her, twisting a piece of wood in her hands, crying. 'Most of us burned out our courage crossing the borderlands. What great task must I now perform to satisfy your standards?'

She threw the wood at Alldera's feet and said, 'Of us two, I'm not the one who's ashamed of who she is.'

The hot weather came full strength. 'Now I'll take you to a place north of here,' Fedeka said. She led them to a small grassy valley among the foothills. She had dug a well there and transplanted trees to shade it. They put up the tent under the trees and drew out Fedeka's great simmering-pots from the brush shelter she had made for them.

Alldera woke the next dawn, while the others slept. She walked the cool slopes alone and looked down on their little encampment, feeling rested but not calm. Her spirits rode high on a tingling wave of anticipation: then the meaning of this place grew clear.

Fedeka had made this, a retreat such as no slave had ever had. But she did not hide here, growing fat and easy. She always returned to the plain with its dangers and its beauties. Because – it must be – out there, alone, was where she had found the strength to make this.

As quietly as she could Alldera got out water bottle, hip pack stuffed with dried food, rope; but Daya heard, raised her head, and said in a voice husky with sleep, 'Where are you going?'

'I'll be back before the dust storms start.'

Running toward the plain Alldera felt light and swift and tireless, at her best.

9

Daya steadied the great pot as Fedeka levered sodden cloth out of it with a pole. Her muscles taut, the dyer transferred the dripping weight to another vessel full of the steaming, smelly solution that fixed the color in the fibers.

The trees had fruited with fantastic colors and shapes: Fedeka's bright pennants hanging up to dry. Daya resented Alldera's escape from all the work there was to do: drawing water from the well with the creaking windlass, tending the fires under the dye pots or scouring out the pots to clean them for new colors, setting out cloth to dry or taking it in.

Was Alldera dead or alive out there, near or far off on the long, flat, empty horizon of the plain? It was months now. The figure of the runner stayed in her mind's eye.

While they worked Fedeka listened with bursts of appreciative laughter to Daya's anecdotes of tea camp life.

Daya sighed. 'You're my best audience, as always. I think I miss you a lot when I'm back in the tea camp.'

'Me too,' Fedeka said. 'Pity we're not better suited. But my nature doesn't much suit anybody in the long run, so it's a good thing I suit myself.' Fedeka sat with the pottery mortar locked between her legs, grinding dried plants to powder with a strong, patient motion of her single arm.

'What kind of company was Alldera before I came?' Daya asked idly.

'Quiet company.' Fedeka dipped a finger into the mortar, withdrew it, and spat on the film of dark material on the tip. She peered at it, and at that moment Daya knew herself to be forgotten.

To get the dyer's attention she said, 'I'm completely healed now, thanks to you; but am I sterile, do you think?'

'Not if you've attended to your prayers.' Daya knew that Fedeka really believed that someday, if it were Moonwoman's will, a free fem would conceive without a man. Her fertility solutions were, to her, merely instruments of the deity.

'Do you think Alldera is alive out there?'

'If she's attended to her prayers, yes,' Fedeka said. Sometimes her piety could be irritating. Now she frowned, grinding the pestle round and round. 'I can see why she had trouble in the tea camp. Nothing suits her, she has no place else to go, but she can't seem to accept herself and the life around her. It's a sickness I have no medicine for.'

Daya said, 'She takes everything too seriously, starting with herself. That's her trouble.'

Fedeka gave a decisive shake of her head. 'She doesn't see. Moonwoman could help her see. When I first saw one of those Marish drum heads of leather all covered in designs rubbed in with red willow juice, I started to see color everywhere; that was a gift from Moonwoman, a great gift. Eyes that always look inward miss everything.'

Eyes that look upward at the moon or down at color plants don't see everything either, Daya thought; knowing and liking Fedeka well, she did not speak her thought out loud. She found with surprise that she was missing Alldera a little. Arguing with the runner could be painful, but it was not as monotonous as discussion with Fedeka could get once the name of Moonwoman was invoked.

Among the rocks topping a knob at the mouth of Fedeka's valley Daya searched for a yellow herb. She paused a while to watch the dust storms drift above the plain like dirty finger smudges on the sky. It was a hot, bright morning.

She saw someone approaching over the plains on horseback. Thinking it was a Mare come looking for Alldera, she ran down the hillside shouting to alert Fedeka. She saw the visitor gallop into their hollow, fling herself from her mount and stride forward to meet the dyer.

It was Alldera, her leather shirt scraped and rent, her hair matted and her lips blackened and split, her teeth white as salt in her brown, grinning face. Her stench was so strong close up that Daya could hardly breathe. She had ridden in on the bare back of a gaunt, shaggy brown horse, trailing two others that followed her like the docile herd beasts of the Mares.

'You've been to the Mares,' Fedeka accused. 'And what have you brought back? Horses! Mares' mates!'

One of the horses lifted its head, made a low, breathy sound, and took a step forward. Fedeka bent to snatch up a stone.

'She's not after you,' Alldera said. 'They smell the water in your well. Let me see to them, and then we can sit in the shade and talk, if I can keep awake. I rode all night to avoid the heat.'

She twitched on the rope that she had tied around the head and jaw of her mount, and the horse followed her. The other two fell in after it.

Daya could not stop staring at her. How strong and brown she looked, how effortlessly she commanded the horses. Her eyes were bright with excitement, and she grinned and grinned like some exuberant spirit. Daya had never seen Alldera like that.

Alldera drew water for the horses and tied their front feet loosely together with leather to keep them from straying out of the hollow. She pulled off her tattered clothes and sluiced herself down with cold water. Then she settled under the trees draped in a blanket. Brewing up tea, she told them what she had done. She kept laughing in the middle of what she said and reaching to clasp their hands as she spoke.

'I never went to the Mares, that wasn't the point at all. These are my horses. They were wild. I caught them, I tamed them.'

Daya marveled. She basked in the vitality of Alldera's muscular body. She had an urge to touch Alldera, to hug her around the waist.

Alldera had gone from watering hole to seeping spring, all the places where water somehow persisted through the Dusty Season weather in amounts too small for the herds of the Riding Women but enough for a wild band. Where she found recent horse tracks, she waited.

The wild horses, a roaming troop of fifteen, returned to drink.

Scenting her presence, they ran away. Alldera followed. She did not need to keep them in sight. She had only to jog along on their tracks until she came upon them where they had stopped to graze. At the sight of her they bolted again. Again she followed, and so it went for a number of days.

'But a horse can run faster than a person,' Fedeka objected. 'Why didn't they just run right away from you?'

Alldera shook her head. 'No horse without a rider covers great stretches at speed. It's only an animal, it runs until the danger is out of sight and then forgets and gets back to its business of eating. Besides, these horses were in poor condition. Even the women have to harden their horses for long trips in the Dusty Season.

'But I was in good shape, and I could eat enough on the run to keep me going and drink water that I carried with me.

'The horses got sore-footed and sore-muscled, and they couldn't get enough to eat because I was always showing up and scaring them off. I know where the water holes are, so I could figure out which water the stud was headed for, cut across to get there first, and scare them off before they drank.

'Mind you, I guessed wrong twice, and had to go track them down again to different watering places. Otherwise, I would have been back long ago!

'I never changed my clothes or washed myself. They could recognize me from a good distance if the wind was right, and they began to get used to my smell. They learned that though they let me get closer and closer, nothing bad ever came of it. A day came when even the old stud could hardly drive them to run from me, they were so tired and gaunt and bored with running away from something just as familiar as a harmless clump of grass or a rock. It was the morning after that that they came down to drink, even the old stallion, though I was right there at the spring.

'When they left, I left with them; just walking, wandering along on the outskirts of the band at first, but later right among them. There was a roan mare that acted as if she'd been gentled before; stolen from some women's herd by the stud, probably. I cut her some grass and she let me handle her a bit. By the time the horses were rested enough to make it hard for me to keep up with them, she let me ride her. I just lay back on her rump at first, until she and the others accepted what I was doing. Then I sat up and rode properly. What a luxury, to be carried after all that walking! But I only did enough riding to keep up. I didn't want to wear her out.

'Meanwhile I began working on some of the others, the way the women gentle their horses: riding alongside and rubbing their backs, leaning my weight on them, getting them used to being handled and laden. Most of the band were scrubs, not worth taking. The old stud, while I was working on them, got into the habit of snoozing all day and leaving the job of lookout to me.

'Signs of sharu or fems or women were all signals for me to give the alarm, just as if I were really a wild horse myself. It didn't happen often. Traveling like that out there, you'd be surprised how few traces of human life you come upon. I talked to the horses sometimes, though I knew words meant nothing to them.

'I brought these away with me. They don't look like much, but they'll fill out, and there's plenty of grass here for just three.'

Fedeka eyed her curiously. 'You never thought of staying out there, living on your own with the horses?'

Alldera sipped tea from her bowl. She said, 'Let me put it this way. One morning the old stud wanted to head the bunch in one direction, and I wanted to go in another. I was riding that dun mare at the time. I had my knife. I could have given the stud a fight and whipped him, too. He stood there snorting, pawing the ground, throwing his head and swelling his neck to threaten me, and I thought it would give me pleasure to beat him, considering how he bullied his mares.

'Then I thought, suppose I drive him off or kill him, what do I win? The leadership of a bunch of horses. So I grabbed up a handful of stones to sling at him if he chased me, cut out my three head, and left.

'And that's all there is,' she finished on a note of happy satisfaction. She yawned.

'But what did you do it for?' Fedeka looked around at the horses in dismay. 'What's to be done now?'

'I wanted to see if I could do it. I'll take care of them, don't worry.'

'One thing I want to know now,' Fedeka said, lowering her voice. 'This old stallion, the leader of the herd – did he ever think you were another of his herd? The Mares get male horses to mate with them; weren't you afraid what the stallion might do to you?'

Alldera blinked at her. 'I didn't say I got to smell like a horse, only like myself,' she protested. 'I never gave off the right odors to rouse the stallion. I don't think a horse has any choice about mating, when the time comes. If I had smelled right, he couldn't have helped it, he'd have had to try to mount me. Since I smelled wrong, I never feared to turn my back on him. The women are right – horses may do things that look like what humans do, but the meaning is all changed.' She stretched. 'I'll go sleep now. I can hardly sit up.'

Daya could not bear to lose contact with her. 'I'd like to come with you,' she said shyly.

After a moment's hesitation, Alldera laughed and pulled her to her feet. Into the tent they went together, getting in each other's way as they laid out Alldera's long unused bedding.

Their lovemaking was not a great success for Daya. She needed to feel overwhelmed by a force of nature, swept to a place of infinite security and delight where she could safely let herself melt. She found Alldera a conscious sort of lover, possibly self-conscious to an added degree with a partner whom she knew to be unusually experienced. Daya could feel her thinking all the time.

It did not seem to matter much. They fell asleep hugged tight together and breathing each other's warm breath.

10

'I hear Alldera doesn't fit in with her own people any better than she did with us.' Sheel and Nenisi sat together in a sunny patch outside the tent of Nenisi's cousins, where Nenisi was staying during the Gather. Nenisi looked just as she always had. The dark-skinned lines hardly aged at all, Sheel thought. She added, 'They say you go and visit Alldera among the free fems.'

Nenisi groaned. 'You and I have been out of touch, Sheel. Don't provoke me here at the Gather. My teeth are already sore enough. I went only once, after the last Gather, to tell her that our child had joined the childpack. She said when we send for her to attend the child's coming out, she'll come.'

'So,' Sheel said. 'What of it?'

'Someday at a Gather like this it will be our daughter, and hers, mating with a stud horse. I know it's hard to think about any daughter that way when she's still only a wild creature running with the pack. But look forward a little, Sheel: when this child comes out, we won't be much help to her as mothers if our feelings about her – and about her bloodmother – aren't warm and loving.'

'Loving!' Sheel snorted. 'I hardly think about the man-used bitch now that our tent family has separated, and it's never with love.'

The women of Holdfaster Family had gone traveling after the years of staying at Stone Dancing Camp to tend their baby. They would reassemble to welcome the child when she was ripe to emerge from the childpack. Meanwhile Shayeen kept Holdfaster Tent running as a shelter for visitors unable, for one reason or another, to stay with their own relatives in Stone Dancing.

Nenisi said, 'What will you do, Sheel, when the family comes back together for this child's coming-out ceremonies?'

'I'll help,' Sheel said promptly, 'but nothing we do will place that child properly and securely among us.'

Nenisi slapped the hard ground between them. 'Why not? Why do you say that?'

Sheel frowned, considering. She disliked talking about ceremonial matters, but it was a long time since she had seen Nenisi and she wanted to be understood. She explained slowly, picking her way. 'We are in touch with strong currents that hold all the things and beings and forces of the plains in balance. Any woman here can be helped to find that balance, or to regain that balance if it's been lost. We help. The horses help. But you can't put in balance something that never belonged at all.'

'We'll make it work, if we try hard enough,' Nenisi insisted. 'We will make that child into one of us, complete with relatives, duties and honor.'

Sheel studied her and saw in the dark, smooth-planed Conor face that tightness of anxiety she had noticed so often in Nenisi since the fem had come among them. Easy enough for me, she thought now; I just hate the fems, no complications. Nenisi's feelings are all gummed up with rights and wrongs. Does she know how she really feels?

She saw Nenisi's pride, the Conor pride in being right. It was a Conor trait and part of Nenisi's beauty. Once Sheel had been comfortable with Nenisi, before Holdfaster Family.

'The horses won't dance with her, Nenisi. Her mothers won't be able to bring her out properly. It can't work.'

Next day the huge camp of the Gather, a camp composed of all the women's camps, was quiet. The games and the races and the settling of quarrels were all over; the time for the mating drew near.

Women filed in and out of the sweat tents all day long. Sheel sat quietly cleaning and repairing the belongings of her tent with other women. They all went inside during a brief, hard shower of rain at midday.

In the afternoon Sheel, among the last women to use a sweat tent, walked out toward the great dancing ground outside camp. She shook out her clean wet hair and swirled her long leather cloak in elaborate passes. The sound of the capes whishing through the air drew the women from their tents. Talking and laughing, they joined the growing procession flowing out of the camp.

Looking back, her arms already aching from wielding the weight of the cape, Sheel saw the sailing cloaks like a camp of tents taking flight over grass still bright with beads of rain.

The childpacks of the camps swarmed among the women, circling, piping and screaming, ducking under the billowing leather, diving into gaps between the walkers. Around and around the dancing ground the procession flowed until it formed a noisy wall of women ringing the flat space. Overhead great ragged cloaks of cloud streamed slowly across the clean blue sky. The moon, a mere edge away from full, was a fragile white disc against the blue.

In a little while the first childpack went racing away from the dance ground, scattering out on the plain. Others followed. Several packs sorted themselves out of a whirling free-for-all and ran in another direction. Too excited by the procession to stay afterward for a dull dance, the children preferred to ambush each other over the thick southern turf or harry the horses left unattended. If they returned too soon, there were women stationed outside the dancing ground to turn them away, with whips if necessary.

As the early risen moon grew more substantial, a channel opened through the women's ranks. Horses poured into the circle, all stallions, nervous at having been separated from the mares. Those women who had walked the horses to the dancing ground closed the gap, penning them in. The horses milled inside the human enclosure, calling, darting one way and then another.

Her arms linked in those of the women on either side of her, Sheel whooped and stamped with them when the horses ran near her sector of the crowd, and the beasts whirled back the way they had come. Her voice skirled joyfully in her throat, she threw her fresh-washed hair from side to side as if it were the mane. Let the land stretch dry and dusty over the rocky bones of the world; the horses were a tumultuous river flowing past her, rough, swift, life-sharing.

Now the young women who had been working with the horses for months had their moment. Dropping their cloaks, they stepped from the crowd and ran naked among the horses. Amid the plunging shadows they swung up onto the studs' backs, where they balanced or leaped. A young woman sprang over a dark colt's back, just touching him in passing, and landed on her feet. Another, a bright-haired Salmowon, stepped from the dipping back of one horse to the back of another as lightly and surely as if crossing a stream on stones.

Sheel remembered, her whole body moved with remembering. Every childpack danced the horses. You skipped over their backs, leaping, vaulting to touch the ground an instant before bounding back up onto another horse's back. Around you and beneath you ran the horses in a chaos of dust and din. You played them until they moved as a group, until they learned the game, you danced them to a lathered standstill. Then next day you laughed at the adults' dismay at finding their horses worn out.

When you were grown you danced the stallions under the round moon before all the women. You felt your strength flow to the horses, and then back again to you, made stronger. All beings found their rightful places in these exchanges, and the balance of all things was reaffirmed.

A young Hont woman came whirling out of the mob, a bay horse with her. It curvetted past her, rearing and shaking its head, and then turned back to come to her shoulder and rub its knobby face against her. The Hont's mothers came out to lead her and the lathered horse quietly away, both to be prepared for mating tomorrow.

By dawn the last stallion and the last dancer had been escorted away, the dust had settled, and the bedding chute was built. The Hilliars had put it together this year, in the neat casual-looking way that they did everything. Some called it 'the saddle' because this was the horse's turn to ride.

It was a rectangular box with three closed sides, an open top, and a high floor. The insides of the floor and walls were padded with leather cushions. Arched across the open top and joining the two long walls was a carefully padded super-structure to take the weight of the stallion and the grip of his forelegs. It would suspend his body over the young woman lying inside the box. There were ropes to release an escape trap for a woman whose mating went wrong and endangered her.

The women assembled as they had for the dancing, forming an

oval of spectators surrounding the bedding chute. Here a voice rose in song, there another. The members of each Motherline sang all the self-songs of the past generations of their line. The singing of each Motherline unfurled like a banner against the paling sky.

'I crossed the Sunset River to raid my enemy's herds,' sang a yellow woman next to Sheel. That was an old song from the days before the camps had discarded streambeds as boundaries because they were places of confrontation and fighting.

Sheel sang the song of her own bloodmother. It was composed largely of affectionate descriptions of the horses the woman had taken during her lifetime of raiding, and the names of women she had faced in feuds and duels. Sheel sang it with passionate pride.

The moist wind stirred the hair of the young Hont candidate who stepped first into the open. She was thickset like all her line, but the simple leather cloak she wore disguised her body's lack of grace. With her clean golden hair falling down her back, she looked her best. You forgot the big-featured Hontish face.

Sheel approved, and found the Hont's showing off appealing. The youngster strolled the circumference of the dance ground, smiling, waving to women who called her name in the midst of their singing.

Someone slipped an arm through Sheel's: Barvaran, her red face shining with happiness. She herself had been to the stud horses three times, and she had three living bloodchildren as robust and good-natured as herself.

Sheel thought of her own two blooddaughters, one lost in the pack and the other to an epidemic of fever. She no longer grieved for them or for her own failure to bring adult daughters to her Motherline. It was true, as women said; no one rides only one horse on a long journey. There were all the daughters of her sisters and her cousinlines, young women as like to her own dead bloodchildren as they were to Sheel and to each other. She sang a brief self-song for the child which had lived long enough to come out of the pack, and then her own self-song of hunts, raids, and the deaths of men.

The Hont climbed into the chute and lay down on her back. One of her sharemothers got in with her to encourage and caress her so she would be moist and open to her stud. Sheel remembered well feeling the smooth wooden rests against which she had braced her bare feet and watching the support frame dark against the sky. Poli Rois, her friend, had lain down with her, kissing her neck.

Poli was gone now many years, struck dead in her saddle by lightning while still a youth.

Into the circle of onlookers came two of the Hont's family. The bay stallion stepped along neatly between them. They walked with their hands on his withers and his neck. They talked into his flicking ears. Small, sedate, groomed so the sunlight shimmered on his hide, he was scarcely recognizable as one of the wild-eyed studs of last night's dance. His feet were filed and oiled, and ribbons of dyed leather were braided into his mane and tail. He was called Tiptoe, and was bred from the home herd of Salmowon Tent in Melting Earth Camp.

Sheel's first stud had been a nameless chestnut with a lop ear. She had looked up and seen his familiar crooked silhouette and the little beard of whiskers on his jaw, so well known to her and so ridiculous that all her fear had dissolved. Awe and joy had filled her, that the instrument of her own joining with the great patterns of the world should be so ordinary a creature. Well, so was she, yet both she and the stud embodied the dependence of all beings on each other and the kinship of creatures. That was the mystery of the mating, its beauty and necessity.

She had spoken softly to him above the singing voices of the gathered women, and he had entered her as smoothly as the staff of oiled leather with which she had stretched herself in practice for him. After the culling that year his flesh had gone to help nourish the child he had started in her belly.

Her second stud, a barrel-bodied gray, had sired a number of fine foals after mating with her. She had ridden him for years until an infected sharu slash had made it impossible for him to keep up with the herd any more. It had taken two hammer blows to drop him for butchering. Poor Cloud.

The singing had sunk to a soft murmur. The faces of other women showed Sheel that they too were thinking of the dead; dead horses, dead children, dead women who had bled to death after bad matings.

The handlers rubbed the neck and chest of the little stallion. They stroked his face and nostrils with pads that had been run under the tails of mares in season. He began to throw his head and snort, and within a few moments they had him erect. Under the touch of hands well known to him he reared high and clamped his forelegs on the padded support frame. He gripped the leather roll at the chute's head and rattled it with his teeth. Standing outside the chute, the handlers stroked his sweating neck and shoulders and bent to guide him.

Suddenly he thrust forward against the wooden braces which prevented him from entering fully. He oscillated his rump, snorting loudly, and his tail jerked, marking the rhythm of his ejaculation. Within seconds, it seemed, he pulled back and stood dark with sweat, droop-headed, quiet.

The handlers praised and patted him as they led him away to rejoin the herd. He left between them as modestly as he had arrived.

Others of her family reached to help the young Hont up, but she was already on her feet in the chute. She swung her robe about herself with a grand gesture that showed as well as anything could her triumphant success. They closed around her, checking her for injury, mopping the milky overflow from her thighs. With her arms on the shoulders of two of them, she walked briskly from the dance ground.

A new candidate had already stepped out from the crowd. A sorrel horse, thick-maned and heavy-headed, came into the circle. Snorting at the crowd, he bounced along half sideways. Sheel knew that horse. She had taken him from the herds of Chowmer Tent in Windgrass Camp last year. She hoped he was smoother as a rider than he was as a mount.

She thought angrily of Nenisi. The black woman was mad to insist that the child of a fem could lie down for a stud like a woman. Holdfaster Tent was just a dream anyway, Nenisi's fantasy of righteousness.

There was a story about a free fem, long ago – she had been taken up briefly by the Golashamets because she had looked so much like them. She had attended a mating, just once. Women said that after the first stud, the fem had turned and vomited on the woman next to her.

11

When the cool months started the three fems returned to the plain. They brought the horses that Alldera had caught. Fedeka's open dislike of the animals abated when she saw that not only could they help carry baggage from campsite to campsite, but they could bear many more than the number of plant samples that she normally packed on her own back.

For Daya, their presence was magical; she rode whenever she could. She had begun, timidly, to learn how under Alldera's tutelage and had discovered a horse's power to transform its rider.

Alldera had made Daya a saddle of padded leather sewn wet onto a wooden frame so as to shrink as it dried to make a strong seat. The saddle was trimmed with straps and strings to lash on bottles, blankets, and other equipment. The leather required frequent applications of soap and oils to keep it supple and uncracked. Daya used the heavy saddle gladly on long rides, but she loved better riding bareback, seat and legs fitted to the horse's body, wearing pants cut off at the knee so that she could feel the living flank of the horse along her calves.

The dun mare had a big, ugly head and at rest its lower lip drooped and exposed its yellow teeth in a comical, foolish-looking manner. But it was responsive, almost tireless, Daya's favorite mount. Alldera said with a trace of jealousy that Daya was a natural rider. She admitted to Daya that she herself did not love the horses; what she loved was having the mastery of them. Daya loved their rich appeal to her senses and the joining of her own meager strength to their power. Crouched on the shoulders of her galloping mount, she reveled in the ecstasy of speed. Alldera often had to remind her that the Mares did not gallop everywhere and that Daya too should practice the slower, less wearing gaits.

Riding under drifts of illuminated cloud, Daya dreamed of tearing down the far side of the mountains scattering terrified men, battering them down with the shoulders of her mount and pounding them under its hooves. Her horse was invincible. She heard in her mind the thudding of heavy, blunt blows on flesh and the crack of bone. Or she dreamed of nothing at all, but lived totally and raptly in the warm, driving reach of her horse under her.

On foot little changed for her. She still spoke softly, moved automatically out of another's way and shed tears instead of shouting when she was angry. She knew these ways were forever part of herself, not to be changed by her joy in the horses and the new strength that they had lent her.

As she rode with Alldera, Daya began to talk about their former lives and even to ask questions about Alldera's adventures with her two outlaw masters in the last days of the Holdfast. Alldera seldom raged against Elnoa's free fems any more. Now when she spoke of them it was painfully, questioning earnestly why they were as they were. Sometimes she would ask Daya for an opinion and then ride silently a while before replying, if she replied at all.

They slept together only occasionally, yet Daya felt them growing closer, knit together by quiet conversations and companionship. The gradual weaving of this connection delighted Daya and frightened her; it was new, an unreadable part of the mystery of the horses.

Sometimes they talked about Alldera's years with the Mares.

'They'll send for me when my blooddaughter, my cub, is ready to come out of the childpack,' Alldera said once. 'The sharemothers come together to receive her, and stay together for however long it takes – a few months, even several years, depending on her maturity – to prepare her for her mating and the forming of her own family.'

'Will you go when they send for you?'

'Yes. Now I have some horses to give for the tent herd. I'll leave the dun mare with you.' After a glance at Daya's face she added hesitantly, 'Unless you'd consider coming with me?'

They were watering the horses. Sitting on the dun mare's back, Daya looked down at the sunlight breaking on the water and spreading in circles from the mare's hot muzzle. Her hands moved over the sleek shoulders, feeling the glide and pull of muscle under the skin as the animal stepped forward, lifting its dripping mouth. A tightening of the rein, a tap of the heels, and it would move on, obedient to the will of the small, weak creature on its back.

A person with this power would not be just a runaway fem among the Mares. If riding were all there was to it . . .

'There's what you call a family waiting for you to join it, Alldera. What would I be, among the Mares?'

'I've thought about that. You'd be my cousin Daya. As my relation, you'd be their relation.'

Daya thought of the tea camp; her place by Elnoa was occupied, but surely not if she chose to return and claim it. It would be dreadful to be abandoned among strangers once Alldera had settled with the Mares again and wearied of the novelty of showing off her pretty pet friend.

She said, 'But what sort of position would I have, myself, with the Mares?'

Alldera looked impatient. 'They have no positions, only relations. You don't need a position when you have kindred.'

Yes, now Daya remembered: waking among the Mares years ago after her own rescue by a patrol and her own healing sleep, and being unable to work out who was important among those who tended her.

'I won't know anyone there, Alldera. You wouldn't – drop me, and leave me on my own?'

'No,' Alldera said. 'I promise.'

'I never thought you'd want me,' Daya murmured.

By the time the Dusty Season came, Fedeka was talking with undisguised anticipation of the rendezvous with one of the trade wagons toward which they slowly made their way. She had been acting more and more distant, and Daya knew that with Fedeka it could not be jealousy. Probably the dyer was just tired of company and hoped that her two guests would join the wagon and leave her to wander on. It seemed to Daya that Alldera was not likely to find a welcome with the tea fems, but there was no point in talking to

Fedeka about that.

The trade wagon was not at the wells of Steep Cloud Camp where they had expected to meet it. Fedeka glared with frustration at the stubbled flats.

'They must be still back at Royo Camp,' she said. 'I need tea. I need cloth. They have to pass this way. We'll wait.'

The hot, dry days dragged past. No one talked about what was to happen when the wagon finally did arrive, and this increased the tension of waiting.

Alldera and Daya endured it, riding out daily in search of grass for the horses. They were returning one evening, discussing the possibility of trading for grain from the Mares to sustain their animals, when a sudden rush of hoofbeats engulfed them. The dark heads and shoulders of running horses dodged around them.

The dun mare bolted, throwing her head forward so suddenly that she jerked the rein from Daya's hand. For thirty long strides, gasping in fear and exultation, Daya clung with her fingers twined in the dun's mane. Then something slammed at her body. Off-balanced, she jumped for her life, rolling like an acrobat when she hit the ground so that she ended up standing on wavering legs.

The dun ran on in the dust of the other horses, holding her head high and to one side so as not to tread on the reins hanging from her mouth.

A rider came toward Daya – Alldera, surely.

Two riders, three, half a dozen; all in a rush they flowed around her, a wall of horses, faces peering down at her past the horses' necks and heads.

'Who's this on foot?' rang a voice she did not know, a Marish voice, rich and imperious. 'Who unhorsed you, woman?'

A new rider galloped up, leading the dun mare. She stood in her stirrups. 'Where is she? Stand back, I knocked her down and I claim the capture!' She pressed past the others and with a swift gesture threw the slack of her bridle rein around Daya's neck. 'I claim ransom! How many horses have you at your tent to give to Patarish Rois of Windgrass Camp?'

Daya was paralyzed by fear of them and dizzy with their stench of sweaty leather.

Someone said in a puzzled tone, 'Looks like one of the Carrals to me, but she hasn't got a big enough behind.'

Then a rider raced up behind the others, leaped from her horse, and rushed into the center on foot. It was Alldera. She snatched the rein from around Daya's neck so fast that it burned Daya's skin.

The first speaker, bending deeply out of her saddle for a closer look, whooped. 'It's that fem Alldera Holdfaster that used to live in Stone Dancing Camp! This must be another one. You've caught two fems, Patarish!'

One woman laughed. Another cried, 'Sorry, fems!' Wheeling their horses they rode away, calling to Patarish Rois to follow them.

She did not. She hung darkly above the two fems, smouldering with outraged pride. Daya moved silently behind Alldera, sheltering from the Mare's rage.

'What are fems doing on horseback?' cried the rider. 'No fems own any horses that I've ever heard of, and any Riding Woman who lets fems ride her mares deserves to lose them. You know who I am. Let the woman who lent you horses come to me to claim her property if she dares!' Her mount danced and snorted. The dun mare tried to break away from its captor, lifting its head and tugging at the reins in alarm.

'No,' Daya whispered, clutching Alldera's arm. The tears of anger welled in her eyes.

Alldera grasped the woman's rein just under the jaw of her mount. 'That dun horse belongs to us.'

'Nothing on the plains belongs to a fem! Stand aside, I'm taking the brown horse too.'

Like a whip lashing, Alldera struck. She spun in the air so that one foot shot high above her own head, and she landed crouched to kick again. There was no need. The Mare's horse had bounced sideways with a terrified snort, and the woman fell like a sack out of the saddle. Alldera caught the woman's horse and stood clutching the stirrup, as if holding herself up.

'See if she's all right, will you?' she said in a strained voice. 'I haven't done anything like that in years. I think I've ruptured myself.'

The high hoops of the long expected trade wagon loomed beside Fedeka's fire. As they rode in, Roona's crew sprang up. Daya saw faces well known to her from Elnoa's camp. It occurred to her that the crew fems may have expected fems on horseback, but never a

Mare riding with them. These closed, defensive masks that greeted her must be what fems often presented to the eyes of the Mares. Now she sat a saddle herself and looked uncomfortably down at her own people.

The captive woman ignored them all. She dismounted stiffly after Roona invited her to. She politely tasted everything they offered her to eat. No one spoke to her. When she went to lie down a little distance off, curled in her blanket beside her hobbled horse, the fems all crowded into the wagon.

Roona turned at once to Daya and said, 'What is this, Daya, what's happened?'

Daya told them. The fems grew furious at Alldera: what would the Mares do in return? they cried; what would happen to the trade, the fems' welcome here? Roona kept pulling off her leather cap, polishing her bald head with her palm, then jamming the cap on again as if she had come to a decision. But all she said was, 'No one has ever done such a thing before!'

Alldera sat on a bale of hides massaging the long tendons of her groin and thighs and the base of her belly. At length she said, 'Listen to me, everyone. It's no use for you to try to figure out what to do. No one is going to be put at risk with the women on my account. I'll see to this myself.

'In the morning I'll start for Stone Dancing Camp with my guest — which is how this young woman is to be treated by all of you. At the first camp I'll stop and have her relatives send word of what's happened to her home tent. It will be up to her own Motherline members and her family at Windgrass Camp to gather horses from their herds and deliver them to me as ransom. They'll object, but in the end they'll pay, and I'll leave the prize horses in the herd of Holdfaster Tent. That way the free fems won't be involved, since no horses will come into your hands.'

Fedeka asked urgently, 'But why go? Turn the woman loose, forget it ever happened, and hope they'll be willing to forget too.'

'I can't. If I just let her go it would mean I thought she was without value, not worthy of a ransom, and I'd be giving her and all her relations a deadly insult. The other way is much better. It's getting near the time my cub should be coming out of the childpack anyway. I'd already decided to go back for that. I'll just start for Stone Dancing Camp earlier.'

There were protests: the Mares would be enraged to see fems on horseback, let alone with a woman prisoner. They would take it out on all the fems. A few said darkly that the whole thing was a trick of Alldera's, too complicated for them to understand. Others, their first panic eased, spoke in tones of shy admiration.

Fedeka gripped Alldera's hand and pumped it to punctuate the single point she made over and over. 'I don't like to see you return to those wild people. They don't believe in Moonwoman.'

She gave up and retreated into silence when Daya admitted that she was going to Stone Dancing Camp too. The atmosphere in the wagon became quiet, but distinctly strained.

Daya went outside to see that the horses were securely hobbled for the night. Clouds masked the moon's bright face, and all the sky seemed crowded with heavy shapes edged in brilliant light. There was so much life in the sky here, she thought, even at night. She went to the horses and stood among them, rubbing their soft noses and lips and the muscles behind their ears, grateful for their unde-manding warmth.

The hostility she had felt in the wagon worried her. Maybe she had made a wrong decision. But she did not want to go back with Roona's crew to the tea camp. She did not want to have to figure out – for her own safety – who had tried to poison her in that whirl of passion and intrigue around Elnoa. The suspicion and self-absorption of the wagon crew tonight had struck her as strange and unpleasant.

Now that she rode a horse herself the idea of staying a while among the Mares seemed less alien. She would have to be careful not to use the insulting term 'Mares' in their hearing, though.

In the morning Fedeka was gone. She had left the gear and belongings of Alldera and Daya in a neat heap on the ground. The horses grazed nearby.

Alldera packed up. Daya did the same. The dark young Mare, Patarish Rois, sat watching in the shadow of her horse while working at her kinky black ringlets with a wooden comb. The fems watched from the wagon.

Daya said, 'Alldera, a couple of the crew fems came to me early this morning and said they would like to go with us.'

'What for?'

'To see what it's like with the Mares. To learn riding.'

'No!' Alldera busied herself knotting the saddlestrings around one end of her roll of bedding. 'We have no horses for them. Besides, it would make more bad feeling than ever between us and the tea camp if we ride off with part of Roona's crew.' The horse swung its head and nipped at her shoulder. She slapped it over the nose, and it jumped. She said, 'What did they pay you to get me to agree?'

'Some good tea,' Daya said, gauging the distance between them in case she should have to duck a blow.

'You'd better give it back to them, then.'

'They paid me for my effort.'

'I thought we knew each other pretty well by now,' Alldera said, mounting and looking down at her. 'I hope I wasn't too far off the mark about you.'

'There's always more to know,' Daya said. You had to keep a little distance from strong people if you were not to be mastered by them.

Two fems from the wagon crew trotted after them for some little distance, shouting abuse. Before turning back one of them threw a rock.

Patarish Rois rode with her eyes fixed politely straight ahead. She did not, during the days and nights that followed, try to take the horses and run away or cut the fems' throats while they slept. Alldera's confident courtesy toward her was at first hesitantly and then routinely returned. The Rois was soon talking animatedly with her, waving her dark hands in this direction and that as they discussed how to thread their course among the women's migratory routes.

They expected Alldera's camp to be on the move in the early rains by the time they reached its range. Their first stop on the way for food, water and grain was to be Singing Metal Camp.

On a hot morning they topped a rise overlooking the Singing Metal herds. They paused, wiping the sweat from their faces, adjusting their gear, clearing their throats of dust. Their own horses, footsore and thirsty, pricked up their ears and neighed to the horses of the grazing herds. The hot wind blew in their faces, tearing away the sound.

The women of Singing Metal Camp, according to Alldera, had a special hostility toward fems. They resented the femmish contention that the women's skills at working Ancient scrap had been learned from fems rather than from the ancestors of Singing Metal women.

Daya was not reassured by the way Patarish Rois sat tugging nervously at the fringes of her sleeve, or by Alldera's silence. They had no choice, however. They needed the use of Singing Metal's wells.

Patarish Rois led them down. They did not make directly for the tents but circled to approach from the side opposite to the grazing herds. Alldera explained. 'We don't want to seem to be sizing up their stock for a raid later on. This young Rois has a lot to lose if we're treated badly or laughed at, so she'll help us. Don't worry; this is going to go well.'

Daya was not convinced. She felt very vulnerable, riding among the Mares' tents. Women peered out at them as they moved toward the largest tent. Tethered horses lifted their heads and whinnied. Someone was working at a forge, throwing out an irregular, clinking rhythm.

Two people stepped out of the big tent as they drew near, handsome look-alikes with coppery skin and black hair.

'Bawns,' Alldera breathed. 'We're all right. Shayeen, one of my own sharemothers in Holdfaster Tent, is a Bawn.'

There was nothing about the two, no insignia or finery or attendants, to show that they were chiefs. They were smiling, but did not speak. They were so clearly at a loss that Daya was embarrassed for them.

Alldera dismounted, took a breath and announced herself. 'Alldera Holdfaster, of Stone Dancing Camp. This is one of my femmish kin, Daya. And this is my guest, Patarish Rois of Windgrass Camp. We're going home to Stone Dancing to see to the horses that Patarish's kindred will be sending to us there, as soon as they hear that she and I are related by the rein.' Meaning, Daya remembered, by Alldera's having captured her.

The younger Bawn looked as if she had been struck.

'Welcome,' the older one said at last. 'Come out of the sun and take tea with us.'

The younger one added nervously, 'Come tell us your news.' As if the greatest of their news was not already told.

The older one embraced Alldera, and Patarish Rois jumped down from her horse and hugged the other. Alldera drew back, signed to

Daya to dismount, and said firmly, 'Will you greet my cousin Daya?'

The Bawns hung back, almost visibly trying to work out in their heads the consequences of any action they might take. Alldera they plainly knew by name if not by appearance; she was a relation, though a fem. Daya, in a femmish smock and Marish pants like Alldera but without headcloth or boots, was so obviously a wagon fem that the Bawns did not seem to know what to make of her as a relative.

Finally, with a gusty sigh the elder Bawn hugged Daya too. Enveloped in a muscular grip and a smell of horse sweat, smoke and the lingering pungency of tea, Daya said through dry lips, 'Cousin,' as Alldera had instructed her to do. She averted her face, hating the scars on her own cheeks.

The younger Bawn took charge of their horses. Daya watched jealously, noting how the woman eyed the dun as she handled it.

In the coolness of the Bawns' wide-winged tent some twenty women of Singing Metal Camp were gathered, and the guests were invited to sit with them. More women arrived, murmuring greetings, patting and embracing earlier arrivals as they took their places to sit. Everywhere were soft sounds of whispering and movement. The first of the tea was passed in shallow wooden bowls holding no more than a couple of swallows each.

Daya took a pouch from her belt and poured some shavings of tea into her own food bowl. Among such rough folk she felt it was only right for a civilized person to make the gracious gesture the occasion called for, even if it beggared her and was not properly appreciated. She passed the bowl.

The Mares looked curiously at this offering. Each one took a bit as long as the supply held out, though none chewed it as fems would have done.

Alldera had warned Daya that to soften bad feeling that might arise over the capture and ransom of a prisoner, it was the prisoner's right to tell the first version of her own downfall. She was entitled to make as much fun of her captor as she liked. Patarish Rois launched into a long preamble. It seemed to Daya that she was narrating all the raids she had ever been on, and acting them out complete with imitations of women involved – and, Daya thought at several points, of horses – to roars of appreciative laughter and comment.

She would stick out her chunky rear and prance in a little circle, or stab her fingers through her wiry hair until it stood up on end. In one or two cases Daya could even see that she produced a creditable impression of someone present in the tent.

Women were elbowing each other in the ribs and grinning. Then Patarish told how Alldera had felled her from the saddle.

Silence and unbelieving stares. Alldera had said once that it was very unusual for a woman on foot to bring down a mounted one, let alone kick her down. The idea of a fem doing such a thing was plainly incomprehensible.

Then Alldera moistened her mouth with tea and took her turn. The women listened intently. At the end, when she said that she would gladly demonstrate the exact kick she had used except that she had nearly crippled herself doing it the first time, there were some smiles.

Someone got up and told a story about Alldera's past among the Mares, something about a hunt. Other stories were told, branching out to feats of her 'family' members at Holdfaster Tent and their relations, and news of their doings since her departure from Stone Dancing. The women seemed a little anxious, possibly because they had never before been confronted with someone who stood in need of several years' news all at once.

They did their best: raids, races, hunts, horse swaps, quarrels sparked and put out, journeys made, gifts given, a death here and a birth there, good seasons and bad, people grown ill or well or staying the same. They did not speak of Alldera's cub, nor did she ask.

She told them about her capture of the wild horses, which seemed to impress them. They asked many questions. Daya felt proud of her.

At length food was brought, and Daya realized that at least some of her weariness was due to hunger. A brace of foals, roasted and cut into steaming joints and chunks, was served on trays of stiff leather. The stringy meat had a strong scent, but a sweet taste.

Daya thought Alldera looked extraordinarily natural in this setting. Indeed she could have been one of the women. Muscular and brown, greasy to the elbows from her meal, she gestured wildly as they did and had swiftly fallen into their patterns of intonation and pronunciation. Her hair, trimmed by Fedeka to shoulder length, was bound back Marish-style with a rawhide thong to keep it from getting plastered to her cheeks with meat juices. She seemed to understand what would interest them most about the pasture and the wells she had passed on the way here.

Abashed by the Mares' frank stares, Daya withdrew into herself. Their yammering dinned in her ears. The odors of unwashed leather and horse sweat, added to the stink of burning dung, made her feel queasy. She sucked at one of her scars where it bulged inside her cheek. She felt very tired, disturbed and put upon. It was a great relief to her when they were told that a special sweat tent had been prepared so the two of them could bathe in privacy.

Much later, outside the sweat tent in the dusk, she and Alldera sluiced each other down with water from buckets left there for them. The sudden cool gush was remarkably pleasant and refreshing. The whole experience of the sweat tent had been unexpectedly agreeable. Watching Alldera drying off, Daya wondered idly what the Mares' bodies looked like under their leather clothing.

No one seemed to be around. The tents glowed faintly in the dusk by the light of small fires. The Bawn chiefs had provided fresh clothing for the two of them, laid out on a leather platter by the sweat tent. Daya had never put on a full Marish outfit before — trousers, boots, breast wrap, tunic, and the striped headcloth of wild cotton. Alldera dressed with obvious pleasure.

'These are wild people, remember,' Daya said, unnerved by a feeling that Alldera was changing into one of them in front of her eyes. 'They despise fems. Why did you leave them before, if it wasn't because they're savages?'

'The trouble wasn't with them, it was with me,' Alldera said. 'I demanded too much of them, I think.' She chuckled ruefully. 'A fault of mine. I'm older now, I think I know a little better.' Then, somberly, she added, 'I liked them even then, and I like them better now. I need to remember who my own people are when I'm here. That's why I asked you to come with me.'

Daya whispered anxiously, 'But also because you love me?' knowing it was only habit that made her worry.

Alldera's hands rested on her shoulders. 'A lot of people have loved you, a lot more will,' she said. 'Perhaps some women of the camps will love you. We both know that you and I aren't much as lovers together. I need your friendship here.'

'I don't know,' Daya murmured, full of anxiety still – was she no longer desirable?

Alldera stood before her, solid, indistinctly outlined in the dusky light, not touching her; waiting.

Daya had never been a friend before.

KINDRED

12

'Heartmother,' Sheel murmured, rising on one elbow in the darkness. She knew the smell of the woman crouching by her bedding: Jesselee Morrowtrow, her own closest mother. She followed the limping woman quietly out of the tent.

There was a faint dawn pallor in the sky against which loomed the low, spreading shapes of the tents of Floating Moon Camp. The air was cold. Somewhere nearby a horse ruffled its breath loudly through its nostrils.

Sheel embraced her heartmother and leaned her head against the weathered cheek. 'I'm glad to see you. Let me get you some tea and some food.'

'Don't trouble yourself. I have food from my travels.' Jesselee lowered herself awkwardly to the ground and laid out a pair of bulky saddlebags, which she set about unlacing.

Sheel crouched opposite her. 'You're the only one with a thought for me. My other relatives have just barged right in and started haranguing me even if it was the middle of the night, regardless of who was with me.'

'I may shout a little myself, Sheel Torrinor. Who else has come to see you?' Jesselee poured something into a bowl and handed it to Sheel.

'Who hasn't come? Women I haven't spent time with in years, Jesselee, women I'd almost forgotten.' She drank; cold tea, not bad. 'Mates from my first raid, my other two living mothers – Derebayan wept buckets and made a spectacle of herself – several cousins and a

Hont woman who familied with my Carrall mother two generations ago! The only person I really wanted to see was you.'

'Tch, I'm not magic, you know,' Jesselee said. 'I'll only tell you what everybody else tells you.' She turned her head from side to side. 'This camp smells of fresh meat. Who slaughtered?'

'Sharavess Tent. They had a feast last night to return gifts they were holding for their tent child. The pack brought its body in yesterday morning – some quick illness, we think.'

'Pity I'm too late,' Jesselee said. 'I know good stories about the Sharavess line that I could have told.'

The sky was lighter, and Sheel could see her better now: a dumpy figure gnawing patiently and with effort on a strip of dried meat with the teeth on the good side of her mouth. She looked smaller than when Sheel had last seen her.

'What's the problem, Sheel? You are a mother of the child of Holdfaster Tent, and she's due to come out of the childpack soon. You should be at Stone Dancing Camp. Even I'm going, as a family member, though I should be taking my last comfort in my own home tent before dying; so what keeps you away?'

As long as Jesselee kept talking about her own death, she was unlikely to do anything about going to meet it. Sheel, loving her, had to smile. Yet she hesitated; daughter and mother of heart closeness were privileged to talk by themselves, but she did not enjoy the idea of being seen trotting out her troubles to her heart-mother like a worried girl.

She said, 'Let me do your hair for you while we talk.' That would relax them both. She settled herself behind Jesselee and began to undo and do up again in a new pattern the small tight braids in which the old woman's gray hair was tied.

'There are fems in Holdfaster Tent.' Word had reached Sheel that Alldera had shown up at Stone Dancing Camp after the last Gather with Patarish Rois as her prisoner and another free fem companion. The Rois had been ransomed and released soon after. Now it was mid-Cool Season, two months later, and women said that Alldera and the other fem were still living in Holdfaster Tent.

'Alldera knew she should be home for the child's coming out,' Jesselee said.

'With another of her kind?' Sheel turned her head and spat. 'Alldera alone is bad enough. Because of her I haven't been allowed to go on a borderlands patrol in years. Because of her the Torrinors had to pay horses for the tent herd of Holdfaster Tent.'

Jesselee moved her head from under Sheel's hands. 'I love having my hair braided up but it always puts me to sleep. Come around here where I can see you, now that the sun's getting up. Good. Now, tell me more about how you feel.'

'I don't want to.'

'Aren't you curious?'

'No.'

'Not about the visiting fems; about your child.'

'No.'

Jesselee sighed. With both hands she eased her leg into a slightly different angle of rest. It always hurt Sheel to see her do that. She could remember her heartmother as an active young woman, lithe and strong. Now every time they met, Jesselee was a little stiffer, her limp more pronounced.

'Let me tell you what I've dreamed three nights since I left Stone Dancing,' Sheel said. 'I dream that I'm back on patrol. I go to the food cache in Long Valley by myself. There I find Alldera, swollen with her cub. I charge her and kill her and throw her body in the river. Then I ride to the others and say no one was there.'

'Feeling – dreaming such anger – I don't want the child to sense that in one of its own mothers!'

'Let me tell you what's been worrying me for some time,' said Jesselee. 'I hear that you've been traveling around lately with one of those Omelly women. Now, I have nothing against the Omelly line; they are women like ourselves and worthy of companionship and affection. But it doesn't do to be careless with them, Sheel. They're dangerous.'

'Grays Omelly and I are thinking of raiding together when the Dusty Season comes,' Sheel said. 'Omellys make raid mates as good as anyone, if you don't let them provoke you and you watch your own behavior so you don't set them off. I can handle Grays.'

'Then you can handle Holdfaster Tent.' Now Jesselee's lined face was fully visible: thick eyebrows arched as if in perpetual surprise, heavy mouth droop-lipped, nose spread out on the face. She looked to Sheel like one of those leather dolls, features lined on with dye, that mothers sometimes made for their daughters. But Jesselee's eyes, drilled deep and small, glittered sharp as stars. Oh, those

Morrowtrows were homely women! For as long as she could remember Sheel had connected that homeliness with warmth and enfolding support.

'Except for you, Sheel, there would be no Holdfaster Tent. You cared for that baby, you nursed it, just as the other sharemothers did. That child will look for you in Holdfaster Tent, and she won't find you in Nenisi or Shayeen or Barvaran or Alldera and her femmish friend. You are the only Sheel Torrinor there is. The child has a claim on your mothering right to the end of her childhood, whatever her background may be, whoever her other mothers are.'

'All right,' Sheel sighed. 'I'll go.'

However obscurely, a heartmother was always on your side.

Jesselee said, 'I'll look for you there.'

Later, while cleaning her horse's feet, Sheel told Grays Omelly that she was returning to Holdfaster Tent. The Omelly breathed, 'Sharu!' and gave her the flickering, nervous glance everyone watched for in women of her line. It meant the onset of the unpredictable anxiety which plagued the Omellys and could make them dangerous.

Sheel said, 'I can't fight off my heartmother.'

'No,' the Omelly said. She had a length of rawhide in her hand and she twisted it first one way and then another. 'I guess she decided you'd spent enough time with a crazy Omelly.'

'Not exactly,' Sheel said, bracing more firmly on her thigh the horsehoof she was picking clean. 'Come with me to Stone Dancing.'

'Ikk. You won't catch me hanging around a tent with fems in it. Fems smell.'

'Everything that lives smells.' The horse jerked its leg. Sheel said, 'Ho, there!' The horse breathed in groans as if Sheel's careful extraction of packed dirt were torture.

'I'm going raiding as we planned,' Grays said. 'Maybe later I'll stop by and give you a horse for your sharechild. I'm curious to see a fem's child.'

Sheel let go the hoof and it clumped back to earth. 'You have seen her. You were at the last Gather. She's in the Stone Dancing pack. Didn't you go out viewing the packs at the Gather like everybody else?'

'You know Grays,' Grays said, snapping the knotted end of the rawhide against the tent wall beside her. 'They all look alike to

Grays, she can't tell one from another till they come out and their families clean them up.'

Someone inside the tent shouted, 'Will you stop that tapping, whoever's doing that? You're driving us crazy in here.'

Sheel said, 'I have to go to my family. It's not any sort of insult to you.'

'Nobody insults the crazy Omellys,' Grays answered. 'You never know what they might do in return.'

When Sheel reached Stone Dancing Camp, the days were beginning to lose their cool bite and turn dry against the skin. She had taken her time, stopping to visit along the way. Jesselee was already in Holdfaster Tent. The tent child had not yet come out.

Alldera looked older, steadier, more muscular than Sheel remembered. They avoided each other.

Shortly after Sheel's arrival, two more fems came. They had deserted their wagon crew to join Alldera and Daya, and they arrived hunched wretchedly on the backs of spare horses belonging to women of Towering Camp. The women had been heading for Stone Dancing and the fems, claiming kinship with Alldera, had begged them to guide them there. Since the Towering Camp women were related to Barvaran and to Shayeen, they had felt bound to honor the kinship claim, and had assented.

The women had not enjoyed traveling with the fems. One of them reported to Sheel, 'They made a fire of their own every night and cooked their own food as if our food were dirty.'

Sheel saw that Alldera herself looked grim to see more fems come. Maybe she was selfish about losing her unique status here. But how could that be, since she had brought the first of them herself?

The new fems draped hides over the inner tent ropes, screening off one wing for themselves. This had never been done before in the camps and mortified Sheel. Alldera sometimes joined them behind this divider, though she seldom slept there at night; she was sleeping with Nenisi again. The scarred one, Daya moved her own bedding behind the divider, however.

According to Nenisi, the new fems said they put up the curtain because they felt they were being watched – and judged – all the time by the women of Stone Dancing.

Sheel fervently wished they would make a tent of their own and live in that, because the curtain of hides did not shut out their femmish voices. They argued incessantly. At first women stopped to listen, but few could follow the rapid Holdfastish speech. One Calpaper woman said, 'When they quarrel they sound like sharu in rut.'

As tormenting for Sheel as their voices was the sweet smoke of the drug the fems called manna. Women occasionally brewed up a medicine from the plant for use in the treatment of certain conditions, but these fems put bits of the leaves on the fire and breathed the smoke. The fumes made Barvaran sleepy and silly, and Shayeen said she got dizzy from them. Sheel found the odor cloyingly sweet and heavy. The fems would not give up the drug or use it outside where, they claimed, the smoke would escape and be wasted.

One evening the fems came out from behind their curtain and joined Sheel and some other women who were gathered outside the tent. The pretty fem called Tua announced, 'Daya is going to tell a story. We thought maybe you'd like to hear it too.'

Everyone was polite and interested, and a few women drifted over from other tents to sit and listen as the little scar-cheeked fem began:

'Let me tell you all how it will be when we fems return to our own country, the Holdfast. We will find the men hiding in burrows in the ground like sharu, sharpening their teeth on the bones of the dead. At night they come out, scavenging for food in the burnt ruins of the City. We'll be able to smell them through the walls. They've let their hair grow to cover their bodies, because they have no clothing without fems there to weave and sew for them.

'One day I find a sick one creeping and hiding. I catch him with my rope, and I bring him back to feed and keep for my amusement. He trots after me for his handful of food, and I kick him or beat him as I like. He won't run away because where else would he get food and a warm place to sleep? He knows nothing of making food grow without slaves to do the work for him, so starvation has tamed him. I ride his shoulders when I choose not to walk, and everyone envies me and pays me to borrow the use of this creature that was a man. We'll have found another way to make cubs by then, so the man I own will keep his genitals only to piss through and for us to mock when we use him as our clown; as the horrible example that we show our children to teach them how debased a human being can be.

'I take my man pet into the City's ruins. I let him visit his former private quarters – he was a rich man – for the pleasure of seeing him weep and sniffle into his beard as he handles the fragments of the statues that once stood in his garden.

'On this day one of the statues leaps up to attack me! It's another man, a wild creature all hair and teeth. He charges me, a broken-bladed knife in one hand, the other brandishing his penis, for the wild men have stories that the fems in the old days worshipped the rod that beat them.

'I draw back my arm to hurl my hatchet at the wild creature, but my man pet throws himself on the attacker before I can do it. The two roll in the dirt, leaving spots of their blood where the splinters of brick and broken tile pierce their skins. My pet gets the other by the beard and smashes the back of his head against a fountain rim. Then he bites his throat out – after all, he was used to eating raw flesh. I whip him back from his prey.

'That's when my pet first sees clearly the bearded face of the dead man. He recognizes his own lover of years before. He screams, he rushes away and hurls himself into the river.

'But I am not unhappy to have lost my pet. Ask any master: a crazy pet is worse than no pet at all.'

It was, Sheel thought, a very peculiar story. Women of other tents who had stopped to listen did not stay to comment and discuss it, but thanked Daya politely and wandered on to chat at other fires. Many women talked about the last remark afterward. No one claimed to understand it.

Sheel said to Jesselee, 'They meant to provoke us. They know we'll never allow them to return to the Holdfast.'

'Go and talk to Alldera about it, if it disturbs you,' the old woman said.

'I don't want to talk to Alldera.'

'Then don't let yourself be provoked.'

The sky was full of tantalizing clouds that Dusty Season. Soft herds of them floated high over the gritty haze which hung above the ground and sifted into a rider's mouth, nostrils and eyes. There was, of course, no rain.

With some help from Alldera the scarred fem, Daya, had taught

the two new fems to ride. Those three borrowed mounts and went
away for a few weeks to catch wild horses. Alldera said she would
wait in camp in case the child should come out; other youngsters of
that generation were beginning to emerge from the childpack.

To Sheel's astonishment the fems brought back fourteen head of
passable beasts which they set about breaking to the saddle under
Daya's direction.

Sheel could not watch. It hurt her to see fems subduing horses.

Sheel sat in Periken Tent with her friend Tico Periken drinking
shake milk together in bed. Grays Omelly, who had gone raiding
and was now visiting as she had promised, was there with them. So
was an older woman of the Caranaw line, a raid mate of Tico's.

The Caranaw sat by the milk cradle and punched and rocked the
bag which hung there, mixing the dried milk and water inside. She
rambled along meanwhile about horse breaking, and ended up
saying that she did not like to see the new fems riding.

'These new 'cousins', Daya and the rest – they don't act like
women. Not at all. What woman stews greens with her meat, or
wears a slave smock over her trousers and a blood rag under them,
or kicks up dust everywhere she goes with those big, stiff sandals
they wear? What woman keeps to herself and speaks like rocks
clacking together, what woman steals?'

Sheel had more to say about the fems than any of them, but she
was bound by the ties of kinship and hospitality not to speak against
any person in her family's tent. She tried to turn the conversation by
saying shortly, 'Complaints about the free fems should go to the
chief tent.'

'Why, Sheel?' Grays said, her blue eyes innocently wide. 'We
don't run to the chief tent with every little thing, like that fem Tua
who went there because she couldn't get Tacey Faller to pay up on a
bet. As if anybody can get a redhaired Faller to pay just by asking! I
don't know why these fems can't go and talk with a person's
relatives and let the lines and families smooth out problems instead
of blowing every spark up into a grass fire.'

'Hush now,' Tico said, rolling onto her belly and reaching for the
shake milk skin. 'You know Sheel can't talk about the fems.'

Grays thumped Sheel on the arm. 'Put their stuff outside the tent
to let them know they should move on, that's the way! Why are

there fems in Stone Dancing Camp anyway? Suppose all the fems come over from the tea camp and move in with you?'

Patiently Tico said, 'There are only forty or fifty of them in the tea camp, and anyway I hear Alldera had some kind of quarrel with them, so it's not likely they'll come here. But those who do come are allowed to stay. I've explained it twenty times to you, Grays. They're blood kin of Alldera. Think of them as a sort of outland Motherline made up of lots of cousins instead of mothers and daughters. Each fem is a distant cousin of each other fem, if you see what I mean. Now, let's leave it at that.'

Maralas Caranaw shifted her bottom on the pile of hides under her. The Caranaws were afflicted with sore joints in middle age. She said, frowning deeply, 'It's our weapons that bring them, our bows.'

'They have their own weapons,' Grays sneered. 'Those little hatchets and those clumsy spears.'

'Never mind what brings them, then,' the Caranaw said morosely. 'Look what's happening because they're here. The trading crews of their wagons are angry because we let the fems stay, so they want to get even. Did you hear how some Hilliars over in Steep Cloud Camp were cheated over salt last month by a trading crew? Women at Steep Cloud are talking of going for salt themselves as we all used to do before the fems took over the trade. Nobody likes salting her food with sand.'

Tico gave Sheel a worried glance. 'We shouldn't bother Sheel with any more of this.'

Grays Omelly had been taking objects from her pockets and lining them up in concentric rings on the floor: bits of bone, scratched Ancient fragments, thread, a horse's molar, buttons, the rubbish with which she made what she called her 'spells'. When she began to glance anxiously around, Tico contributed her own striking flint to complete the design.

Grays said, 'Sheel won't mind hearing that Alldera Holdfaster sleeps with Nenisi Conor. Or that Daya sleeps with me. Sleeping with Daya is like sleeping with a child, a child you hate. She makes you think she's helpless, as if you're somehow taking her by force. And you do, in a way. It's exciting, like hunting. You should try it, Sheel. She will come to your bed willingly, now that she's come to mine.'

Tico tried again: 'Let's drop it now. Look, you're getting Sheel angry with all this talk.'

'Magic of circles, tell me now,' Grays continued, bowing over the floor, 'if I killed a fem, if she had a spirit, where would it go? It couldn't rise to the spirit country above the clouds and rejoin its Motherline because it has no real Motherline. It had no share-mothers to love it and no bloodmother and no horses and no sharu —'

'You're raving, Omelly,' the Caranaw said sharply.

Grays flung herself headlong into Sheel's lap. 'Love!' she said. 'Sheel's love is what all the fems need.' She nuzzled Sheel's groin. 'I pinched Daya's nipples till she wept, but afterward she hugged me and said it was all right, it was because I am a wild woman and don't know how to control myself.'

Sheel pulled violently away, and her feelings burst out. 'You hug that filthy, man-used fem as if you were her master, you kiss her scars — they marked her like that, and she let them, and never fought back! You drink shame from her body, and now you come to me? Get away from me!'

The Omelly hugged Sheel's legs in both her arms, pleading, 'It's a plot of the Conors. Nenisi and her line are corrupting me, making me play with these fems!'

'Get — off!' Sheel shouted, and kicked at her. Grays hit back at breasts and groin, sobbing as she fought. Sheel kept pulling her punches, trying not to hurt her.

Their struggles scattered Grays' design all over the floor.

One morning Sheel stopped Alldera in the tent when Alldera came in alone from running. She held out an iron bit she had missed two days previously.

'I went behind your friends' curtain, there, and I found this in the bedding of one of the new fems. I also found a dozen arrow shafts that belong to the Bawns and a lot of smaller things — leather lace, sharpening stones, ornaments — who knows how long the fem has had them? You tell her she'd better not take anything again.'

'You know the culprit,' Alldera replied. 'Tell her yourself. She's a relative of yours.'

'Not of mine! This stealing is a coward's kind of raiding — to live with us and take our belongings little by little! If I catch the thief, will you ransom her?'

Alldera said, 'Let her alone, Sheel. Let them all alone. They're not what I'd have them be, but I share a long past with them. I'd speak for them in the chief tent.'

Goaded by Alldera's cool refusal to apologize, Sheel burst out bitterly, 'It's thanks to my own blundering that you came here! I had a feeling someone was at that food cache. Not a man; I can smell them miles off. One of your kind. So I said, Shayeen is sick, let's not take the time to stop. I was careless. I should have taken my lance and made sure, as I have in my dreams since. I didn't realize how dangerous you were.'

'Then you missed your chance, Sheel, because we are kindred now,' Alldera said, and moved to pass around her.

Maddened, Sheel caught Alldera's shirt in both hands, as if to raise her up and dash her to the ground. But the fem said grimly, 'Remember, Sheel – we're kindred. If you so much as bloody my nose, you'll be outlawed for it and have to run south.'

Sheel released her. 'Your lips are white, you're scared, fem!' she sneered, her own voice breathless with rage.

'Yes,' Alldera said, pulling her shirt straight. 'You're a formidable woman, Sheel, and your anger is frightening. But I think you know as well as I do that we're way past this kind of scuffling. What you and I started in the desert between women and fems is out of your hands and mine now.'

Sheel sat soaping her saddle outside the tent where Grays Omelly was staying. Nenisi came and sat with her. Nenisi looked worn and tired. Like all women of the Conor line, she was outgrowing her painful teeth at last. But now she kept scratching at her sore, red-lined eyes. The inflammation showed bright as blood in her black face. She had been having eye trouble since the hot winds had begun to blow.

'Are you thinking of leaving?' Nenisi said.

'This camp is like living in a dust storm for me.'

'Be patient, Sheel. The tent child is growing breasts, and there's hair between her legs. She's bound to come out soon. Then it won't be so difficult, you'll see.'

Sheel heaved the saddle into a new angle in her lap and lifted the stirrup leather so that she could reach underneath. 'I can hardly talk to my friends without getting into a fight. My own tent is full of strangers that I hate, my enemy speaks to me as if she were my mother – and it all goes back to my own mistake, Nenisi. How can I hold up my head here?'

Nenisi sat with her a long time, saying nothing, looking as troubled and unhappy as Sheel felt.

On the way to the squats the following evening, Sheel saw that Grays had taken up one of her frozen stances on the dusty dancing ground outside the camp, arms outstretched, face blankly fixed. She could stand that way for hours, captive to the visions that were an Omelly trait.

The two new fems walked past, returning from practice with their bows. One of them shouted something at Grays, who did not answer.

Sheel hesitated, half expecting Grays to leap at them. Someone should have told them to keep away from the Omelly.

The fems called to Grays again. They walked on. Then one of them wheeled suddenly, stooped, and shied a stone at the motionless woman.

Shouting, Sheel took a step after them. A rock whizzed past her own head. She yelled for help.

Women swarmed out of the nearer tents and a brawl spread on the dancing ground. Sheel, barred from fighting against her own kindred, ran for the Shawden chiefs. Hard on her heels came a crowd of women dragging the two fems, so that the chief tent was soon filled with shouted accusations and insults.

Grays, unresisting, had been stoned by the two fems. They said they had done it because she had mocked them by refusing to speak to them, and that they had not recognized Sheel, their cousin, when they had thrown a stone at her. The Shawden chiefs set them stiff fines of skins and salt, and that was that.

Sheel avoided the discussions of the incident at other tents and even in Holdfaster Tent, which bore the brunt of the fines. She thought about what had happened through several sleepless nights. It outraged her that women did not seem to know how to deal with these upstart fems, and so fell back on treating them as if they were women.

The herds had been culled at the beginning of the Cool Season, before the fems came. Now the grass was too sparse, and it was agreed that a second culling would be necessary this year.

The night before the culling was scheduled Daya slipped away alone after dinner, heading out of camp quietly on foot. Sheel saw. Taking one of the night horses tethered outside the tent, she followed.

There was a bright moon. Out by the tent herd she found the tracks of Daya's favorite mount, a stripe-legged dun that Daya had brought with her to Stone Dancing Camp. The tracks led eastward, away from the camp.

Riding through the moonlight like a real person in a ghost-white world, Sheel could feel the distress in her bones that meant cruelty from the past was accumulated here or nearby. The women called these feelings 'ghosts'. Not that anything tangible or even visible would arise here to startle her horse or raise her own hair; but in some places you could feel the lingering vibrations of long-ago cries of pain.

Her horse stopped and stood flicking its ears this way and that. The night hung still around her. Sheel turned in her saddle, seized with a sudden anxiety. Why had she left her tent to wander solitary by moonlight like a person without kindred? Had hatred for the fems done this to her?

Someone was moving over there, on foot, heading back toward camp: a fem, slender and very graceful. Sheel heard the faint chime of the little bells, love gifts that Daya had taken to wearing bound into her hair.

Sheel waited.

Daya did not alter her course but walked right past as if Sheel were invisible. She seemed to be following her own tracks back to Stone Dancing, singing some sorry femmish song under her breath.

Sheel turned her horse and followed, thinking, No one would know if I did it out here. I might smash Holdfaster Tent once and for all.

She said, 'Stop singing. The sharu sleep lightly.'

'My song is a prayer,' Daya said, not looking up.

'A prayer won't save you.'

'Not a prayer for me,' the fem said in her soft, deceitful voice that never seemed angry. 'A prayer for the safety of my dun mare. She was marked for the culling. Alldera gave her to me for my own, not to be your food.'

Sheel stood in her stirrups and looked out, away from the camp. 'You drove the dun off, did you? I suppose you think Moonwoman will take care of her?'

Daya said, still soft-voiced, always soft-voiced, 'You have no right to speak of Moonwoman.'

'Why not? The moon shines on my head too. I grew up beside water with tides that answered to the moon – the Great Salty River to the west. I would know if there were some single great moon-being controlling all movement in the world – the tides, the growth of plants and creatures, the weather. That's the sort of thing the Ancient men believed in. We women know better. We celebrate the pattern of movement and growth itself and our place in it, which is to affirm the pattern and renew it and preserve it. The horses help us. They are part of the pattern and remind us of our place in it. What can a horse do for you, a stranger?'

Daya raised her hand to touch the shoulder of Sheel's mount. Sheel reined the horse aside, out of her reach.

Daya said, 'A horse can trust me.'

'Trust you for what? Why? Because you think it's love if you save one horse from the culling? That's not love, it's silly and useless.' She looked contemptuously at the fem's bent head. 'There is no way you can make a place for yourself in the pattern.' She knew what she was saying to herself: it would make no rent in the pattern if I killed you; it would be no crime. Carefully, she chose words Nenisi had spoken once.

'Our bond with our horses is old and true and the center of our lives. The horses lend us their strength, their speed, their substance for food, their own dim wisdom. We protect them from the sharu, we dance with them and look after them and put our bodies in their power, too, in our own way. Then when we die our corpses go to feed the sharu, and what do the sharu do in turn? They dig in the earth for roots and to make their burrows, which prepares the soil for the grasses the horses eat.'

'The dun mare was a wild horse,' Daya said almost inaudibly. 'She belonged to me, not to you women. I had my own understanding with her.'

She looked up at last, and Sheel saw the glitter of tears, the vulnerable face, the delicate line of the cheek rutted with slave scars. She felt no pity. This was a creature who would throw stones at an

Omelly.

A preliminary thrill of violence tightened the muscles of her hands and arms, and the mare pulled protestingly at the bit. Sheel slackened the reins, annoyed with herself for having needlessly hurt her horse's mouth.

She remembered who she was, and that was much more important than who or what this miserable fem was. Fems had no kindred to teach them how to behave. They were not women.

I am never alone, she said to herself. My line and my kindred and our ways are always with me. If I killed now, I would not be a woman. I would be responsible to no one, solitary, worthless. I would be like this fem.

'I'll show you the way back. You can't see any more,' she said. 'Look, the moon has set.'

The fem trudged on, head at the level of Sheel's hip. 'I can find the camp myself.'

'You claim to be cousin to the bloodmother of my sharechild,' Sheel said acidly. 'My sharechild wouldn't want me to ride on and leave you wandering here to be eaten by sharu.'

By morning the dun horse had drifted back to the tent herd, having nowhere else to go. It was butchered with the others.

'Don't be foolish – my horse has never mounted a woman,' Sheel said impatiently. She hated being fussed over in the middle of a game of pillo. 'He's much too big to mate with. You're safe from him, Shayeen.' She tightened the reins of the red stallion dancing under her.

At her side Shayeen said, 'All the same, he's got his hanger out. I wish you'd ride a mare, like everyone else.'

'Not in a pillo game,' Sheel said. 'Have you seen the rump on that Faller woman's horse?' She pointed disdainfully with her chin. 'Imagine entering the game on a mare in season! That's why this stud is all excited.'

Sheel was winner of the previous round in their game, so she was now the quarry. She crouched on the back of her sweating mount, the heavy braided rope supple in her hands. One end of the rope was tied to the pillo itself, a stuffed sharu skin; the other end was knotted. In the hands of a skilled rider the ten meters of rope were a strong weapon, the only weapon permitted on the pillo field. The red dye with which the stuffed skin was saturated left marks like blood on an opponent that took her out of the game, just as if she or her mount had been slashed by a real sharu.

Sheel craved the cleansing power of violence, the release. A good, rough game of pillo gave that. She could hardly wait for the coming clash, and part of the red horse's impatience he had picked up from her.

The twelve women who were Sheel's opponents lined up at the opposite end of the field. They held their lances points downward, aslant beside their horses' shoulders. Hidden behind these riders was the 'burrow', a sheet of leather propped up on sticks like a tent. Sheel's object was to ride through the opposition without losing the pillo, which she would try to sling into the mouth of the burrow and earn a goal. Each other rider would try to prevent her goal by pinning the pillo to earth with a well-placed lance thrust.

Around Sheel friends and rivals laughed, called bets and counter-bets, commented on the states of the horses and riders in this second half of play. Shayeen moved around the red horse, checking its gear and its feet. She need not have bothered; nothing short of a broken leg would stop the stud, a five-year-old named Fire. Like other stallions, he was no use in a real race or a raid, either of which entailed a run of three days or so; only the wiry little mares had that kind of endurance. For a day's hunting or a pillo fight, he was superb.

'What are we waiting for?' Sheel groaned.

In the center of the field a dark woman of the Clarish line sat on her horse, lance raised straight in the air. From its end drooped a white horse tail. When the horse tail dropped the play would resume. She was looking from one end of the field to the other.

The sky was overcast, presaging the end of the Dusty Season and the coming of rain. Over the distant mountains seams of sunlight opened in the dark, rich layers of cloud. Assured of new grass by a week of thunderous skies, the women had used the last of their precious grain to strengthen their fittest horses for the game.

Sheel shivered in the breath of a breeze. She was wet with the sweat of anticipation. If fems were permitted in the game, there might now be femmish blood spilled by a woman of the Torrinor line. But pillo was a clean game, not for slaves from the lands of men.

The red horse snorted and mouthed the bit. He had gone four rounds already and his coat was dark with sweat. He jigged and fretted for the start of his run, one eye on the Faller's high-tailed mare.

The Clarish's lance dipped.

'Go!' the women screamed.

Fire shot forward. Sheel lay along his neck, riding him with weight and legs. Her right arm yanked back the taut rope with the pillo bounding at the end of it, preparing a low, skimming whip-stroke to catch the legs of the oncoming horses.

The riders came like a dust storm, yelling and jostling, their lances cocked shoulder high to jab at the pillo. Sheel slung the pillo forward on its line, and the horses rushing toward her sprang aside.

The red stud ignored the gap they left. He veered toward the Faller woman on her foam-streaked bay mare, fifteen meters down the field on the left. Sheel hauled on the reins and beat him over the shoulders with the knotted end of the rope. He would not turn.

'I'll kill you!' she screamed into his back-laid ears. 'You're dead as you run, sharu-vomit!'

The Faller's mare, trying to stop and piss, swung broadside across other riders coming up along her flanks. Women on the sidelines shrieked warnings to their friends and curses at the Faller.

Then someone swept up alongside and punched the distracted Faller out of her saddle. This player lashed the mare across the rump with her rein ends and headed her back full tilt the way she had come, while the Faller skipped about on foot in a panic, trying to avoid being trampled. A friend caught the Faller up and carried her out of the melee.

Fire stopped trying to stand on his hind legs. He plunged after the Faller's mare at a dead run, and into a swarm of riders. Other horses cannoned against him; Sheel felt him stagger. Flying clods were hurled up by the hooves of the horses as they dug for purchase. Sheel shortened the rope swiftly with both hands so that it would not drop slack and foul her own mount's legs. She laid about her with the knotted end, beating the riders, whooping.

She was at a disadvantage. Everyone was too excited to feel much pain, force was all that mattered. They hooked at her with knees and elbows. To beat them back she used the rope with both hands. Women swung aside, dripping red where the pillo had struck. The press thinned about her. She brought Fire's blocky quarters over hard against the shoulder of a pursuing mare and had the satisfaction of hearing the rider curse as she was jarred from the saddle. At last Sheel was in the clear.

She clamped the shank of the rope hard between her leg and the saddle, leaned forward with both hands on the red horse's mane, and summoned breath to call to him. He groaned and stretched out over the ground in a flat run. If anyone caught the pillo now as it streaked and bounded along at the rope's end, it would tear free, unhorsing her, but she did not care, did not even look back. Fire ran on, laboring. The women roared.

Judging her moment, Sheel caught up the rope and with a triumphant sweep of her arm she slung the pillo at the burrow. The frayed rope parted in midair, the heavy leather bag flew wide. Groans came from the sidelines.

'Sharu drink my blood!' Sheel swore. She turned the red horse in a long, faltering curve off the field. Dismounting, she stepped away to keep from hitting him. Her eyes stung and her legs shook under her.

Women crowded around, patting her on the back, hugging her, congratulating her on a game well played despite the bad rope. Her bruises began to ache.

Close at her side Nenisi said, 'I hate that lumpy red horse of yours, but he is a pusher in a game – once you get him to concentrate on the business at hand, that is.'

Women laughed.

Limping back to Holdfaster Tent, Sheel leaned on Nenisi. A flying stirrup iron had struck her in the calf; she remembered the impact, now that she felt the pain.

Good pain; she was still well within reach of other women's hands, their buffets as well as their caresses. She still belonged despite Daya and Alldera and the other fems.

She hugged Nenisi's shoulders more tightly and flinging back her head shouted out a victory song that pressed at her chest and throat like the onset of weeping. There were no words to the song, there was only her rough, glad voice.

13

Under a wet-season sky ripe with clouds the mothers and the child of Holdfaster Tent moved in procession around Stone Dancing Camp. Alldera found the slow pace maddening. Nenisi's descriptions of the coming-out ceremonies kept settling in her mind. This was the last stage of their child's absorption into the lives of the women, and she kept wondering if some unexpected intrusion might yet break it all up and leave the child unclaimed – or even back in her own hands. She did not know how she would take that.

The child walked close at Barvaran's side, a naked, dirty rain-streaked figure, its face half hidden by its mat of greasy hair. Looking at it, Alldera felt detached. She reminded herself many times as they wound their way among the tents, this is the child of my body. It was incredible! The child had matured rapidly into a young adolescent.

She seemed to Alldera rather stocky, certainly not tall. She had a wide, well-shaped mouth and her alert eyes looked everywhere, at everyone and everything. Sometimes she licked her lips, or clenched her hand on Barvaran's so that her dirty knuckles paled. Alldera saw she was afraid, but there was no whimpering or shrinking. Alldera approved in an abstract way.

This is the child of my body.

At every tent women came out smiling to embrace the share-mothers, laughing, congratulating them, eyeing but not touching the child. Each clasped Alldera's hands or stroked her shoulders or straightened her hair. Alldera was continually reminded of the day, years ago, when she had given birth among them. To this child.

The sweat tent was not quite ready. The five sharemothers waited outside wrapped in their leather capes while other relatives – including free fems from the wagons, four of them now besides Daya – finished preparations for the ritual. Jesselee, as a grandmother, directed all this.

Alldera could not stop yawning with nerves. Her belly rumbled, and her left side, where she had been hurt once in the tea camp, ached from the Rainy Season dampness. She looked at Nenisi standing close by, her face lit with joy. The child had come out late, a month after the pack mates of her generation, and she was small. She would not mate at this year's Gather, or even next year's. But she had come out, and Alldera could see the women's relief and was glad of it. Now it was only required that this go well, that the gift to the women – to Nenisi, really, who wanted it so badly – be accomplished, whatever else might happen.

As they went inside the sweat tent, Nenisi's hand brushed Alldera's and tightened briefly on her fingers.

Scrapers had been laid out on a leather mat, fresh white slivers of soaproot gleamed, and the floor had been strewn with aromatic grasses. The sharemothers spread their leather capes on the floor and sat upon them, nude.

The child crouched by Barvaran's side. Her instant affinity for the red-faced woman meant that Barvaran would be her heartmother. Alldera felt relieved. For the moment there was no necessity of close contact between herself and the youngster, contact for which she felt totally unready in spite of all Nenisi's preparations.

Barvaran began to speak softly to the child in the quick, fluid slang of the childpack. Alldera felt a startling stab of jealousy. If she were to address the child in Holdfastish, there would be no understanding between them. Never mind, she thought; what would I have to say to her?

She sat down near the stone pit, feeling the heat tighten her skin. Nenisi, squatting next to her, began pounding soaproot into paste. Cheerful Barvaran, handsome Shayeen whose reserve Alldera had never pierced, and Sheel, more wiry than ever and seeming very deliberate today, the family was gathered again. Naked, all but Nenisi and coppery Shayeen were pale-skinned except on their hands and faces, which sun and wind had weathered.

Alldera looked down at her own thighs – once brown from exposure below the short working garment of the fems, now pale from the protection of the pants she had adopted from the women – her own darkened hands resting on them.

It amazed her to think that Sheel the raider, Sheel the fierce who rode stallions, killed men and hated fems, had once entered a tent like this as a child among her own mothers. But so had all the women.

At the first hiss of steam from the stone pit the child shrank back into the enclosure of Barvaran's arms. Gently, still speaking in a low voice, Barvaran scooped up a handful of lather and soaped the child's shoulder while the others watched. The child glanced from one of them to another and back down at the shining film of soaproot that Barvaran spread with great tenderness on her skin.

'She has clear hazel eyes,' Shayeen commented, 'and her teeth look good and straight.'

Sheel said, 'I think a horse bit her there, on the arm.'

'Neat hands and feet,' Nenisi said. 'She isn't big, but she's well shaped, with good proportions.'

Barvaran held up one of the child's arms and gently moved the hand in a circle with both of hers. 'Something happened here,' she said with concern. 'A break, I can feel the knob where the bones knit. But the wrist moves smoothly.'

The tricky part of the ritual bath was coming; apparently all the youngsters fought against the discomforts of having their hair washed and untangled. Nenisi said that this was good: in her struggles to avoid her mothers a child learned that though they overpowered her, they did not harm her; she could trust them.

'I think she's going to give us a good fight,' Shayeen predicted approvingly.

Barvaran began lathering the child's hair. In a moment the youngster let out a yell of outrage and tried to lunge away. The women rushed to help hold the slippery, thrashing limbs so that Barvaran could finish the hair wash.

Alldera hung back, reluctant to lay hands on this strange young body.

'Come on,' Shayeen shouted to her, 'get the feel of your child, and let her get the feel of you!'

Alldera thrust her own body among the bodies of the others. They were all dripping and lathered now. Helping to pinion the thin, flailing arms, Alldera kept her head pressed next to the child's head to avoid being smacked in the face by her hard skull. Stinging soap had gotten into her eyes and she could not see, but she could feel the muscles pull and thrust under her grip, and she smelled the first blood flow which had led the childpack to expel the child. She kept remembering with disbelief that these straining limbs belonged to her own offspring.

A douse of rinse water left them gasping and ready for the next stage.

Barvaran blotted the child's long, tangled hair in a blanket. The child still tried to pull away, abusing them all in pack slang. She yanked out her menstrual plug twice before Barvaran could get her to accept its presence in her body. Barvaran sat with her, grooming her sleek hair and talking quietly in her ear while the other share-mothers washed their own hair and scraped each other down. They showed off to one another the red marks where the child had hit them and ruefully compared bruises.

The entryway was tightly laced. Alldera saw how the child's eyes kept flashing in that direction; she no longer fought back, but she had not given up.

Alldera thought, this child would never have lived to come out of the Holdfast kit pits. The older fems would have judged her too ready to fight. Before she could break some man's teeth for him and bring a flood of femmish blood in reprisal, we would have killed her ourselves. An ordinary idea, in my old life.

The child watched each of the adults warily. For an instant her eyes met Alldera's. There was no spark of special feeling. She seemed rather ordinary now, a draggled youngster, hair dark with moisture, skin dark with years of running naked, flickering eyes of an indeterminate color in the silvery light of the sweat tent; hazel, Shayeen had said.

Alldera looked away. What came next would exclude her because she was not a Riding Woman. Nenisi had prepared her. She withdrew to watch and sat with her back against one of the tent poles.

The others rose to their feet and stood in a group near the stone pit, leaving the child apart for a moment.

Something very small and simple happened. The child jumped up and glanced quickly at the entry; as she did so, the women turned their heads toward her. That was all, but there was something in the carriage of their heads, the wideness of their eyes. They seemed to Alldera to mimic with extraordinary power the way that horses lift their heads from grazing to look and listen.

Then Sheel squatted, and moving backwards on her haunches she began to smooth the sand outward from the pit toward the sweat tent wall behind her. Time had touched her, Alldera saw; veins and tendons stood high under the skin of her forearms and hands. Nenisi and Shayeen did as Sheel did, palming the sand flat. Barvaran stood with a hand on the child's shoulder and still talked to her, pointing, smiling, as the smoothed sand was marked by the others with lines, dots, circles, zig-zags, all oriented to the stone pit, which symbolized the present campsite of Stone Dancing.

This was how women gave a child the plains.

As heartmother, Barvaran took the first turn, leading the reluctant youngster about the tent by the hand. The other women walked in attendance as Barvaran named all the places that were special to her, places mapped by the markings on the floor. She walked the child over their world; all heads bent to follow Barvaran's stubby, pointing finger: 'The Star Saddle,' Alldera heard her murmur, 'where we found water just in time coming back from a long, hard patrol, and here is the spring of the split-hoofed horse . . .'

There could be no turn for Alldera in this, Nenisi had said; 'The first place you show the child is where the bones of your own bloodmother were left for the sharu.'

Nenisi came out of the group and sat by Alldera at the tent wall. With the back of her hand she pushed aside the hair plastered to her gleaming black forehead. Her eyes were on the other women. 'It's going well. Is it making some sort of sense to you?' she said.

Alldera thought of that moment of magic when their heads had turned. 'I think so.'

'Good!' Nenisi hugged her. 'A great day, finally, this coming out. Some say that on such a day all elements of the world are placed fresh: living and nonliving, past and future, the spirits of animals and of grass and wind and time passing and even the spirits of stars. Each time we make again the web that is the inner pattern of all things, all things are balanced, the world is made steady.'

Alldera did not say aloud, Are not the men and fems beyond the mountains elements of the world? She did not want to disrupt the ceremony or the triumphant mood of Nenisi, whom she loved.

Then it was Nenisi's turn to take the child walking over the world. Alldera sat back, thinking.

She recalled Nenisi's joy at her return, months back now, and her own almost sensuous delight at what had taken on the color of a true homecoming, so familiar had everything seemed.

Coming from her years away with the free fems, she had at once noticed the changes that only a woman of Stone Dancing Camp would notice: this person gone, these horses newly arrived or newborn, such and such a family richer than before while another once prosperous group used other women's cast-off tent leathers and awaited its turn of luck. Rayoratan Tent had gone, having packed up after a quarrel with the Shawden chiefs and joined Waterwall Camp in the north. Shan the bow-maker who had made Alldera's first bow was dead, carried off by a bout of lung fever. When Alldera expressed her shock and even a touch of real sorrow, the women nodded and patted her just as if she were one of them and had a right to mourn.

She was no longer trying to catch up with them. Their distance from her — when she felt it — was now simply part of their nature and their beauty. She found that she did not need Daya to remind her of who she was.

From the first the little pet had been much more than a shadowy companion. She had become a teacher of other fems and lover of Grays Omelly, of all women! Alldera knew she had underestimated the pet fem. She had asked Daya to come as a companion of her own kind, thinking it could make no difference to the women. The effect that Daya made among them delighted her. Despite the women's low opinion of free fems, the little pet's grace, her elegant manners, her beautiful marred face as serious and watchful as an animal's, intrigued them. Also, they could not hide their startled admiration of her skill with horses.

Alldera had never considered the free fems who admired Daya and who would be attracted and reassured by tales of her presence here. Four had come, and maybe there would be others. Their presence made Alldera uneasy.

They brought friction. There was their inveterate stealing, their pathetic arrogance, their clannishness. And Daya's affair with Grays

Omelly — how long before other free fems moved into the beds of other women, with what consequences? Fems were intense and jealous lovers, totally opposite to the casual behavior of women. They insisted on wearing sandals, chewed tea instead of drinking it, spat everywhere in a way that the women found offensive . . .

So many irritating matters, so difficult to cope with and to explain. Even Nenisi did not fully understand; and there was an aspect of the fems' presence that Alldera could not even try to explain at all. Perhaps Sheel felt it too — the unpredictable influence of a number of free fems living in a women's camp.

Alldera had wanted to make changes, first in herself and then in the free fems, but never in the lives of the women. Now changes had followed her to Stone Dancing Camp, and she could not see where it would lead. It frightened her.

Alldera felt that she and the black woman were closer than ever. She no longer took lessons at Nenisi's knee. Often they did not speak together at all, but clung close in simple gratitude for each other's presence. They shored each other up; maybe Nenisi was not as confident as she seemed. Don't think that. She's no more perfect than anyone, but grant her her strengths . . .

There were traces of gray in Nenisi's kinky hair now, like curls of pale ash in charcoal. Nenisi was not afraid, and she was wise. Didn't the women say, Those Conors are always right? If Alldera said what she was thinking, Nenisi would say, Why these gloomy, anxious thoughts? This is a day of gladness for your child's sake, our daughter's sake.

The women were sitting grouped around the stone pit now, home from walking over the world. They hugged the child and patted her, and she shyly accepted their embraces.

Barvaran murmured something to the child, who rose from among the women and came to stand in front of Alldera. She put her hands on Alldera's jaw and tilted her head back to study her face: warm hands, light and steady, that Alldera did not resist.

'Is my nose flat in the middle like yours?' the girl said, frowning over the unfamiliarity of the language of adults or perhaps over the idea of having a flat nose.

'No.' Alldera paused. She searched the bold young face before her. 'You'll be better looking than I am.'

The youngster laughed like metal chinking on metal. 'But we're blood kin, how could one of us be prettier?'

Alldera found that she could not now remember the face of either of the two men who might have been this child's father.

Jesselee, in charge of the coming-out arrangements, did not alter the traditions in any way for this unique child. There was feasting, dancing on the dance ground, gift giving, and gift acceptance, all centered on the child and her introduction to the women of other tents. These ceremonies involved the rest of the family, but not the bloodmother. The bloodmother always tended the tent herd. The effect was to insulate the bloodmother and the child from each other.

The bloodmother looked at her child and saw her own image made young, her replacement in the world, Nenisi said. The child saw in her bloodmother the pattern for her own being. Women said it was best not to let this powerful connection unbalance all the other relationships that guided their two lives, and so it was appropriate that the bloodmother and child be separated for a time.

'Such a fuss,' Daya said, riding with Alldera on the second morning after the coming out. Daya had brought a flask of blood broth from which Alldera drank gratefully. 'Not that we ourselves hold back. Tua's given the cub a tooled leather belt. The other three made her sandals.'

'She'll never wear them. What did you give?'

Eyes downcast and showing some embarrassment, Daya said, 'Fedeka's here, traveling a while with a trade wagon. I got the kit a jar of perfume in case she should ever want to smell like something besides horses, sweat, and old leather.'

Alldera said soberly, 'Couldn't you persuade the other fems with us to go back to the tea camp with the trade wagon?'

'They didn't come here just for me, Alldera, and they won't leave just because I tell them to. Maybe if you said something to them –'

'I'd look pretty foolish, telling them to go home to Elnoa after what I used to say about her. Look, Daya; I have something on my mind.' Although there was no one near them on the green and glistening plain, Alldera lowered her voice: 'It's the naming. Nenisi told me how it's supposed to be – I smile and produce a name and use the formula: that the name came into my mouth with the food I ate or with the water I drank from the wells.

'Only no names come. Nothing.'

'How about "Tezera"?' Daya said hopefully. 'That's a pretty name.' She listed several others: 'Fenessa, Maja, Leesha, Tamsana.'

Alldera disapproved. 'Those are all femmish names that a master would give a new-bought slave.'

She saw Daya's eyes widen slightly. 'She is a femmish cub, Alldera.'

'Is that what they say at the trade wagon?'

'Yes,' Daya admitted. 'They think she should have a femmish name, ending in "a". We've all kept our slave names, in respect for our past. And she was conceived back there.'

Alldera laughed. 'A femmish name wouldn't make any difference. The women would just drop the "a", since to them she's a woman, not a fem – unlike ourselves, who wobble along somewhere in between.' She kicked her horse into a brisker stride.

Daya kept pace alongside. 'Some fems are saying that we should insist on taking the child and dedicating her to Moonwoman. They'd be furious if they knew I'd told you.'

'Why do they care about her all of a sudden?'

'You know many fems in the tea camp thought from the beginning that you were wrong to leave the cub with the Mares,' Daya replied. 'They thought you should have brought her with you to the tea camp so she would grow up with her own people. These Mares are admirable in their way, but she doesn't belong with them.'

'The fems talk as if I owe them something.' Alldera thought angrily of her broken ribs. She pressed Daya: 'What about you? Do you believe I owe you and Fedeka and the rest of the wagon fems?'

'No; but I think that we do need, for our own sakes, to make a claim on that cub.'

'What's this "for our own sakes", Daya? Is this you?' Daya looked older, more beautiful and less mischievous – something of a stranger. 'Go and tell them that I won't have them – or anyone – meddling with the child's life, not in any way. This cub has nothing to do with them. You had nothing to do with her. That's the men's disease, thinking they're so important that everything connects to them and their schemes and desires. How I hate that mixture of the worst in both men and fems – cowardice and conceit together! That's what they'd teach the child if they could get her.'

'Alldera, don't turn on me,' the pet fem said unhappily. 'I'm not your enemy.'

The rough words had not been meant for Daya, Alldera knew. She was sorry, and they rode on without speaking. Then she tapped Daya's knee. 'I've got to find a name! Not a name from the old life, like those you've suggested. Think of a name that's not the property of the fems and not the property of the women either.'

Daya smiled her scarred smile. 'Call her "Alldera".'

The flaps of Holdfaster Tent's front wall were pinned back to make a wide entrance. The women of Stone Dancing Camp had assembled outside, all but the Holdfaster sharemothers, who sat expectantly within. Alldera, seated by the fire cage, could see the child coming flanked by Sheel and Shayeen. The two women were bringing the last of the child's presents. It was time for the naming.

All the femmish names from Alldera's memory seemed harsh and ugly. My mother, whoever she was, never named me, she thought as the child drew nearer. I chose no names for my other two cubs. The master did that. Why do they leave the naming to me? Her palms and her face began to sweat, and she sat there thinking over and over, the one who gives the name is the master.

Sheel and Shayeen brought the child into the tent, and she went right to Barvaran, her heartmother. Standing before the red-faced woman, the child said formally what she had been told to say: 'Heartmother, I am not wild any more. Stone Dancing Camp has welcomed me among women. I need a woman's name.'

Barvaran said, 'Your bloodmother has a name for you.'

The child turned to Alldera.

It was two days since the beginning of the coming out. Looking at her now, Alldera saw something new: the color of her hair, which hung dry and clean and fire-glossed. She saw very suddenly and strongly the color of the two men who had fucked her shortly before her flight from the Holdfast: one tawny, the other pale-skinned with thick black hair. She said the first thing that came into her head:

'You haven't got the color of either of them. Your hair is like the coat of Shayeen's sorrel mare.'

She saw the look of consternation on the women's faces.

Then the child of the tent, oblivious, laughed her shining laugh and announced with her thin arms outflung, 'My name is Sorrel! I'll ride nothing but red horses all my life, so watch out for me, you who keep red horses in your herds!'

'A lucky beginning,' old Jesselee muttered. She got up and closed the tent. The naming part was over.

Shayeen began her self-song:

> My blaze-faced bay carried me for seven days,
> From Red Sand Wells to the Great Salty River,
> And she was twelve years old then,
> The year I first raided for horses —

Each sharemother was to sing her self-song, and Alldera was to sing last. With Nenisi's help she had put together lines telling of her escape and her life among the women. She hoped she could remember them. She was still shaking inwardly with relief that the naming had gone off all right.

Something noisy was happening outside. Alldera stopped breathing. Shayeen turned, glaring as she sang.

There were furious voices, and someone fought loose the pins that closed the edges of the entry flaps. Fedeka strode inside, fierce-faced, a one-armed vision. Fems from the wagon crew peered in past her.

'Alldera! You forgot us!' Fedeka cried.

Sheel had her hand on the haft of her knife.

Alldera sprang up. 'What are you doing here, Fedeka?'

'Why is she singing? Why the women's songs?' Fedeka demanded. Her eyes glittered hard as metal, and below the drooping line of her long nose her mouth was grim with anger. 'You should be singing for the cub, Alldera.'

'Get out of here,' Shayeen commanded, outrage cracking her habitual calm. 'You're not supposed to be at this ceremony.'

Panic gripped Alldera, she could not think well. Who knew what the invaders from the trade wagon might do? Didn't Fedeka understand that Alldera's turn to sing would come later? Was she infuriated by the child's non-femmish name? With relief Alldera saw that Daya was sidling into the tent at Fedeka's back. She would appeal to Daya for support; but then Fedeka shouted, 'We have our songs too!' and opened her mouth wide and wailed out a verse:

> The greedy whip scorches, the load burns me down, the
> eyes of my master are everywhere.

My lover has fled, I will not pursue her.

Shall I see her bloody footprints halted by a closed City door

And the flames of the masters' eyes suck at her face and hair?

The greedy whip scorches, the load burns me down . . .

It made the women flinch. Sorrel stared open-mouthed.

When the singing stopped, Daya said in her soft manner, 'Women of Holdfaster Tent, that is a song of Alldera's bloodline. Not a self-song – we fems had no self-songs – but we did sing our lives.'

'We'll go back outside now,' Fedeka said, 'but not far. We know whose cub it is, so we came.' She stared reproachfully at Alldera. 'Even though the dam forgot us.'

Daya put a hand on Alldera's arm. 'I said they should come,' she whispered under the sound of Shayeen's renewed singing.

'You want to tear me in two, you want to force me to choose,' Alldera whispered back.

Daya replied, pleading, 'You said I shouldn't let you forget who you are.' She left. No one looked at Alldera except Sorrel with her wide, dazed eyes and Nenisi.

Sheel sang next, her voice breaking with fury. Barvaran sang, Nenisi sang, Jesselee sang. The tea bowl was handed to Alldera so she could moisten her throat. She sipped, hiding her face with the bowl. Into the silence came the singing of the wagon fems from outside. Muffled by the walls of the tent, their voices were to Alldera like the voices of generations of ghosts far away in the Holdfast.

Alldera said over the singing, 'I resign my right to sing for my bloodchild. Let my femmish kindred sing in my place.'

They listened in silence to the fems singing:

Wash all clean, black sea, roll stones,
Break walls, salt sand, spare none.
Men will moan, and fems will roar.
We breathed earth all our generations.
We can breathe an ocean of dead men and not care.

In the trading fems' wagon late that night the fire bowls were lit, and there was a scent of manna. Alldera came because she could not stand the angry looks of the women, and she did not want to be alone tonight. The naming of the child had made her feel old and unimportant.

She needed to find out how the free fems would greet her.

They made room for her without fuss, and she sat down with weary relief amid the tea-scented bundles of trade goods and the rolls of bedding of the crew. The atmosphere in the wagon was vibrant with victory. From their triumphant glances at her she guessed they felt they had repossessed not only the child but its mother.

Daya was telling an ugly Holdfast story about a man who betrayed his lover and how his lover killed him with a whip and ran his flayed skin up the flagpole of their company hall next morning.

'Mother Moon,' sighed Tua, leaning her head back against the wagon wall, 'I don't miss the men and their mad, mean city, but how I miss the smell of the great salt sea!'

A flood of reminiscence followed.

'The sea,' they said. 'The taste of fresh laver, when we could steal it.' 'Remember the look of the beach at Lammintown on a bright morning, with the town coiling up the hills behind it?'

'Once we got hold of some prime manna that belonged to the master of a friend of mine –' 'Remember how quiet the City got when the men went dreaming on manna? You could sit in your quarters, cool and waiting, and listening to how quiet it was. You could think about how it would be if those quiet buildings belonged to us, no masters there at all.' 'Remember the sound of the sea, and the beaches shining hot in the sun?' 'The moon was better. A poor fem could look straight at the moon and not be roasted or blinded by it, and it spread the sea with a cool, silver light.'

'In my company's hall they had four different sets of tableware and another dozen small sets for the Senior men – all the colors you've ever seen, each set to go with a different meal. The eating hall used to glow with the brightness of it. We never minded washing up, it was such a pleasure handling those glossy plates and platters.' 'I never handled anything but a weed hoe and a ditching shovel, but I remember how the land smelled. We used to stumble around half dreaming at manna harvest time.'

'I used to polish my master's jewelry for him and pin it on my lover when the master was gone,' Daya said. 'We made ourselves splendid for each other! There was a brooch of silver in the form of a kneeling boy, with eyes of colored stones . . .'

They spoke of greenness all year round, the smell of the river, fog in the morning, storms that shook the cliffs of Lammintown and threw the sea up against the sky; of good, strong beer from the City breweries, of the excitement of inter-company skirmishes fought in the big square, of the brutal, crazy arrogance of the men and the sly, perilous stratagems of fems.

Alldera listened with her head bowed, for she knew they did not see what she did: the vast rift between these cherished memories and the songs of pain they had sung for Sorrel. The fems' blindness made her feel dismal and exhausted.

For years they had sat around their fires here in the Grasslands and carefully picked over their Holdfast lives, extracting the few bearable bits, embroidering them for their own and others' comfort.

Pity for their need wrenched at her. Pity for herself, too; their cheering stories were just fantasies to her. She shared only the anguish of their bitter songs.

What are we, here? Alldera thought, looking around at the rapt, firelit faces. Outsiders, eking out a living at trading, which women must have handled perfectly well for themselves before free fems ever came here. The women don't need us, there is no next generation of fems that need us, we don't need ourselves. If we vanished tonight, whisked away like dream people, who would miss us?

Someone was absent from the gathering, the one fem who had always seemed to her to belong to the Grasslands. Leaning nearer to Tua, Alldera murmured, 'Where is Fedeka?'

'She left,' came the answer. 'She said that with the rest of us staying in Stone Dancing Camp, she wouldn't have to worry about leaving the child here among women.'

'The rest of you are staying?'

Other conversations ceased. Everyone was looking this way. Several of them said yes, nodding, and a fem back in the shadows called, 'Daya says we're all your cousins, that's the way the Mares think of us. Your cousins can visit you, can't they? Your cousins can learn from you what Daya has learned.'

They came for the child and now they mean to stay and have me teach them to ride and shoot and track . . . It was what Alldera had feared, or part of it. She felt anger – would they never cease to complicate her life? – and yet some pride. It did not do to underestimate them, ever. They needed to show that they mattered; they needed to make their marks on the Grasslands.

Eagerly they told her of what had been suffered already in her cause. They spoke of fights and bitterness in the tea camp between fems wanting to join Alldera and those remaining loyal to Elnoa. Many said they had wished to come to Stone Dancing Camp sooner, but a fading allegiance to Elnoa had held them back, till now; till Sorrel's coming out. The Plan was just the Plan, always in the future, but Alldera's child was real now, and they kept hearing of real things happening now at Holdfaster Tent – free fems on horseback, free fems with bows.

So they came, newly bold, animated with the daring of their decision. Telling her, they watched her face. She blinked water from her eyes, shook her head without speaking because she did not trust her voice.

Daya said, 'Time for another story.' She sat alert, resourceful-looking since she had taken up riding; grown-up, Alldera thought. As these others will soon be.

'This one is about Kobba. She's with a group of us that goes to Bayo to rescue some fems that are said to be trapped there by men. The free fems try to storm Bayo town, but the men have fire throwers and dart throwers and slings, and the fems run out of arrows. Kobba and her troop are driven back into the swamp, up to their thighs in water, struggling southward through the sucking mud among the reeds and the roots. In the night they hear the prisoner fems singing, calling for help as we all used to speak to each other in songs.'

'I don't like this story,' Kenoma said. Others shushed her.

'Deeper into the swamps, Kobba sees her companions cut their own throats rather than fall into the hands of the pursuing men. She refuses to die or be caught. She eats roots, she drinks marsh water and doesn't let sickness slow her down. She forces herself on even when the swamp is silent and she knows the men no longer follow. She thinks she has caught the smell of smoke. She finds a broken sandal strap.

One day she stumbles onto the shore of a huge island in the marsh, where reeds give way to trees. Someone is watching there – a

fem, scar-backed, solid, one of those who slipped away from Bayo
and hid in the swamp. There are many others with her.

'They have houses of reeds and clothes of grass, and they've
found live creatures to catch and eat in that warm southern water.
Some creatures the fems have tamed and trained to attack men.

'The swamp fems welcome Kobba. They say they thought all the
fems of the Holdfast were dead, for none have slipped out to join
them in a long time. But Kobba tells them, Come and help me, the
men still hold Bayo and twenty of our kind prisoners there, many of
them pregnant with cubs we need. This time we will surely batter
through the walls.

'We have a better way, say the free fems of the south. They follow
Kobba carrying not bows or even spears, but cages full of swift
water creatures with poison in their mouths. Kobba and a few
others go close to the walls of Bayo and from hiding shout taunts at
the men. The men attack and chase them into the swamps as before
– but the fems step onto solid ground that they have marked in their
minds, and they release the water creatures.

'The creatures swim along the channels of the swamp and find the
men and fasten onto their feet and legs, flooding their bodies with
poison. The men die loudly. They have no discipline, they scream
and cry and flounder in the water, they beg to be saved. The fems
listen from hiding. They want to laugh, but they stay silent.

'Dead men drift in the water and lie on the banks where they have
hauled themselves up to die. Then the swamp fems call their water
creatures by slapping the water quickly and lightly, and the creatures feel this through the water and return.

'The fems still do not laugh. They hug Kobba, but silently. They
will not laugh, they will not triumph, until the prisoners are rescued
– and that's another story for tomorrow evening.

'We won't laugh either when we go back, armed with our new
strengths and new weapons, until we've rescued all the fems still
living there.'

There were murmurs of approval. They were all looking at
Alldera.

She left the wagon, descending into the dark. She walked among
the tents, keeping to the dark places, sorting out her thoughts.

They want to go back to the Holdfast. They are sure of me now,
and they want me to teach them fighting and riding so they can

invade the Holdfast like women going to war – that's the fantasy Daya has woven for them with her stories!

Fems have always learned what they needed to survive. They could learn to ride and shoot, not like women who've done those things all their lives, but well enough. But what would they be once they learned? They'd still be no stronger than I am, no more skilled or brave, just people like me – not witches armed with killing spells. We'd be a pathetic little band, desperate fems trusting to tools only recently come into our hands, keeping each other's courage up with stories and lies. It's impossible.

But suppose we did it: went back, found the Holdfast in ruins but some men alive, took it all over, made it ours. How many of us are fit to bear a new generation? How many captured men would be young enough to father healthy cubs? Would we all want to bear cubs if we could?

They envision taking over the masters' luxuries but the Holdfast must be in ruins. We might have to kill our horses for food, assuming we could get them that far to begin with. What good is an archer if she can't move around quickly on horseback? In seconds a man can charge too close for an arrow shot and break her head with a rock.

No one has come across the borderlands since I came, ten years ago, or is it eleven now? The Holdfast people may all be dead. We could spend our last months wandering an empty land, turning on each other in our hunger before we finished.

If we ever got there to begin with. Free fems have already come to blows over joining me here. Elnoa has lost a whole wagon crew to me now; she'll defend her place as leader harder than ever. And the women will fight to keep us from going back. They have to protect themselves too. The men would only have to catch sight of us, armed and mounted, to know that over the mountains there's more than emptiness and the monsters of their foolish legends. They would come, they would invade the Grasslands looking for slaves. I would do anything rather than endanger the freedom of the Riding Women.

I once wanted to move the free fems to action. Now they move despite me, and they mean to sweep me with them. It doesn't matter to them that I am happy with the women. No wonder I've been afraid.

She walked in the darkness among tents murmurous with the voices of women still awake, or silent with sleep. It seemed to her that the surface of the plain stirred slowly, purposefully, inexorably beneath her feet, carrying her and all of them east toward the mountains like waves to the rocks.

When it was time for the Gather, the free fems of Holdfaster Tent – twenty-one of them now, with Alldera – went off to work on the Stone Dancing granaries. They labored hard, well, and without incident.

On the way back Daya rode with Alldera, fiddling with the string of small bells she wore in her hair, a gift from Grays Omelly. She said, 'They're very attractive, these women. At best they have a crude sort of power. Sheel has it, all armed against you – against me, too. Haven't you felt it? She looks at you as if she'd like to bite the heart out of your body, but you're too strong for her, so she just glares and glares.'

Daya's intrigues, Daya's sensitivity, Daya's fantasies – today they exasperated Alldera beyond measure. There was much else on her mind that she needed to speak to the pet fem about, but somehow whenever they managed to get a moment alone lately there were other matters in the way, or the time felt wrong. She saw now that Daya wanted to talk, not listen, and she held her tongue. She watched Daya twine the bells into her horse's mane.

'It bothers you, doesn't it – me and Grays? Well, you've never feared finding your bed empty, like me,' Daya said. She pulled the bells out, looped them around her wrist.

Alldera tried to answer evenly. She knew by now the feelings of small worth that sometimes unreasonably afflicted the pet fem. 'Grays Omelly wouldn't have been my choice.'

'No, I know your choice, but it's different for me. I'm not strong Alldera the runner, proud Alldera who brought a cub over the mountains, tough Alldera whom women respect and fems learn from. Look at me: Daya that was a man's pet, a man's toy, good at games. So your Marish friends see me, though they know little enough what it means. I had to take those who'd take me, like Grays.' She added in a voice turned half playful, 'Were you jealous, a little, of Grays and me?'

They rode quietly. Alldera thought again of bringing up the whole question of going back to the Holdfast; the other fems had dropped back a little. But the fact was, Alldera could not seem to get it straight enough in her own mind to discuss, even when an opportunity came.

Daya said. 'There'll be no more games with Grays, anyway. She came into the wagon nights and listened to us telling stories. She said she knew the stories were spells to get us home to the Holdfast, and she wanted to hear them. Then, a few mornings before we set out for the granaries, she came to me and said she couldn't be with me any more. She told me she felt like someone moving without sound or weight through our femmish dreams. She asked me to kiss her. "Make me as real as you," she said. I tasted tears when I kissed her.'

Alldera and Daya entered Holdfaster Tent, weary and dusty.

'You just missed your child,' Jesselee said, as if this were Alldera's fault. 'She's out hunting. Why did you stay away so long?'

Shayeen, the only other woman in the tent, added, 'We were beginning to worry about you. It takes only a day or two to patch a leak in a granary roof and not much longer than that to put on a whole new layer of oiled hides.'

Alldera said, 'We stayed out to build a new granary building, out of stone. The sharu will never be able to get in and eat the grain again. We even paved the floor.'

'Paved – ?' Shayeen was clearly unfamiliar with the word.

Alldera explained.

No one commented at first. Shayeen sat frowning at the tangle of straps in her lap, a bridle she was mending.

At length Jesselee said, 'Mud-walled, earth-floored granaries have served for years. Why change?'

Daya said, 'The sharu have always raided your granaries. Now in the Dusty Season the horses can have the grain the sharu used to take.'

Jesselee shrugged. 'We steal stores from sharu burrows sometimes. It's a proper thing that the sharu should sometimes steal from us.'

A low voice said, 'This work of the fems is surely meant as a gift.' It was Nenisi, lying unnoticed till now in her bedding, deeper in the recesses of the tent.

'What's the matter with Nenisi?' Alldera asked, full of alarm.

'Her eyes still, but worse today,' Jesselee said. She turned her head and added solicitously, 'If we're annoying you, Nenisi, we can go outside to talk.'

'Stay,' Nenisi said. 'I want to hear you.'

The old woman sighed. 'You won't like it.' To Alldera she said, 'All you were to do was make the old granaries rainproof. Anything else should have been the decision of the whole camp.'

Alldera drank from the shake milk bag hanging by the entry. She said, 'My cousins have skills that you women lack. Can't you give them recognition for what they've done, instead of complaining?'

'What Alldera means,' Daya said sweetly, 'is that we aren't afraid of a job that lasts more than a few days or needs careful planning. We're not too proud to dig a foundation ditch or trim a stone.'

Shayeen snorted. 'You fems make no sense about what you call work. Women need time to talk and play and ride out hunting, not just to work. You work all the time, learning something, building something. We do what satisfies us.'

'Yes,' Daya said, 'women are satisfied to do the same things over and over, year after year. It's a woman who is satisfied when every year her horses fall to the butcher knife to keep them from starving for lack of grain.'

Jesselee's reply crackled with anger: 'A person is in the world to live in it, not to make it over. Only a creature who belongs to nothing has to keep making things to belong to. A woman isn't like that.'

Alldera saw the glittering tears of anger in Daya's eyes and swiftly said to her, 'Our cousins are growing hungry while we stand here arguing. You'd better start setting up for a meal. I'll come later.'

With Daya gone, Alldera felt free to go to Nenisi. There was a bowl of water by her. Alldera took the cloth from Nenisi's eyes, dipped it and wrung it. She saw that Nenisi's eyelids were swollen shut and crusted around the lashes. She replaced the cloth across the black woman's face.

Nenisi said, 'I bet you wish you hadn't come back. Excuse our bad tempers – the Gather was out of balance this year. There were some fights, and two women got hurt in the mating.'

'And more will be hurt,' Jesselee said ominously.

They told Alldera about some quarrel that had sprung up at the

Gather between the Conors and the Periken women. Insults, warnings, scuffles that ruined games and races – it was a messy affair of obscure roots, which Jesselee was trying to explain when Nenisi said finally,

'Oh, leave it, it's not worth talking about, I'm sick of it!' She groped for Alldera's hand and clasped it with her thin, dark fingers.

'This quarrel of yours isn't connected with my femmish cousins in some way, is it?' Alldera said.

'It's an old dispute come alive again, that's all,' Nenisi said. 'You don't really think that everything that happens among us involves you, do you?'

In some years vast numbers of sharu swarmed over the plain devouring everything. They could overrun a camp and consume food, grain, leather gear, even tethered horses or women immobilized by accident or illness. They ravaged the grazing land, gnawing the grass down to the subsoil and scattering the women's herds beyond retrieval for months after.

Sorrel, Barvaran and Sheel came back from their hunting with reports of large bands of sharu traveling roughly east to west toward the Great Salty River, on a path which would bring them across the Stone Dancing lands.

Stone Dancing Camp became a moving war center against the sharu. Groups of women ranged in all directions, each rider armed with two bows and several quivers of arrows, to destroy or deflect any sharu hordes they could find a day's ride from camp.

The free fems wanted to join the hunt. Alldera explained that fems would be more useful taking over camp duties so that more women could go after sharu.

There was no argument against her advice. Daya simply came to her and said, 'Tua and Lexa and a couple of the others want you to know: they are going out of camp to hunt sharu on their own.'

'When?'

Eyes down, Daya said, 'I can't tell you. We need to go. We're not old women or children in the pack.'

'So you're going too?' Alldera said. 'Eager for sharu blood yourself?'

'Oh, no,' Daya said, looking very domestic. 'I don't like the bow, you know that – I'm not proportioned for the thick arms that archery can give you. But I'll find a way to be useful.'

Alldera spat out the dregs of the milky tea she was drinking. 'What am I supposed to do?'

Daya waited silently.

Alldera said, 'Tell Tua and the others to meet me out by the herds in the morning.'

They were changing. The quarreling and lying and stealing were giving way to other things: pride in new skills, ambition, some kind of group spirit. Standing together openly against her mistrust of their old competency, they forced her to look again and re-evaluate them.

She assessed the abilities of each of the fems with horse and bow, consulting with Daya in front of all of them in the cold dawn. The fems stood eagerly soaking it all in, their breaths misting before their faces. Alldera assigned each fem to accompany one of the groups of women going out that day. She had talked with the women the night before, enlisting Nenisi to help overcome the reluctance of some who feared they would be distracted from their work against the sharu by having to save the lives of incompetent fems. A schedule had been made by which fems would take turns riding out just as women did.

Since their arrival at Sorrel's coming out, the fems of the wagon crew had been working furiously with horse and bow. What they had not yet mastered they now learned fast under pressure. There were no complaints from women about the free fems' efforts, once it was apparent that they really were able to handle their mounts and their weapons. Suddenly, Alldera's worrisome 'cousins' were transformed into useful allies.

Sorrel came clamoring to her mothers to be allowed a part in the killing, saying that if even her bloodmother's cousins were involved, she could surely be. It made Alldera uncomfortable to think of this handsome youngster, with her alert, quick-smiling face and beautiful hair, at risk among the sharu.

There was risk. A woman of the Shawden tent fell from her horse when her girth strap broke; she was torn apart by sharu before she could be picked up. Another, her arrows spent, met a sharu's charge with her lance. The sharu took the point in its breast and kept coming, impaling itself but ripping her knee with his teeth and claws as it died.

Alldera did not have to speak against Sorrel's pleas. The women in the tent said firmly that Sorrel might help with weapons, child-pack, horses, or with any work in the camp, and perhaps in emergencies she might run messages; but that was all.

'Just like your age mates from the pack,' Jesselee said.

'Most of them are pregnant,' Sorrel objected. 'I'm not.'

'And you never will be, if some sharu claws your insides out.'

To Alldera's surprise, Daya did not turn to making arrows or to some other protected, camp-bound task. She became a collector of arrows for the archers. Looking back, Alldera would see her riding in long sweeps back and forth behind a shooting party, leaning steeply out of her saddle to retrieve arrows from dead and dying sharu. Daya rode gauntleted and booted in boiled leather like that which shielded her horse's legs. Unwounded sharu sometimes turned from devouring their own injured to attack a passing rider, and even in dying the beasts could be lethally quick and strong. Daya's leather armor was soon black with blood. She looked like some dream warrior, the more terrible for her stained armor, her neat, small figure, her scarred beauty.

She worked closer to the sharu than anyone. Alldera noted with satisfaction that even Sheel received her arrows from Daya with a civility verging on respect.

Sorrel did get into the field, in a fashion, by racing out one morning to tell Alldera that Daya had been injured.

Dropping back from her group of archers, Alldera said, 'Tell me, quickly.'

'A big sharu jumped on her horse's rump and raked her down the back. She had an arrow in her hand, and she jabbed the point right into the sharu's eye and killed it. They say they found her bent down from her saddle, streaming blood, trying to work the arrow back out of the eye socket, but the barb had caught, and Tico says it was the coolest thing she ever saw, but Daya was weeping and screaming the whole time and kept throwing up all the way back.'

Sorrel had come armed with a lance, not a bow, so there could be no excuse for her staying. The plain shifted and rippled with moving sharu only thirty meters off.

'Thanks for the message,' Alldera said. 'Now go back.'

'Aren't you going to ride home and see how she is?' Sorrel cried. 'I could relieve you here. Jesselee says —'

'I'll come like everyone else, when I'm out of arrows.'

'But I want –'

'A good messenger takes back the answer as soon as she has it.'

'I'll tell Daya you're all right, I'll tell her you'll come.' Sorrel galloped away.

Later, Alldera found the pet fem sitting by Holdfaster Tent, her torso and one arm wound in a band of soft leather, a bloody shirt draped over her slim shoulders. She looked very white but composed, and she was stirring one of Jesselee's pots of medicine with her free hand.

'Poor Daya,' Alldera said. 'More scars.'

'I got the arrow back.' Daya invited her, with a graceful wave of the stirring spoon, to sit.

'I need to change horses,' Alldera said.

'You need to rest,' Jesselee said. 'I can see the muscles in your arms jumping with fatigue. If you go right out again, you'll only shoot wildly and make more work for others.' She got up stiffly, laying aside the leather she had been cutting into strips. 'I'll go shift your saddle to a fresh horse, if I can find one.'

She limped away, chirruping to Alldera's mount which plodded at her shoulder.

Alldera sat down with Daya in the sun outside the tent. 'What horse were you riding?'

'Dark Tea. She was cut badly, but Jesselee has stitched her up. Poor beast, she'll have scars worse than mine.'

'They could have given you something younger. I rode that horse when I was first here, years ago.'

'That sharu jumped right up onto her. She staggered, but she didn't fall or bolt, so I had my balance and could put some thrust behind the arrow in my hand. She's a good, steady mount, Dark Tea. Though my dun would have been better.'

Daya stirred the steaming brew erratically. Some of it slopped over the rim of the kettle now and then and made the fire underneath hiss.

The camp was unusually quiet. Most of its inhabitants were out shooting sharu, and the childpack was confined safely in the sweat tent. There was a faint smell of decay on the wind. Not enough sharu were swarming in this area any more to eat up their own dead.

'How long can this last?' Alldera muttered.

'We needed the practice,' Daya said. 'We need to be thoroughly blooded before going back. It's different, wearing armor, seeing the teeth of a ravening sharu snap shut only a hand's breadth from your face. I feel strong – the way I did when I first learned to ride.'

Alldera leaned forward, elbows on knees, looking out past the tents at where wheeling groups of mounted archers drew gouts of dust from the plain. Her arms and chest and back ached. She felt as if she had had no rest for months. Wearily she surrendered to the inevitable subject: 'You really mean it, don't you. Going back,' she said.

'You've never talked about it with me,' the pet fem said. 'It's been on everyone's mind for so long. What do you think about it?'

'Daya, must the free fems go back to the Holdfast? Not the free fems of your stories, mind you. The real ones.'

'I can only tell you about myself. Look at me, Alldera – a first-quality pet fem, marred certainly, but still –! Here I am, dressed in stinking leather, with dirt caked in the roots of my hair, living among beasts and very little above them in houses of their skins. I own my clothing, my saddle, a few ornaments, and the knife on my belt. Oh, and that gray horse the tent gave me to make up for butchering my dun. I spend my time tending animals or fixing things or talking – about old times, another life. I drift over the plains as aimlessly as the clouds, my direction dictated by weather, by grass. I love the horses, the women too; but my life is just floating past me here.'

Angrily Alldera said, 'Must the free fems go back because you are bored?'

Daya touched her lightly, pleadingly. 'Don't you ever think of the richness, the excitement and color of the old days in the Holdfast? It wasn't all horror and pain. Nenisi is certainly a splendid person in her way – even rather stylish; but what about the brilliance, the music –'

'I have only pain and anger from those times.'

'Maybe that's what we have to go home to do, then,' Daya said. 'To give the pain and anger to our masters, if there are any of them left, and take the brightness for ourselves. It was all built on our backs. Can you blame us now for wanting to claim it?'

'And if we find nothing but bones?'

'Then we'll make something beautiful out of bones,' Daya replied, her eyes lustrous with excitement. 'Here, everything is already made and it all belongs to the women. We can only borrow. At home, what we find and what we make will be ours.'

'Ours. All twenty-two of us?'

'The others will come too. Except Fedeka, probably, and Elnoa.'

'Elnoa! She's led them for years. They won't all desert her, she won't let them.'

'She's a leader only as long as we follow her,' Daya pointed out.

Women's reasoning, Alldera noted with grim amusement, and in the women's country, true.

She laughed ruefully. 'Recently a woman came to me and asked me to interfere in the private affairs of one of us. I said no, and she said in a sneering way, "Why not, you're their chief." I told her I hadn't spent all that time alone here in Stone Dancing without learning a few things – like how not to be a master. I thought that was a pretty smart answer at the time.'

'Left to yourself you'd stay here forever, wouldn't you,' Daya said. 'I'm sorry. It's a pity that we should require you after you've made peace with this place, but you're part of what draws the free fems. It isn't me, you know. I'm like the others, I make my peace with the people around me, moment by moment.

'Don't look so astonished. I know you expect to hear such clever things only from Nenisi. The Conors are wise, the Conors are always right, and besides you love Nenisi and you still don't think much of me.'

It was still so shamefully easy to forget that Daya's feelings could be hurt. Alldera shook off the pain of having caused pain and capitulated. 'You win, Daya. I can't see fems come galloping in, red with the blood of sharu and grabbing for more arrows, and pretend not to know that the free fems are spoiling for war. It's my doing, some of it. I'm even proud of how strong they've grown, but that doesn't make going back any less wretched for me.'

'I told them you understood, I told them I knew you!' Daya exclaimed. 'Some fems said you'd been bewitched by Nenisi, but I knew better. Alldera, if word gets to the tea camp that we'll take in anyone else who wants to learn to ride and shoot, they'll come – they'll all come. Say you want them and I'll get them for you. We can be more than forty strong when we ride home!'

'Go ahead,' Alldera said, kicking savagely at the edge of the fire with her booted foot. 'It's the best story you've had for them so far. They'll trample each other finding places for themselves in it. Put it all down to the will of Moonwoman, that's what Fedeka would say. Only I wish you'd told some stories about fems staying with the Riding Women, living good lives here, instead of about going home.'

'I tell the stories that come to me to tell; don't be bitter,' Daya begged. 'Even you say "home" now when you mean the Holdfast. It's your triumph too, that we turn homeward at last.

'Listen, here's a story for you: we are a small, grim army drawn up on some high path on the far side of the mountains, looking out in silence – except for the stamp of an impatient pony's hoof, the creak of leather as someone rises in her stirrups to see better – over our own country, green to the horizon line of the sea . . .'

EPILOGUE

14

Sheel was making a new boot patterned on the leathers of an old one. Outside the air was crisp. The tent was closed and the fire glowed under the draft of the smoke hole.

Sorrel lay on the bare floor of the tent, kept in on account of various abrasions and one furiously multi-colored eye. She had put on muscle and weight since coming out, but she was no match for a crowd of her pack mates.

The tent was quiet. Guests had come, a daughter of Barvaran's traveling with a couple of cousins. They and the fems and the rest of the family were all out gossiping and borrowing extra bedding and supplies for tonight. Jesselee was home doing nothing, Shayeen was in charge of the food, and Sheel was in charge of Sorrel.

Sorrel said, 'I don't like Saylim Stayner.'

'You still shouldn't have tripped her with the dung rake,' Shayeen scolded. She was pounding dried meat for the evening meal. 'You made gossip for the whole camp. If the others hadn't given you a licking for what you did, you'd probably come up in the chief tent for a fine.'

Her words were barely audible over the pounding. Sorrel was making faces at Sheel, trying to convey the joke of not being able to hear the rebuke.

Sheel said, 'Shayeen's right about the dung rake.'

'Oh, Saylim didn't get hurt or anything. Just insulted.'

'Don't sound so satisfied.'

'She insulted me first!'

'How?' This was Jesselee, listening from her bedding.

Uncharacteristically, Sorrel paused. Sheel watched her push the floor sand around with her fingers, making ridges and valleys. Then Sorrel said, 'Saylim said the self-song I was making left out the most important part: about my bloodmother being from over the mountains, and how she had a master there. She said it sly and droopy-eyed, as if it meant something rotten.'

Shayeen whacked the meat one last time, scraped it into a bowl, and marched off.

The youngster brushed the hair back from her face, showing the bruised eye in all its splendor. 'I don't much like my mother Shayeen Bawn either,' she muttered.

'Why not?' Sheel began punching holes around the edges of a leather piece with an awl.

'She's always telling me what to do.'

'Let's talk about the Stayners for a minute,' Sheel said. 'Myself, I don't like that line. The Stayners pick their noses.'

'Rosamar says —'

'I know, they always say they have some kind of funny crookedness inside their noses that bothers them. I don't care. They could still blow their noses as other women do.

'And I don't like the Ohayars because they're sneaky. The Fowersaths are quick-tempered, the Mellers borrow things and don't return them, the Churrs have ice cold hands, the Hayscalls mumble till you think you're going deaf.'

Jesselee joined in zestfully, 'The Clarishes are vain, the Perikens exaggerate everything, the Farls are lazy and their fingers turn back in a sickening way and make a horrible wet cracking noise doing it besides. As for the Morrowtrows' — she was one herself, of course, gappy-toothed and wide in the jaw — 'they like to stick their noses into everything that happens, especially to children of their own families.'

'However,' Sheel said, 'there isn't one of those lines that we don't both have kindred in. I forgot to add the Bawns. I don't love the Bawns, but here I am, sharemothering you with Shayeen Bawn.'

She wished she had not said that. After all, it was not a matter of choice that she was familying with Shayeen.

'You don't know, though, what it's like to have Shayeen as one of your mothers,' Sorrel said, doodling a frowning face in the sand with her finger.

Sheel set her foot into the curve of the boot sole. She had cut the thin sole wet and set it days earlier to dry in a sand mold of her footprint. It was a comfortable fit. 'No, but I do have mothers I don't love.'

Jesselee interrupted. 'Sorrel, you'll be related to women all your life whom you don't love or even like – raid mates, pack mates, relatives of your mothers, captives – you may even find that you don't care for your own bloodchildren. Liking women has nothing to do with being related to them, and you might as well work that out and get used to it right here in your own family.

'Have you slept with anybody yet? Since the pack, I mean.'

Her face burning, Sorrel nodded.

'A pack mate who came out ahead of you? Yes. Well, when you start yearning after a grown woman see that you go and lie with Shayeen. Then you'll like her better.'

'You shouldn't talk that way about things like that,' the young-ster whispered hoarsely.

'Save me from foal love,' Jesselee groaned. 'Who are you sleeping with – that young Bay that lost a finger roping a sharu instead of lancing it like a woman?'

Sorrel's blush deepened. 'Not everybody would be so brave.'

'Not everybody would be so stupid. Archen Bay risked herself and her tent's best hunting horse just to show off.'

'My leg hurts,' Sorrel said disconsolately. 'One of those piss faces kicked me.' When no sympathy was forthcoming she tried a new subject. 'I don't know why you bother making yourself a pair of boots, Sheel. I have three pair. You're not much bigger than I am in the hands and feet. One of my pair would fit you.'

'Then the woman who gave that pair to you would be unhappy with both of us.'

Sorrel brushed the sand flat. 'Do you like my bloodmother?'

'No,' Sheel said.

'Why don't you like the fems?' Sorrel had spent more time with them since the sharu swarming.

'Why do you like them?'

'Oh . . .' Sorrel made a ludicrously long and dreamy face. 'I think they're very strong and sad because of their terrible lives.'

'They're from the Holdfast,' Sheel said. 'I don't like things from the Holdfast.'

'Am I from the Holdfast too?'

'You're one of us.'

'I am a little Holdfastish in my blood, and special.'

Irritably Jesselee said, 'Don't get stuck on yourself. Everyone's flawed, everyone is still a woman.'

'I know my faults,' Sorrel said, sulky again. 'I ought to. Everybody's always telling me.'

'So they should,' Sheel answered. She refrained from adding, they should because you have no real Motherline to look at and see your faults mirrored in it. There were always the oddest gaps in her conversations with Sorrel.

'What's it like, beyond the borderlands?' Sorrel asked.

'No one's been there.'

'My bloodmother and her cousins have.'

'Then ask them.'

'I don't always understand what they say,' Sorrel admitted, 'and if I say they don't make any sense, they get angry or shrug and change the subject. Is it true that a man has a hanger-and-bag, just like a stallion, and hair on his face like the Chowmers?'

'More hair than the Chowmers,' Jesselee said absently, mouthing a bit of food or the memory of a bit of food, 'less hanger than a stallion.'

Sorrel snorted. 'It sounds silly and clumsy, like carrying a lance around with you all the time.' She sighed. 'I wish my bloodmother liked me. Maybe she will after I make a good raid.' She rolled over and sat up, wincing slightly. 'Why can't I go raiding with Shelmeth's band?'

'No. Shelmeth Sanforath is not experienced enough to lead a raid,' Jesselee said.

'But nobody will be expecting us, it's so early in the season! It's going to be a triumph!' Sorrel blazed with enthusiasm.

Sheel began to stitch the uppers to the sole. 'Early raids have been tried before. It takes good judgment to pull them off successfully.'

'I want to go!'

'No,' Sheel said. 'You've asked about this before. Jesselee says no, Shayeen says no, Barvaran says no, I say no, and Nenisi says no.'

'You all treat me like a baby, but I'm too big to ride in a hip sling, you know. I have to go on my maiden raid sometime. How am I supposed to find women to sharemother my first child with me if I don't start now to get a good reputation?'

'Try avoiding the reputation of the sort of person who attacks other women with a dung rake,' Jesselee suggested.

Ignoring this, Sorrel went on, 'I want to have a dozen wild raider daughters and then go wandering with you, Sheel, and the bravest of my pack mates. I'll be the scourge of the plains and make my daughters rich with gifts of the finest horses in the camps.'

'A dozen daughters?' Jesselee said. 'After a dozen daughters you'll be lucky if you can still get your legs together around a horse's ribs.'

'Really?'

'No, not really, silly. Worry about real dangers, like having your arm broken in a fight.'

Sorrel laughed. 'I'll get Alldera to teach me kick fighting so I can kick Saylim's eye out if she comes after me again.'

'I don't like that kind of bloodthirsty talk,' Jesselee began in a tone that promised a lecture; but then some youngster put her head into the tent and shouted,

'Pillo fight starting!'

'I'm coming,' Sorrel said, jumping up.

Sheel said, 'Youngsters' rules – no rough stuff.'

'It's no fun then,' Sorrel objected.

'We'll be careful,' said the girl at the entry, having learned more than Sorrel about placating her elders. 'Come on, Sorrel. I bet you my old gray horse can –'

They were gone, their voices already locked in argument.

Jesselee lifted one knee and began kneading her calf. 'Cramp,' she groaned. 'Hits me even in the middle of lovemaking, no respect for an old woman's last few pleasures . . .' She sighed. 'The child is right, Sheel. She should get one good raid behind her so that women will start to think of familying with her for her own children. I'd like to see her show everyone her quality myself, before I die.'

'You want me to organize her maiden raid for her?'

'Which of her mothers would do it better than you?'

Why am I hesitating? Sheel thought, frowning over her work. Sorrel has courage and intelligence, there's no sign yet of her femmish heritage. But after her first raid – the next step is preparing her for her mating. That's where it could come out.

'Heartmother, what's going to happen to that child if she turns out not to be fertile to a stud horse but only to a man, like her femmish bloodmother?'

'You, daughter of my heart, know better than I do that a woman's worth doesn't lie only in the children of her body – though sometimes women do lose sight of that truth.'

'It would make a difference,' Sheel said. 'Sorrel has no blood relations to keep her line among us. If she has no children of her own body, after her death she'll just – disappear.'

'Would you forget her?'

'Never.'

'The self-songs of many lines have words in them about women who "disappeared" that way when whole chains of descent ended. Those women are not completely lost.'

Sheel said, 'I don't want Sorrel to be lost at all.'

Sheel asked Sorrel to come with her to choose horses for the raid they were planning. Delighted, Sorrel dug out her favorite gift, a light leather shirt covered with big flakes cut from the hooves of dead horses and sewn into a sort of armor of overlapping scales.

'I want to see how it feels,' she said as they rode out toward the grazing grounds. 'Maybe I'll take it with me when we go raiding. I like to hear the little pieces all click and rub together.'

'A fancy shirt like yours is only a gift thing, something to make bets with. Women don't wear them.'

Sorrel promptly wrestled the shirt off over her head and tied it behind the cantle of her saddle.

A little distance from the grazing horses most of the new fems had gathered, sitting like Riding Women in the shadows of their mounts. One of them walked a spotted mare back and forth before the others. Their voices carried clearly. They were agreeing, more and more confidently, that the horse was lame.

Alldera, sitting chin on fist among them, demanded, 'Which leg?'

'Off fore,' said a blond fem. What a pale people they were under their sunburn, not a black skin among them, Sheel thought.

'How can you tell?'

'By the way she walks.'

Alldera directed that the horse be led away and then toward the group again, head on. 'Which leg?'

'Near foreleg,' Sorrel whispered to Sheel. 'See how she drops her head?'

'I know,' Sheel said dryly.

Alldera spoke to the fems with the faintest trace of weariness. 'The leg she drops her head over is the leg all her weight is going on, to spare the sore one.'

'Near foreleg,' someone volunteered.

'Good. Now, leg or foot?'

Some of the fems had noticed the two onlookers and a few called to the child to join them. She had become immensely popular with them after a period of shyness on both sides.

'Go on, then, if you want to,' Sheel said. She settled to watch and listen herself a while, one leg crooked across her saddle bow.

Sorrel hobbled her horse and sat down next to Daya, who seemed to be her favorite among the fems; not so terrible a choice as Sheel would once have thought. The little fem with the scars had done all right during the sharu swarming.

Alldera continued her instruction with only a glance at her child: 'If she takes a short step, the foot is sore. Soreness in the shoulder would make her swing her leg out stiffly to keep from using those muscles. See? Maybe it isn't the kick she took that's bothering her at all. Lora, go ahead and find out what the trouble is.'

'Can somebody hold her for me?' the blond fem said nervously.

Sorrel whispered, Daya whispered back, knotted cheek close by smooth one. Sheel could see that the slow method of instruction was not for Sorrel, who had grown up with these horses while in the childpack.

Alldera said, 'You have to be able to handle your own horse, Lora. There may not be anybody with you when trouble comes up. If she were skittish – which she isn't, but suppose she were – how would you control her while you looked her over?'

Visibly unhappy, Lora untied a strip of soft leather from her belt and bent to hobble the horse's front feet.

'But you'll have to lift her forefoot to look at it,' Sorrel pointed out politely to her. 'Better hobble the back feet instead.' She flung Sheel one bright, amused glance over her shoulder.

'She won't kick me?' Lora inquired, looking anxiously at the mare's shining eye.

Alldera said tartly, 'Not if you do as our expert there suggests.'

It had all been gone over before, and would be again. How could they bear it? Sheel supposed that by femmish standards they were quick learners, or they would never have survived their deadly crossing from the Holdfast. Yet all these lessons seemed so excruciatingly repetitious. Alldera worked away session after session, as if she were polishing hard stones.

Hard stone heads, Sheel thought, looking over at the big one, Kobba, a relatively new arrival, fierce and melancholy. All of the free fems were living at Stone Dancing these days except for the one said to be so huge that it would take two horses to carry her, and one or two who had stayed behind with her. Women of Royo Camp, returning from cutting tea in the hills for themselves, reported the tea camp deserted and its great central wagon shut up tight. Hearing this, Daya had said that the fat one, the free fems' former leader, must have withdrawn to the caves where she kept her books, to stay with them until they were found. No one understood what she meant by this but the fems, who seemed subdued by the idea. A few even wept.

The one-armed one, Fedeka the wanderer, still wandered. She stopped at Stone Dancing often, however, and always took time to talk privately with Sorrel before leaving again. Sorrel said she told even stranger stories than Daya did. Daya had assured the women of Holdfaster Tent that the dyer meant no ill, and had appointed herself a sort of special guardian to Sorrel for some vague time in the future when the girl would need her.

The newly arrived fems studied horses and the bow so hard with Alldera and Daya that women joked about how they must be meaning to make Riding Women of themselves. They had given up their ungainly wagons and now had their own fem tent pitched next to Holdfaster Tent.

Even Sheel, unwilling as she was, had to admit to herself that the longer they lived here in the camp the more their slavish ways fell away from them. Everyone noticed that they all quarreled and intrigued far less among themselves than they had when they had been only a handful. With women, their manner was no longer brashly alien, but guarded and self-contained. Except for Alldera, they chose their lovers only among their own ranks now; even Daya did.

'I don't sleep with Daya anymore,' Grays Omelly had told Sheel. 'When she looks at me, I feel like a ghost. They see us and hear us, but they're all gone away.'

These days Grays's circular spell designs were turning up everywhere, and Grays was found crying among the tents that everything was losing its place. Sheel had brought her back twice from outside the camp where she had been sitting, beating on a drum at the full moon 'to make it stay where it belongs'.

Here was Alldera surrounded by her own kind, obviously in her place. Yet to Sheel she did not look happy, only intent and serious.

Lora edged closer to the spotted mare again, her face tight with fear and determination.

'Help, if you're going to, Sorrel,' Alldera commanded suddenly. 'I don't want this horse to think it can frighten us.'

Covertly Sheel studied Alldera's face. No humor there; hardness and hostility showed in the set of the wide mouth. No wonder; Sorrel knew in her blood and bones from her earliest life so much that these clumsy, thick-headed outlanders were laboring to grasp. The youngster would make a better teacher than her bloodmother, if she were patient enough to command the fems' attention for long.

Sorrel went to the mare's head and took hold of the reins, patting its nose and scolding it in a cheerful voice. Her cheeks were flushed; she knew when she was the center of attention and enjoyed it. She looked down at Lora, who had bent to lift the horse's hoof in her hands.

'You tap the foot lightly all around with a stone,' Sorrel explained, 'to find the sore place.'

She looked over the ground for a stone. The horse, taking advantage of Lora, leaned more and more of its weight on her. Lora did not realize that the horse was using her as support, but Sorrel saw, called it a sharu's foal, and gave it a punch in the shoulder with advice to mend its manners.

Sheel and the watching fems grinned, and even Alldera smiled. Sorrel was clearly playing to her bloodmother. She turned toward Alldera her most appealing glances to make sure Alldera would miss nothing that she did.

Sheel thought of other bloodmothers she had seen with their daughters. There was always a period of assessment; then each began to think about taking the first tentative steps toward the other. The coming together always took time. Without the pull of identically patterned minds and bodies to help, it might take unusually long for Alldera and Sorrel to meet. But Sheel recognized the beginning – on one side that cautious attention to the child, a touch perhaps of wary pride, and, on the other, curiosity and eagerness to please. A strange thing, the start of such closeness between a femmish bloodmother and a woman-child.

Yet Sheel had to admit to herself that Alldera was no longer the anxious, touchy, self-absorbed young fem who, thanks to Sheel's own error, had come to Stone Dancing years ago and lived as a woman. Now she had no time for the women, only time for her own. Sheel hardly saw her in Holdfaster Tent. Alldera was like a hard, scarred stud nursing a wild band along through a dry, dry season toward water. Her face bore what the women called 'chief lines', marks of unremitting concern.

Startled, Sheel thought, Why, she came to us still in her youth, and her youth has been long gone.

Moved in some way that she did not wish to be moved, Sheel pulled her mount's head up from its browsing and rode slowly toward the tent's horses. Sorrel would soon tire of the instructor's role and catch up with her. As she rode, her practiced eye noting the condition of each mare and of the grass they grazed, Sheel became more and more convinced that Grays was right: if things were not exactly out of place, they were at least in a new alignment, moved by some deep, slow, powerful shift of events, long in the making and still only dimly perceptible.

Sheel could remember now how it had been once: thinking about correcting her original mistake and killing Alldera; rejecting that course because she would not stoop to be outlawed on account of a dirty little fem. The thoughts came back and even some of the fierce feeling, but none of it seemed to apply in the least to Alldera Holdfaster sitting over there teaching her followers about horses.

Which was strange, because plainly the thing Sheel had always feared – that the free fems would truly determine to return to the Holdfast, with unforeseeable consequences for all women – was clearly happening. As a nightmare, the idea had maddened her. Now, with the phantoms of angry imagination vanished in the face of reality, it became simply a fact of the future to be dealt with in its time.

She felt saddened by the loss of her hatred. There would be no brilliant, satisfyingly violent clash between herself and Alldera. The fems, and Alldera among them, belonged to whatever current had drawn them to Stone Dancing Camp, where now they toughened themselves to be drawn elsewhere on that current.

Sheel looked back again. The wide plain, the deep sky glowing blue overhead, the curves of the leather tents, even the drifting horses, were like a picture painted on a tent wall, against which were thrown the free fems' coarse shadows.

15

Alldera would not have believed that a woman's death could affect her so strongly. Everyone was stunned: who could have imagined Barvaran, red-faced and crude and good-hearted, caught up somehow in Nenisi's quarrel with the Perikens and rushing into a duel on the dancing ground?

Returning from a ride to check the location of the next campsite, Alldera found the Holdfaster women assembled by Barvaran's bedding. Barvaran lay gasping, her mouth frothing blood. There was a wound in her chest that opened with every breath she drew. The woman who had struck her had fled to seek refuge with relatives in another camp.

Barvaran was dead by morning. They took her body, lashed limply over the back of a horse, to abandon it in the grass far from camp. They laid the body down, washed clean and clothed, and they left it for the sharu. That was all. Women did not speak over corpses. Their farewells had been taken during the night, while Barvaran's spirit still lived and struggled.

Shayeen said, 'Later we will think of who should die for this, which well-loved woman of the guilty line.'

Sorrel argued furiously with Jesselee all the way back to the camp and wept and insisted she was going to find the killer and cut her throat. She lashed her horse into erratic bursts of speed and blood ied its mouth with her wrenching on the reins until Sheel rode up, yanked her from the saddle, and set her on her feet on the ground.

'The horse has done no harm,' Sheel said. 'If you can't ride like a woman, walk like a fem.'

The youngster hugged her mare around the neck, remounted, and on a slack rein let herself be carried homeward, crying bitterly.

Alldera trailed behind them, wondering what would be good to say to comfort Sorrel; thinking that it was better the fems had stayed behind rather than coming along to criticize the women's death customs; thinking most of all of Barvaran's red face looming above her in a gully in the desert years ago before Sorrel was born, the way Barvaran's breast had yielded under her hand, that first touch of a Riding Woman, that first amazement . . .

Who would have thought that Barvaran and I would live together as members of a family? My family, the family of my child that I brought to them, gave to them.

Shared, she thought suddenly; I shared her with my share-mothers. One part of Sorrel isn't given and can't be – my share.

I really did it. I was no mother, I didn't know how to become one – I was just a Holdfast dam. But I got her away from the men and I found her a whole family of mothers, and saw her into her free life as a young woman. Not that I set out to do it, and it's not all I've done on this side of the mountains, but it's done.

She looked at the dejected figure of Sorrel up ahead. Will she ever realize, and thank me for it? Not that a family is forever, your mothers leave you – Barvaran, maybe Jesselee, myself, soon. Still, it's something.

What's she going to be like, I wonder? I'll come back and find out, if I can.

Nenisi rode up alongside Alldera. Strapped to the bridge of her nose she wore a wooden mask with a slit across the center, used for protecting the sight from flying stone slivers when chipping flint. Now it protected her swollen eyes from the sun and the wind.

Along the hard ground flickers of light seemed to dance: leaves from a brush bank, curled and dry, were being driven in skipping circles by cool eddies of air. The sky was half skinned over with high white clouds, against which there floated smaller cloud puffs of exquisitely modulated grays and silvers. To the south the sky was clear, a blue of burning intensity in which these same subtly shaped and tinted clouds hung with a melting softness, sweet to Alldera's eye.

Nenisi said abruptly, 'You will leave us.'

'No!' That was a lie. 'I don't want to.' The truth.

Nenisi went on as if Alldera had not spoken: 'For generations women have watched so that no free fems would go back to the Holdfast and turn the men's attention toward the plains. That was right to do as long as we were few and the men were many, and as long as the free fems were strangers to whom we owed nothing.

'Now that relationship has changed. The free fems are kindred of the camps and free to go where they like – and I'll say so, as a Conor, when the question arises whether we should let you all return across the borderlands. But women like Sheel may charge that I can no longer speak as a Conor in this matter because of my feelings.

'Let me warn you, my friend. What others say on the question will matter. Some may even say to kill, and take no chances on these fems, or on you.'

Alldera fixed her eyes on the steadying sight of her own hands clasped one over the other on the peak of her saddle, as she groped for a response.

Nenisi turned toward her, her smooth black face masked, red lipped where the wind had bitten her mouth. 'You've lain in my bed, you've bathed my eyes as tenderly as a woman; yet you've told me nothing about your feelings. It's as if we were back when you first lived in Stone Dancing Camp and you were not yet yourself and didn't dare speak. Well, I know you better now; you lie in the dark in the distress of your thoughts and breathe harshly, like a woman toiling over the plain on foot. Your hands wind together sometimes like struggling enemies. But never a word, no speech to knit us together.

'Making love is much the same for all, but each person speaks only her own words. I have few of your words from days past to keep with me.'

Words, Alldera thought blankly. I was a messenger, and a messenger should know the importance of words without being told. I haven't paid enough attention.

She said, 'I thought you had so much trouble already – your eyes, and this cursed Periken feud – look, Nenisi, nothing is certain yet.' She stopped. Nothing was more certain, nothing more strange – she had been sent from the Holdfast to find allies, and not finding them she had somehow helped to make them; now she must return with them, years late. She recoiled. 'Nenisi, you're a Conor! Find a way to make it right for me to stay here!'

Nenisi shook her head. 'It's right to go with your close kindred. All Conors may not agree with me, but there are other women who will – perhaps enough of them to insure safe travel back for you. These last years our borderland patrols have found no signs of men venturing near the plains. No fems have come to us from your country since you came. Many women now think that the Holdfast is a dead place and men no danger.

'And as you know, there are women of Stone Dancing Camp who would cheer to see you and your people leave our tents, no matter what the long-range risk. Women of my Motherline want you gone for my sake – they see that your otherness, your singleness, has captured me, and they worry that I have become a stranger to my own. It frightens them that we are so close for so long.

'Don't worry about Sorrel. We'll look after her. She has a future with us: tent mates, raid mates, lovers, perhaps even a Motherline to found – everything that matters.'

Everything that matters! Alldera drew her headcloth closer around her shoulders, too dismal to speak.

Nenisi glanced back the way they had come.

'Tonight we'll sit in the tent and tell stories about Barvaran,' she said. 'Tonight you are with family. Tomorrow and the days after, you'll be busy with your cousins Daya and the others, talking about returning to the Holdfast. That will take a lot of planning. Later, on the other side of the mountains, maybe you'll tell some stories of us and this place. We'll tell about you and how the fems lived among us and left us their child. Most of that will be mine to tell; we Conors remember well, that's why we're always right.

'You and I, Alldera, had better talk now, while we have the chance.'

Alldera stared ahead where Sorrel rode, bowed and weeping, among Shayeen, Jesselee and Sheel. Suddenly she felt the downward drag of her own shoulders, the sting in her own eyes. She turned toward Nenisi and spoke.

Riding slowly toward Stone Dancing Camp, leaning in her saddle toward the dark figure beside her, she stumbled and struggled to say what she needed to say: that she, like her child up there, both grieved and was comforted; that Sorrel was not the only one whose world had been gladdened with kindred, nor the only one to find and lose the mother of her heart.